Madness,
Masks,
and Laughter

Madness, Masks, and Laughter

An Essay on Comedy

R. D. V. Glasgow

Madison • Teaneck
Fairleigh Dickinson University Press
London and Toronto: Associated University Presses

Associated University Presses
440 Forsgate Drive
Cranbury, NJ 08512

Associated University Presses
25 Sicilian Avenue
London WC1A 2QH, England

Associated University Presses
P.O. Box 338, Port Credit
Mississauga, Ontario
Canada L5G 4L8

The paper used in this publication meets the requirements of the American National Standard for Permanence of Paper for Printed Library Materials Z39.48-1984.

Library of Congress Cataloging-in-Publication Data

Glasgow, R. D. V. (Rupert D. V.), 1964–
    Madness, masks, and laughter: an essay on comedy/
  R. D. V. Glasgow.
        p.   cm.
    Includes bibliographical references (p.) and index.
    ISBN 0-8386-3559-8 (alk. paper)
    1. Comedy—History and criticism.   2. Comic, The, in literature.
  I. Title.
  PN1922.G43   1995
  809.2523—dc20   94-21586
                                                                          CIP

PRINTED IN THE UNITED STATES OF AMERICA

for Mum, Dad, and Faith

Contents

Acknowledgements

Many thanks to Martin Amis for permission to quote from *The Rachel Papers*, *Money*, *London Fields*, and *Time's Arrow*, N. F. Simpson for permission to quote from *A Resounding Tinkle*, and the University of Wisconsin Press for permission to quote from "News, Sex, and Performance Theory" by Richard Schechner, which originally appeared in *Innovation/Renovation: New Perspectives on the Humanities*, edited by Ihab and Sally Hassan (Madison: University of Wisconsin Press, 1983).

I should also like to thank the following people: Mark (Jeff) Astle, Robert Baldock, James Bell, Buddy Bendick, Ingrid Bietz, Richard Bluett, Dave Collier, Claus Daufenbach, Helen Delingpole, Elke Diener, Ralf Edelman, Jez Faulkner, Uwe Fechner, Bertram Gerber, Felix Grigat, Tina Grothoff, Ulla Hans, Lothar Hönnighausen, Holger Hörz, Christoph Irmscher, Ann Jefferson, Phil Jenkins, Bronwen Jones, Lisa Jones, John Kampfner, Mirjam Kasperl, Monika Kaup, Tordis Knees, Nina Knippschild, Stefan Koch, Dick Laycock, Meirlys Lewis, Jules Marshall, Anne-France Morand, Nicola Morris, Jim Reed, Renate Ruge, Tim and Christiane Swain, Deborah Sykes, Jane Szita, Stephen (Tommo) Thompson, Lois Thorley, Stefan Troisch, Alan Valentine, Graham Ward, Sacha Ward, Bill Weir, Andy and Nicole Weisz, Nick Williams, Sarah Wynick. Most of all I wish to thank my parents, Barbara and Wilfred Glasgow, and my sister, Faith Glasgow. The book is dedicated to them.

Madness,
Masks,
and Laughter

Introduction

Laughter

"Laughter as such is of no significance for an understanding of the comic."[1] This assertion is diametrically opposed to the assumptions on which this essay is based. It represents the sort of perspective that inspired the more or less completely unfunny sentimental "comedies" of the Enlightenment, that "species of Bastard Tragedy" (as Goldsmith put it)[2] written at a time when many playwrights were allowing their emotional nobility to get the better of them. General usage suggests that laughter is in fact the lowest common denominator for all comic forms worthy of the name and that, while not everything that makes us laugh is necessarily comic, everything that is comic has at least the potential to make us laugh. The inward and intellectual smiles favored by some commentators of the comic are (to adopt Goldsmith's tone) but a species of bastard laughter. For this reason, comedy is here interpreted primarily in its capacity to cause laughter, and, in an attempt to avoid too many overnice technical distinctions at the outset (for example between farce and satire, burlesque and travesty), all comic subgenres and modes are tossed into a single terminological melting pot that is intended first and foremost to filter out what they have in common as laughter-inducing phenomena. It is to be hoped that the differences will come to light in the process.

A methodological query here raises its tiresome head: Who is this "us" who is made to laugh by comedy? For a start, the first person plural incorporates a first person singular, i.e., "me." To a certain extent, therefore, what follows inevitably revolves around a "personal" selection. Yet it is not merely this. Not *all* of it makes me laugh (although it may have had past audiences or readers hooting, roaring, or guffawing uncontrollably), nor do I mention *all* of my favorites. Accordingly, at another level, "us" can be taken to mean "anybody" or "people in general"—although efforts to understand this "anybody" (which includes "me" of course) can only ever take place through thick-lensed hermeneutical bifocals, spectacles that become more and more speculative as temporal and geographical distance increase. Forays outside the Western tradition are consequently tentative and brief. While even such limited and provisional references to "us" may irritate dogmatic relativists, some degree of consensus about what is comic *has* to be assumed. "I" have no option but to presume that someone, somewhere, laughs at some of the same things "I" do if the essay is to have any sort of general relevance or be of any interest to anyone other than a solipsistic "me" gurgling and chuckling and chortling contentedly away in splendid but fairly idiotic isolation.

Yet related methodological bogeymen persist in getting up the nose of the comic theorist. One such question is whether laughter is to be viewed primarily as a sign, insofar as it is a culturally dependent function of a specific communicative context, or as the bodily manifestation of a pan-culturally identical physiological state. On the one hand, laughter fulfills a signifying role within a culture-specific, differential system of social signs, and, according to context, it may signal mockery, complicity, embarrass-ment, ebullience, snide superiority, pleasure, playfulness, relief, or in-credulity. On the other hand, it is a tangibly corporeal phenomenon that has a habit of exploding or defying all rigid systems of signification or classification, involuntarily escaping like a fleet-footed fart or an unan-ticipated belch. It may—in especially favorable circumstances—degen-erate into self-perpetuating meaninglessness, its infectiousness causing what starts out as a seemingly restrained titter to end up with weeping and wetness. While functional grins and giggles belong to the "inten-tional" communicative weaponry of a sovereign subject, the comic situa-tion may on occasion produce a characteristic power-reversal whereby laughter assumes mastery over its subject, reducing him or her to a gib-bering wretch rolling about on the floor and clutching his or her sides. The sixteenth-century French thinker Joubert describes the symptoms of such a paroxysm in his *Traité du Ris* (1579), noting that "when we laugh, our face suddenly becomes excited, our mouth grows wider, our eyes sparkle and water, our cheeks turn red, our chest shakes, our voice breaks off: and if the fit of laughter persists for longer, the veins of the neck swell, the arms quiver and the legs dance, the abdomen contracts and feels great pain: we cough, we sweat, we piss and shit ourselves for laughter, and sometimes we faint as a result of it."[3] Part of the reason for the infectiousness of the phenomenon is that laughter itself—by the time it has people bepissing their pants—is a comic happening.

Referring to the "intentional" subject in the grip of hilarity, the philo-sophical anthropologist Plessner writes: "He himself does not actually laugh, but there is laughter within him [*es lacht in ihm*], and to a certain degree he is but the scene and the vessel for this process."[4] The human body, as it were, turns the tables on the human subject and bestower of meaning who is supposed to control *it*: instead of me being master of my body, my body becomes master of me. Indeed, in response to the sup-posed sovereignty of the Cartesian cogito (the claim that "I" am the boss of my own mind), a whole series of thinkers, including Lichtenberg, Nietzsche, Russell, and Mach, have made a counterclaim analogous to Plessner's "*Es lacht in mir/ihm*" with regard not to laughter but to thought in general: "*Es denkt (in mir/ihm)*"—it thinks, or there is thought (in me/him). The fact that, despite these claims, "I" continue in practical terms to be the one who is doing the thinking and laughing even though there may be some "it" who is doing the thinking and laughing (within me) hints at the impossibility or futility of ultimately separating the semantic from the somatic, mind from body. They are different aspects or levels of the same phenomenon. The following essay is thus based on the assumption that laughter is both a sign with a culturally variable meaning and a physical phenomenon with its causal roots in the biological constitution of the human body. Appropriating a "Freudian" (or Hobbesian) model of (social) mask and (asocial) face, the orientation of this essay is intended to bridge the gap between the two levels, doing justice to the fact both that we exist within a specific social system (with different structures of signification from other systems) and that—as individuated or autonomous biological units—we necessarily stand in a not unproblematic relationship to the structures of this system.

That these various levels of explanation tend to be no more watertight than Joubert's hearty laugher gives rise to confusions and ambiguities, as shown by the question of authenticity. If laughter is a cultural gesture mimetically acquired in the context of social interaction, it may be asked then, is it possible to speak of "genuine" laughter? At one level, the answer would seem to be no, for being something we learn (and by imitation at that), all laughter is equally histrionic. In practical terms, however, the answer is again of course yes: understanding "spontaneity" as we usually employ the term, laughter may indeed meaningfully be said to represent an outburst of physical spontaneity, say, an unpremeditated rush of merriment, or a sense of sudden bewilderment. Equally, though, it *may* be used to simulate ebullience or to hide embarrassment or fear. At this level, the attribution of authenticity or its opposite to laughter is a contingent and not a necessary one.

A widely held and not completely unjustified prejudice, harbored in particular by those who would wish to veil humor in inscrutability, is that people who attempt to theorize about laughter of all things must be pedantic windbags and wearisome party poopers. As Voltaire put it, "A joke explained ceases to be a joke: any commentator on quips is a fool,"[5] while Jean Paul commented that "from time immemorial the definitions of philosophers have failed to accommodate the ridiculous—except involuntarily."[6] More recently, comedian Ken Dodd, himself a buff in the workings of the "chuckle muscle," has made the telling point that Freud never had to play the second house, Friday night, at the Glasgow Empire.

This is not merely a warning to put off all readers except those who enjoy the dry, the tiresomely overexplained, and the utterly factual, but also an attempt to justify a somewhat relativistic tack whereby the phenomenon is approached primarily with the aid of a *metaphor*—or, more specifically, with the aid of a cluster of semantically contiguous metaphors from the field of theatre: the metaphors of mask, appearance, and illusion, understood in their opposition to a face or to an underlying reality (of whatever nature this may be). The aim is less to provide THE TRUTH about comedy and laughter than, casting a side-glance at some of the ways it has been traditionally apprehended and explicated in philosophy, to synthesize these explanations into a more comprehensive system that will throw light on how comedy is related both to our understanding of the world and to certain modes of understanding our understanding.

Play

Psychological research into laughter in developmental terms seems to reveal two distinct signals which converge in adult laughter. On the one hand, psychologists point to cooing and vigorous smiling in babies as an early reaction to the recognition of a *repeated pattern* of stimulus and response, as when an indulgent parent makes silly sounds every time the child wiggles its legs. This is seen as an intense expression of the baby's pleasure in ascertaining its control of the environment, the joy of anticipation and fulfillment. The child repeats its actions for the fun of mastering them, laughing at its own power. On the other hand, laughter may occur as a response to something unusual performed by the mother. It is significant that those pranks and antics most likely to generate laughter when played by the mother are the ones most likely to produce tears when the prankster is a stranger and that the baby's first laughter corresponds developmentally with the first recognition of the mother at four months. This laughter seems to be dependent on two factors: first, the occurrence of something unsettling, abnormal, new, or frightening (something that might otherwise make us cry, such as being chucked up and down in the air), and, second, the fact that this abnormality takes place within a safe context, a play situation which neutralizes the threat. It is the mother who is generally first able to play anything as alarming as "peekaboo" with the child.[7] These findings hint by homology that adult laughter too may be a response either to reassuring repetition or to a disconcerting surprise and that the play-context is essential.

Recent investigations by psychologists into the phylogeny or evolution of laughter and smiles similarly imply a convergence in human beings of a number of signals also found in other higher primates. In this context, laughter primarily emerges as closely connected to communal aggression and self-assertion. The rhythmic emission of barking sounds resembles the behavior of many primates in collectively threatening or asserting themselves in the face of a potential enemy, an act that binds and generates solidarity among the members of the group. This aggressive gesture is to be distinguished from the smile or "silent bared teeth display," which generally signals appeasement or submission, a toothy snigger manifesting fear or humiliation. A few species are now known in which the display can also be given by an unthreatened dominant creature towards a subordinate one, indicating reassurance, attachment, but perhaps even related to the human smile of condescension as well as to the broad smile indicating a nonhostile or friendly attitude. A further category of display is the "relaxed open-mouth display," known as the play-face, which is normally an accompaniment to such play activities as mock-fighting and mock-chasing. This functions as a metasignal creating a play situation and indicating that the rough-and-tumble is not serious. It is also elicited by tickling.[8] If (for our purposes here) we therefore ignore the traditional claim that laughter itself is something uniquely and essentially human and thus qualitatively different from whatever it is other species may do, these laughterlike signals lead us to conjecture (by homology) that human laughter too is inherently associated both with power-situations, where it may demonstrate collective aggression, mastery, and superiority, or fear and embarrassment, and with play situations, which render a potential threat harmless. Given, however, that human laughter is sited at a confluence of a number of discrete signals, it may well become impossible in practice to hold these different categories definitively apart and thus differentiate with certitude between, say, masterful and fearful or servile laughter.

Studies of babies and higher primates alike, therefore, link laughter in a fundamental way with the notion of *play*, and—using the theatrical metaphors of mask and illusion to elucidate the phenomenon—this essay will look at adult, human laughter above all insofar as it arises in a mutually acknowledged or "officially" designated play-context. This will entail taking not only theatrical laughter as a focal point, but also directing more occasional attention towards other play frames such as joke-telling situations and the temporary licence sanctioned by plebeian festivities and carnival celebration, for these run parallel to and in certain respects illuminate the laughter generated by the comic dramatic play of the theatrical institution. It has indeed been posited that the comic is an aesthetic category, whereas the merely risible, laughable, or funny is an existential one, and this is certainly a useful distinction in reminding one of the ordinary usage of the terms. Yet it is also an oversimplification, for laughter itself may imply an aestheticization of the existential,[9] or, to put it less pompously, when we laugh at some everyday occurrence, we are treating it with the same emotional distance that is also characteristic of our attitude to aesthetic phenomena, such as theatrical performances. Laughter is not simply dependent upon a play-context; it may create such a context, just as the play-face of the frolicking monkey turns fighting into mock-fighting and just as a sense of humor permits its lucky possessor to view the vicissitudes of the world with a detachment akin to that of the theatrical spectator. A distinction has been commonly made between comedy, a theatrical or fictional genre, and humor, defined in its most general sense as a laughing response to certain everyday situations. In this respect, comedy is relegated to a type of institutionalized humor. Accordingly, while comedy might be seen as providing ready-made distance through its formally established play-frame, humor requires do-it-yourself detachment.

If a provisional definition of "play" therefore pinpoints it as a *context*— a "less risky situation," a "severance from life's serious aims," a "relaxed field"[10]—neither play nor laughter allow themselves to be restricted to "art" or institutionalized play situations. In daily encounters, laughter tends simply to presuppose safety, a nonthreatening situation, or some form of distance from its object—be this emotional, spatial, or temporal, as with danger overcome. The humor response to socially deviant behavior occurs when there is no significant awareness of personal or social threat. It is an alternative to regarding such conduct as evil, mad, or not worthy of attention.

As the psychologist Bateson has observed,[11] the play-face, or "this is play" signal, is fundamentally paradoxical. Like Epimenides's example of the Cretan who held that all Cretans are liars, it consists of a negative statement containing an implicit negative metastatement. It signals that "this—my present behavior—is not to be taken seriously"; my actions do not signal what they would usually signal (in the sense that, say, squaring up might signal aggression). But this toothy metasignal is also a part of my present playful conduct. Is it to be taken seriously itself? If it is, then it is not, for its message is "don't take present signals at face value"; if it is not, then it is, for the signals are to be taken seriously after all. This equivocacy is essential to the realm of play, a locus where danger or threat can be classified as nondangerous or unthreatening. Play both is and is not real. It is serious, but simultaneously unserious. Theatre and theatrical performance may here be viewed as paradigmatic, for what the spectator sees is on one level "real" (it is not a subjective delusion), but on another level it is "just pretend." Play is permeated by an ontological ambivalence that echoes the ambivalence of laughter, situated as this is on the crossroads of culture and nature, structured order and disorderly transgression.

There are specific aspects of theatrical comedy that—analagous to a play-face—generate the distance or play-context necessary to allow its audience to laugh. These are a function of the spectator's expectations regarding what is being—or is about to be—watched, and they may operate at a number of levels. In a very broad sense, the aesthetic context in general fulfills this role by distancing the spectator from the spectacle. The act of buying a ticket and entering an auditorium specifically set aside for the purpose of performance "frames" the events that are to follow, demarcating the real from the illusory or lusory. It has indeed been pointed out that the term "aesthetic distance" is tautological, in that "wherever there is aesthetic apprehension there is emotional and in-tellectual detachment"[12]; the Russian formalist Schlovsky characterized art as "beyond feeling."[13] The aesthetic is thus paradoxically *anaesthetic*, a paradox (again) that parallels the paradox of play. If the aesthetic is a feeling that is beyond feeling, it corresponds in this to the duality of identification and distance with which one regards the fictive theatrical characters, suspended as these are somewhere between being and non-being. All in all, one is less likely to laugh at someone if one thereby runs the risk of being bopped on the nose by way of recompense. The fact that one is sitting in a theatre means that (by and large) one is immune from the consequences of what takes place on stage—and the same applies to reading a book or watching a film. Farce in particular yields the piquant pleasure of seeing *someone else* being harassed, hit, and hurt. In this sense it is only the ludic or playful element that differentiates art and savagery.[14] It is to the extent that we willingly suspend our disbelief, "forget" the play-context, and start to identify with the fictive figures that we start to take acted discomfort seriously.

Distance has two vectors, the horizontal and the vertical, though the two are, of course, often inextricably interrelated. The former is the purely situational fact that, as aesthetic observers, we are invulnerable and are able to distinguish the theatrical event from the seriousness of reality outside the auditorium. The latter refers to the superiority of our perspective as privileged, godlike contemplators, knowing more than any of the fictive characters and in a position to appraise and judge the situation in which they are *immediately* enmeshed. This is why the Olympian gods (and certain Olympian philosophers) derive so much amusement by withdrawing from the hurly-burly of the human comedy, looking down from the celestial circle as we mortals make a complete hash of a worldly drama utterly beyond our control—a reassuring and self-affirming form of laughter if ever there was one (more on this in chapter 2).

Within the comic genre itself, therefore, the element of play and dis-tancing may be reinforced by various means. Here it is a question of expectations not merely produced by the theatrical or fictional context, but of what might be termed generic expectations. Traditionally, comedies have been typified by their happy ending, and, secure in the knowledge that everything will turn out fine, the spectator is less troubled by the hitches encountered on the road towards this guaranteed felicity. Carnival plays and German medieval *Fastnachtspiele*, for example, normally ended with a dance in which the audience was also invited to partake and, deriving as it does from phallic rites and fertility rituals, comedy down the ages has made a point of concluding with marriage and the prospect of concerted baby-making. This motion from disorder to order—or from order via disorder back to order—is something that the archetypal comic plot has in common with the scriptural canon. Accordingly, the morality plays of th Middle Ages, such as *Mankind*, could be regarded as essentially comic by medieval criteria, for the conventional certainty of redemption permitted the security of a comic perspective. This applied even more in the case of the mystery plays: whereas the moralities were concerned with urging Everyman to mend his ways in order to secure his personal salvation (and thus confronted at least the possibility of perdition), the Corpus Christi cycles followed a preestablished and generally recognized pattern in leading up—via a sequence of Biblical events—to theological triumph and the salvation of man in general. Dante's *Divina Commedia*, which has its roots in the same worldview, in his own words "introduces a situation of adversity, but ends its matter in prosperity. ... at the beginning it is horrible and foul, for it is Hell, but at the end it is happy, desirable and pleasing, for it is Paradise."[15]

Our responses are indeed governed by our awareness of watching a drama (or reading a novel) designated a comedy and heading towards paradise (be it secular or heavenly) with an inevitability transcending the strivings of any particular individual within the fiction. The literary theorist Culler in fact defines genre as a "conventional function of language, a particular relation to the world which serves as a norm or expectation to guide the reader in his encounter with the text."[16] To ensure the happy ending, for example, it is essential that the fool, rogue, or butt of the laughter should not be portrayed as exceeding a certain degree of power, menace, or competence in his folly or roguery, just as social "deviance" can only elicit a humorous response if it is regarded as nonthreatening or harmless. In Plato's *Philebus*, Socrates introduces the stipulation that comic fools must be "weak and unable to revenge themselves when they are laughed at"[17] in order to be genuinely ridiculous, and Aristotle likewise saw the ludicrous as a "defect or ugliness which is not painful or destructive."[18] *A Midsummer Night's Dream* is exemplary in the way it repeatedly reminds the audience that short-term snags will be overcome and all will be well. Virtually at the outset, Lysander's remark that the

"course of true love never did run smooth" prompts a duet with Hermia
on the obstacles that are a customary feature of love (and equally of the
comic/romantic plot of which love forms the mainspring), generating an
awareness that such conventional trials are only there in order to be sur-
mounted (1.1). Later, at the end of act 3, Puck, mischievous imp though
he may be, emerges as the spokesman and representative of this comic
principle, promising that "Jack shall have Jill," or, less flatteringly, "the
man shall have his mare again" (3.2).

Shakespeare's festive comedies differ from other comic subgenres in
that they are pervaded by this holiday humor and characterized by an
exceptionally high degree of ebullient self-assurance as they steer towards the happy ending. In such cases, signals within the fiction—as well
as or instead of generic conventions—serve to reassure the onlooker that
the comic confusion will resolve itself into harmony and order. Such
happy endings embody an ambiguity allowing them to be interpreted
either as mimetic reflections of a possible or an actual reality or as ironic
inversions of the way the sordid world really is. In fact, however, the
happy ending hovers elusively between these two poles, its blithe indeterminacy arising because celebration is less mimetic than affective,
something to be done, not watched. As will become clear with time,
comedy was never a genre to stay on one side of the footlights. Like
Shakespeare's green world, carnival festivities provide the perfect comic
context—a place where proclivities for madness, folly, love, and revelry
can be indulged with scant concern for the consequences. This topsy-
turvy, celebratory frame of mind pervades the work of one of the most
comic of all comic writers, François Rabelais, and Aristophanic comedy is
similarly inseparable from the context of Dionysian festival at which it
was performed. Restoration comedy was seen by Charles Lamb as a
"passing pageant"[19] peopled by profligates and strumpets, fools and
knaves, and, in the twentieth century, Joe Orton's manic *What the Butler
Saw* displaces the context of anarchic, anything-goes folly into a psychiatrist's clinic. Such comedy explicitly creates a mood in which the sobriety
of normality is out of place and laughter instead becomes the norm, the
original, limited notion of play as distance or freedom from danger expanding to incorporate a sense of freedom from the pressure of maximum
rationality, the freedom to behave nonfunctionally. In these circumstances play by extension becomes a locus of comic irrationality, nonsense, and madness, where one can afford to oaf about, be creative, silly,
illogical, and babyish. As anthropologists point out, play thereby turns
into an opportunity to experiment with alternative forms of comportment
and thought.

Emotional distance (and the likelihood of being moved to laughter)
may be further enhanced if the comedy is not illusionistic or if it is ac-

tively anti-illusionistic, for the more we identify with the figures and forget that what we are watching is a fiction, the less we are prone to laugh
at their misfortunes. Plays that remind us that they are play (for example
by drawing attention to the props or by talking about the audience), fantastic, absurd, and irrealistic comedies (which do not engender the illusion of being "real" or "true"), as well as plays that contain the device of
a play-within-a-play—all tend to distance the audience from the proceedings. The masks worn by the figures of the commedia dell'arte have a
similar effect, at times bringing Arlecchino and Brighella close to the
status of puppets, while the more modern figure of Père Ubu has his origins in the anarchic puppetry of the French *guignol* or Punch and Judy
show. Bad acting too consistently, if involuntarily, directs attention to itself as *acting* and not "reality" and has the magical ability to turn a tear-
jerking tragedy into a rip-roaring burlesque; the exuberant irrealism of
festive comedy likewise makes no bones about its ludic nature (such
techniques will be more exhaustively examined in chapter 5). In these
cases, comic play may become explicitly paradoxical in a manner analogous to the play-face, both meaning and not meaning what it says and, in
the bargain, drawing attention to this nonsensical ambivalence. Like
Epimenides the Cretan who claimed that "all Cretans are liars" or the
philosopher who asserts "this statement is false," the fictive fool who
steps out of the action and reminds the spectator that what is being
watched is not real may be plunging into a vicious semantic whirlpool.

Two (related) provisos remain to be made at this point. Critical or
emotional distance need not arise as a result of the theatrical factors
mentioned above, but may be, as it were, internalized within the particular observer. Bergson located within the individual the distance or detachment necessary for laughter, claiming that laughter "has no greater
enemy than emotion.... Step back from life, observe it as an indifferent
spectator, and many dramas will turn into comedy.... In order to produce
its entire effect, therefore, the comic in fact requires something like a
momentary anaesthesia of the heart. It is addressed to the pure intelligence." Moreover, "the characters of real life would not make us
laugh if we were not capable of looking upon their actions as upon a play
observed from the heights of our box at the theatre."[20] Walpole judged
that "the world is a comedy to those that think, a tragedy to those that
feel."[21] Laughter outside the comic theatre thus results from an attitude
analogous to that within the comic theatre, stimulated as it is by an
awareness of all the role-playing, acting, and deception of self and others
that takes place in human life. This type of emotional distance may end
up tantamount to a universalized play-context (an inability to value anything as serious in itself) and is of course the speciality of those Olympian
philosophers who observe the human farce with critical detachment from

above. Black humor and sick jokes also necessarily incorporate some form of distance from the suffering to which they are a reaction, just as gallows humor, like other sorts of self-mockery, must require what might be termed self-distance—intellectual or emotional detachment from one's own suffering, be it present or future. Glossing Nietzsche's observation that the *Witz* is an "epigram on the death of a feeling,"[22] Plessner adds that it is an epigram that hits the nail in one's coffin on the head.

What comes to light in the case of gallows humor is that the laughter may itself *create* the distance, giving rise to a viciously circular situation in which laughter creates distance creates laughter creates distance.... While psychologists tend to stress that laughter operates as a *release* of psychic tension, the sociological perspective by contrast emphasizes that humor is a means of "tension management,"[23] a way of *coming to terms* with social pressures, just as the periodic legal anarchy of carnival enables the members of society the better to cope with the rigors of normal, structured, hierarchical life. Many tribal societies indeed establish special joking-relationships that permit a certain fusion of playfulness and aggression between in-laws, generally taking the form of sexually obscene pranks and mock insults;[24] in British culture, the stand-up comedian with his in-law jokes is perhaps contributing to tension-management in an analogous manner, helping his audience to attain distance with regard to their own more traumatic or distressful personal relationships. Almost two centuries ago, the German poet, dramatist, and critic Schiller pinpointed the essence of comedy itself and its opposition to tragedy in this generation of detachment: "If tragedy thus proceeds from a more important starting-point, it must on the other hand be admitted that comedy moves towards a more important goal, and it would, were it to reach it, render all tragedy superfluous and impossible. Its goal is one with the highest aim to be striven for by man: to be free from passion, always looking clearly and calmly into oneself and upon one's surroundings, finding everywhere more chance than fate, and quicker to laugh about folly than be vexed or weep about wickedness."[25] The primary pedagogical value of comedy is to teach us to view the world as a comedy. Again, the perspective thus acquired is the perspective of the gods, and this clearly implies both horizontal and vertical distance, both divine invulnerability and the cognitive superiority of the divine overview.

As ludic distance may in practice be a product of the laughter that was first judged to presuppose it and may be located moreover within the laughing observer, the boundary separating play and nonplay, and therefore a definition of play, is clearly problematic. On the one hand, comedy is to be equated with the generation of laughter in an aesthetic (i.e. play) context, while, on the other, laughter itself seems to produce what has been called an "aestheticization" of the real, creating the distance that is constitutive of a play-context. It is partly for this reason that the theatrical metaphors of mask and illusion seem particularly suited to explain the phenomenon. Comic laughter may be taken as representative of laughter in general, for laughter is both a response to comic theatre and a way of turning the world into a (comic) theatre. Even when it assumes the form of blatant mockery, signaling aggressive derision and the overcoming of an antagonist in combat (seemingly a million miles—or evolutionary years—from the comparatively civilized amusement to be found in the theatre), it may still be associated with an overcoming of danger, a sort of unilateral play situation that only counts for the victor, not his humiliated opponent. To this extent the boundaries of play and nonplay must be provisionally left open.

Anti-illusionistic drama on occasion openly plays with its own playful nature, thematically focusing upon the blurred borderlines between the fictional "reality" it depicts and its own illusionary status, while the experimental theatre of the twentieth century has progressed even further in addressing these questions. In the late seventies and early eighties, the New York performance group "Squat," for example, turned to account a window that looked out from the rented building in which they performed on to the bustling daily life of Twenty-Third Street.[26] This window both permitted the theatrical spectators to view "real" passersby passing by behind the "fictional" action and allowed these passersby to look in at what was going on inside, which was frequently scandalous enough to make them look twice. It thus functioned as a transparent breach in the theatrical frame which is normally flawless in its demarcation of play and life. This breach was cheerfully exploited by the group as a means of producing startling coups de théâtre. When a man strolled past with his arms on fire, the audience remained uncertain whether what they were witnessing was a "real" or a "fictional" occurrence, and the following scenario, described by Schechner, puts both the "real" audience and the passing-by spectators on the horns of a similar dilemma:

> In *Mr. Dead and Mrs. Free*, a jeep drives up on the sidewalk and stops close to the glass door adjoining the storefront window. Two soldiers in battle dress unload a bloody passenger from the back seat and carry him through the door into the theater. They put him in a hammock. A priest and nurse attend him. Spectators gather outside the theater, peering in and staring at the jeep on the sidewalk. Soon a police car arrives. It is an actual New York City police car. Why did it arrive? Did someone in the theater call for it? Or did a passerby? Do the police come every night? Don't they know that a "play" is going on? *Dead/Free* had been running more than a month when I saw it. Does Squat have permission to use Twenty-third Street? To drive a jeep onto the sidewalk? Two cops get out of the car and talk to the performers next to the jeep. Then the cops enter the theater through the glass door. The audience laughs. They

laugh some more, and gasp, when a city ambulance, with all its lights flashing, drives up nose to nose with the police car. The cops confer with the performers in the theater; one cop writes in his notebook. They leave. The ambulance leaves. The cop car drives off. Then the jeep drives away. The cops and the ambulance are "life"—but when the cops enter the theater they are also "art." The jeep on the sidewalk is "art," but to some passers-by it is "life."[27]

What such drama makes clear is not only that the play being watched is real, but also that the real itself involves performance. Again Schechner elucidates this reciprocal interaction between "art" and "life" in a way that runs parallel to the relationship between comedy and laughter: "There are two main realms of performance theory: (1) looking at human behavior—individual and social—as a genre of performance; (2) looking at performance—of theater, dance, and other 'art forms'—as a kind of personal or social interaction. These two realms, or spheres, can be metaphorically figured as interfacing at a double two-way mirror. From one face of the mirror persons interested in aesthetic genres peep through at 'life.' From the other side, persons interested in the 'social sciences' peep through at 'art.' "[28] This two-way mirror Schechner sees embodied in the window incorporated in the performances of "Squat." It is the point of convergence between seeing life as theatre and theatre as life.

Mask, Illusion, and Appearance

The metaphor of the *theatrum mundi*, the idea of the world as a stage with man as an actor, can be traced back at least to Plato's *Philebus*, where Socrates refers to "the tragedy and comedy of life."[29] It recurs in his *Laws* and is to be found in the Cynics, Horace, Augustine, Erasmus, and Luther, reaching a heyday in the baroque period.[30] The fundamental conception underlying the metaphor at this point is that, the world being a stage, man is but an actor or puppet or marionette in the hands of an all-powerful playwright. The world, in other words, is a mere illusion behind which the truth or reality of God is hidden. The image similarly occurs in the fictional work of Cervantes, Shakespeare, and Calderón, fiction here considered as having the advantage of at least admitting its illusory nature (unlike the world in its pretence to reality).[31] While in the baroque era man's role-playing and the human comedy is seen as directed, produced, watched, and reviewed by God the director, producer, audience, and critic, the romantic era uses the metaphor with greater emphasis on the fact that man's fate is guided by gods or forces unknown (and primarily for their sadistic amusement). With time, indeed, man comes to be regarded as a social role-player, acting and experiencing according to a script that is biologically or culturally determined, but at any rate beyond his ken and control. The duality of the original trope (theatrical performance contrasting with the reality of that which transcends the performance) is frequently ignored or rejected in favor of a monistic perspective that, in some extreme cases, may end up seeing nothing but the script as real.

Twentieth-century sociologists and role theorists such as Goffman thus interpret the human actor as *necessarily* donning a sequence of roles and costumes, reciting a script determined by his social context. From such a perspective it is questionable whether there is anything "hidden" behind this social mask: if performance is a necessary rather than a contingent condition, then the distinction between performance and non-performance loses any practical applicability, and art and life cannot ultimately be separated. The unsuspecting policemen who enter the play area of the Squat company, it can be argued, are in fact "playing a role" even before they enter the theatre, even before they pull up outside the theatre and enter the line of vision of the audience. It is a role that may be professional in nature and may be taken for granted as a normal part of social intercourse; nonetheless it involves the adoption of a persona acquired by a process of more or less unconscious mimetic interaction over time, a performance the underlying structure of which transcends the individual actor concerned. Thinkers as different as Hobbes and Freud have also regarded man as fundamentally an actor, one who dissimulates an essentially anarchic core beneath a cultural mask. The real self, the face beneath the mask, is private and asocial (and in a sense unknowable) and is concealed or partly concealed behind the mere appearance of sociality.

In the case of Freud, the "real" face behind the cultural mask is designated the *unconscious*, the sphere of dynamic bodily drives and energies insofar as these resist conformity to the social mold, and, in its various modulations, this term has had a pervasive influence on twentieth-century thought. Operating with a similar "repression" hypothesis, for example, the early Foucault regards folly and madness since the Enlightenment as constituting a sort of *cultural* unconscious, speaking a language that is excluded and silenced by the prevalent rational discursive order. According to Foucault, post-Enlightenment reason is a tyrannical force that masks or conceals the voices of "otherness." (Chapter 6 in particular looks into the comedy that arises when folly has its say, while the chapters 7 and 8 are concerned with the way in which comedy is related to the social mask insofar as this mask curbs the folly of our tendencies towards social disorder, the madness of our sexual and aggressive impulses.) The terms "folly" and "madness" thus stand in a very broad sense for that which cannot (officially at least) be known or shown. Although this may of course include the area of clinical illness (once after all an accepted source of amusement, back in the days when trips to the madhouse offered fun for all the family), institutionalized mental disorder is now too often viewed as pathetic or sympathetic to be comic. In this essay, folly functions as a more general metaphor for spiritual abnormality or otherness, frequently associated either with truth-speaking or with untruth-speaking (depending on one's evaluation of the discursive norm). The fluidity of the term is betrayed by the fact that acting itself—as a confusion of appearance and reality, identity and difference, self and other—has often been judged a form of madness. The metaphorical and primarily heuristic nature of this mask/face (or appearance/reality) model is underlined by its reversibility. While this essay will concentrate largely on the Freudian or Hobbesian perspective, the unanswerable question posed by Mary Mungummory (the Traveling Whore o' Dorset) in John Barth's *The Sot-Weed Factor* hammers home its relativity: "Is man a salvage at heart, skinned o'er with fragile Manners? Or is salvagery but a faint taint in the natural man's gentility, which erupts now and again like pimples on an angel's arse?"[32] Does our civilized rationality mask an atavistic brutality, or is it not the rationalized brutality of civilization that has displaced and eclipsed a more genuine sanity?

If human conduct in a social context is to be viewed as consciously or unconsciously structured by cultural codes and norms, it would equally seem that an element of patterning is essential to human experience in general, a development of the baby's cooing recognition of repetitions. At a perceptual and a conceptual level, experience of the world is necessarily and intrinsically structured by the limitations of our cognitive faculties.[33] This and related ideas are as old as the philosophical hills, going back to Anaxagoras's claim in the fifth century B.C. that, whereas the universe was originally homogeneous and motionless, a sort of murky, tepid, and rather unappetizing soup, the whirling influence of mind caused the universe to become differentiated and ordered. Perhaps the most sophisticated statement of the idea was formulated by Kant, who argued that our experience is *necessarily* structured by certain epistemological principles known as the "Categories," which include (most importantly for us) causal order and permanence of substance. These principles, Kant claimed, are essential to the structure of cognition but not to the thing as it is *in itself*, independently of our apprehension of it. The laws of causality and substance apply at the level of appearance (*Erscheinung*), that is, but not to the "reality" of the thing in itself, which thus remains well and truly beyond our grasp. Our experience of the world is necessarily restricted to the way it appears to our cognitive faculties. (Chapter 9 delves into the comedy that may be derived from breaches in these cognitive structures.)[34]

Various followers of Kant, including Schopenhauer, were led by his psychophysical and physiological idiom to see these principles as psychological instead of epistemological laws. Coupled with the influence of the Eastern mystical belief in *Maya* (the illusionary veil of individuation and differentiation, which distracts the human mind from the underlying unity and oneness of *Brahman* or reality), Schopenhauer's appropriation of the Kantian model can be regarded as fundamental to his notion of the Will (*Wille*) as the thing-in-itself. For Schopenhauer the Will is the primary reality, a chaotic, impulsive, primeval force, while human cognition only has access to what he calls *Vorstellung* (or representation), a flimsy veil hiding the perpetual flux of the transcendental reality behind an illusion of differentiated order. Interestingly, Schopenhauer's metaphysical vision is pervaded by theatrical metaphor, the German word *Vorstellung* itself meaning both mental image or idea and theatrical representation or performance. Human life is seen as a farcical burlesque featuring puppets driven from within by this blind (sexual) force that is beyond their conceptual comprehension. The attempts of the human intellect to attribute motivations and causes is but a grotesque masking and distortion of the unfathomable.[35] The human self does, however, possess a sort of direct, noncognitive access to the Will in the displaced, temporal (but not spatial) form of its own will, for the human "I" is both cognitive and volitional subject at once[36]—both one who knows and one who wills or wants. Schopenhauer's identification of the metaphysical Will with the human will encourages him to get carried away by his own metaphor, ignoring the Will's unknowability and turning his transcendental force into an irrepressibly randy thing-in-itself that defies all the rationalizing attempts of reason to master or conceal it. Freud reformed Schopenhauer's Will into the human unconscious—an equally irrational, sexual, and aggressively amoral reality, ultimately sharing the same epistemological status, that of the unknowable.

Severing "reality" from the spatio-temporal frame of reference (space and time being but the forms of our cognitive intuition, not inherent in things as they really are), such models at one fell swoop remove the distinction between appearance and reality from the realm of significant application and thus teeter uneasily on the brink of incoherence and nonsensicality. Even the possibility of apprehending things as they are is rejected. Kant's notion of the thing-in-itself has indeed generally been regarded as his biggest philosophical howler, for how can we conceive or conceptualize that which is beyond our conception? In response to the Kantian position, Hegel went to characteristically unintelligible lengths in the *Wissenschaft der Logik* to show that, whereas ordinary consciousness understands appearance as a screen before reality, in fact there is nothing behind. For Hegel, the way things appear *is* the way they are. Instead of arguing for the fundamental hiddenness of the transcendental real as Kant had done, Hegel's notion of appearance expresses that reality is essentially manifest; the essence must appear, for appearance is the essence.

Of all claims that appearance is reality, Hegel's is perhaps the most interesting because of his untranslatable idea of *Aufhebung*, which contains the meanings of annulment, suspension, and preservation. Put briefly, the difference between essence and appearance is *aufgehoben*, which means that, whereas the distinction may continue to exist for a certain level of consciousness, a higher stage of philosophizing awareness will recognize the fundamental identity of the two terms. In the *Ästhetik*, Hegel was accordingly able to define the ridiculous in the following terms: "Any contrast between the essential and its appearance can be ridiculous, a contradiction through which appearance is annulled/suspended in itself."[37] For Hegel, appearance both is and is not reality, and the ridiculous arises from the discrepancy between the two. Although Hegel's thoroughly rational essence is very different from (for example) Schopenhauer's thoroughly irrational Will, and the analogy is a purely formal one, the point at this stage is that the distinction between mask and self, appearance and reality, may still be of value for an understanding of the comic even if we should choose to suspend this dualism in the higher synthetic awareness of the unity of the two differents.

If appearance both is and is not reality, in this it corresponds to play, and the difficulties of drawing a meaningful distinction between appearance and reality on a cognitive level echo those of differentiating between a performing self and a nonperforming or true self at a social level. Fortunately, however, the metaphor of man as an actor is a two-way metaphor, life being theatre-like as much as theatre is lifelike, and the problems exist both at a theatrical and an existential level. While, for example, the theatrical actor in one sense *is* the part he plays (even when he simultaneously maintains a distance from his role) and for the duration of the performance at least his mask *is* his face, at another level the actor never truly becomes the person he is acting, for it is "just pretend" after all. It is thus more accurate to say that the mask both is and is not the face, the actor both is and is not the character he portrays. By the same token, while sociologists might argue that a self *is* but the sequence of roles he plays and the "real" subject—understood as a creative ego or soul orchestrating or pulling the strings behind the social performance— is a nonexistent fiction (or at best unknowable), the human individual is also equipped with possibilities of intellectual self-detachment or self-distance, which as it were split us in two and allow us to observe ourselves and our role-playing as if from the outside. Of course, it can be countered that even our transcending consciousness of "role" is but a role, and our most private self-evaluation is all part of our publicly or socially determined script. We in other words even act our own audience. But here—as with the appearance/reality dichotomy—it is a question of levels of analysis.

We may be inclined to bridle at the "role" metaphor because it seems to rule out creativity in describing the social actor as reading a prewritten script. But actors can always improvise, and frequently they are indeed meant to do so. The rigid masks of Arlecchino and Brighella hid an endless potential for doing the shocking, the surprising, the unusual. A greater danger in the metaphor is that it tends to reduce human life to a farce and human beings to actors alienated from any sense of self or reality, and this can be rather demoralizing. At an ordinary level, therefore, a distinction between theatrical and social acting is indispensable. Theatrical acting is always in practice delimited by its play context (even if this play context is itself made problematic and flexible) and by the fact that it has no direct effect on the "real" world. Social acting is not (necessarily) play, for the simple, tautological reason that it is (often) too serious. The claim that everything is play is best viewed as a claim about language use, not about the world.

Taking such considerations into account, the following essay will hover indeterminately and inconclusively between two versions of the metaphor of mask or appearance: a dualistic one based upon an actual distinction between mask and face, appearance and reality, and a monistic one that, claiming the impossibility of ultimately transcending our behavioral role or the limitations of our cognitive faculties, posits that there is in the end nothing behind the mask. In the course of the study, this "nothing" will itself become a thorn in our theoretical flesh, owing to the perennial problems of referring to nothing (which ought to be, but are not, the same as those of not referring to anything).

The implication of this motley crew of metaphors is that because the patterning and structuring apparent in life is a function of human cognitive or social organization, it is in some sense different from reality, from what would be the case if the human mind was not there to do the organizing. Order is a mask hiding the chaos of the real or of the unknowable. Our normal perception of the world is thus essentially like our perception of an illusionistic play—a structured "appearance" that masks a reality we cannot usually know (not during the play) and that we tend to forget about because the appearance is so convincing in its role that it kids us it is real. Social behavior is likewise patterned role-playing that —in normal circumstances at least—is convincing enough to "take us in" and allow us to forget that it is merely "acting," the performance of a part. What this essay attempts is, first, (in chapters 1 to 5) to show how the interplay of mask/illusion/appearance and reality works *within* theatrical comedy and related contexts, and, then, (in chapters 6 to 9) to suggest that the experience of certain kinds of comedy may on occasion—by association and identification and on account of the metaphorical relationship of "theatre" and "reality"—imply a release for the *audience* from its normal social and cognitive mask. (For ease of understanding there follows a skeletal overview of the essay's argument. Those who wish to follow the argument as it unfolds are best advised to skip this and move straight on to chapter 1.)

Chapter 1 ("Mask and Repetition") starts with the masks characteristic of Old Greek Comedy and the commedia dell'arte, understood as being comic above all because of the element of repetition, thereby giving the onlooker the pleasure of recognition. The mask is then taken as a metaphor for the type of comic effects produced by iteration, structural patterning, and fixity of character. Chapter 2 ("Mask and Acting") moves on to the idea of the mask as *hiding* a true face and thus to deception, roguery, and knavery. A discrepancy is here opened up between appearance and reality. Various brands of irony are described in these terms, and the problematic notion of self-deception is looked into. Chapter 3 ("Language as a Mask") focuses on language, understood primarily as a mask in some sense mediating what is meant or intended. This chapter both echoes themes already mentioned and prefigures arguments to come. The concept of cliché relates to language as repetitive and—rather like a caricatural mask—an agent of distortive simplification, while the opaque linguistic mask of gibberish shows language on holiday, released from functional transparency and rejoicing in its own materiality. While "wordplay" refers to wit insofar as it is structured by patterns and repetitions, the word "pun" in the following section draws attention to the potential of language to *hide* meaning and, unlike functional language, to do so explicitly (for those in the know). Verbal inversions are seen to point up the arbitrary nature of the linguistic mask.

Chapter 4 ("Cracking the Mask") explores role-playing not so much for the state of discrepancy between appearance and reality as for the moment of disillusionment when the mask falls, the appearance is shown to be deceptive, and the expectations are shattered. Imposture may be unmasked both from without, thanks to the insights of a perspicacious hero, or the mask may crack owing to pressure from within, the congenital incompetence of a bad actor. Bad acting often takes place on a stage-within-a-stage. The bathetic comedy of parody and burlesque may also incorporate this element of surprise. Chapter 5 ("Rupturing the Illusion") is concerned with breaks and flaws not in individual role-playing but in the theatrical illusion as a whole. By spotlighting those theatrical conventions normally taken for granted, so-called "metatheatre"—like comic language and imperfect imposture—functions as an illusion or mask that draws attention to itself as such.

With Chapter 6 ("Discarding the Social Mask"), attention now switches to the other side of the footlights, to investigate the way a comedy may cause its spectators empathetically to "drop" their own social posture or role in identifying with what takes place on stage. The ambivalent and paradoxical concept of folly is introduced, both in its festive and its sinful variations. Correspondingly, it is conceived both as a natural or "true" self and as the negativity inherent in a person's potential to deviate from the social norm, to do what is not done. Folly is approached firstly as a context, a "holiday humour" in which madness and foolery is the order of the day, and then as a phenomenon embodied in such comic fools as Shakespeare's Falstaff, Rabelais's Panurge, Jarry's Père Ubu, Harlequin and Brighella of the commedia dell'arte, Grimmelshausen's Simplicissimus, and John Kennedy Toole's Ignatius.

In Chapter 7 ("The Political Mask"), the metaphoric "mask" is considered as "political" to the extent that the social actor plays out a series of behavioral roles that are necessarily determined within a hierarchical structure of interpersonal relationships. Comic breaches in established social roles and reversals in power relationships afford pleasurable release from the restrictions of the normal order. Such reversals are most commonly between servant and master, or husband and wife. Chapter 8 ("The Ethical Mask") explores what is here termed the ethical mask, the mask that conceals our natural tendency to violence, sexual excess, and anarchy. Farce and satire are seen as offering releases for aggressive impulses, while the second section focuses on the complex relationship between comedy and sexuality. Finally the mask is described as cloaking cloacal messiness, and in this respect comedy functions as a letting off of scatological steam. Toilet humor and related issues are here the theme. "The Cognitive Mask" of chapter 9 operates at a rather different level of abstraction and is preceded by a theoretical section explaining (in broadly Kantian terms) the idea of an ontological distinction between appearance and reality and of the nothingness of this reality. When this cognitive mask is transgressed, the play with our perceptual and conceptual structures produces the comedy of nonsense, the grotesque and the surreal, as well as the lunacy of the topsy-turvy world.

1

Mask and Repetition

Most of the cognitive and linguistic patterning and structuring of experience is taken for granted rather than actively registered or interpreted. Our understanding and our application of concepts, for example, are processes that generally occur "on automatic." One may use the concept "cat" to apply to scores, hundreds, or thousands of particular furry purrers, yet the repetition of the concept in a myriad of contexts and denoting any number of different individual specimens is not something that as a rule disturbs, surprises, or bowls us over. If structuralists (rightly but one-sidedly) stress that meaning depends on difference, the concept "cat" having a significance by virtue of *not* being "mat," "vat," or "dog," this metaphor recalls to mind that meaning is also necessarily dependent on identity—that is, repetition of the same. The concept "cat" has a significance as long as a cat is a cat is a cat is a.... One could say that such repetition makes itself scarce, hiding itself like a translucent mask or a convincing illusion. Comic repetition is more obtrusive, reducing us to babies cooing with satisfaction at the predictability of the world. It is as if the structure of our experience is drawing attention to its own structuredness.

The masks worn by the figures of the commedia dell'arte show the connection between mask and repetition in a way that can be taken as paradigmatic. The very sight of the demoniacal half-mask of Arlecchino, or Harlequin, afforded the Italian audiences of the sixteenth century the comic pleasure of predicting and recognizing his standard behavioral patterns—his acrobatic wit, his powers of impersonation, his muddle-mindedness, laziness, and naivety, and his vaguely diabolical charm. The Neapolitan Pollicinella, or Pulcinella, would have a similar effect through his hooked nose, his baggy white costume, and his sugarloaf hat, just as the masks of such characters as Pantalone, il Dottore, and Brighella would prompt anticipations of amorous folly, stuttering pedantry, and sly cunning, respectively. Masks had been worn as early as the Aristophanic comedy of ancient Greece, where—quite apart from any ritual significance—they not only served to facilitate the actors' role-swapping and

add to the visibility of the spectacle, but also generated comic predictability in the recognition of stock characters. Roman New Comedy too
(the plays of Terence and Plautus) was rife with stock figures such as the
braggart soldier, the parasite, and the aging bawd.

In such instances, the physical masks impose a grid of rigidity on the
action (a grid within which improvization can of course flourish), which is
relished for the pleasures of anticipation and fulfillment it yields. Whenever the character in question turns in an appearance, the audience
knows it is going to witness a certain pattern of conduct. Human behavior
in general naturally has a tendency to slip into standardized routine and
regularity, to congeal into repetitive fixity, our traits of character being
modes of comportment seen as *recurrent*. It is when the element of recurrence comes to the fore and a persona emerges as dominated by a
specific trait that a potential for comedy is created. Clearly, therefore, the
"mask" need not be taken literally. Any old hackneyed cliché of a figure
is likely to raise a titter so long as the sameness of his recurrent appearance is recognized. Feydeau's nineteenth-century comedy *La Puce à
l'oreille* can be taken as representative of boulevard farce in general in
its exploitation of masklike stereotypes that are geographical as much
as vocational in nature, presenting a jealous, rantingly homicidal
Spaniard called Homenidès as well as a randy English no-hoper by the
name of Rugby, both of whom behave throughout with consummate
predictability.

In the case of this type of caricature—be it malicious or not—the
identity to be identified is above all a national one: Homenidès's and
Rugby's actions are but "self-evident" extensions of those seemingly immutable racial abstractions, The Spaniard and The Englishman. To cite
one modern and popular example of a figure whose comedy results in
part from the predictability of a self-generated myth, Basil Fawlty of the
BBC television series *Fawlty Towers* is a "mask" of middle-class insensitivity and prejudice and manic British incompetence. In his presence, we *know* we are about to be confronted with the behavior of a
bullying, cringing bastard for whom everything is going to go catastro-
phically wrong. It is ultimately the same process (fulfillment of expectations) that is at work when—or if—we laugh at the catchphrase of the
professional stand-up comedian, or at the stock joke—such as Aristophanes's standard jibes about randy or bibulous women.

A particular satisfaction is granted when a specific "mask" turns up in
a variety of contexts, giving the audience the self-congratulatory pleasure
of perceiving the identity within the difference. This is illustrated by the
figures of the commedia dell'arte, whose well-known and well-loved
masks woula put in an appearance in an endless range of standard
plots—yet always in character. From the world of early cinema, Buster

Keaton's "stone face," one of the most haunting and evocative of all masks, never fails to retain its characteristic unsmiling silence (in the pre-MGM films at least), whether Buster is playing a model pupil, an engine driver, or a rich loafer; in more recent times, Woody Allen's angst-ridden, bespectacled mask has likewise kept its essential features wherever he has turned up. Even when Woody is playing the role of a sperm about to be dispatched into the beyond (in *Everything You Always Wanted to Know about Sex*), it is a safe bet that he will be a bespectacled sperm plagued by worries about being splattered onto the ceiling or propelled headfirst against a wall of hard rubber.

Imitation itself is a form of repetition and one characteristic of dolphins as well as human beings,[1] both subaquatic and terrestrial mimicry being playful duplications of a perceived identity. Yet its ludic aspect coexists with a functional import: as psychologists have pointed out, the development of man's mimetic impulse may be traced back to the initial assimilative urge to repeat actions for the sake of mastery.[2] The elements of playfulness and of power converge more specifically in derisive or mocking imitation, which consists in the selection and reproduction of repeatable facets from the victim's conduct or appearance with the intention that these facets should be recognized—and in turn derided—by a third person or by the victim himself. This is a principle underlying much satire and caricature. The Aristophanic masks referred to above served for the recognition not only of stock characters, but also of widely known public figures, politicians, and poets. The German philosopher Schelling was aware of this feature of comedy. In his *Philosophie der Kunst*, he defines comedy's essence as consisting in a reversal in the normal relationship of necessity and freedom such that, instead of the human subject being free and the nonhuman object governed by necessity, the subject's behavior seems to be dictated by necessity (i.e., determined by predictable laws) and the object behaves as if it were free. In this general context, Schelling maintains that the best comic method for achieving the appearance of necessity in the subject is to make it a public figure having a recognizably fixed character: "The highest manifestation of comedy thus necessarily requires public characters, and in order for maximum concreteness to be attained they must be real-life persons of public character who are presented in comedy."[3] Like Hegel and Schlegel, Schelling saw in Aristophanes a comic paradigm. Nietzsche likewise attached especial value to the *public* nature of Aristophanic comedy and opposed it to what he considered the private and domestic pettiness of Plautus. Whether or not one accepts these rather dogmatically held points of view, it is clear that such satire constitutes a form of comic repetition dependent largely (though not solely) on being *identified*. A caricatural mask is a product of the twin processes of synecdochic or metonymic simplification (that is, the selection of specific features belonging to or associated with the "face" in question) and hyperbole (the amplification of the abnormality or grotesqueness of these features). Such a lampoon thus involves recognition through a mask of distortion. Once again, it is left to the audience or public to recognize the identity within the difference.

Of course satire and caricature need not be personal. Even when it is directed at social and political institutions or indeed at society in general, however, a similar process of selective simplification and exaggeration seems to be at work. Boccaccio's satire of the religious orders in his *Decameron*, for example, focuses on their venality, ignorance, and lechery— commonplaces of the time doubtless received with (among other things) the laughter of recognition. Molière's satire of doctors in *Le Malade imaginaire* similarly seizes on a trait widely attributed to the medical profession at the time (the use of latinistic jargon) and inflates it to the level of grotesque gibberish. As Freud points out, topicality is essential to such comedy:[4] the identity that is repeated should be something fresh in the public mind.

The repetition and predictability of comedy is not restricted to a *human* mask (individual or collective), but may also occur as a structural patterning at the level of the aesthetic experience as a whole. Aesthetic experiences are of course by nature highly structured without necessarily being comic: it is when the patterning insistently pokes us in the mind's eye that the repetition may provoke laughter. Obtrusively repeated leit-motifs, customized catchphrases associated with a particular character, and crassly stylized verbal exchanges or sequences of action all function in this way, also tending to break the theatrical illusion and drag the performance away from the realm of dry realism.

Der Talisman, a socially critical *Posse* or farce written by one of the greatest of German-speaking comic playwrights, the Austrian Nestroy, exemplifies this comic exploitation of structure and repetition at a number of levels. The play is indeed dominated by disguise and linguistic mimicry as Titus, the "carrot-headed" comic hero, tries to overcome prejudice against redheads and climb the social ladder by donning a wig and pretending to be "normal" in matters pileous. At a verbal level, however, Titus is not merely a skilled actor able to repeat and adapt the style and register of his conversational partner (although not always flawlessly so), he is also a sophisticated rhetorician. As an aspiring gardener, he on one occasion displays his verbal dexterity particularly impressively, proving that a knowledge of plants is essential for a knowledge of mankind in a speech structured around a series of syntactical repetitions used to force the point that most people do not live but vegetate (1.ı7). At a formal level, the play in its entirety revolves around a comic interplay of repetition and difference as it follows the rise in the social fortune of its wig-wearing hero, who successively courts the gardener's widow, then the chambermaid (also a widow), and finally the Lady herself (also a widow) and who—social differences notwithstanding—is successively offered the costumes worn by each of the three late husbands. To make matters worse, Titus's repeated mimicry is accompanied by repeated moments of near exposure as the impostor comes within a (red) hair's breadth of being recognized, not merely by the audience, but also by the rest of the protagonists.

A variant of such structural repetitions is the tit for tat pattern of much slapstick comedy. In *Big Business*, one of Laurel and Hardy's great early films, what starts out as controlled and measured reciprocal violence develops into an orgy of destruction in which Laurel and Hardy trash James Finlayson's house and he annihilates their car. *Tit for Tat* is a later variation on the theme, but it is pale and staid beside the earlier anarchy. *You're Darn Tootin*, another of the older films, reaches a crescendo of equally structured violence in which everybody rips everybody else's trousers off, Hardy furthermore punching his foes on the nose, Laurel kicking his on the shin. This example also illuminates the role of patterned complementarity in creating comic predictability. Comic partnerships are an oft-noted phenomenon, in which each partner has his or her specific mask. Laurel's naivety and Hardy's blustering clumsiness, Laurel's lips-down, eyebrows-up, headscratching attempts to stave off tears and Hardy's resigned finger-tapping after yet another (really painful) catastrophe regularly turn up throughout the years and regularly raise a laugh of satisfied anticipation. Perhaps the model for such relationships based on complementarity is that of Don Quixote and Sancho Panza, in which the former's monomanic obsession with chivalry and his ascetic idealism (and madness) comically contrast and interact with the latter's earthy simplicity and lusty common sense. This opposition is supported by a thick-thin, short-tall contrast that has persisted down the ages not only in Laurel and Hardy, but also in Andrew Aguecheek and Toby Belch (of *Twelfth Night*), Clown and Pantaloon (of the Victorian theatre), Abbott and Costello, Morecambe and Wise, Little and Large, Cannon and Ball....

Stylized dialogue, to be found—in different forms—in both Shakespeare and Molière, is also characterized by structural repetition. In *A Midsummer Night's Dream*, Hermia and Helena alternately describe their relationship with Demetrius:

> *Hermia.* I frown upon him, yet he loves me still.
> *Helena.* O that your frowns would teach my smiles such skill!
> *Hermia.* I give him curses, yet he gives me love.
> *Helena.* O that my prayers could such affection move!
> *Hermia.* The more I hate, the more he follows me.

Helena. The more I love, the more he hateth me.
Hermia. His folly, Helena, is no fault of mine.
Helena. None but your beauty; would that fault were mine!

(Act 1, scene 1)

These lines are not hilarious. Highly structured as they are by phonological and syntactical parallels together with semantic antitheses, however, they seem to come somewhere on the borderline between comedy and poetry, thus anticipating a point that will be frequently re-encountered: that wit and poetry often have in common an exceptionally high degree of phonological and semantic patterning. Frye claims that there is a "perilous balance in paronomasia [i.e., wordplay] between verbal wit and hypnotic incantation."[5] In other words, there exists a certain sort of repetitious pulsing rhythm that, instead of provoking laughter, can charm the listener, even send her to sleep.

That repetition itself may even become not only soporific but downright *boring* is a point illustrated by Büchner's *Leonce und Lena*, a play whose wit is characterized primarily by morphemic repetition. Witness Valerio trying to stave off his master's attempt to drown himself: "Ich werde Sie lassen, sobald Sie gelassen sind und das Wasser zu lassen versprechen" (2.4), which could be freely rendered in English as "By your leave, I'll leave you when I believe you calm and you leave the water." Another rather tedious example of Valerio's wordplay entails the repetition of the word "kommen" with six different prefixes. Yet this is appropriate, for the play is a comic poem on the repeatability of experience and is permeated by the problem of tedium. In a context where all the characters, Leonce and Lena included, are shown to be predictable, puppet-like automatons enmeshed in routine, mechanical role-playing, and cliché, the wordplay becomes a sign of artificiality rather than verbal vitality and ebullience. The mask here functions as a central symbol of alienated or inauthentic identity, and, in a final self-reflexive coup de theatre, Leonce draws attention to the repeatability not only of the fictive world but also of the theatrical performance. When he sends the Council home ("Go home now, but do not forget your speeches, sermons, and verses, for tomorrow we shall at leisure go through the whole lark from the beginning again" [3.3]), the words apply equally well to the real-life audience.[6] Büchner's vision of the *theatrum mundi* has man as a theatrical marionette, puppet, or mask without any genuine sense of identity and playing a role that is essentially repeatable. The repetition of the theatrical performance echoes the repetition in life.

Beckett's *Waiting for Godot* is another comic poem on the repetitiveness of life, the play's iterative structure making an existential point. The second act reflects and modifies the first, while the recurrence of the words of the title, for example, serves as a verbal backbone holding the two halves together. Like Leonce, Vladimir and Estragon are battling to fill the emptiness of time, and this uphill struggle provides another example of the borderline between comic repetition and hypnotic lyricism.

Estragon. In the meantime let us try and converse calmly, since we are incapable of keeping silent.
Vladimir. You're right, we're inexhaustible.
Estragon. It's so we won't think.
Vladimir. We have that excuse.
Estragon. It's so we won't hear.
Vladimir. We have our reasons.
Estragon. All the dead voices.
Vladimir. They make a noise like wings.
Estragon. Like leaves.
Vladimir. Like sand.
Estragon. Like leaves.
        Silence.
Vladimir. They all speak together.
Estragon. Each one to itself.
        Silence.
Vladimir. Rather they whisper.
Estragon. They rustle.
Vladimir. They murmur.
Estragon. They rustle.
        Silence (...)
Vladimir. They make a noise like feathers.
Estragon. Like leaves.
Vladimir. Like ashes.
Estragon. Like leaves.
        Long silence.
Vladimir Say something!
Estragon. I'm trying.
        Long silence.
Vladimir. *(in anguish).* Say anything at all!
Estragon. What do we do now?
Vladimir. Wait for Godot.

(Act 2)

As with *Leonce und Lena* the circularity of the play, underlined by a parallel sense we have that Vladimir and Estragon are performing to fill in the emptiness of *our* time and pad out *our* silence with the comfort of diversionary words, works as a link between the repetitiveness of the world and the repetition of theatrical performance. Vladimir and Estragon too will be back to repeat their stint and forget their words on the next day, and the next, and the next, and the....

Since the romantic era, masks have taken on a disconcertingly grotesque quality, symbolizing a sense of alienation, a lack of identity, an absence of selfhood. Human beings who behave like automatons have been presented as frightening rather than funny.[7] Brecht's play *Mann ist Mann* demonstrates this sinister aspect of repetition (and thereby straddles another of comedy's borderlines). Portraying the transformation of the protagonist Galy Gay from a simple and well-meaning docker into a fighting robot, the play shows man as a machine that can be taken apart and put back together again with a new identity. The replaceability and functionality of the character is underscored by a number of thematic repetitions and leitmotifs (recurrent phrases such as "Mann ist Mann" and the elephant and train motifs, which are comically fused and confused). Such puppetlike repeatability (the fact that a man is a man is a man is a man is a ...), whether making an existential or a political point, is unsettling to the extent that it seems to deny such (bourgeois?) notions as individuality and human uniqueness. If man is determined by social forces and society is felt to be essentially sick and cankerous, then the idea of man as a puppet—although it may have comic potential—takes on a horrific dimension.

More obviously comic is the repetition characteristic of monomanic obsession. Lanson and others have pointed out the derivation of Molière's comic figures from the tradition of the commedia dell'arte, explaining the unalterable fixity of such personae as Argan, Harpagon, and Alceste in terms of the unalterable fixity of the Italian masks.[8] Molière's protagonists to this extent *are* masks, simplified repetitions of a dominant trait, and the principle of predictability is essential to the laughter they generate. Harpagon's monomanic mask of miserliness manifests itself repeatedly in his constant exits to check his stock of money, and the psychological predictability is underlined by verbal repetitions, the most renowned of which is the reiterated "sans dot" indicative of his eagerness to marry off his daughter without a dowry. Compulsive verbal repetition equally characterizes Argan, Monsieur Jourdain, and Orgon, to name but three of Molière's most famed protagonists.

Harpagon is of special interest for he is one in a long line of obsessive misers, variations in which shed light on the comic potential of excessive avarice. He is a direct descendant of Plautus's Euclio, whose conduct is equally predictable and typified by an equally paranoid distrust of all and sundry. Yet the motif turns up as far afield as thirteenth-century China, where Yo—in the love-comedy *Yüan-yang-pi*—combines features of the miser with the sort of leering senescent lechery that by comic consent is an invitation to physical manhandling (which is what he gets). Marlowe and Shakespeare offer rather more complex examples of extreme rapacity. While Marlowe's Barabas is avaricious and mean, however, the comic possibilities of the trait remain occluded because this never develops into a compulsive behavioral pattern affording the audience the pleasure of anticipation and fulfillment. Indeed, he is such a nasty piece of work that he may seem fearsome rather than funny. Even so, Marlowe's melodrama does come close to the comic (if not becoming a downright hoot) when Barabas's nastiness itself turns into a repetitive pattern and the spectacle of a bloodbath veers towards a grotesque and farcical parody.

Of all five misers, Shakespeare's Shylock is the most highly developed and subtle in psychological terms, a fact that tends to increase identification with him and reduce the emotional distance on which laughter depends. Whereas Harpagon remains above all a mask and Barabas more often resembles a psychopathic puppet wanting to kill everyone in the world, Shylock is always first and foremost a human being—and a human being, moreover, who is not just dangerous and dastardly but also a pitiable victim of social prejudice, a lonely pariah. Inspite of the intricacies of his portrayal, the comedy of his character is at times allowed to prevail, and he vacillates between the pathetic and the ridiculous. One scene in particular demonstrates his comic potential, showing Shylock the predictable marionette whose swings of mood can be manipulated with ease by Tubal and anticipated with pleasurable regularity by the onlooker.

Tubal.   Yes, other men have ill luck too—Antonio, as I heard in Genoa,—
Shylock. What, what, what? ill luck, ill luck?
Tubal.   —hath an argosy cast away coming from Tripolis.
Shylock. I thank God, I thank God! Is it true, is it true?
Tubal.   I spoke with some of the sailors that escaped the wreck.
Shylock. I thank thee, good Tubal; good news, good news: ha ha! heard in Genoa!
Tubal.   Your daughter spent in Genoa, as I heard, one night, fourscore ducats.
Shylock. Thou stick'st a dagger in me—I shall never see my gold again—fourscore ducats at a sitting, fourscore ducats!
Tubal.   There came divers of Antonio's creditors in my company to Venice, that swear he cannot choose but break.
Shylock. I am very glad of it—I'll plague him, I'll torture him—I am glad of it.
Tubal.   One of them showed me a ring he had of your daughter for a monkey.
Shylock. Out upon her!—Thou torturest me, Tubal—it was my turquoise; I had it of Leah when I was a bachelor. I would not have given it for a wilderness of monkeys.
Tubal.   But Antonio is certainly undone.
Shylock. Nay, that's true, that's very true.

(Act 3, scene 1)

The case of avarice is of further relevance because not only is it a mono-manic mask, it is also a trait that we (i.e., "we") morally condemn. Misers are comic butts therefore not merely for being repetitive, but also for being socially abnormal, reprehensible, or "inferior." Obsession in itself is often regarded as a stigma. Bergson's famous theory of the comic, which drew attention above all to the comedy of predictability and repetition, of fixity and rigidity of character,[9] viewed laughter as a social corrective prescribing human flexibility. When human beings start behaving with the fixity of masks or machines, laughter steps in and normalizes them, stamping out excess and eccentricity.[10] It sounds like some particularly insidious form of secret police: be flexible, or else we'll send the boys round and humiliate you into flexibility. The seventeenth-century English political philosopher Thomas Hobbes likewise developed a theory of laughter primarily as prescriptive derision: "Joy, arising from imagination of a mans own power and ability, is that exultation of the mind which is called GLORYING.... Sudden Glory, is the passion which maketh those Grimaces called LAUGHTER; and is caused either by some sudden act of their own, that pleaseth them; or by the apprehension of some deformed thing in another, by comparison whereof they suddenly applaud themselves."[11]

Laughter is a gesture of self-applause. Not only, therefore, does the recognition of patterns, the "getting" of a joke, in itself produce a sort of self-approving laughter, but compounded with this may be the self-congratulation arising from the recognition of a social defect in another, measured against the yardstick of one's own "normality." Again, laughter does not seem to cut a particularly savory or gallant figure, and Hobbes consequently regarded it as a sign of pusillanimity: after all, it is only the weak who *need* to assert their power. Hegel too recognized the element of self-congratulation inherent in the simultaneous awareness of a norm and acknowledgement of a deviation from it: "Laughter is then but an expression of complacent cleverness, a sign that they (the public) too are wise enough to recognize such a contrast and know themselves above it."[12] Fortunately, however, this is only half the truth. Laughter can equally well *celebrate* abnormality, deviance, and eccentricity.

It tends to be satiric comedy that most unequivocally mocks obsession. Ben Jonson used the term "humour" to refer to such excessiveness, which he saw as a kind of physical and mental imbalance. His figure Lady Politic Would-be, herself unable to stem the flux of her own logorrheic humour, puts it thus in *Volpone*:

There's nothing, more, doth overwhelm the judgement,
And clouds the understanding, than too much

Settling, and fixing, and (as't were) subsiding
Upon one object.

(Act 3, scene 4)

Mosca later echoes this sentiment, a sentiment in fact that applies to the whole Jonsonian ship of knaves and fools. Being (of course) a strictly moral audience consisting only of very decent and well-balanced people, we laugh at the fixity, the one-sidedness, and the deviance from the moral norm because *we know better*—and, what's more, we really enjoy knowing better. The victims of an obsession are prey to deception and self-deception, while our moral (and theatrical) overview puts us in the position of the undeceived.

It is from our knowing better that the comedy of naivety tends to arise, as well as from the potential for repetition that obstinate naivety generates. Voltaire's *Candide*, for example, is structured by the eponymous hero's persistent optimism in the face of the biggest catalogue of catastrophes imaginable, his reiterated "tout est bien" coming to sound more and more hollow as time passes and he witnesses more and more people being swindled, betrayed, drowned, and butchered. Sade's *Justine* has an analogous structure and can likewise (with the requisite emotional distance) be regarded as an exceedingly black comedy. The heroine's intransigent candor leads her on a direct route from one sexual nightmare to the next even bigger one with a remarkable (predictable, stylized) regularity. Hasek's (and Brecht's) Svejk offers a subtle variation on the theme of naivety, for in his case we can never be sure to what extent the candor is feigned. Svejk too is a mask, his face wearing an expression of benign equanimity and unshakable good-nature that is a comic constant throughout the novel. But feigned or not, naivety becomes a skill in his hands, a way of coping with the harsh madness of military life. It is an admirable naivety.

Monomania and predictability need not therefore be objects only of normative mockery. N. F. Simpson's *One Way Pendulum* is packed with repeated idiosyncrasies treated not scornfully but with amused detachment. To take but three examples, Kirby Groomkirby is obsessed with singing weighing-machines, Sylvia with the length of her arms, and wheelchaired Aunt Mildred with methods of transport ("What's happened to my tricycle, Mabel?" and related questions forming the backbone of her conversational offerings). The whole business seems to celebrate barminess and a sort of understated lunacy. Laurence Sterne's Old Shandy and Uncle Toby (from *The Life and Times of Tristram Shandy*) are a lovable comic partnership based on idiosyncratic complementarity, Old Shandy's tendency to abstraction opposed by Uncle

Toby's remoteness from anything vaguely abstruse, Shandy's outbursts of choler countered by Toby's implacable gentleness (this in turn prompting Shandy's immediate remorse). Each has his particular hobby horse on which he goes digressively trotting through the entire novel. Whereas Old Shandy is possessed by his hypotheses and theories, Uncle Toby has a passion for military works that colors his whole vision and repeatedly distracts him from his companion's wordiness. As the narrator puts it at the outset: "have not the wisest of men in all ages, not excepting Solomon himself,—have they not had their HOBBY-HORSES?"[13]

2
Mask and Acting

To say that Harlequin, Harpagon, Svejk, and Basil Fawlty are masks is to use the term in a clearly metaphorical way. This notion of *being* a mask (referring to rigidity and predictability of character) can be distinguished from that of *wearing* a mask (which refers to dissimulation, role-playing, disguise, and deception). Correspondingly, two levels of comic mask come to light: to the extent that the theatre itself is a form of role-playing, there is the mask (whether literal visor or metaphorical persona) worn by the actor performing the part of Harlequin or Harpagon, and, to the extent that the theatre portrays a world full of figures themselves capable of pretence and imposture, there is the mask optionally donned by characters within the fiction for purposes of trickery or deceit—the mask *of* the fiction or the mask *in* the fiction. Molière's hypochondriac embodies this distinction for, on one level, Argan the stage presence *is* a mask of hypochondria (a stock comic type—The Hypochondriac—whose conduct presents pleasurable patterns of repetition and predictability), while, on another, he is a figure within the fiction himself *wearing* a mask of illness—a mask that consistently falls to reveal a perfectly healthy figure chasing about the room and sturdy enough to survive even the treatment meted out by the medical profession. Argan's pretence of infirmity in fact convinces nobody except himself. Likewise, Molière's Tartuffe—as the quintessential Hypocrite—*is* a mask of hypocrisy, a recognizable persona fixed in its underlying features, yet within the fiction, this hypocrisy consists in *wearing* a wobbly mask of piety beneath which his baser instincts are very much in evidence, to the audience at least.

The comedy of watching people act a part or don a disguise lies above all in the recognition of the difference between appearances and what is assumed to be really the case. Aware (smugly) of the true face behind the false mask, moreover, the onlooker's laughter testifies to a cognitive superiority over those who are taken in by the acting, the fools and gulls who are deceived by the masks of the knaves and rogues. The vertical distance that results from an awareness of the plot as a whole bolsters the spectator's sense of having access to the truth (unlike most of the characters), perhaps supported by asides and soliloquies that yield an insight into the impostor's "real" intentions or by glimpses of the mask falling when the actor gives himself away in moments of weakness. A number of factors may be at work in such comedy, including mockery of the dupe coupled with self-applause on recognition of the discrepancy between appearance and reality. The theatrical overview furthermore allows the audience to anticipate the ways in which the deception may bring the gulls to behave predictably, performing like marionettes following the logicality of their own position and blindly careering into a stream of mishaps. This is the dominant impulse behind situation comedy, the comedy of plot and intrigue, misunderstanding, disguise, and mistaken identity.

The mask-wearer—the actor, the trickster—is an inherently ambivalent figure, as exemplified by such naturally histrionic comic personalities as Harlequin, Falstaff, and Panurge. On the one hand actors are dangerous for they can hide their vices and exploit their powers of mimicry in the cause of deception, while on the other the mimetic impulse is in itself pleasurable, theatre keeps us entertained, and actors moreover have an enjoyable knack of deflating pretension and deriding gullibility and vice. Accordingly, imposture (seen as ethically dubious) is regularly debunked and unmasked by comedy's corrective impetus, while mimetic agility and flexibility (seen as positive attributes) tend to be applauded and rewarded. The medieval Vices of the morality plays often bore such names as Counterfeit Countenance and Cloaked Collusion, alluding to their status as "seemers" who employ disguise to cheat and swindle and are thus to be ridiculed and condemned; comedies of manners down the years have regularly pilloried those who hide their own rough edges and protrusions under a veneered social mask. In his preface to *Joseph Andrews*, Henry Fielding indeed pinpoints human affectation as the primary source of the ridiculous. "Now, affectation proceeds from one of these two causes, vanity or hypocrisy: for as vanity puts us on affecting false characters, in order to purchase applause; so hypocrisy sets us on an endeavour to avoid censure, by concealing our vices, under an appearance of their opposite virtues."[1] An appreciation of the ridiculous therefore becomes a matter of exposing the *reality* behind *appearances*, for example by apprehending the gap between what people say and what they do (when they believe themselves unobserved). Whence the comedy of Tartuffe, whose pious pose fails to conceal the ruttish rogue beneath.

Much of the comic energy in such instances is devoted to unmasking what is masked. The English Restoration comedies in particular reveal a society that, underneath the facade of respectability, is gunning for sex and money. The laughter here may indeed be three-pronged, aimed not only at what is masked (the infringement of the ethical norm), but also at both the attempt to mask it and at the failure of this attempt. It is to the extent that such comedy unmasks imposture, debunks pretension, exposes illusion, and discloses deception and self-deception that it has frequently been associated with a movement towards truth, culminating in the cumbersome enlightenment of the "recognition scene," or what an Aristotelian tradition of scholarship has called *anagnorisis*.[2] Although used by Aristotle himself to denote a device characteristic of epic and tragic poems, over the years this term and the related (but somewhat broader) Latin terms *cognitio* and *agnitio* have come to be seen more and more as designating a feature belonging to the realm of comedy (indeed unworthy of tragedy insofar as the device relies on chance and coincidence). The late Latin grammarians Donatus-Evanthius thus characterize the Roman New Comedy as concluding with a *cognitio* that unravels the knots of the plot and unearths what has really been going on, Dionysius of Thrace claims that "whereas tragedy has its consummation in slaughter and bloodshed, comedy ends in recognition," and the Renaissance scholar Robortello prescribes the placement of recognition at the close of the comedy as a tidying up of all the misunderstandings. In his *Essay of Dramatick Poesie*, Dryden uses the term "discovery", likewise conceived as an unravelling and leading to "that resemblance of truth and nature, that the audience are satisfied with the conduct of it," while in the twentieth century, Frye has identified the role of *cognitio* as a device dispelling the misconceptions fostered by imposture, affectation, obsession, and unknown parentage and bringing about "a movement from illusion to reality."[3] Yet comedy is not simply an overcoming and a rejection of illusion. This would be to deny its own essence. Comedy may equally well celebrate acting and revel in the temporary madness of disguise and play.

Jonson's Volpone incorporates this duality, using his histrionic skills both to fleece fools who deserve their fleecing and to hide his own rather shady intentions. Posing as an invalid, Volpone wheedles money out of his rich old dupes by separately promising each of them the inheritance of his fortune on his death, thus mocking and exploiting the avarice of those who would seek to have the better of him. The play is pervaded by this interplay of knave and gull, which is given a further twist when Volpone has the tables turned on him by his rascally servant Mosca. The audience shares the perspective of the knaves (Volpone and Mosca, and later just Mosca) and is able to gloat with self-satisfied complicity at the expense of the gulls (themselves also money-grabbing rogues) taken in by Volpone's performances. Volpone is above all else an actor, a trickster, a con man, unlike Harpagon glorying more in the cunning purchase of his wealth than in the glad possession. Even his opening eulogy on gold seems to show him revelling more in his own verbal dexterity than in the wealth itself. While we enjoy—and the comedy depends upon—his skill as a crafty rhetorician, however, Volpone is still presented as reprehensible and vicious. Above all in the unsuccessful wooing of Celia, the sophistication and measured artifice of his oratorical spiel is eventually shattered to reveal the ugliness of the potential rapist underneath. Yet inspite of his nastiness, the severity of Volpone's final punishment on being exposed has tended to disconcert critics and viewers rather than satisfy a sense of poetic justice. Beside the colorless goody-goodies, Volpone's ingenuity and audacity make him the charismatic focal point of the play.

The audience is often brought to give the actor or deceiver less ambiguous support and sympathy. One of the stock comic themes has been the wile and wit employed by young couples to outmaneuver domineering parents or vigilant guardians, the dashing hero gaining entrance to the otherwise inaccessible household for example by posing as a music teacher or some such tutor. Whatever the specific form of the role-playing and intrigue that takes place, the important comic point is that the audience—unlike the troublesome old *senex*—should be in the know. Where lovestruck youth is too witless or incompetent to devise its own trickery, moreover, a more general comic handyman-in-roguery is required. In this capacity, Plautus's Pseudolus is an archetype of the sympathetic schemer, the artisan of untruth working in the name of comic justice, i.e., young love. Indeed, right at the outset of Plautus's play, of which he—as much as Plautus—may be said to be the orchestrator, he takes the precaution of warning the audience of his mendacious nature, thus ensuring its collusion. Unlike his future dupes, the spectators are allowed to see his acting as acting, to recognize his performance for what it is. A continuation of this Plautine tradition is the Italian comedy of the Renaissance, where such tricksters as Pseudolus are reincarnated in the guise of Machiavelli's Ligurio or Aretino's Rosso, and where the *beffa* or practical joke comes into its own. In English Restoration comedies the true wit was usually also a true rogue. Wycherley's *The Country Wife* is structured around the sparklingly amoral roguery of Horner, who elicits the support of the spectator if only because his deception is carried out at the expense of dupes who merit nothing better. Passing himself off as a eunuch, he does himself down in order to outwit others, rather like the age-old comic figure of the *eiron* (the precursor of the Socratic ironist). Yet the onlooker is in on the imposture. Horner hides his horn beneath a pretence of impotence obtrusively broadcast to the public, but this fakery enables him to blow his own trumpet (or have it blown) in private: when the husbands are gone Horner drops his pretences and reveals his true end to both the audience and the ladies.

If deception is an ubiquitous comic theme, then lies and exaggeration are archetypal modes of comic discourse, largely dependent upon being seen through for their effect. Plautus's *miles gloriosus* or braggart soldier Pyrgopolynices is thus mocked for his boastfulness, amatory pretensions, and military braggadocio and for the rift discerned between attempted appearances and less flattering reality. When he comes out with tall stories of bravery and heroism (and claims to have slaughtered 7,000 of the enemy in one day), his slave superficially plays along and pretends to confirm the facts, but reveals the truth in asides to the audience, establishing their complicity and justifying their scorn. The stock type lives on in the form of *il Capitano* (sometimes known as Spavento) in the commedia dell'arte, a cocky coward none of whose lies is believed and who, like Pyrgopolynices, always ends up the loser (that is until, in the charismatic hands of the actor Fiorilli, he frees himself from the mask and becomes Scaramuccia, ancestor of Scaramouche). Falstaff too is among many other things a relative of the *miles gloriosus*, an aspect of his Protean nature that comes to light in the lies he tells after he has been set upon and pasted by Hal and his men incognito. That the audience has witnessed his humiliation makes the woolly fabrication he spins all the more see-through, but Falstaff—ever the performer—subtly turns his physical defeat into verbal victory by hyperbolically expanding his figures beyond all credibility. "I am a rogue if I were not at half-sword with a dozen of them two hours together ... if I fought not with fifty of them, I am a bunch of radish" (*1 Henry IV*, 2.4). Lies are not merely a mask hiding a cowardly nature, but also signs of imaginative versatility and fertility. As the roguish Brighella of the commedia puts it: "When you tell lies, tell big ones."[4] Rabelais's Panurge—armed as he is (or says he is) with an implacable plonker—couples cowardice and sexual bravura in inimitable manner, and his claim to have swonken 417 wenches within the last nine days clearly comes right up to Brighella's standard. In the case of Rabelais, moreover, there exists a patent link between lying that takes place within the fiction and fiction itself as a sort of lying. Rabelais's tall stories of exaggeration and fantasy are fictions that question and throw into doubt their own truthfulness (in spite of and indeed because of the asseverations and threats of the narrator), and the Rabelaisian narrator—and ultimately Rabelais himself—reveals himself as a kind of liar. Plautus's Pyrgopolynices pales into insignificance besides Frère Jan who, we are told, effortlessly debrains, eviscerates, and dismembers 13,622 of the enemy, not counting the women and small children, of course.

Rabelais's Panurge is as much as anything an avid practitioner of the practical joke, a form of comedy closely linked to comic deception in that the third party—reader or audience—colludes in the worsting of a victim, this worsting often being of a sexual or scatological nature. Having been rejected by a noble lady with whom he wishes to mate, Panurge gains his revenge by sprinkling the lady's dress with the diced genitals of a bitch, thereby causing 600,014 dogs to follow her in procession and bepiss everything she touches. The cruelty of such comedy is only a more manifest variation on the cruelty of any mockery, but here it is clearly focused on the victim's embarrassment and discomfort. The medieval sense of humor seems to have been buttressed by a robust insensitivity in such matters. The surrealists of this century, merry pranksters that they were, went in for practical jokes of an equally excremental but less cruel order, such as plastic turds. Not merely an attempt to *épater les bourgeois*, this jolly jape also relies upon the comic discrepancy between appearance and reality, what it is and what it seems to be. The Sex Pistols, also merry pranksters, exploited the same gag on one of their album sleeves.

In the realm of the Renaissance comedy of Italy the wit of the *beffatore*, or practical joker, comes to gain at least equal status with virtue. This tradition is traceable in particular back to the comic tales of Boccaccio, whose *Decameron* devotes all ten stories of the seventh day to the *beffe* played by women upon their husbands, all of them in the highly laudable name of an extramarital swyving. In Machiavelli's *Mandragola* too the *beffa*, stage-managed by the ingenious parasite Ligurio, is a skillfully contrived means of enabling Callimaco to have sex with the beautiful Lucrezia—with the approval of her doltish husband Nicia. Ligurio, Callimaco, and the corrupt clergyman Fra Timoteo succeed in convincing Nicia that a fertility potion made of mandragora (which Lucrezia is to take to guarantee Nicia the son he desires) will kill the first person to sleep with Lucrezia after she has taken it, and they persuade Nicia to allow someone (Callimaco in disguise) to be dragged in off the streets and "made" to lie with her. This entails a sequence of mask-wearing episodes: Callimaco must pretend to be a learned doctor, the friar must disguise himself as Callimaco, and Callimaco must also assume the role of the "unfortunate" passer-by. The audience all the while maintains the distinction between appearance and reality and mocks the gullible old dope blissfully unaware that the "learned doctor" is scheming to dighte his wife.

Cuckoldry is also central to the medieval tradition of French farces such as *Un Amoureux*, where the sexual deception is supplemented by a healthy measure of fecal and uretic humor, throughout depending upon the superiority of the audience perspective. On the husband's unexpected return, there is thus the standard comic situation of the lover (the village curate) hiding, as well as relaxing his sphincter, under the marital bed, but the comic irony is increased when, seeing his wife (pretending to be) ill in bed, the husband asks her if she wishes to have a word with the curate. The bawdry also encompasses the inadvertent swapping of a bottle of wine with a bottle of freshly produced urine (to be taken to the doctor), both of which are imbibed with gusto.

The confusion of the bottles shows the comic potential of the inadvertent, as opposed to the intentional, misunderstanding. Again, the effect normally depends upon the audience or reader being above the confusion and knowing better and is often spiced up by being located in the sphere of sex. Misunderstanding characterizes the relationship of Old Shandy and Uncle Toby, these two veteran hobby-horsemen frequently trotting off in completely different directions. Indeed *Tristram Shandy* contains one of the most celebrated of comic misunderstandings when Toby offers to show the eager Widow Wadman where he sustained his war wound and even let her put her finger on the spot. The comic capacity of misunderstanding is in evidence both in Molière's *L'Avare* and in its source, Plautus's *Pot of Gold*. The former contains a confusion lasting over 100 lines, in which Harpagon accuses Valère of stealing his money-box, and Valère confesses in the misapprehension that his crime is to have "stolen" Harpagon's daughter. In Plautus's play the same situation has Lyconides admitting to having got Phaedria pregnant. In both cases the audience recognizes the illusion or error leading both parties astray and has the satisfaction of knowing better.

The action of Feydeau's boulevard farce *La Puce à l'oreille* is impelled—like so much farce—by the perennially dangling carrot of extramarital sex. Starting from the attempt to deceive the husband (or wife) and working on the principle of consistently (and predictably) bringing together the wrong people at the wrong time, Feydeau creates a dizzying maelstrom of misunderstandings, mistaken identities, and confusions in which the figures chase around like manic clockwork puppets and not even the spectator always knows what's what. The loudest laughter inevitably comes when the misunderstanding is either sexual in nature (when, thanks to the rotating bed, two complete strangers have a close encounter under the covers) or when it leads to violence (beatings being meted out to the wrong person, for example).

The comedy of deception and misunderstanding or confusion depends upon the vertical distance of the audience or reader, the superiority of perspective that allows him to know more than the fool and register the difference between the way things *seem* and the way they *are* or to anticipate the network of calamities into which the implicated figures are flung headlong. As self-congratulatory onlookers, we bask in our omniscience and revel in our godlike invulnerability. This is the ironic perspective: "He that sitteth in the heavens shall laugh: the Lord shall have them in derision" (Psalms 2:4). Nietzsche too has produced a graphic image of the divine laughter of a Dionysian creator reverberating around the cosmos as he watches the pathetic human comedy on earth with its cast of fools caught up in the illusion of their own significance. "There ought to be more spiritual creatures than human beings simply in order to appreciate the humour inherent in man's view of himself as the purpose of the entire universe.... If a god created the world, then he created man as *God's ape*, as a constant source of amusement in his interminable eternities. The music of the spheres around the earth would then be the derisive laughter of all other creatures around man."[5] The gods or higher forces stand in the same relation to us as we stand to the theatrical pawns on stage floundering about in ignorance and illusion, whence the (not necessarily comic) poignancy of the *theatrum mundi* motif when used by one of the few enlightened fictive figures who senses that he is but a character in a play. Whence also the symbolic potential of the play-within-a-play.

There is, however, one kind of character who tends to share the over-view to a certain degree. The plot-weaver is a certain cast of comic figure who creates laughter above all by generating comedies within the comedy, by manipulating the action according to *his* plots and controlling the "actors" rather like marionettes. This description clearly applies to such Shakespearean characters as Prospero or Puck who, on account of magical powers, attain something akin to the privileged panorama (even if the case of Prospero shows his theatrical artifice to be insufficient for procuring the happy ending and ultimately reliant upon the natural force of Ariel). But at a different level, Machiavelli's Ligurio, Brighella of the commedia, and Molière's Scapin use native wit rather than magic to control the plot. *Les Fourberies de Scapin* is virtually a one-man show. In a single episode Scapin hides one of his victims in a sack, and then, playing a number of parts at once (including himself), he acts out a scene in which—loyal servant that he is—"he" (i.e., Scapin) tries in vain to protect his victim from the blows meted out by a group of aggressors, also acted out by himself. Scapin's ancestor, beyond Brighella and Ligurio, is perhaps Plautus's liar Pseudolus, an equally crafty plot-weaver; indeed, he is one who explicitly likens his role to that of the poet, making a "fiction look very much like a fact." Again, mendacity *within* fiction and the mendacity *of* fiction are exposed as parallel phenomena.

Superiority of perspective additionally permits the spectator to recognize and enjoy recognizing such potentially comic patterns as dramatic irony. Dramatic irony is the irony that arises when, unbeknown to the utterer, an utterance has a double meaning, one for the situation as it appears to himself, another for the situation as it is in reality, as revealed to the all-knowing audience. Such scenes of course need not be comic, especially if it is a question of life and death in a gripping play, but they can be funny, as in the famous eavesdropping scene of *Love's Labour's Lost*, here supported by a sophisticated arrangement of patterns and repetitions. The scene opens with Berowne's entrance and his rhetorical declaration of love. Perceiving the King, he stands aside and observes the latter rhetorically declaring *his* love. Perceiving Longaville, the King stands aside and the two of them, unbeknown to one another, observe the latter rhetorically declaring *his* love. Perceiving Dumaine, Longaville stands aside and now three people observe the new arrival rhetorically declaring *his* love, debunked by Berowne's asides to the audience. Berowne relishes this ironic constellation of observers:

> All hid, all hid—an old infant play.
> Like a demi-god here sit I in the sky,
> And wretched fools' secrets heedfully o'er-eye.
>
> (Act 4, scene 3)

Having witnessed that Berowne too is a wretched fool with a secret, however, it is the spectator, strictly speaking, who is the demigod. Shakespeare then doubles and reverses the irony with a stylized process of unmasking. Firstly, Longaville advances and chides Dumaine for breaking the vow of continence taken together by the four of them; then the King advances and chides Longaville for hiding the fact that he too is in love; then Berowne advances and chides the King for hiding the fact that he too is in love (and he really does rub it in: "Now step I forth to whip hypocrisy . . ."). Finally Jaquenetta and Costard enter with a letter that reveals that Berowne too is in love: the hypocritical scourge of hypocrisy thus himself takes a lashing that confirms the ultimate ascendancy of the audience over the fictive fools who are unaware that they are being observed. Structural repetitions combine with an ironic overview which allows us to know more than any of the characters on stage.

The knowledge of the discrepancy between appearance and reality may equally well be retrospective, giving rise to what is known as the irony of events. Here the irony of an occurrence only comes to light when future developments put it in a new perspective, the temporal dimension revealing a situational reversal. Hindsight proves things not to have been as they had seemed to be (but often the opposite). Whereas dramatic irony relies more upon a spatial overview, irony of events hinges on the overview derived from an extended temporal perspective. Although such irony may easily be tragic and indeed is frequently associated with catastrophic reversals of events that seem to imply, once again, that man is but a plaything in the hands of that implacable blackguard Fortune, it has great comic potential, involving as it does the recognition of patterns and of the discrepancy between appearance and reality. The most basic example of a (possibly) comic irony of events is the thief, swindler, or rogue who revels in his trickery but is in fact with time outwitted by his gull and himself turns out to be the real fool. Seeing a knave duped, a robber robbed, a judge brought to trial satisfies not only our sense of justice, but also our love of patterns and structures. These two impulses—the ethical and the cognitive or recognitive—here prove their radical proximity.

The configuration of the trickster-tricked or the knave-duped is an ubiquitous comic form, again highlighting the ambivalence of acting: imposture is outwitted by benevolent ruse. Volpone the rogue comes to be duped by his aide Mosca, just as Lesage's fleecer Turcaret is in turn fleeced by his Machiavellian servant Frontin in another play absolutely suffused with deception, although in both these cases it would be truer to describe the (provisionally) triumphant trickery as vindicated by circumstance rather than motivated by goodwill. Frontin sums up the whole sequence of knaves, fools, and knaves fooled: "How I admire the course of human life! We fleece a coquette; the coquette clips a tradesman; the tradesman plunders yet others: all in all the most delightful ricochet of ruses in the world" (1.10). Because the irony is based in this instance on a simultaneity of knavery and gullibility that exists from the outset as much as on a syntagmatic progression from knave to dupe, this example forms a borderline between dramatic irony and the irony of events. Whichever term is adopted, however, the comedy of the irony consists in the contrast between the appearance or semblance of ascendancy deluding the proud protagonist and the reality of the comic justice to which he is to fall victim. That such ironic reversal may be linked to a socio-political reversal in which the servant gets the better of the master is illustrated by both *Volpone* and *Turcaret* and even more clearly by Beaumarchais's *Le Mariage de Figaro*, where the outwitting of the trickster is also a political victory.

Irony of events may then be tied to a spirit of vengeance akin to poetic justice. It can be found in this form in the grotesque and comic tales of Edgar Allan Poe. In "Hop-Frog" for example, the court dwarf proves himself to be not after all just an *object* of mirth and target of derision, but also a comic jester, a *creator* of jokes, a laughing subject, gaining gruesome revenge on the tyrant who had laughed at him. The underdog has the last, demonic laugh. The comedy of Poe's "Cask of Amontillado" is pitch-black in its depiction of the narrator's settling of scores for a past insult, the irony of events supported by intentionally created semantic patterns. The narrator, snubbed by a freemason (Fortunato), gets his own back by burying him alive: whereas initially it is Fortunato—unlike the narrator—who has the privilege of being a freemason, the reversal sees Fortunato incarcerated and the narrator, trowel in hand, playing the part of a "free" mason. Chaucer's *Reeve's Tale* is also founded upon the principle of just deserts and the outtricking of a trickster, as two wily students put one over on a churlish miller who cheats the locals on his corn. Not only is the thief robbed (they take *his* corn), but also his proud wife and his daughter are into the bargain merrily "swonken al the longe nyght" ("So myrie a fit ne hadde she nat ful yoore"). The tale ends with the salutary moral that a "gylour shal hymself bigyled be" (*Canterbury Tales*, 1: 4230 and 4321).

These reversals often amount to reversals in a subject-object relation to the verb or activity in question and, as in the Chaucerian summary, it is the *repetition* of the verb in conjunction with the difference in its form that constitutes the ironic pattern. The object of laughter becomes the laugher, the swindler comes to be swindled, the servant assumes the status of one who is served. A standard slapstick gag during farcical pursuits consists in the chaser finding himself being pursued by the person he is chasing (as when two people are running round a tree), while the sophisticated irony of Kleist's *Der zerbrochne Krug* presents the corrupt judge, Adam, as the one who ends up being judged. Alternatively the reversal may be an adjectival turnabout: the proud wife becomes the well and truly swonken, the *free*mason ends up incarcerated. The permutations are infinite. Boccaccio's *Decameron* (3:4) describes how pious Friar Puccio performs a penance taught him by Dom Felice, while Dom Felice and the Friar's wife snatch the opportunity to take a trip to paradise.

Related to these ironic reversals are such scenes as the lovers' tiffs, or *scènes de dépit amoureux* as the French call them, to be found on a number of occasions in Molière. These episodes constitute power reversals based on the battle of the sexes and structured around the principle that the (normally) male aggressor be forced on the defensive and compelled to renege. *Le Bourgeois Gentilhomme* offers a typical example (3.10) in which Lucile turns the conversational tables on Cléonte and the dialogue between master and mistress is echoed and parallelled by an analogous tiff between the servants, Nicole and Covielle. These highly structured exchanges generate the comic pleasures of anticipation and fulfillment, of predictability and recognition. What emerges is that the lovers' indignation is but a wobbly mask that ends up being seen through, as exemplified by Valère in *Le Tartuffe*, who makes one of those invariably counterproductive attempts at a dramatic exit grounded upon the hope of being called back in the nick of time (but which normally only meet with a stubborn silence).

The wobbly mask, bad acting, the sight of a role unconvincingly performed, has proved itself an essential comic principle. In the context of this chapter its primary relevance is its (perhaps retrospective) contribution to our awareness of the role-playing *as* role-playing, possibly confirming the audience's sense of superiority both over the gull who does not notice how bad the acting is and who fails to distinguish between illusion and reality, and over the actor who is mocked for the inadequacy of his performance. As with irony the comic moment amounts to a flattery of the spectator. Central to Molière's vision in particular are moments of self-betrayal revealing a reserve of healthy humanity beneath the self-imposed monomanic mask.[6] Yet this principle applies not only to Argan, who in his anger forgets his hypochondria to chase his cheeky servant around the room, or to Tartuffe, who drops his mask of piety in order to try his hand at undoing Elmire's spiritual chastity belt. It is at work in the romantic comedies of Marivaux (*Le Jeu de l'amour et du hasard*) or Eichendorff (*Die Freier*), in which aristocratic suitors line their time by indulging in disguise and role-playing to win their loved ones, as well as at the heart of comedies of social climbing and imposture, where the social mask just *will* insist on playing tricks upon the rogue-cum-fool whose aspirations lie "above his station."

One of the best-known of Russian comedies, Gogol's *The Government Inspector*, is based upon such an interplay of misunderstanding and deception in the context of the social pecking order. Seeing a down-and-out junior official from St. Petersburg (Hlestakov) unable to pay for a meal at the local inn, the town's chief authority (the Mayor) mistakenly convinces himself that the figure in question is the government inspector expected in town who has turned up incognito and that his requests for money signal a desire to be bribed. From this basic misconception is spun a web of deception and self-deception that structures the play as a whole. The Mayor's ensuing behavior, as well as that of his fellow officials and family, is a performance put on to mask the corruption that normally permeates their bureaucratic Tsarist system, but the spectator—unlike Hlestakov—sees through the mask having witnessed earlier their true sentiments. The knavish bureaucrats, however, are in this instance themselves fools and gulls led astray by their mistaking Hlestakov for the government inspector, a mistaken identity with which Hlestakov starts to play along, coming to relish his new role, to indulge in flights of fancy, and under the influence of alcohol even to *believe his own lies*. The deceivers are deceived (mutually), and only the audience retains the overview.

Self-deception is a problematic term, but one so central to comedy that it would be a pity to sweep it underneath the comic carpet. The idea of a rogue and a dupe subsisting within one and the same person either implies some form of self-division (say, a divided mind, of which only a part is conscious) or remains inherently paradoxical, as it does with Sartre, who—refusing to acknowledge the existence of an unconscious—seems to revel in the contradictions entailed by the phenomenon. "In bad faith (*mauvaise foi*) it is from myself that I mask the truth ... the person being lied to and the person doing the lying are one and the same, which means that insofar as I am deceiving I must know the truth masked from me insofar as I am being deceived."[7]

Self-deception has been interpreted by some as a simultaneous belief that a proposition is the case and that the same proposition is not the case, frequently with the stipulation that one of the beliefs be unnoticed or remain unconscious. Others have defined it as the belief that a proposition is the case under "belief-adverse circumstances," the import of which the subject must recognize (though here self-deception is hardly distinguishable from merely making a mistake).[8] Both these approaches to self-deception link it implicitly to irrationality, it being considered "irrational" to form a belief that is not supported by the evidence or is in patent contradiction with it and even more so to hold two contradictory beliefs. These definitions are applicable in varying degrees to Hlestakov, whose inebriation together with all the attention lavished upon him causes him to get carried away by his own flights of imagination, to "forget" his lowly station, indeed temporarily to believe (or half-believe) that he is the government inspector and that tomorrow he is to be made field marshal.

An even more illustrious self-deceiver is Cervantes's Don Quixote, who, because of his desire to be a gallant knight, interprets everything in terms of a chivalric novel of which he is the hero. He believes, under circumstances that are belief-adverse to put it mildly, that the inn he comes across is a castle, that the whores he meets are fair maidens, that the sow-gelder is a musician, that the passing barber's shaving bowl is the renowned Mambrino's helmet. He charges a flock of sheep under the delusion they are a band of warriors, attacks a group of monks believing they have abducted a damsel in distress, and sets about a windmill that he mistakes for a sword-wielding giant, an encounter in which he comes off decidedly the worse.

Wherever one draws the line between being self-deceived and making a mistake, an important point from the comic perspective is that the spectator or reader knows better, enjoying a position of rational superiority and privileged undeception. The emphasis is on the self-deceiver as a dupe (deceived) rather than as a knave (deceiver), and such celebrated self-deceivers as Don Quixote are generally charged with irrationality (or incoherence or inconsistency) rather than immorality. Like Hlestakov, the Don illustrates that self-deception of this order may be interpreted primarily as a confusion of illusion (or appearance) and reality. Because of his monomanic obsession with chivalry, he is trapped at the level of illusion, whereas—initially at least—the rest of the fictive figures, as well as the narrator and the reader, see the truth. After receiving a few beatings Don Quixote does admittedly come to recognize this dichotomy between illusion and reality—but on his own terms. Turning the "normal" perspective on its head, he redefines his illusions as reality and reality (the prosaic, nonchivalric world) as a set of illusions produced by a wicked enchanter who has it in for him. This imaginary projection constitutes a new form of self-deception that justifies and perpetuates the old. When self-deception externalizes its deceiver in this way, it may end up coinciding with that state of delusion commonly known as paranoia.

Just as moral deviance is comic insofar as the spectator knows and values the norm (even though the laughter might signal a more or less secret approval of the deviation), so the madness of self-deception presupposes an audience that is, or considers itself, undeceived and sane. Such is the arrogance of the comic perspective, but it is an arrogance pervading all assumptions about knowledge and normality, barring radical relativism. It is the same principle that is at work in jokes about stupidity, such as those told about the Irish in England and about the Belgians in France. Even antiquity had its "stupid" towns, notably Sidon in Phoenicia. Whether the stupidity is associated with an ethnic minority, a geographically neighboring country, or a provincial town, the underlying logic is the same: *they* are woodenheaded and irrational, *we* are clever and rational. Likewise, the spectator's laughter on witnessing an act of self-deception is an indication among other things of rationality patting itself on the back for being able to hold illusion and reality apart.

Yet self-deception cannot be reduced to irrational belief formation, for it tends to be deception not just *of* self *by* self, but also *about* self. In other words, it is a two-pronged phenomenon that results in its knave-cum-gull being unaware both of the suppressed belief (or of the evidence that would refute the illusion to which he is subject) and of the wishful thinking motivating the irrationality. Consequently, a further definition of self-deception characterizes it as a wrong belief that a proposition is the case, where a desire that it should be the case leads the subject to manipulate data relevant to the proposition's truth-value in such a way as to justify his belief.[9] This misinterpretation of the world thus coexists and coincides with a misinterpretation of one's motives in interpreting the world as one does. Sartre's paradoxicality can be relocated in the fact that self-deception is its own cause.

The examples from Gogol and Cervantes demonstrate further that this ignorance of self is intrinsically linked to some form of role-playing. Just as Hlestakov is taken over by his role as government inspector, Don Quixote is so firmly ensconced in his performance as a chivalric hero that he is duped by his own acting. It is perhaps this histrionic element that distinguishes self-deception from mere stupidity or making a mistake in the manner of Grimmelshausen's Simplicissimus, who out of sheer naivety and childish ignorance throws a bucket of water on the picture of a house on fire. Acting a role tends to imply a fixity of perspective and performance that blinds the victim to the nuances of reality in the cause of a monomanic delusion. In this sense, the monomaniacs of the last chapter are also self-deceivers, (unconsciously) imposing a mask of rigidity upon their behavioral possibilities, and this adoption of a self-justificatory persona goes hand in hand with the rationalization of the irrational, which allows the self-deceiver to be unconscious of the irrationality of his beliefs or of the fact that they are caused by wishful thinking in conflict with his own interests. This rationalization functions in the same way as a transparent or a badly worn mask: anyone can "see through" a chain-smoker's refusal to kick the habit because cigarettes "don't really do any harm anyway."

The association of self-deception with role-playing brings one back to the Sartrean notion of self-deception, which he termed *mauvaise foi*, or bad faith. For Sartre, beliefs about oneself (as well as about such matters as politics, ethics, and religion) are necessarily mixed with disbelief, the paradox resulting from the imperfection of belief as opposed to the certainty of knowledge. In the state of *mauvaise foi*, belief—in its imperfection—is satisfied with itself in spite of its imperfection. Beliefs about oneself, one's nature, and one's character traits and personal relations pass themselves off as true, as it were, even though one simultaneously (and for Sartre consciously) recognizes the impossibility of such an unambiguous stance. A person may claim, for example, that his religion or his political beliefs demand a certain conduct from him, or that his social, political, or racial status justifies or necessarily entails a particular line of comportment. He may even maintain that he behaves the way he does owing to some inherent nature or essence that cannot be changed. The significant point about such *mauvaise foi* is that it tends to manifest itself as role-playing, the adoption of a fixed mask, exemplified by Sartre's case of the waiter who almost self-parodically launches himself into his role as a "waiter" and presents himself to the world as essentially a waiter, denying or suppressing the mutability and radical freedom of the human self.

> Let us consider this waiter. His movements are animated and accentuated, a little too precise, a little too quick: he approaches the customers a little too speedily, he inclines a little too eagerly, his voice, his eyes express an interest a little too full of solicitude for the wish of the customer.... He is playing, he is enjoying himself. But what is he playing at? You need not watch him long to realize: he is playing at *being* a waiter.[10]

Acting the rôle of a waiter, he loses himself in his role, comes to believe that he *is* a waiter (in some essential way), and thus falls victim to the self-deception of bad faith.

According to Sartre's conceptual system, we resort to *mauvaise foi* as a means of concealing from ourselves our own fundamental negativity. Characterized by its capacity to project what is *not* the case, by its freedom to deny and negate, and by its awareness of possibilities, human

consciousness is in a state of perpetual self-difference: as a conscious being (or *pour-soi*), I am always in a sense not what I am. *Mauvaise foi*
constitutes a retreat from this radical freedom through the comforting
adoption or assumption of an identity (an *en-soi*), a persona that allows
me to tell myself that "I am what I am." The fixed nature of a self-imposed identity serves as a justificatory origin for my acts ("I do such and
such a thing because I am such and such a person"), hiding the realm of
possibility opened up by the temporal dimension ("I could be ..."). The
mask of *mauvaise foi* permits us to conceal from ourselves and from others the radical ambiguity both of the human subject (I both am and am
not myself) and of the subject's beliefs (which—lacking the certitude of
knowledge—can only ever be half-beliefs).

Molière's Argan may in these terms be regarded as having imposed
upon himself the *mauvaise foi* of his role as an ailing father, while Harpagon has clamped a straitjacket upon his existential freedom by adopting the identity of a miser. The obsessions of Molière's monomaniacs are
a form of semiconscious role-playing, blinding them to the possibilities
with which human consciousness is necessarily invested. It makes just as
much sense, however, to suggest, in contrast to Sartre, that the imposition
of the role or mask may be unconscious. Indeed, if aware that we are only
playing a role, we are not fully taken in by our performance and cannot
properly be said to be self-deceived. It is only if we forget that our performance is but a role and become the fools of our own deception that
self-deception occurs. Whereas deception of others involves the intentional wearing of a mask or creation of an illusion (for the purpose of
besting a fool), self-deception is the unwitting or unconscious wearing of
a mask for motives not immediately evident or accessible.

Don Quixote may likewise be read as above all prey to *mauvaise foi*:
having donned a mask as a chivalrous hero, his vision of himself and of
the world is repeatedly and compulsively couched in the appropriate
terms. He *is* the knight whose identity he has adopted. Peter Barnes's
play *The Ruling Class* yields a further victim of the folly of self-deception,
a further gull to his own role-playing, in the guise of the Earl of Gurney,
who is convinced he is God. This fantasy is in itself funny on account of
the logical implications that come to light in the figure of the would-be
deity ("When I pray to Him, I find I'm talking to myself" [1.4]; "What a
beautiful day I've made" [1.5]; "For what I am about to receive may I
make myself truly thankful" [1.6]) as well as the emphasis he lays on being a God of Love, who unzips his fly on being asked to reveal his God-
head and who takes pleasure in embarrassing respectable old ladies.
The comedy of the play becomes progressively less as we follow the path
of his disillusionment and normalization after he comes out the worse in
a test of strength with an aggressive Scottish God of Vengeance who

threatens to burn him to a crispy noodle. The second half of the play takes a turn for the sinister and grotesque as Barnes shows the consequences of un-(self)-deception and normalization.

Self-deception frequently exists in a relationship of reciprocal interaction with deception of others, requiring social assistance just as deception requires people who allow themselves to be deceived. It is as a result of finding his lies and fictions corroborated by the bureaucratic gulls he is deceiving that Hlestakov ends up drunkenly believing in the role he has adopted. Similarly, monomanic self-deceivers, denying the freedom of possibility and choice and mistaking the mask they wear for the truth about themselves, are the most common victims of rogues and knaves. It is as if the mask held in front of their face (or instead of their face) not only distorts their "true" nature in the eyes of the world, but also functions as a prism distorting *their* vision of the world (witness, for example, the paranoia of Don Quixote and Molière's Harpagon). This both subjects them to illusions about the world, and, via the mirror of intersubjectivity, reinforces their illusions about themselves.

Such fools impose a straitjacket upon the world and are punished for it by the vital flexibility of the *beffatore*. Volpone's gulls are all themselves monomanic misers, their vision warped by their passion. Likewise Argan the hypochondriac is deceived not only by himself, but also by almost every other character in the play: he is milked by the lunatic medical profession, Béline dupes him with a performance of doting affection with which she seeks to win his inheritance, Toinette and Cléante trick him with an eye to the happy ending, and even his wee daughter Louison exploits his gullibility by playing possum when threatened with a beating. Indeed the comedy ends with a communal act or performance humoring Argan's obsession, combining the carnival happy ending with a ceremony initiating him as a doctor (a show that is seen through by everyone except the initiate). Molière's social climber, M. Jourdain, undergoes a similar ceremony in which the credulous old fool obsessed with rank is to be made a *Mamamouchi* or paladin. Of course, the butt of the mockery is the only person to mistake this miniplay for reality. *Don Quixote* contains an even crasser example of the way the self-deluded come to be deluded by others. The Duke and Duchess in book 2 play along with the hero's madness not in order to exploit him for financial gain but for the sheer prankish pleasure of play and the self-confirmatory satisfaction of laughing at the fool who mistakes the imaginary for the real. The Don has indeed become a good excuse for the aristocracy themselves to escape from the real into a realm of illusions.

In short, comic self-deception incorporates the idea of a confusion of illusion and reality, often resulting from unintentional or unwitting role-playing, a confusion of mask and self. The resultant conceptual straitjacket imposed by the rogue-cum-fool upon both his behavior and his cognition causes him to misinterpret or ignore facts or evidence obvious to the nondeceived omniscient reader or onlooker. The self-deceiver's misreading of the world, that is, arises from a misreading of himself. The misinterpretation of the self has indeed been recognized as a fundamental comic principle ever since Plato had Socrates posit that the ridiculous is the result of an infringement of the Delphic command to know thyself. If jokes about stupidity suggest that ignorance in general may be the cause of laughter as much as ignorance specifically about oneself, Socrates's point is perhaps that self-ignorance is the root of ignorance in general. One notable example (often considered unfunny by critics) might clarify the claim. Molière's Alceste, at times an admirable figure in his misanthropy, is comic not only because his misanthropy becomes a rigid, inflexible mask, an oversimplification and distortion both of Alceste's self and of his view of the world, but also because, unaware of his *mauvaise foi*, Alceste is unaware of his real motivation, his own need for recognition, his individualistic and self-assertive desire to be different. Alceste chides others for their mask-wearing but, absorbed in his role as a moral castigator, ignores his own theatricality.

Part of the comedy of self-deceivers, therefore, arises because we, the undeceived, can read into them a motivation of which they are themselves ignorant, as is patently the case with the wish-fulfillments of Don Quixote, Hlestakov, and Alceste. The self-deceiver is unaware of his motivating "irrationality," (unlike us) having access only to the "mask" of self-deceptive rationalization and not to the level of the unconscious desires that have motivated him. *We* by contrast interpret or "see through" his rationalizations with all the assurance of a sovereign rationality, of course ignoring the unflattering possibility that our interpretation of human motivation may in turn have its roots on a level of unconscious desire that we keep strictly hidden from ourselves. (This is *our* self-deception). The realm of the unconscious means that we all necessarily have an infinite potential for comic self-ignorance.

Sartre explicitly rejected the Freudian unconscious, objecting to the fact that, locating mental causes in the past, it constitutes the sort of psychological determinism that—itself a form of *mauvaise foi*—denies the absolute freedom of the human subject in the present. Sartre's own interpretation of Alceste would presumably be analogous to the reading of the "champion of sincerity" proffered in his hypothetical case history of the homosexual who denies he is one brought face-to-face with the sincere person who says he ought to admit he is one. In fact, both figures are prey to *mauvaise foi*, for both operate with an essentialism that steamrollers over the freedom of the individual at any particular moment of his life to be or not to be a homosexual. While the homosexual is in bad faith in denying his possibilities of homosexuality, the champion of sincerity is in bad faith in his desire to lay down the identity of the other as if it were a preestablished and immutable fact. The sincere man himself—with his aim of being who he is, his compulsion to be "himself"—thereby also (half-)conceals his own possibilities and masks the negativity at the heart of his being. In Sartre's words, "the sincere man constitutes himself as what he is *in order not to be it*," the goal of sincerity being to "make me be in the mode of *en-soi* what I am in the mode of 'not being what I am.'"[11] The fact that sincerity necessarily misses its target indeed lies at the heart of the possibility of bad faith in general. Put simply, even "being oneself" is a pose.

3
Language as a Mask

Cliché

When reading Sartre, one may be unclear to what extent *mauvaise foi* is a necessary part of the human condition. Although Sartre does talk of authentic existence, it is difficult to envisage how this could be possible in practice. Given that conscious beings have no essence and that *mauvaise foi* is a mode of being that masks this absence of an essence, the donning of some sort of persona seems an inevitable step, for the pure fluidity of absolute freedom is utterly vacuous. Without some kind of role to play, we are nothing.

Heidegger's notion of inauthenticity, which predated and profoundly influenced the one developed by Sartre, is pervaded by a similar ambivalence. In the case of Heidegger, inauthentic existence conceals from man the authentic possibilities of selfhood and, in particular, the primary ontological possibility, that of not being. One of the ways in which the everyday mode of existence hides what it means to be and not to be is through what Heidegger terms *Gerede* or "chatter" (the authentic counterpart of which is *Rede*, "talk"). *Gerede* can be characterized as an empty or hollow regurgitation of secondhand truths passing for authority, a verbal screen of unthinking reiteration concealing the realm of possibility: "The thing is so because so they say."[1] As a consequence of *Gerede*, the self loses itself in the mediocrity of Mr. Average and hides from its own existential possibilities (and especially the possibility of not being[2]). Like a permanently running walkman, such chatter smothers the nothingness at the heart of Being with a blanket of sound. For Heidegger, however, authentic existence is not essentially different from inauthentic being, but merely a modification of a fundamental state from which one can never definitively escape.[3] At a certain level, therefore, *all* are self-deceived, prey to the unintentional self-delusion that comes to light verbally in *Gerede*.

Intentional role-playing in a social situation uses language as a mask to hoodwink a gull, as a medium for hiding "true" feelings and "genuine" motivations and keeping secret what is "really" being thought or meant. Tartuffe veils his venality and lustfulness behind a verbal cloak of religious devotion for the express purpose of deceiving others. Jonson's Volpone, Shakespeare's Berowne, and Nestroy's Titus are all in their various ways actors and rhetoricians who manipulate words as a mask in order to captivate their listeners. Yet these deceivers are also self-deceivers, and , as such, they show that the implicit duality of the mask/face metaphor, presupposing a clear-cut dichotomy between a true and a false self, may be inherently problematic. In the case of Berowne, for example, the verbal mask of amorous eloquence cannot be said to be a cover or front for anything essentially different from itself, such as baser instincts or financial motivation. Berowne thus represents the unintentional role-player who *is* his mask, as displayed above all in his histrionic rejection of histrionics.

> O, never will I trust to speeches penned,
> Nor to the motion of a schoolboy's tongue,
> Nor never come in visor to my friend
> Nor woo in rhyme, like a blind harper's song.
> Taffeta phrases, silken terms precise,
> Three-piled hyperboles, spruce affection,
> Figures pedantical—these summer flies
> Have blown me full of maggot ostentation.
> I do forswear them.
>
> (Act 5, Scene 2)

Sancho Panza gets in a similar mess when, on Don Quixote's prompting, he pledges to renounce all proverbs except the strictly necessary ones. In his renunciation he immediately drags in four more unsuspecting maxims by the hair:

> I know more proverbs than a book, and so many of them come all together into my mouth when I speak that they fight one another to get out.... But from now on I'll take care to bring in only those that suit the gravity of my office. For in a well-stocked house the supper is soon cooked; and a good bargain doesn't hold up the business; and the man who sounds the alarm is safe; and giving and taking need some sense.[4]

Even the abjuration of *Gerede* is but another form of *Gerede*. As the modern-day graffito has it, "I used to talk in clichés but now I avoid them like the plague." Sancho's indiscriminate use of proverbs is part of the monomanic mask that constitutes rather than hides his comically predictable nature. Berowne by the same token *is* rather than *wears* a comic mask, that of the witty and wordy lover, and in this capacity, he is unable to transcend the psychological consistency of his character.

Within the fiction itself, Berowne's behavior and speech are predictable because as a social actor he necessarily plays a "role" (or sequence of roles) determined by a nexus of socio-cultural givens, his rank, gender, and upbringing. Self-awareness does not allow Berowne to escape from his socio-linguistic script any more than from his theatrical one. If sociologists are justified in seeing the human being as necessarily and ineluctably a role-player, divisible into a temporal sequence of social masks or parts with no remainder or inner core, then being one's own spectator, as in a sense Berowne is, may well increase the theatricality of one's performance, but it cannot permit the shedding of the mask or grant access to what lies "behind." In the twentieth century, Martin Amis's figure Charles Highway will prove to be equally entangled in the snares of introspection and self-awareness. As with Berowne, his self-consciousness makes his performance all the more literary (or theatrical), but fails to unearth a "real" or spontaneous self.

Seen in this light, the linguistic mask (of *Gerede*) is not a ludic option or a mode of intentional deception (although it may generate ludic options and possibilities of deception), but an essential aspect of existence. Our experience of the world and our articulation of this experience is structured by a language that precedes us and that we have learned mimetically during a long process of social interaction. We are condemned by our existential condition to recite from a social script over which we have only an illusion of control and from which we cannot escape. Even self-awareness is just another kind of role. In its second-hand status as something that has already done the rounds before being appropriated by us, it is the cliché that seems to typify language, assuming a special significance as archetypal *Gerede*.

Whether such linguistic determinism is to be accepted or not, the mask metaphor may have other implications. *Gerede* can also, for example, be characterized as patterned, repetitious, and distortively simplifying, imposing a grid of rigidity either upon the fluidity of experience or on the multiplicity and endless heterogeneity of the world. In this, it is rather like one of the crudely caricatural masks of the commedia; words seem to caricature the subtlety inherent in what they represent. A single concept may be repeatedly applied to any number of individual objects or myriad experiences, cavalierly lopping off the differences and focusing on the area of common ground, pruning a leaf down to a "leaf" whether it be beech or birch, tea or clover. Normally, of course, habit blinds us to the repetition that imparts a (fictive?) sense of structure to experience. But, as Nietzsche points out: "Every concept arises through an assimilation of the dissimilar. Just as surely as one leaf is never completely the same as another, so the concept leaf is formed by arbitrarily discarding these individual discrepancies, by forgetting the differences, thus creating the

impression that besides leaves nature contains something that is a 'leaf,' a
sort of archetype after which all leaves are woven, designed, delineated,
colored, puckered and painted ...: truths are illusions which we have
forgotten are illusions, metaphors which have become worn down and
lacking in sensuous force.''[5] Language is a mask that hides its distortive
tendency, a fiction that disguises its fictiveness, much as the social roles
we play have a habit of self-deceivingly passing themselves off as spontaneous and concealing their theatricality. Again it is the cliché that appears to epitomize language in its self-effacing repetitiousness. Stock
phrases (such as the soccer manager's "take each day as it comes," "go
out on the park and give 100/110/200% on the day," "the boys done
brilliant," as well as a whole hierarchy of less obtrusive ones) are pat
responses picked up in day-to-day dealings and equally applicable to an
infinite range of situations.

The more extreme version of the mask metaphor would indeed have it
that, being in a sense all we can ever know, language is a mask with
nothing behind it. Whereas earlier (e.g., Enlightenment) conceptions of
language were based upon a "representational" model, according to
which language constitutes a verbal *Vorstellung* representing mental images or thoughts, philosophers such as Wittgenstein and Ryle have col-
lapsed this duality separating language from the intentional content
underlying it. If the proposition is no longer seen as a verbal mask or
surface "standing for" a nonphysical semantic entity located somewhere
in a ghostlike mind, and if its meaning is considered instead to reside in
the way it is actually *used* (in the rules of its use), then the cliché emerges
once more as an archetypal proposition and the boundary between cliché
("empty" words) and noncliché (words "filled" with meaning) becomes
deeply problematic. As a behaviorally functional reaction to situational
stimuli (rather than an expression of "meaning"), the cliché in turn stim-
ulates cognitive, emotional, and volitional responses in the person addressed, while seeming to preclude reflection on what is meant. It is
masklike language, but it is as if there is no meaning or intention "behind" the mask. The words are hollow, said without thought, as though to
plug the silence.

In short, if it is suggested that conceptual thought or language in general may have three aspects (which may vary according to model):

1. it is repetitious, simplifying, therefore distortive
2. it is constituted by a script that is not our own, a mimetic reiteration
   rather than a spontaneous effusion from a private self; it is a hand-
   me-down received from a discursively ubiquitous big brother (and
   that explains in part why it never fits perfectly)
3. there is no "deeper" meaning or intention "behind" it

then the cliché may be taken as paradigmatic. Indeed, the claim that all social behavior and human intercourse is role-playing reduces all linguistic behavior, all language, to a type of cliché. Like the assertion that social interaction is "play," the proposition that language is cliché of course amounts at one level to little more than a claim about language use, a request for a redefinition of the terms in question. Ignoring practical differences within discourse, it overlooks the fact that, while verbal communication may resort to a fixed expression, language may equally well be employed in innovative ways. Yet it is not necessary here to come down on one side or the other in this matter. A good many thinkers have sharpened—or broken—their teeth on this well-chewed bone of contention.

Cliché of course (indeed by definition) normally passes unnoticed, if not constituting our discourse in its entirety then insidiously pervading it. Habitual and repeated scripts and fragments of scripts *pretend* to be spontaneous expressions, creative products of a "self" who is master in his own verbal workshop. The comic use of cliché, however, is cliché that draws attention to itself as cliché, the excessive repetition becoming so obtrusive that it rams home its own origins in habit. It is a fragment of that prewritten script we have mimetically picked up, but a fragment that admits to the fact that it is but a repeated scrap from a script not our own. Comedy makes the mask of cliché visible, but (if all language really *is* cliché) it thereby runs the risk of revealing that there is nothing underneath the mask.

Excessive repetition as a symbol of hollowness is a timeworn comic motif. It comes to light for example in the morality play *Everyman* (ca. 1520). This most sombre of plays corresponds to the medieval idea of comedy in that it begins in adversity and ends in harmony, as well as vaguely mocking the hypocrisy of such characters as Fellowship, Kindred, Cousin, and Goods (who anticipates the Vice of later morality plays), all of whom leave Everyman in the lurch when he is called to settle his metaphysical bank balance. The hollowness and formulaic nature of their protestations of friendship is above all underscored by repetition ("I wyll not forsake the to my lyues ende," "wete you well, we wyll lyue and dye to-gyder," "in welth and wo we wyll with you holde," [ll.213, 324, and 325]). Similar, equally vacuous protestations come from the mouths of Strength, Five Wits, and Beauty: "And I, Strength, wyll by you stande in dystres," "We wyll not departe for swete ne soure," "No more wyll I vnto dethes houre," (ll.684, 687, and 688). Sure enough, not long afterward they are on their way, leaving only Knowledge and Good Deeds to see Everyman through to the happy ending.

In this play, the hollowness (half-)masked by repetition stands out by contrast with the genuineness of Good Deeds. The same can hardly be said of such twentieth-century plays as Sternheim's *Die Hose*, Beckett's *Waiting for Godot*, or Ionesco's *La Cantatrice chauve*, in which cliché and repetition seem to hide a psychological or a metaphysical void. In Sternheim's play, written shortly after the turn of the century, the repetition primarily takes the form of conformity to a literary or a social stereotype. Not only are the protagonists tellingly called Herr and Frau Maske, but the pervading impression is that every figure is hamming away at some mindless social role, shaping the mask they present to the world according to a premolded cliché. If Herr Maske is a caricature of bourgeois boringness and *Spießbürgertum*, this satirical aspect only emerges in a displaced and indirect form, owing to the absence of an ethical measure, an unmasked self (such as Good Deeds), anywhere else in the play. When Frau Maske inadvertently exposes too much of herself in public (the nearest we come to any sort of unmasking), Herr Maske's response of outraged philistinism is no more ridiculous than the literary and philosophical banalities churned out by Mandelstam and Scarron, who fall in love with her—or at least fall in love with the role of falling in love with her. The pseudo-Nietzschean Scarron, for example, is unable to stop seeing himself as a heroic lover creating poetic history, and, even when Luise has lowered her middle-class defences and is shaping up for a smacker, he frustrates everyone by popping off and transforming the experience into poetry. Ultimately the universality of the mask leaves a feeling of ethical instability. Where any moral standpoint emerges from the mouth of a mere mask, a fixed sense of truth goes by the boards, for our perception of the truth, no less than our perception of the face, is relativized by the everpresent mask.

In the theatre of Samuel Beckett, the clichés are of a different kind, constituting less regurgitations of literature or philosophy than fragments of language that are repeated until they themselves turn into cliché within the duration of the play itself (although Winnie in *Happy Days* enjoys playing around with literary fragments as well). Such reiterated verbal morsels as "We're waiting for Godot," "Something is taking its course" (*Endgame*), and "Oh this is going to be another happy day!" (*Happy Days*) are recurrent throughout Beckett's drama, serving above all as a technique employed by the characters for killing time. The repetitions not only serve dramatically as structural focal points, but also stress the desperate endeavors of the figures to overcome silence and avoid thought, which after all only exposes them to the hush of the cosmic vacuum, the meaninglessness of the whole existential caboodle. The following exchange exposes the vacuity of their dialogue in a comic and poignant way:

Vladimir. You must be happy, too, deep down, if you only knew it.
Estragon. Happy about what?

Vladimir. To be back with me again.
Estragon. Would you say so?
Vladimir. Say you are, even if it's not true.
Estragon. What am I to say?
Vladimir. Say, I am happy.
Estragon. I am happy.
Vladimir. So am I.
Estragon. So am I.
Vladimir. We are happy.
Estragon. We are happy. (*Silence*) What do we do now, now that we are
            happy?
Vladimir. Wait for Godot.

                                                                    (Act 2)

Happy Days is even more riddled with cliché, this being Winnie's natural idiom in her fight against nothingness, isolation, and silence. Habitual verbal time-fillers keep her spirits up, and, when she runs out of
words, she dips into her bag for some object to hold her interest for a
while. In Winnie's case the bitterly comic effect of her banalities consists
in part in the contrast between the superficial joviality of her comments
and the depth of the nothingness they are an attempt to hide.

The contumely to which cliché is exposed in the (anti-)drama of Ionesco comprises not only metaphysical lamentation on the vanity of words
in the face of the meaninglessness of existence, but also specifically social
critique. *La Cantatrice chauve* mocks, among other things, the triteness of
everyday conversation, showing it in the end disintegrate into gibberish
based on alliterative word association. The conversation between Madame and Monsieur Martin who, after bringing to light a remarkable sequence of "coincidences," eventually ascertain that they have met one
another before—indeed that they are married—exemplifies how habit
and cliché stultify perception, the whole dialogue being dominated by
exclamations such as "how curious" (ad nauseam) and coming to a climax with M. Martin's "how curious how curious how curious and what a
coincidence!" Ionesco's later play *Rhinocéros* is an even more overtly
critical mockery of the ubiquity of unthinking discourse, presenting a
provincial township all of whose petty burghers (except the protagonist
Béranger) respond to the sight of a rhinoceros charging through the town
with the same set of pat platitudes, firstly "My word!" (again repeated ad
nauseam) and later "Oh! a rhinoceros." This startling lack of originality
in turn causes them to turn into rhinoceroses. The play furthermore reveals not merely cliché and platitude to be dangerous, but also slogan,
generalization, and dogmatic logic as well, transforming us all into big,
ugly, green beasts.

One of the masters of banal conversation is Harold Pinter, who likewise regards the triteness of language as functioning rather like a mask covering up the nakedness of true silence.

> There are two silences. One when no word is spoken. The other when perhaps a torrent of language is being employed. This speech is speaking of a language locked beneath it.... The speech we hear is an indication of that which we don't hear. It is a necessary avoidance, a violent, sly, anguished or mocking smoke screen which keeps the other in its place. When true silence falls we are still left with echo but are nearer nakedness. One way of looking at speech is to say that it is a constant strategem to cover nakedness.[6]

Pinter's *The Birthday Party* demonstrates the way speech may serve to mask utter vacuity, Petey's and Meg's dialogue perpetually teetering on the brink of tautology.

Meg. Petey?
Petey. What?
Meg. Is that you?
Petey. Yes, it's me.
Meg. What? (*Her face appears at the hatch*). Are you back?
Petey. Yes.
              . . . . .
Meg. Is Stanley up yet?
Petey. I don't know. Is he?
Meg. I don't know. I haven't seen him down yet.
Petey. Well then, he can't be up.
Meg. Haven't you seen him down?
Petey. I've only just come in.
Meg. He must be still asleep.

(Act 1)

Tautological sentences ("I'm here"), perhaps even more than mere commonplaces, are the epitome of language as a pure mask, verbal configurations that tell us nothing about the world, but merely reveal the logic of their own construction: "I" am necessarily "here," for this is how we use the word "I." In the case of tautology, the linguistic mask discloses nothing except its own constitution, which depends upon the self-evidence that a cat is a cat, a leaf is a leaf, and that "I" am "here" at the time of speaking. *The Serial*, Cyra McFadden's parody of the psychobabble of the seventies, furnishes a further example of tautology used as a way of hiding (but also expressing) complete mental hollowness. Its characters are so mellow and laid-back that even exemplary drivel like the following is allowed to go unpunished: "When Jody told me you were back at the house, you know what I said? I said, 'Wow, Harvey's back at the house.' That's just how I felt."[7] Foolish figures in Shakespeare also resort to tautology. In *Much Ado about Nothing*, the old man Verges makes the boldly vacuous claim to be "as honest as any man living that is an old man and no honester than I" (3.5), and Sir Andrew Aguecheek of *Twelfth Night* is probably "thinking" along the same (circular) lines when he professes to be as good (at revels) "as any man in Illyria, whatsoever he be, under the degree of my betters" (1.3). Bardolph's explanation of the word "accommodated" demonstrates Wittgenstein's point[8] that definitions themselves have a habit of leading us round in circles for all the ostensive vigor with which we repeat what we mean. "Accommodated: that is, when a man is, as they say, accommodated, or when a man is being whereby a may be thought to be accommodated; which is an excellent thing" (*2 Henry IV*, 3.2). In parodies of scholarship and learning, tautology is a recurrent expression of academic windiness.

In the case of *The Birthday Party*, however, part of the fascination is owing to a certain tension present in the play. Speech is on the one hand a mask hiding the emptiness of mental vacancy, the avoidance or absence of thought; on the other hand, as is evident from Pinter's comment cited above, it seems to mask a hidden, silent language to which we are normally oblivious, in this case the nonconformity or otherness represented by the mysterious figure of Stanley. Exactly what—if anything—is "wrong" with Stanley, we are not told: the play is not about the abnormal, but about the way the abnormal is masked or silenced. The deluge of words with which Goldberg and McCann flood Stanley (describing how they intend to normalize him) is the most graphic illustration of the point, itself a comic enumeration that generates its own locomotion.

Goldberg. We'll watch over you.
McCann. Advise you.
Goldberg. Give you proper care and treatment.
McCann. Let you use the club bar.
Goldberg. Keep a table reserved.
McCann. Help you acknowledge the fast days.
Goldberg. Bake you cakes.
McCann. Help you kneel on kneeling days.
Goldberg. Give you a free pass.
McCann. Take you for constitutionals.
Goldberg. Give you hot tips.
McCann. We'll provide the skipping rope.
Goldberg. The vest and pants.
McCann. The ointment.
Goldberg. The hot poultice.
McCann. The fingerstall.
Goldberg. The abdomen belt.
McCann. The ear plugs.
Goldberg. The baby powder.
McCann. The back scratcher.

Goldberg. The spare tyre.
McCann. The stomach pump.
Goldberg. The oxygen tent.
McCann. The prayer wheel.
Goldberg. The plaster of Paris.

(Act 3)

And so it continues. Stanley is reduced to speechlessness by the brute force of the verbal bombardment and afterward can manage but a few stammered burblings before being carted off in the back of a van. This is black comedy of a most menacingly grotesque and sinister stamp.

Comic cliché is often deployed as a weapon of *parody*. Just as the examples above use everyday cliché to show how we unthinkingly lapse into behavioral patterns and roles in order to eschew the need for reflection, so literary cliché may be exploited to expose theatrical roles that have become hollow, hackneyed, empty of their original relevance. Tom Stoppard's *The Real Inspector Hound* does this, ridiculing the stock features of the country-house mystery by presenting a specimen of the genre as a play-within-the-play—although it soon comes to merge with and take over the outer play itself. Stoppard simultaneously uses the opportunity to parody the stock jargon of the critics. The play is structured around a repetition and modulation of the "key" scenes and especially of such "key" phrases as "I'll kill you for this, Simon Gascoyne!" "We can't go on meeting like this!" and "I'll kill anyone who comes between us!" The comic ramifications are further developed when one of the critics, Birdboot, enters the play and starts spouting the same sort of melodramatic regurgitations. Stepping with ease into the stereotypical part performed by a fictive figure, Birdboot exemplifies the interchangeability of the hackneyed roles we play, the functionality of identity. He *becomes* Simon, the cad in the country-house mystery, merely by swapping positions with him. Mrs. Drudge, the housekeeper, functions as the primary agent of the clichés, pointing out the remarkable sequences of coincidences and the ominous symbols, repeatedly entering the scene in time to hear the death threats, and putting the audience in the picture with an exaggerated comprehensiveness logically incompatible with her perspective as a character *within* the play. Her phone-answering technique serves as a parody of dramatic scene-setting:

Mrs. Drudge. (*into phone*) Hello, the drawing-room of Lady Muldoon's country residence one morning in early spring? ... Who did you wish to speak to? I'm afraid there is no one of that name here, this is all very mysterious and I'm sure it's leading up to something, I hope nothing is amiss for we, that is Lady Muldoon and her houseguests, are here cut off from the world, including Magnus, the wheelchair-ridden half-brother of her ladyship's husband Lord Albert

Muldoon who ten years ago went out for a walk on the cliffs and was never seen again—and all alone, for they had no children.

(Act 1)

Gibberish and Logorrhea

Language is structured by repetition in that it is infinitely repeatable and adaptable in its application. This is exemplified by clichés, tautologies— indeed by concepts in general. The mask metaphor might put it that a linguistic system (considered statically or synchronically at least) consists of a finite number of sememes, or units of meaning, taken as representing an infinite number of objects, events, or experiences. It works by simplification and distortion rather in the way that the commedia mask simplifies and distorts the face. Yet language is also constituted by repetitions in its phonological properties, the finite number of sememes being "represented" by an even smaller number of phonemes, or minimal phonetically distinctive articulations of sound. As Jakobson would have it,[9] the defining attribute of poetry is an especially (obtrusively) high level of such repetitions and patternings, both grammatical and phonological as well as semantic, language as it were drawing attention to itself as a medium, a physical mask. Once again, the proximity of the poetic and the comic Muses comes to light. Excessive repetition, in poetry as in comedy, accentuates the repetition that normally goes unnoticed. Poetry of course does not necessarily do so for comic reasons, often preferring to present itself as beautiful rather than grotesque and distortive, its repetitions functioning hypnotically, satisfying an innate desire for regularity, or formally structuring the poem. A serious or a didactic context may likewise prevent repetition from turning into comedy, the patternings seen as hiding a "deeper" truth. As an extension and perversion of this principle, however, phonological repetition may be taken to excess as a debunking of poetic pretension, just as the inane and mindless reiteration of literary clichés parodies empty poses and stale roles. Swinburne's self-parody "Nephelidia," for example, exaggerates his own tendency for mechanical alliteration and bombastic sound-patterns:

From the depth of the dreamy decline of the dawn
   through a notable nimbus of nebulous noonshine,
Pallid and pink as the palm of the flag-flower that
   flickers with fear of the flies as they float,
Are they looks of our lovers that lustrously lean from
   a marvel of mystic miraculous moonshine,
These that we feel in the blood of our blushes that
   thicken and threaten with throbs through the throat?

> Thicken and thrill as a theatre thronged at appeal of
>   an actor's appalled agitation,
> Fainter with fear of the fires of the future than pale
>   with the promise of pride in the past;
> Flushed with the famishing fullness of fever that
>   reddens with radiance of rathe recreation,
> Gaunt as the ghastliest of glimpses that gleam
>   through the gloom of the gloaming when ghosts go aghast?
>
> (lines 1–8)

As Swinburne shows, it is not far from inane repetition making fun of itself to the realm of complete and utter gibberish, a realm where alliterative and assonantal sequences alone (if not pure chance) generate the verbal movement and language lays down all claims to meaning or sense and revels in its own audio-visual properties as a physical mask. Gibberish is frequently regarded as a negative phenomenon, an absence of signification or a failure to fulfill the criteria of normal discourse. Dante's giant Nembrotto (Nimrod) is punished for his hubris in building Babel and causing the confusion of languages (as in the Bible) by being condemned to speak a gibberish accessible to no one else and mocked by Virgil: "Raphèl may amèch zabì almì" (*Inferno*, 31.67). Ionesco's *Les Chaises* ends with an orator coming to reveal the meaning of life, but in fact not managing to do anything more than burble a grotesque parody of meaning. Both instances show gibberish as the outcome when language overestimates itself. Traditional mockery of intellectual pretension has likewise often consisted of portrayals of the pedant in question as a mouthpiece for absolute rhubarb, occasionally seasoned with a sprinkling of dried Latinisms. The quacks of the medieval mystery plays, il Dottore of the commedia, Shakespeare's schoolmaster Holofernes (in *Love's Labour's Lost*), and Molière's celebrated doctors are all massacrers of meaning who, as Mote says of Holofernes, have stolen the scraps from a great feast of languages. In their hands gibberish becomes a form of deception, nonsense passing itself off as sense for professional purposes.

Related to gibberish in this sense is the monomanic deluge of logorrhea spouted by Ben Jonson's Lady Politic Would-be. When speech becomes as compulsive as it is in her case, the torrent of words seems to dissociate itself from meaning. It is as if repetitive banality issued on automatic or overdrive (or overkill) merely lines the time and plugs the void of silence rather than expressing thought or reflection. The following "exchange" shows Volpone desperately struggling to stem the conversational tide:

> *Volpone.* The poet,
>   As old in time, as Plato, and as knowing,
>   Says that your highest female grace is silence.

Lady Would-be. Which o' your poets? Petrarch? or Tasso? or Dante?
             Guarini? Ariosto? Aretine?
             Cieco di Hadria? I have read them all.
Volpone. Is everything a cause, to my destruction?
Lady Would-be. I think, I ha' two or three of 'em, about me.
Volpone. The sun, the sea will sooner, both, stand still,
           Than her eternal tongue! nothing can scape it.

                                                    (Act 3, scene 4)

And on she goes, undaunted in her compulsive prating.

As much as anyone, Rabelais took constant delight in pillorying the scholastics for their pretentious prattle, a case in point being Maistre Janotus de Bragmardo, an ancient member of the Faculty of Theology, who hawks up a garbled jumble of dog-latin and chop-logic in pleading, on behalf of the populace of Paris, for the return of the bells of Notre-Dame: "Omnis clocha clochabilis, in clocherio clochando, clochans clochativo clochare facit clochabiliter clochantes. Parisius habet clochas. Ergo gluc."[10] The argument between Messieurs de Baisecul and de Humevesne is equally unintelligible, and a variation on the comedy of gibberish is the ridiculous sign language in which the debate between Thaumaste and Panurge is conducted, embracing a wealth of codpiece play from Panurge and Thaumaste beshitting himself ("un gros pet de boulangier, car le bran vint apres"—possibly loosely translatable as "a carpenter's fart, so-called because it produced a stool"). The whole of the third book is a study in the comedy of nonsense.

Yet Rabelais's gibberish is not necessarily to be seen as a deficiency or lack. There is no one who has reveled more than he has in the pleasures of language in itself, celebrating its physical properties as much as mocking its misuse. In the early parts of the sixteenth century, Erasmus of Rotterdam had already drawn attention to the inherent ambivalence of language, its duality and duplicity. For Rabelais too, language can be either a manifestation of spirit (of cornucopian plenitude) or of windy emptiness. The ambiguity is exemplified by the Rabelaisian lists and enumerations, which hover between hollow repetition and fertile creativity. In the third book for example, when Panurge asks Frère Jan whether he ought to marry or not, the question is preceded by an apostrophe to the addressee's bollocks or *couillons* (or, strictly, to the addressee considered as a bollock) that comprises 166 phrases. "Escoute, couillon mignon, couillon moignon, couillon de renom, couillon paté, couillon naté ... couillon belutant, couillon culbutant, couillon hacquebutant, couillon culletant, Frère Jan mon amy," the overriding impression being that the bollock addressed is above all a procreative, fertile, bouncing bollock. This bouncing bollock's reply, however, is preceded by an apostrophe consisting of some 169 phrases that above all call Panurge's sexuality into question: "Dis, couillon flatry, couillon moisy, couillon rouy ... couillon fébricitant, couillonas au diable, Panurge mon amy."[11] The two litanies are formally the same in that they are propelled by an alliterative force that creates an almost incantatory aura, yet Frère Jan's disparagement, in conjunction with Panurge's praise, thematically enacts the ambiguity not only of sexuality but also of narrative activity itself, which hovers between creativity and repetitiousness. Poor Panurge is a diseased, withered, and unproductive old bollock, but Panurge and Frère Jan are ultimately two sides of the same cullion.

Pantagruel and Panurge's antiphonal singing of the praises of Triboullet the fool is an equally ebullient comic enumeration and hints at the origins of such lists in the French *sottie*, the satiric drama performed by the fools' societies of the fifteenth and sixteenth centuries. In the *sottie*, lexical enumeration, often culinary or sexual in theme, is exploited as a means of generating a verbal euphoria to match the general aura of acrobatic madness and folly. In the *Farce Nouvelle nommée la Folie des Gorriers*, having dissimulated her true nature throughout the play, Folly finally reveals herself with a litany that clearly prefigures Rabelais:

> Je suis cornue
> Et si suis Folie cornarde,
> Cornant, cavilleuse, coquarde,
> Coquillarde, coquillonnee ...
>
> (lines 565–68)

The repetitive verbal delirium, which in this case continues for another thirty lines, may come close to being hypnotic, or merely downright boring (for the sober), but, in this context of universal folly, it serves as an infectious invitation to join in the madness. A comparable catalogue in the *Carmina burana* generates a convivial sense of folly and revelry in like manner. Song 196 is a praise of wine-drinking that eventually resorts to the principle of "Everybody's doin' it," listing the ranks of the bibulous as a way of persuading us to join in:

> Bibit hera, bibit herus,
> bibit miles, bibit clerus,
> bibit ille, bibit illa,
> bibit servus cum ancilla,
> bibit velox, bibit piger,
> bibit albus, bibit niger,
> bibit constans, bibit vagus,
> bibit rudis, bibit magus ...
>
> (lines 33–40)

The rhetorical force of the song lies not in its lyrical beauty, but in its repetition, which is both incantatory and celebratory.

That verbal inventiveness is linked to festivity and the ludic context is further demonstrated by the lexical leviathan in the closing song of Aristophanes's *The Assemblywomen*, a word that contains 170 letters and twenty-six components, each denoting a dish to be served at the concluding feast:

τάχα γὰρ ἔπεισι
λοπαδοτεμαχοσελαχογαλεο-
κρανιολειψανοδριμυποτριμματο-
σιλφιοπαραομελιτοκατακε-
χυμενοκιχλεπικοσσυφοφαττοπε-
ριστεραλεκτρυονοπτεκεφαλλιο-
κιγκλοπελειολαγωοσιραιοβα-
φητραγανοπτερύγων.

(lines 1168–75)

Just as the wind that propels the Rabelaisian text may be both the fullness of the spirit or soul and the emptiness of mere repetition, so verbal profusion can be linked with the fetid winds blowing down below as much as with the festive and creative *pneuma* up above. As Rabelais's fourth book explicitly brings to light, wind (emptiness) and spirit (plenitude), *vin* (wine) and *ven* (wind), are antitheses that are never far apart and are often indistinguishable.[12] Burgess's *Inside Enderby*, written over four centuries later, testifies to the potential for verbal inventiveness in the realm of wind, his eponymous hero producing conversation stoppers such as "Grerrrrkhrapshhhh" and, repeated at various times through the narrative, "Pfffrrrummmp.... Perrrp.... Querpkprrmp.... Porripipoop.... Bopperlop."[13] The Greeks seem to have come up trumps with their onomatopoetic term "borborygmus" to denote the phenomenon. Helping to structure the novel as it does, the borborygmus is a variation on the theme of comic repetition. In the "Sirens" episode of James Joyce's *Ulysses*, Leopold Bloom's blowings as he leaves the Ormond Hotel are transcribed with an equally onomatopoetic gusto: "Pwee! Little wind piped wee.... Fff! Oo!.... Rrrpr. Kraa. Kraandl.... My eppripfftaph. Be pfrwritt."[14]

The Joycean love of lists, as found for example in *Finnegans Wake*, is likewise very much in the Rabelaisian tradition. Indeed one of the most enjoyable ways of setting about reading this verbal deluge, so resistant to the attempts of the interpreter to stem the semantic flow, is simply to yield to it as a torrent of language in the purely physical sense, enjoying it as a complex structure of patterns and repetitions. The texture of the text is fundamentally dependent upon a musicality generated by words not as sense but as sound. The following enumerative depiction of the stinksome inkenstink room of Shem, the room of a sham and a penman and packed with verbal clutter, exhibits in typical manner the linguistic celebration running through the whole work:

> My wud! The warped flooring of the lair and soundconducting walls thereof, to say nothing of the uprights and imposts, were persianly literatured with burst loveletters, telltale stories, stickyback snaps, doubtful eggshells, bouchers, flints, borers, puffers, amygdaloid almonds, rindless raisins, alphybettyformed verbage, vivlical viasses, ompiter dictas, visus umbique, ahems and ahahs, imeffable tries at speech unasyllabled, you owe mes, eyoldhyms, fluefoul smut.... magnifying wineglasses, solid objects cast at goblins, once current puns, quashed quotatoes, messes of mottage, unquestionable issue papers, seedy ejaculations, limerick damns, crocodile tears, spilt ink....[15]

The description resists all attempts at definitive visualization or *enargeia*,[16] leaving one in the dark as to whether (for example) Montesquieu's *Persian Letters* are used as shutters (as implied by the Italian words *imposte* and *persiane*), whether the seedy ejaculations are to be found in the burst loveletters or in the unquestionable issue papers, and whether one can eat once current puns or quashed quotatoes. Instead, it draws attention to itself as alphybettyformed verbage of a most unashamedly substantial, concrete kind.

It is the emptiness of the list as a linguistic form that above all comes to the fore at the hands of Joyce's compatriot Samuel Beckett in his novel *Watt*. Here the enumerations prove to be ultimately tautological, saying nothing, expressing, if anything, only that Watt knows nothing. Rather than functioning as playgrounds for flamboyant lexical acrobatics, they as often as not consist in the working through of a series of logical possibilities, self-mocking in their monotonous futility. Regarding the sound of voices that distract Watt from his conversation with Mr. Spiro, the reader is told:

> Now these voices, sometimes they sang only, and sometimes they cried only, and sometimes they stated only, and sometimes they murmured only, and sometimes they sang and cried, and sometimes they sang and stated, and sometimes they sang and murmured, and sometimes they cried and stated, and sometimes they cried and murmured, and sometimes they stated and murmured, and sometimes they sang and cried and stated, and sometimes they sang and cried and murmured, and sometimes they cried and stated and murmured, and sometimes they sang and cried and stated and murmured, all together, at the same time, as now, to mention only these four kinds of voices, for there were others.[17]

The sequence of repetition is as dry as a mathematical table. In exploring the logical permutations of the situation in their entirety, the narrator ends up telling the reader nothing (except, by chance, about a brief period called "now" when pandemonium reigns). The false hope of a meaning or point tricks and captivates the reader before deflating itself in semantic emptiness, a waste of breath or ink. The narrator seems to be lining the reader's time with spare verbiage.

It is perhaps misleading to describe Joyce and Beckett as being in the Rabelaisian tradition for they can be sited above all in an Irish tradition, the Gaelic roots of which seem to have been conducive to a predominantly playful attitude to language and to be responsible for the Anglo-Irish heritage of wits.[18] Another pun-loving Irishman, Jonathan Swift, developed what is known as phonetic writing ("Eye mash aimed off knott wry tin two yew"), a comic code that may appear to be vacuous gibbering but in fact, when read "correctly," has a perfectly graspable meaning.[19] Verbal garbage and garbled verbiage are also signs of protest, assertions of otherness. Just as, in the fifties, the Goons evolved an antilanguage as an alternative to the boring functionality of normal language, the Victorian working class, like the vagabonds of Elizabethan England centuries earlier, invented a secret language known as gobbledygook.[20] The Dadaists too used language's phonetic properties as a comic release from and critique of ordinary discourse. Kurt Schwitters's recorded recitations come across as systematic aberrations from a norm he despised. It is language stripped down completely to the absurdity of its sound, vocal silliness allowing one to take pleasure in its materiality rather than its functionality. Instead of being unthinkingly taken for granted as a means to a useful end, language is enjoyed in itself for its physical texture.

Wit and Wordplay

As in the case of Harlequin, whose fixed half-mask came to be a signal of the fixity of his character, the metaphor of language as mask, therefore, incorporates two aspects: on the one hand, its (phonological or graphological) physicality, on the other its meaning. A linguistic system, that is, is composed of a finite number both of phonemes (and graphemes) and of sememes. Wit and wordplay is a conscious patterning and interplay of the two aspects such that repetitions and similarities give rise to ego-boosting pleasures of recognition. A somewhat wearisome example from Büchner's Valerio in *Leonce und Lena* (of which just the first half is quoted) shows the extent to which wordplay may be informed by a conjunction of semantic and phonological repetition. "Kommen Sie jetzt meine Herren! Es ist eine traurige Sache um das Wort kommen, will man ein Einkommen, so muß man stehlen, an ein Aufkommen ist nicht zu denken, als wenn man sich hängen läßt, ein Unterkommen findet man erst, wenn man begraben wird." (1.3). (A free translation, using and developing analogous wordplay possibilities in English and borrowing a grave pun from Shakespeare's Mercutio, might be: "Come now, gentlemen! The word 'come' is not a comely one: one must thieve for an income, the gallows are the only outcome, and comfort comes only with burial, a deadly comeuppance and a grave comedown indeed."). The art and skillfulness of Valerio's contrived wordplay consists in bringing together a number of words containing the unit *komm* (or come/com) into a single referential context, here the theme of worldly misfortune. Such wordplay exploits sound repetitions enjoyed not merely as sounds, as in gibberish, and semantic repetitions that have not simply been unthinkingly churned out, as with clichés. It is a highly self-conscious skill, in which the repetition displays relevance of some sort.

The donkeywork of wordplay is most commonly done by sound repetitions that, through a process of association, bring together two or more semantically remote concepts, at the same time showing that the concepts do after all have something in common, a shared semantic attribute or a referential context. Wordplay thereby yokes components together that are revealed as sharing an area of common ground but that belong together only contingently. Freud cites the example of "alcoholidays,"[21] in which the repetition is condensed into one word and thus exacts a slightly greater effort of recognition on the part of the hearer. He termed this process of condensation *Verdichtung*. The wit of the wordplay consists in the fact not only that the two words "alcohol" and "holiday" repeat the syllable *hol* and can therefore be phonologically yoked together, but also that the two concepts in a sense, though different, belong together, holidays being commonly recognized as ideal opportunities for quaffing. The semantic pattern here echoes and underscores the sound pattern. Nestroy's Titus comes up with the comic coinage "*millionärrisch*" (another example cited by Freud), which links stupid and rich people through the repeated syllable *när* common to *Millionär* and *närrisch* (foolish); while Barnes's Earl of Gurney coins the term "insinuendo," a compound of insinuation and innuendo, with an inkling of sin for good measure.

The notion of yoking discrete elements together brings to mind the rhetorical figure *zeugma*. Redfern cites Hugo's example of Lisbeth, who at bedtime "souffle / Sa chandelle et ma raison" (blows her candle and my mind).[22] Here the yoking is syntactical rather than phonological: recognizing an implicit repetition of the verb (*blowing* the candle and *blowing* my mind), the effect is supplemented by the jarring juxtaposition of the literal and the figurative, the physical and the mental. The outcome is comparable if (like Dickens's McCawber in *David Copperfield*) we take our hat and our leave, if we make love not war—or tea or water, not love—or if we commit the social perfidy of passing wind and the buck.

Jakobson makes the point with regard to poetry that "similarity superimposed on contiguity imparts to [it] its thoroughgoing symbolic, multiplex, polysemantic essence."[23] Wordplay too may use phonological repetition in order to create links between semantic elements and bring to light hidden patterns of meaning. Repetitive wordplay slows a reader down, calling for interpretation and reinterpretation. By deviating from the unobtrusive linguistic norm, both poetic and comic repetition tend to make one dwell on what is repeated, seeking a significance, just as puns and metaphors require one to unearth the "hidden" meaning. In the twentieth century, novels such as Coover's *Spanking the Maid* and Robbe-Grillet's *La Maison de rendez-vous*, again forming a borderline between comedy and poetry, have been structurally and thematically based upon a principle of insistent repetition and modulation. Coover's novel reports the repeated action (or repeatedly reports the action) of a master waking up and a maid entering the room, a textual or fictional repetition that is echoed by the repetition of certain key phrases. (They become "key" precisely because of the repetition). With time, modifications in the repeated elements start setting up metaphoric links between clusters of more or less related terms such as humility, humor, humidity, tumidity, tumor, hymnody, humanity, and homonymity, or ledger, lecture, lecher, and elixir. The theatrical repeatability of the action and the text indeed call to mind the puppetry of Büchner's *Leonce und Lena*. The repetitions have an analogous effect in Robbe-Grillet's novel, prompting the reader to reread and repair his normal slovenliness, as well as contributing to an aura of narrative playfulness and self-generative textuality.

On the one hand, the components coupled by wordplay are the same (and the comedy consists in recognizing the repetition of identity, the similarity); on the other, they are different (the comedy lying in the playful absurdity, the incongruous implications of this juxtaposition of elements that are different). For classificatory purposes, one might call the first aspect of wit "wordplay" and the second "punning," though this neither conforms to everyday usage nor does justice to the interdependence and inextricability of the two aspects.[24] To the extent that the classification is seen as useful, "wordplay" emphasizes those features of wit that yield the intellectual, rational pleasure of a recognition of identity, an enjoyment grounded in the *patterns* of the linguistic mask, while the "pun" lays greater stress on the difference, the subversive, irrational, and absurd side of wit, being founded on a desire to see *behind* the mask, to perceive that which is hidden, forbidden, or excluded from rational discourse.

Alice's encounter with the Mock Turtle and the Gryphon in Wonderland perhaps illustrates the distinction. The reader learns, for example, that shoes under the sea are composed of soles and eels and are polished by a whiting, and that no wise fish would go anywhere without a porpoise. The homophony of soles and eels (as fish) and soles and heels (as parts of the shoe) means that their phonological identity is complete, and "getting the joke" involves recognizing the two senses hidden under the same set of sounds or written symbols. Yet these two senses can only coexist within a shared referential context that could be called "shoe-cleaning under the sea." That the semantic difference between the terms necessitates the invention of such an unlikely (absurd, nonsensical) context constitutes, crudely speaking, the "irrationality" of the pun. When, however, shortly afterwards in Alice's adventures, the King of Hearts answers the Mad Hatter's "I'm a poor man, your Majesty" with "You're a *very* poor *speaker*,"[25] the wordplay hinges on the repetition of the word "poor" with different meanings. Although dependent upon recognition of the difference between "poor" meaning impecunious and "poor" meaning low in standard, the identity of the two terms is so great that the comic effect, slight as it is, is primarily one based on recognition of repetition.

In the thirties and forties, the variety and film partnership of Abbott and Costello utilized misunderstanding as a pretext for punning wordplay:

Abbott.   Didn't I see you at the race-track today?
Costello. Yeah, I was there. I like to bet on the nags.
Abbott.   (*grabbing him*) Don't talk like that about horses! Do you realize that I have one of the greatest mudders in the country?
Costello. What's your mother got to do with horses?
Abbott.   My mudder *is* a horse.
Costello. What? I will admit there's a resemblance.
Abbott.   My mudder won the first race at Hialeah yesterday.
Costello. You oughta be ashamed at yourself, putting your mother in a horse-race.
Abbott.   I take very good care of her. If she don't feel like running, I scratch her.
Costello. And what do you give the old lady for breakfast—oats?
Abbott.   Don't be old-fashioned! Modern mudders don't eat oats. They eat their fodder.[26]

The comedy relies firstly on the mistaking of "mudder" for "mother," with the homophonic similarity bringing together two concepts that are normally distinct. It is the difference between the terms—and the somewhat disrespectful juxtaposition of horses and mothers—that forms the more subversive aspect of the wit. The wordplay is all the more skillful, however, because, as Costello says, there is—or there may be—a resemblance between mudders and mothers (or rather, the dialogue unearths one), an analogy that is rammed home in the punch line that mudders eat fodder.

In the seventeenth century, the English philosopher John Locke defined wit by contrast with judgement: "For, wit lying most in the assemblage of ideas, and putting those together with quickness and variety wherein can be found any resemblance or congruity, thereby to make up pleasant pictures and agreeable visions in the fancy; judgment, on the contrary, lies quite on the other side, in separating carefully from one another ideas wherein can be found the least difference, thereby to avoid being misled by similitude and by affinity to take one thing for another."[27] Wit is a synthetic capacity to recognize similarities, while judgement is an analytic skill in telling things apart and recognizing differences. Laurence Sterne's perceptive gloss on Locke's distinction, to be found in his "Author's Preface" halfway through *Tristram Shandy*, is that wit and judgement are as different as farting and hiccuping, a comment that implicitly renews the age-old, above all Rabelaisian, association between the (presumably unsmelly) breath of spirit and the more foul reeking bodily winds. Thomas Hobbes makes a distinction extremely similar to Locke's a few decades later: "Those that observe ... similitudes, in case they be such as are but rarely observed by others, are sayd to have a Good Wit; by which, in this occasion, is meant a Good Fancy. But they that observe ... differences, and dissimilitudes; which is called Distinguishing, and Discerning, and Judging between thing and thing; in case, such discerning be not easie, are said to have a good Judgement."[28] This definition of wit as a capacity to perceive similarity, above all between seemingly unrelated terms, has not been universally accepted. La Rochefoucauld for one rejected the separation of the two mental faculties, claiming that "judgement is but the magnitude of the light cast by wit (*esprit*) ... it is the scope of the light cast by wit which produces all those effects we attribute to judgement."[29] Yet the distinction was to exercize an extraordinary influence on a German tradition of theoretical ponderings on wit starting in the eighteenth century with Christian Wolff, who regarded wit as "the facility with which we perceive similarities," and perpetuated through Mendelssohn, Lichtenberg, Kant, Schlegel, Jean Paul, and Hegel.[30] To the German romantic Novalis, moreover, is owed an important modification: "Wit is creative—it *makes* similarities."[31] The creativity of wit consists in its potential not merely to point out similarities that are evident anyway, but to unearth identities that have not been perceived before, to yoke together things that resist juxtaposition. These philosophers indeed elevate the faculty of wit to the status of a fundamental epistemological principle, the ability to recognize similarities being seen as a basic prerequisite for the formation of con-

cepts in general. In this very broad sense, wit is coterminous with what
has been referred to as the cognitive mask, and *comic* wit results from the
cognitive mask being obtrusive as a mask, drawing attention to its patterned and structured nature.

Schopenhauer likewise deemed the play of similarity and difference as
central to the ridiculousness of incongruity, this interplay in his eyes occurring not between two disparate concepts or semantic fields, but between conception and perception/intuition. Human conceptuality, as he
sees it, can never do justice to the infinite shades of difference in concretely intuited reality, and comic incongruity arises from the disparity.[32]
According to Schopenhauer's classification, wit starts out with the perceived object or objects (a performing horse who drops his load on stage,
to take Schopenhauer's illustration) and then intentionally subsumes this
percept under a concept that is technically applicable but also in some
way incongruous (the "witty" showmaster telling the horse that improvization is not allowed on stage). Laughter is provoked (allegedly) on
the one hand by the incongruity of the perceived reality and the abstract
concept (defecating and improvizing respectively), but on the other hand
also by the juxtaposition of congruity and incongruity. At a certain level,
defecating *is* a form of improvization. The immediate real both does and
does not correspond to the abstract. "Now, on the one hand the more
appropriate the subsumption of such realities beneath the concept and on
the other the greater and more glaring their incompatibility with it, the
more intense is the effect of ridiculousness springing from this contrast.
All laughter thus arises as the result of a paradoxical and therefore unexpected subsumption."[33] In other words, the laughter again depends
upon a recognition of the similarity or common ground (shared by concept and percept) in conjunction with an enjoyment of the disparity or
dissimilarity. In case the reader has any doubts about the validity or applicability of this explanation, Schopenhauer adds: "This is in short the
correct explanation of the ridiculous." So now we know.

Just as wordplay's phonological patterns or repetitions serve to couple
ideas and concepts together in such a way that we recognize the identity
in the difference and thus make some more or less fundamental but normally overlooked identification (alcohol and holidays, millionaires and
folly, mothers and mudders, fish and shoes), so the rhetorical tropes
known as metaphor and simile operate by conjoining disparate elements
that are nonetheless in some way similar. The comedies of the Restoration specialize in comic similes, drawing parallels that are often
"naughty" or slightly subversive in nature between two spheres not normally associated. In Wycherley's *The Country Wife*, for example, Horner
exhibits his wit by forging a thematically explicit bond between sex and
trading in his cheeky assertion that "great ladies, like great merchants, set

but the higher prices upon what they have, because they are not in necessity of taking the first offer" (5.4), while Lucy—with the aid of parallelism and sound repetition—structures a double analogy on the theme of
loveless marriages undertaken in the hope that things will get better with
time: "The woman that marries to love better, will be as much mistaken
as the wencher that marries to live better. No, madam, marrying to increase love is like gaming to become rich; alas! you only lose what little
stock you had before" (4.1). The laughter—or the smile, or the inner
smirk—signals both applause for the rhetorical skill and syntactical patterning and self-applause for being equal to this skill in recognizing the
balanced effect and the aptitude of the simile. Such wit is not unique to
the Restoration. Shakespeare's Dromio proves equally accomplished in
unearthing the hidden analogy as he takes the audience on a geographical
tour of Nell's body in *The Comedy of Errors*:

> *Antipholus of Syracuse.* What's her name?
> *Dromio of Syracuse.* Nell, sir; but her name and three quarters, that's an ell
> and three quarters, will not measure her from hip to hip.
> *Antipholus.* Then she bears some breadth?
> *Dromio.* No longer from head to foot than from hip to hip; she is spherical,
> like a globe; I could find out countries in her.
> *Antipholus.* In what part of her body stands Ireland?
> *Dromio.* Marry, sir, in her buttocks; I found it out by the bogs.
> *Antipholus.* Where Scotland?
> *Dromio.* I found it by the barrenness, hard in the palm of the hand.
> *Antipholus.* Where France?
> *Dromio.* In her forehead, armed and reverted, making war against her heir.
> *Antipholus.* Where England?
> *Dromio.* I looked for the chalky cliffs, but I could find no whiteness in them.
> But I guess it stood in her chin, by the salt rheum that ran between
> France and it.
> . . . .
> *Antipholus.* Where stood Belgia, the Netherlands?
> *Dromio.* O, sir, I did not look so low.
>
> (Act 3, scene 2)

Dromio exploits a medley of phonological links (her forehead being like
France in that it is in conflict with its heir/hair), morphemic connections
(her pudenda being likened to the Netherlands because both are *low
coun*tries), and metaphoric-metonymic associations (her nates being
compared to Ireland because both are on the boggy side). In Congreve's
The Way of the World, by contrast, Witwoud the would-be wit demonstrates how it is not done:

> *Millamant.* ... I have denied myself airs to-day. I have walked as fast through
> the crowd—

Witwoud.   As a favourite just disgraced; and with as few followers.
Millamant. Dear Mr Witwoud, truce with your similitudes: for I am as sick of
     'em—
Witwoud.   As a physician of a good air.—I cannot help it, madam, though 'tis
     against myself.
Millamant. Yet again! Mincing, stand between me and his wit.
Witwoud.   Do, Mrs Mincing, like a screen before a great fire. I confess I do
     blaze to-day, I am too bright.

(Act 2, scene 5)

Witwoud gets in the same monomanic tangle as Sancho with his proverbs
and Berowne with his eloquence. In the sophisticated world of Restoration comedy obsessive wits (and, by Congreve's time, bawdy wits as well)
were liable to be turned into the butts rather than the creators of the
joke.

A similar, and often bawdy, recognition of repetition and reversal is
required in the case of the spoonerism, which broadly defined may either
constitute a syntagmatic reversal of an established phrase (defining a
hangover as the wrath of grapes, for example),[34] or a transposition of the
initial consonants of a group of words. Panurge embarrasses the Parisian
lady with whom he wishes to mate by drawing attention to the spoonerism of "A Beaumont le Vicomte" ("A beau con le vit monte"),[35] and he
forges an ineradicable link between religiously fanatical and soft-but-
tocked wenches when he observes "qu'il n'y avoit qu'un antistrophe
entre femme folle à la messe et femme molle à la fesse."[36] The old jokes
about performing artists with cunning stunts and bathing nuns with hope
in their souls (viz., "Where's the soap?"; "Yes, it does, doesn't it.") work
on an analogous principle, not unlike the old tongue twister on the
pleasurable subject of pheasant-plucking.

Just as Restoration wit elicits the applause of laughter for its balanced
similes and patterned analogies, much twentieth-century prose (and poetry) has taken pleasure in exploring the boundary between comedy and
poetry in its use of offbeat or unorthodox tropes or similes.[37] Arno
Schmidt is one such writer whose prose is often comic in its striking
originality of vision. His use of moon imagery, recurrent in the novel *Aus
dem Leben eines Fauns*, exemplifies this trait: "The moon was stuck on
the back of the night as a red, round tail-light (Only the number-plate
was missing, otherwise everything in order)."[38] The metaphor of the
moon as a rear light is in itself not particularly comic (nor particularly
striking), for the two elements implicitly compared have a clear area of
identity (their circularity, the brightness they project against a dark
background) that is fairly obvious anyway. Schmidt's unusual perspective, coinciding with the predictably bureaucratic perspective of
the office-working narrator/protagonist, consists in the extension of the

metaphor. Taking his own figurative vision literally, he logically assumes that if the moon is a rear light, then the night is a car, and, if night is a car, then it strictly speaking ought to have a registration plate. Although the two terms "night" and "car" do have attributes in common (they are both punctuated by a bright circular patch, and they share a possible metonymic link between cars and night travel), the metaphoric association that yanks them together is characterized more by comic difference than identity.

Schmidt's narrator additionally develops his moon imagery in a different direction. "Moon appeared and observed me icily from beneath yellow-silver cloudlids."[39] Such comic personification is likewise the expression of a whimsical imagination calling both for an act of creative identification on the part of the reader, yet where the difference between the elements identified (moon and physiognomy) locates the identification emphatically within the realm of fantasy. Walking through the wood, the narrator correspondingly describes the discomfort of the carnations on being confronted with his smelly feet: "The carnations reluctantly moved their delicately carved heads (probably because my smelly feet were standing next to them in greased leather pods)."[40] The prose of the American writer Richard Brautigan is pervaded by strikingly unusual metaphors, both comic and forceful in their understated eccentricity. *The Hawkline Monster* develops the comic personification even further than Schmidt, describing a shadow, for example, who feels as if it is going to throw up (in response to the mischievous tricks played by its light), who lies on top of the gravy pretending that it *is* gravy, who drags its feet and tumbles along goofily in trying to keep up with its light, but who eventually gains its revenge. "The shadow had a burst of unbelievable physical fury and shadows are not known for their strength."[41]

As in the case of poetic repetition versus repetition comically taken to excess, the boundary between comedy and poetry is skirted on one side by parody. Excessively absurd tropes generate a comedy of incongruity in which the difference between the terms implicitly or explicitly compared is greater than the identity. Buckingham's seventeenth-century burlesque *The Rehearsal* parodies bad theatre and bad poetry, using, among other methods, the technique of taking a metaphor to the point of absurdity. The following metaphor used by Prince Pretty-man ought to serve as a warning of the effects of love: "All hearts turn ashes which her eyes controul: / The Body they consume as well as Soul." But Prince Volscius, not to be outdone, counters by revealing that even an all-consuming passion can have its good sides:

My love has yet a power more Divine;
Victims her Altars burn not, but refine:

Amidst the flames they ne're give up the Ghost
But, with her looks, revive still as they roast.

(Act 4, scene 2)

Fielding's *Tom Thumb*, written over half a century later, shows a comparable liking for absurd metaphors, again mocking second-rate poetry. The King displays a tactfulness to match his lyrical subtlety when he asks his weeping wife, "Whence flow those Tears fast down thy blubber'd Cheeks, / Like a swoln Gutter, gushing through the streets?" (1.2), and he adopts an equally flattering tone in conversation with his daughter: "Your eyes spit fire, your Cheeks grow red as Beef"—a simile to which the Princess replies by pointing out that her happiness is enough to turn her into beef indeed. In more recent times, N. F. Simpson has gone over the top with his similes less with parodic intentions than in the name of a general aura of barmy playfulness: "You've got about as much satiric vision as a hawk with bi-focals has got eyes like a lynx.... You remind me of a cormorant with a beak a yard long, tapping out a manifesto to the cosmos on a second-hand typewriter" (*A Resounding Tinkle*, 1.1), while in the TV series *Blackadder*, the utterly clodpated Prince Regent produces rhetorical humdingers such as "You look as happy as a man who thought his cat had done its business on his pie but it turned out to be an extra large blackberry." Here they clearly function as signs of silliness.

Allied to such excessive and obtrusive metaphors and similes is the comic technique of taking the metaphorical literally, a technique that is generally also founded upon the fact that we know better, that as cognitively superior readers or onlookers we are able to tell the figurative and the literal apart. The literalization of the metaphorical, seen as an unintentional cognitive weakness or deficiency, is the consequence of a failure to recognize the absurdity caused by the element of difference, while the comic pleasure consists in spotting precisely this (as well, perhaps, as enjoying the absurdity in itself). Aristophanes's *The Frogs* provides a celebrated instance of this comic moment in the contest between the poets Euripides and Aeschylus. Playing upon the metaphor of *weight* applied to verses (that is, in the sense of being heavy with significance), the judge Dionysus decides to weigh some of their words in order to determine who is the better poet. Aeschylus, whose words are weightier, wins the day.

Bergson explains the comedy arising from taking the figurative literally in the following terms: "We obtain a comic effect by pretending to understand an expression literally when it was meant figuratively.... As soon as we concentrate our attention on the materiality of a metaphor, the idea expressed becomes comic."[42] Like the excessively absurd or incongruous metaphor, where the element of difference is so great that it pokes one in the eye, the metaphor taken literally, where the element of difference is—intentionally or not—ignored by the speaker but not by the laughing spectator or reader, is a category of metaphor that *draws attention to itself* as a metaphor. In the same vein is the sort of mixed or misused metaphor found in Private Eye's *Colemanballs*, which includes such verbal balls as "That's the gravy on the cake," "Logie (the cricketer) decided to chance his arm and it came off," and "Celtic will be glad to be sitting in the bath now with two points tucked under their belt."[43]

The absurd or comic metaphor is a mode of language that admits its figurative nature, implicitly divulging that it does not mean simply what it says, but as it were masks its meaning. Now if, like Nietzsche, one further regards *all* language as metaphorical insofar as it is radically different from what it refers to (the nonlinguistic "reality" being ultimately unknowable, if not a fiction or sort of nothing), then there is a sense in which openly metaphorical language can be granted a certain integrity, for it at least concedes its metaphorical status, drawing attention to itself as a mask. Whereas functional or literal language—feigning transparency—pretends to be identical with what it means, to mean what it says, the unabashedly metaphorical admits its difference, its "untruthfulness."

Semantic self-identity—ensuring that the moon is the moon, not a rear light; that tears are tears, not swollen gutters—is a prerequisite for what has been termed the cognitive mask. Rational thought depends upon such tautologies; determinate cognition presupposes the recognizable recurrence of identity. "Behind" this mask of self-identity, the metaphor might have it, lies a realm of difference, a realm of infinite potentiality where moons can be rear lights and shadows can feel like chundering. This is the world of the irrational, of the fantasy. The comic metaphor, highlighting its status as a mask, concurrently gives an intimation of this unknowable world.[44]

Wit and Puns

This whole chapter is grounded upon the metaphorical assumption that language is a mask, and, as such, it is complicated by the fact that a mask can hide a diversity of things. It may hide a face, but it may also *be* a type of face (hiding the absence of any "real" face). It may be a ludic option, yielding the comic pleasures of peeping behind it, or it may be an existential necessity, an immovable front. In this case, what is behind is unknowable, and therefore as good as nothing.

At the simplest, binary level a comic trope or figure comprises an immanent or latent layer of meaning hidden beneath the superficial sense. Just as a metaphor is in a sense a *disguising* of what is meant (and the absurd or overdone metaphor has the same effect as a flamboyantly implausible imposture), so the trope known as verbal or rhetorical irony masks its intent to the literal-minded. Its most direct form, antiphrasis, consists in saying the opposite of what is meant with the intention of being misunderstood by one hearer or set of hearers, but correctly understood by others. Yet it is also possible to be ironic by not saying *exactly* what one means, again with the aim of selective deception. One may say less than one means, as in litotes and meiosis, or more than one means, as in hyperbole, but in all such cases the key point is that the initiated (say, a theatrical audience) should recognize the difference between what is said and what is meant, between the manifest verbal mask and the hidden intention. The ironic difference may come to light either through clues in the immediate textual context or through the "enlightened" reader's or onlooker's application of general contextual assumptions, a shared moral code or field of experience. To this extent, irony is not only collusive (a sharing of a code) but also exclusive (excluding those who are not in the picture),[45] possibly even functioning as a secret code for the purpose of hoodwinking "stupid tyrants" or "censors."[46] As with dramatic irony and the irony of events, however, it can be classified above all as a discrepancy between appearance and reality, a discrepancy accessible to some but not others.

This discrepancy stems from the much lamented capacity of words to deceive. The following exchange from Joe Orton's *Loot* testifies to the sort of comic problems caused by language's inherent duplicity:

Truscott. Have you never heard of Truscott? The man who tracked down the limbless girl killer? Or was that sensation before your time?
Hal. Who would kill a limbless girl?
Truscott. She was the killer.
Hal. How did she do it if she was limbless?
Truscott. I'm not prepared to answer that question to anyone outside the profession.

(Act 2)

Not two but three possible meanings are latent beneath one set of words, the truth in this case remaining concealed, to be found, if anywhere, in the files of a lunatic policeman.

Tom Stoppard's *Rosencrantz and Guildenstern Are Dead* demonstrates the havoc that can be wreaked by a slovenly use of pronouns in the following exchange between the Player and Rosencrantz. Here the unspecified "he" (does it refer to the old man or to Hamlet?) together with the unspecified "his" mean that the initial assertion could—grammatically at least—equally well imply an incestuous relationship between the old man and his daughter, an incestuous relationship between Hamlet and *his* daughter, or even an affaire between the old man and Hamlet's daughter: in fact none of these permutations is what is meant.

Player. The old man thinks he's in love with his daughter.
Ros. (*appalled*) Good God! We're out of our depth here.
Player. No, No, No,—*he* hasn't got a daughter—the old man thinks he's in love with *his* daughter.
Ros. The old man is?
Player. Hamlet, in love with the old man's daughter, the old man thinks.
Ros. Ha! It's beginning to make sense!

(Act 2)

Like irony, verbal ambiguity (polysemy, homophony, or homonymy) may be intentionally turned to account for the purpose of deception. In Beaumarchais's *Le Mariage de Figaro*, the rakish Bartholo uses a pun on "où" (where) and "ou" (or) to try to persuade the court that Figaro has pledged to marry Marceline. Having borrowed a sum of money, Bartholo claims, Figaro signed a contract containing the clause: "Laquelle somme je lui rendrai dans ce château où je l'épouserai" (The which sum I shall render him in this castle where (or) I shall marry her [3.15]). Figaro is saved from this fate by a timely revelation of identities: not only does Bartholo turn out to be his father, but Marceline, the woman he has allegedly pledged to marry, is his mother.

Words have further comic potential in their capacity to deceive their own user, as in the case of malapropism or catachresis, a foible so often gently mocked in Shakespeare's so-called "low" characters. The misuse of words depends for its comic effect upon the recognition by the spectator or reader that what is said (unintentionally) differs from what is meant. When Bottom exhorts his fellow Mechanicals to rehearse "most obscenely" (for "seemly") in preparation for their performance, or waxes lyrical in his description of "the flowers of odious savours sweet" (for "odorous"), the laughter generated in both cases hinges on an awareness of the blunder and a sense of knowing better, as we see through the verbal surface to the intended meaning. Yet the comedy is frequently supported by an ironic hint of hidden truthfulness or appropriateness in the meaning inadvertently expressed or by an involuntarily fitting irreverence or bawdiness. The verbal clanger dropped by Costard in *Love's Labour's Lost*, for example, contains a concealed depth of relevance: "Such is the sinplicity of man to hearken after the flesh" (1.1).

At this level, the comic effect is still a function of the perception of a new, self-identical, unambiguous meaning. Just as a mask hides a face, the superficial word hides a latent, " true" sense. A new factor enters into the picture, however, when this hidden sense furthermore happens to be the sort of sense that remains "hidden " in the normal run of social discourse and that is generally concealed by the cultural mask of order, propriety, and decorum. Two levels of hiddenness are here at play: on one level, the "inner" meaning is being hidden by the external word, while on another level, it is the socially subversive, the aggressive, the sexual, the irrational or nonsensical, which may be regarded as being hidden by a cloak of discursive decency. Freud's theory of jokes may throw an interesting light on the metaphor. Distinguishing between the harmless and tendentious joke, Freud sees the latter as a processing of four basic impulses or drives that, normally repressed by cultural education, from time to time well up from that antisocial bastard within us, the unconscious. He correspondingly distinguishes four types of tendentious joke: (1) the sexual; (2) the aggressive; (3) the cynical (comprising aggression directed against institutions and social beliefs); and (4) the sceptical (querying the logical basis of knowledge in general). Freud himself lays greatest emphasis on jokes as a channeling of sexual and aggressive drives, a circumvention of the social obstacles placed in the way of asocial or anarchic instincts—our "real" self in its presocial form. This simplified version of a Freudian model would thus have it that, as babies, we learn to don a social mask in response to the threat of castration at the hands of the father, who requires us to stop desiring our mother (his wife, after all) and to check our aggressive sexuality. Having been intimidated into hiding our real self, we enjoy jokes as a release from this social role-playing. Just as "normal" discourse in its functionality excludes (as nonsense) the world of irrationality and logical contradiction (where the moon is a rear light and shadows feel like puking), so it—in its "decency"—excludes and suppresses (as taboo) certain categories of aggressive and sexual behavior and discourse. Jokes allow the "hidden" to rear its antisocial, irrationalistic head.

In terms of the metaphor, and returning to the distinction between wordplay and punning, it can thus be posited that, whereas wordplay involves the recognition of repeated identity or similarity, the pun revolves around the perception of difference as well as an instinctual enjoyment of the elements of fantastic illogicality, of suppressed sexuality, or of hidden aggression. Punning words are *wobbly* masks that disclose a hidden disparity normally masked more efficiently by social discourse. Identifying with the sexuality, aggression, or nonsense, we may vicariously enjoy a temporary release from our constraining social mask of rationality and ethical order. At this stage, however, the point is primarily that, in the form of puns, the mask of language reveals itself as a mask (different from what it means) and thus simultaneously exposes the you-know-what or the we-know-what-you-mean beneath. It is the bawdy pun or innuendo that typifies this structure.

Consisting of two or more levels of meaning in coexistence or tension, the bawdy pun hinges upon the recognition of a sexual sense beneath a mask of verbal decorum. The Roman rhetorician Quintilian had drawn attention to the jest that involved taking another person's words in a sense other than the one intended.[47] In the ribald Shakespearean world, conversational wit consists in great measure in being able to pick up a bawdy quibble in the speech of one's partner and playfully extend it. This is the form, for example, of much of Sir Toby Belch's wit in *Twelfth Night*, and Falstaff and Pistol spar with verbal cut and thrust in *2 Henry IV*:

> *Falstaff.* Welcome, Ancient Pistol! Here, Pistol, I charge you with a cup of sack; do you discharge upon mine hostess.
> *Pistol.* I will discharge upon her, Sir John, with two bullets.
> *Falstaff.* She is pistol-proof, sir; you shall not hardly offend her.
> *Hostess.* Come, I'll drink no proofs, nor no bullets; I'll drink no more than will do me good, for no man's pleasure, I.
> *Pistol.* Then to you, Mistress Dorothy! I will charge you.
> *Doll.*   Charge me? I scorn you, scurvy companion.
>
> (Act 2, scene 4)

Falstaff starts by playing on Pistol's name, for "to charge" can mean not only to toast but also to load for action. This military image is itself, however, rapidly transformed into a bawdy metaphor, loading for action being an activity of the sexual as well as the military battlefield. "Discharge" likewise means both to return the toast and to go off like a firearm (in both senses), and this quibble is continued during the course of the exchange for the purpose of embarrassing or teasing the women, thrusting at them with their verbal weaponry. Doll clearly recognizes the sexual provocation barely masked beneath the verbal surface. The play is indeed suffused with military metaphors: stabbing, foining, thrusting, using one's weapon, firing bullets, charging and discharging, occupying, serving, using one's pike—all regularly imply a meaning different from the military one. This set of metaphorical linkages intimates not only the aggressiveness inherent in sexuality (or male sexuality at least), but also the element of hostility so often latent in wit, as realized by Sheridan's Lady Sneerwell in *The School for Scandal*, who saw "no possibility of being witty without a little ill-nature" (1.1). The bawdy quibble is an equally fundamental feature of Sterne's *Tristram Shandy*, be it in the form of such epigrammatic wisdom as "(a man) may be set on fire like a candle, at either end—provided there is a sufficient wick standing out,"[48] or the somewhat more masturbatory musings on the gashliness of unrequited love:

> The duce take her and her influence too.... By all that is hirsute and gashly! I cry, taking off my furred cap, and twisting it round my finger—I would not give sixpence for a dozen such!

—But 'tis an excellent cap too (putting it upon my head, and pressing it close
to my ears)—and warm—and soft; especially if you stroke it the right way—but
alas! that will never be my luck—(so here my philosophy is shipwrecked again)
—No; I shall never have a finger in the pie (so here I break my metaphor)—[49]

One of the characteristic charms of the *Decameron* is the twinkle of the
eye with which Boccaccio accompanies his narrative, regularly hiding a
humanistic plea for the harmlessness of humping beneath a verbal surface
from the spiritual sphere and thereby combining a measure of religious
irreverence with the sexual naughty-but-niceness. It is the same thematic
configuration that has Masetto da Lamporecchio cheekily feigning
dumbness as a tactical ploy enabling him to induce a whole nunnery, including the Abbess, to swap their conventual habit for a riding habit (so
to speak), the weaknesses of the flesh here masked by the muteness of
the gardener and the silence and religious isolation of the nuns (3:1).
Priests and friars are likewise perpetually to be seen on the lookout for
an opportunity to play the two-backed beast (1:4; 7:3). The seventh story
of the second day portrays its heroine as the victim of a catalogue of catastrophes prefiguring *Justine* in its (comic?) repetitions and modulations
and its depiction of a silent female sufferer. Unlike in *Justine*, however,
sex proves not to be a violation, but the Great Consolation for the hardships of the victim. After the death of lover number one, number two
keeps the ball rolling with the God-sent aid of St. Harden-in-hand ("col
santo Cresci-in-man che Iddio ci diè"), quickly bringing her to forget her
grief. When eventually called upon to give an account of her adventures,
which incorporate a number of such spiritual encounters, it is this saint
whom she invokes (the reader, unlike her father the sultan, knowing what
she really means), and she is married as a virgin. *La risurrezione della
carne*, the resurrection of the flesh, is both a celebration of sex and a disrespectful parody of the Church, a metaphorical copulation of the sensual
and the spiritual, the physical and the metaphysical.
    Another story in similar vein (3:10) has the monk Rustico persuading
innocent Alibech that one can serve God by the simple act of putting the
Devil back in Hell ("rimettere il diavolo in inferno"), Alibech turning out
to be a God-loving girl plagued by her Hell, and Rustico's Devil not
equal to the task. Elsewhere (4:2), Frate Alberto, who disguises himself
as the Angel Gabriel in order to have his way with a credulous Venetian
woman, is described as flying without wings, Dom Felice goes to paradise
with Frate Puccio's wife (3:4), Gianni Lotteringhi's wife teaches her lover
a good half dozen of her husband's lauds (7:1), and the Priest of Varlungo
makes Monna Belcolore a kinswoman of the Lord God (8:2). This story is
particularly indicative of Boccaccio's wit, demonstrating his skill in coupling his puns with their context. Monna Belcolore, married to a farm-

worker, is presented at the outset as better accomplished than most in the grinder's art ("atta a meglio sapere macinare che alcuna altra"), and the local priest, who has long since harbored a yearning to get his nose to the grindstone in question, extends the metaphor to boast of the sexual potency of his vocation:"noi maciniamo a raccolta"—his grinding is all the more vigorous for being intermittent. This frictional imagery is continued with the introduction of the pestle and mortar, which become the focus of attention in the second half of the story, after Monna Belcolore has become a kinswoman of the Almighty. Having been tricked out of payment by the priest, she sends a message to him swearing that he will never again be allowed to grind his sauces in *her* mortar, to which the priest—a master in one-upmanship—replies that a mortar is no good without a pestle anyway.... This sexual metaphor enables the two of them to communicate their sexual discord unbeknown to the unsuspecting farmer, who does not see beneath the verbal mask. "Capturing the nightingale" functions similarly in Caterina's attempt to deceive her parents and meet her young lover (in 5:4). She does indeed capture the nightingale she is after, but the problems arise when she falls asleep with the exhausted bird in her hands.

The German theorist Joachim Ritter describes the comedy of the saucy allusion in terms of *masks*: "It is the sphere of the 'indecent' which is addressed, but not directly and as such; it puts in its appearance in the mask of decency ... i.e., in innuendo."[50] The glimpse of naughtiness and indelicacy that is caught through the mask of decorum is the comic principle informing innuendo, sexual understatement, and the even more muffled up sexuality of euphemism. Boccaccio can again illustrate the comic euphemism, for in his hands even consoling one another or making peace after an argument—accompanied by an implicit narrative nudge nudge wink wink—come into service as alternative metaphors for riding, grinding, and praying to Saint John Thomas. Sterne too takes the bawdy innuendo to a logical extreme, where he indeed takes almost every other narrative device as well, replacing whole sentences by asterisks where he can be sure we know what he means. The narrator's recurrent denials of bawdiness also work paradoxically as signals to read beneath the surface for a "hidden" indecency. The word "it" is the simplest English vehicle for the saucy innuendo, a verbal factotum that, given the appropriate "say no more, say no more" context, can turn virtually any sentence into a sentence about sex or the male member. Sticking it out in adversity, being told to diet (what color?), or being asked how long it is since the wife left home[51] is all grist to the comic millstone, and "As the actress said to the bishop" has a similar transformative magic. In the right frame of mind, one can use almost any transitive verb to denote coition, and the

French do it with "faire" as their verbal factotum that will stand for anything.

Joyce's *Finnegans Wake* employs a special method of using language to hide and simultaneously reveal (to the initiated) the sexuality of his text. His polyglottal versatility gives him the opportunity to use foreign obscenities which remain unrecognized or simply not understood by those without the relevant prior knowledge. In describing the eternal geomater (the paradismic perimutter), for example, Joyce, alias Shem the Penman, alias Shun the Punman, utilizes his familiarity with German to disguise his naughtiness, referring to "those fickers which are returnally reprodictive of themselves,"[52] and thereby linking the eternal circularity of mathematics and of sex within the phonological yoke. Elsewhere he speaks of his "bestpreserved wholewife, sowell her as herafter," the modification of the German construction "sowohl ... als" (as well as) helping to fuse the notions of posterior and posterity beneath the German word "After" (anus).[53]

Just as the absurd metaphor represents an expression of that fount of fantasy and nonsense that refuses to be subjugated by the cognitive mask, so the bawdy quibble is a welling-up of our prelinguistic, asocial sexuality, which pops up its angry conk as if to spite the social mask that would cut it off. Yet this simple, binary latent/manifest distinction proves itself inherently problematic. For a start, it is possible to read even Freud as understanding desire itself to be fundamentally mimetic, the little boy's desire for his mother originating in an imitation of the father with whom he identifies in all things, going as far as to desire what he desires.[54] Even sexuality is a performance acquired by mimicry. As a result, the language of desire is itself necessarily a structured script, making it difficult to see the joke in particular as an outburst of some sort of undiluted or original sexuality. Take such puns as "there's a vas deferens between children and no children" or "a defective condom is a 'Welsh letter' (because it has a leek in it), or a 'Scotch letter' (once it has been repaired)."[55] While on the one hand exploiting puns that operate as two-tiered structures, the sexual theme cannot truthfully be said to be "hidden" in either instance, nor is there any mask of chaste decorum veiling the unmentionable: the jokes clearly depend above all upon the self-congratulatory acknowledgement of semantic patterings and repetitions.

That even bawdy quips may be highly structured units and, as such, dependent upon the recognition of repetition is exemplified by the sequence-joke, as when one newspaper headline reading "Convict evades noose. Jury hung"[56] is followed up by an escalation of the same: "Sex convict evades noose. Jury well hung." Not only are the quips in question based on gratifyingly patterned wordplay, they are also, by today's standards at least, relatively harmless and inconspicuous. Although touching upon matters in the past considered taboo, such as contraception and the male member (of the jury), the element of shock or sexual "release" is at most secondary. The metaphor of instinctive drives that "well up" and find an outlet in such punning is clearly not always equally satisfactory. It does not seem to be some source of raw, untapped sexual energy that bubbles to the surface, but a product that is already processed and refined. The irrationality of the pun cannot ultimately separate itself from the mask of wordplay.

It is here that the model of the mask that hides nothing or "nothing" again comes into action, for if we can indeed never truly escape from our social role-playing, then the asocial core, the "real" self, cannot be anything other than a fiction, a nothing, an absence, or a gap. Freud himself shows an underlying awareness of the unconscious as an "unknowable" of the order of the Kantian thing-in-itself. At this level of interpretation, the real subject is purely negative; the "reality" of the subject in itself is nowhere to be found—or at least nowhere other than its appearance. Notably, however, this may amount to an assertion of its ubiquity.

While the simple Freudian model would thus maintain that it is only the occasional joke or slip of the tongue (or dream, or neurosis) that allows the unconscious to surge up, post-structuralists (such as Lacan) go further: all language is a slip of the tongue, all communication is a skeptical joke, and every utterance is invaded and pervaded by the unconscious. Again, Freud himself seems to have been aware of the "symptomatic" character of speech, regarding *all* propositions as "compromise formations" (a disguised emergence of repressed bodily drives or wishes), even when not patent parapraxes. Despite its claims to the contrary, therefore, *all* language is a sublimation of our desire and has its origins in the unknowability of the body. In this respect, sexual and aggressive jokes can consequently be seen as exhibiting a certain sort of honesty analogous to that of openly metaphorical language, in that they at least *admit* that they are but a front to bodily drives rather than mimetic signposts to the "world." While most language tries to conceal its origins in desire and efface itself in objectivity, the saucy allusion and the bawdy pun—though themselves (half-)masquerading as decency—also (half-)admit their pretence. They are self-confessed masks, which reveal what they veil.

The Lacanian model provides a third interesting perspective to shed light on the limits of the binary mask/face opposition, yet it is one that can in fact be severed from its psychoanalytical context. The structuralist point that signifiers are but arbitrarily "attached" to what they signify (that is, through social convention) entails that signifying words have an infinite potential for meaning and that a given signifier could be attached to any number of signifieds. Functional discourse can only work by provisionally nailing down words onto meanings, giving an illusion of stability (as if a particular word "belonged" with its meaning), and hiding the dynamic potentiality of language. If the word is a mask arbitrarily stuck onto a meaning, therefore, then it generally conceals the arbitrariness of this coupling and pretends to yield transparent access to its sense. Although Lacan himself would have objected to the mask metaphor and the implication that there are two levels of structure, he thus refers to the unconscious as "a perpetual sliding of the signified *beneath* the signifier"[57] (my emphasis), an image that suggests a reservoir of semantic fluidity or potentiality hidden by the fixity of the signifying mask. The ego, the consciousness, can only function by repressing this turbulence, a turbulence that in its myriad permutations coincides with what has already been encountered as the realm of the irrational, the fantastic, the grotesque, and the surreal, where identities are blurred and forms fused.

The radical separation of signifier and signified, which means that we can never ultimately say what we mean nor mean what we say, is pasted over and played down in functional discourse, which imposes a unilinear straitjacket (a rear light is a rear light) upon the plurivalent potential of language (a rear light *could* be a moon, or an orange, or a face ...). The pun is in this sense a means of escaping this straitjacket and signifying a number of things at once. Yet like the Kantian thing-in-itself, which is a purely *negative* conceptual construction, the pure potentiality of "unconscious" language is an empty notion. As Hegel pointed out (although in a different context), the possible either exists as grounded in the actual or real, or it becomes completely vacuous.[58] A word that "could" mean anything fails to mean anything. If the verbal mask is thus hiding a semantic vacuum (nothing), or if what is "behind" the mask—i.e., reality or the unconscious subject—is unknowable, then the pun can only ever be, at most, a hint of the inadequacy of the mask, or a masked intimation of the unknowable within us or outside.

It is perhaps Joyce's *Finnegans Wake* which illustrates these points more than any other work. More often than not, the semantic components of the puns that permeate this verbal behemoth resist classification into the latent and the manifest, working simultaneously on a multiplicity of levels at once. A brief phrase such as "I never open momouth but I pack mefood in it," a repetition and modification of the earlier "for every dime he yawpens that momouth you could park your ford in it," exemplifies this complexity.[59] Eluding all attempts to appropriate a single self-identical meaning, the sentence not only contains elements of opening one's mouth to speak, opening one's mouth to eat and putting one's foot in it (making a verbal blunder), but also, by referring us back to the earlier variant, it prompts the reader to make a web of metaphoric connections between mouth (of river) and ford (as river), and between ford (as river) and ford (as car). Parking, packing, and putting, food, ford, and foot, rivermouths, eating and speaking mouths are all blurred in a welter of semantic fluidity that links eating, talking, driving, and flowing as part of the same vicus of recirculation (our wholemole millwheeling vicociclometer) that characterizes the river.[60] The text clearly refuses to be tamed by a bipartite distinction between manifest meaning and latent subtext. Just as the comic metaphor was described as highlighting its status as a mask and thereby simultaneously yielding an insight into an unknowable realm of the irrational, *Finnegans Wake* presents itself as a dazzling verbal surface in its phonological materiality while also—concurrently—exposing itself as a semantic flux that echoes the fluvial motion of the river anna livia plurabelle as well as imitating the fluidity of dream.

Wit and Inversion/Reversal/Subversion

Wit may be interpreted as containing an element of hidden subversiveness in the form of the pun, which masks its bawdry or its irreverence under a pretence of verbal decorum, or it may be seen as embodying a semantic plurality that undermines the notion of meaning in general. Yet wit may also be much more openly subversive.

Etymologically, the word "wit" has its origins in the semantic field of knowledge (and ultimately vision), as is shown by its German cousin "Witz," which is descended from the Old High German *wizzi*, an overall designation for natural and acquired knowledge in general. As late as Leibniz, *wiz* can still be found denoting mental capabilities in the broadest sense. In these terms, wit is seen to be linked to a moment fundamental to comic hero and audience alike: that of knowing better. The comic hero is one who *outwits* his gulls, exploiting a superiority of knowledge shared by the audience. To the extent that the gull is normally also a rogue of some cast or other, the act of outwitting tends to constitute a situational reversal, frequently a power reversal. The rogue is *turned into* a gull by an act of "wit," wit here coming to mean something akin to trickery, wile, or guile. Although wit does not seem to be directly related to wile in etymological terms, a certain spiritual proximity is hinted at by the fact that wit stands in the same etymological contiguity to wizard (in the semantic field of knowledge) as wile does to witch (in the semantic field of sorcery). The English had in fact initially imported the word "wit" in the second half of the sixteenth century to translate the Latin *ingenium*, a word stemming from *gignere* (to beget, produce) and responsible for such terms as genius and engineer. Wit was at this stage felt to be synonymous with ingenuity in general, and not necessarily verbal ingenuity.

Boccaccio's *Decameron* testifies to the power of wit, in the form of *ingenium* or ingenuity, to "turn the tables", above all in the recurrent comic motif of guileful wives outwitting jealous or inadequate husbands who spend their time applying what little wit they have to the maintenance of the marital yoke. Yet the tales also furnish examples of purely verbal alacrity reversing a situation as when Maestro Alberto da Bologna uses his wit to embarrass a woman who had intended to embarrass him (1:10). The prankster is turned by wit into the butt of the joke. On the sixth day, devoted in its entirety to rhetorical skill and the witty retort, Neofile describes how "a ready wit (*il pronto ingegno*) ... will frequently yield a fleet phrase, graceful and to the point, from the lips of the speaker."[61] *Il pronto ingegno* is thus the mental agility and flexibility capable of begetting that swift response that can upturn or invert a situation. Michele Scalza (6:6) combines his wit with an element of what Lady Sneerwell would have called ill-nature. Claiming to prove the ancient descent and nobility of the unpopular Baronci family, he argues that it is signaled by their ugliness. Being the oldest family, not only in Florence but in the whole world, they were created at a time when God was still learning the rudiments of his business, which explains what a mess he made of them. Under the guise of praising the nobility of the Baronci, Michele Scalza mockingly insults them by inverting normally accepted values and forging a link between nobility and ugliness.

Figaro likewise exemplifies the politics of wit as an ability to turn the tables, his gift for guile and intrigue running parallel to his skill in verbal repartee (this latter, as with Michele Scalza, coming closer to "wit" as the word is normally used). Not only does Figaro prove himself in every respect conversationally superior to his master, he also uses his perspicacity to question the existing order. His perspicacity manifests itself, for example, in his keen eye for situational analogies and divergences (a fusion of wit and judgement in the Lockean or Hobbesian sense):

Count. The servants here ... take longer to dress than their masters!
Figaro. That's because they don't have a valet to help them.
(Le Mariage, Act 3, scene 5)

and his use of paradoxical inversions of an ethical/normative order:

Count. I remember you being quite a varlet in my service.
Figaro. Egad, Monseigneur, can you expect a poor chap to be beyond reproach?
Count. Lazy, disorderly....
Figaro. Given the virtues you demand of a valet, does Your Excellency know many masters worthy of being a servant?
Count. (*laughing*) Not bad....
(Le Barbier de Séville, Act 1, scene 2)

Indeed, at the end of *Le Mariage de Figaro*, Figaro himself stresses the role of wit in inverting hierarchies, turning the social order upside down, or rather back the right way up (the word "esprit" he uses having likewise been taken by the French as a translation of the Latin *ingenium*):

> Through the vagaries of birth,
> One is shepherd, one is king:
> Fortune makes a person's worth;
> Wit alone shifts everything.

(Vaudeville)

The case of Figaro brings to light a further factor constitutive of wit. The wit of comic tropes and similes consists not merely in an ability to spot identity, but more essentially in a capacity to yoke concepts together that do not on first sight tolerate such a juxtaposition. As such it is related to a creative power of the imagination, a reservoir of fantasy that is able to picture the possibility of otherness, of difference (the moon as a headlight, a shadow throwing up). Analogously, wit of the political sort manifested by Figaro springs from a capacity to imagine a different social order, to perceive the identity between master and servant (a common core of humanity), and to visualize a world in which the differences are irrelevant—or even the relations inverted (master becoming servant and servant master), as well, moreover, as enacting this inversion through both verbal and practical wit. It was perhaps to take account of this element of fantasy inherent in wit that the eighteenth-century German philosopher Christian Wolff, in addition to adopting the Lockean inheritance, felt able to dissect *ingenium* into *acumen* (or perspicacity), *memoria*, and *imaginatio*[62] (although Gottsched was subsequently to separate *acumen*, *imaginatio*, and *ingenium* into three discrete faculties again). As a vehicle of fantasy, wit is thus radically opposed to a torpid, dogmatic, or unthinking acceptance of the world as it is, to an uncritical disregard for possibility in the name of actuality, or to thought patterns molded and formed entirely by social habit and consequently sunk in a quagmire of predictability. Of course political awareness, like imaginative awareness, may itself quickly become stereotypical and predictable: the comic moment resides in the initial jolting reversal that wrenches us out of our linguistic torpor. Wit consists in precisely this ability to come up with a conversational surprise, rupturing normal patterns of linguistic expectation. The inversion need not be overtly political; it may be ethical or aesthetic. Indeed, it may simply be a reversal of (humdrum) common sense. The factor common to all such wit is the perception of a new, shocking, unusual, or inverted perspective, a knack of turning the conversation on its head.

It is perhaps Oscar Wilde who is the master of the subversive epigram, Lord Henry Wootton in *The Picture of Dorian Gray* producing a sequence of conversational corkers such as "Punctuality is the thief of time," "It is only shallow people who do not judge by appearances," "I can believe anything, provided that it is quite incredible," "Ugliness is one of the seven deadly virtues," and "One can always be kind to people about whom one cares nothing."[63] The Wildean inversion generally takes the form of self-contradiction or paradox. All the preceding examples, that is, are reversals or negations of tautologies or near-tautological commonplaces; in their turn negated, they would possess the soporific quality of truisms: "Shallow people judge by appearances," "I can believe anything that is credible," ... (yawn). Such tautologies and near-tautologies, being inevitably and unthinkingly true, are the epitome of the cliché, pat truths trotted off unquestioningly. Wilde's technique consists in structuring a sentence that initially gives the appearance of being an easy self-evidence, but then—with an inserted negation or a carefully placed antonym instead of the expected word—startles, jolts, and jars us out of the self-satisfied mental torpor that can hear and respond to an assertion without questioning, interpreting, or thinking about it. The element of surprise has long since been recognized as a key to laughter, Hobbes referring to the "*sudden* Glory" leading to it and Kant defining the phenomenon as "an affect resulting from the sudden transformation of a suspenseful expectation into nothing,"[64] a definition that will be encountered again later. The point here is that the comic surprise (the unexpected antonym or negation) as it were rips down the mask of linguistic self-evidence and complacent truism, reawakening us to the possibility of difference.

That the Wildean bon mot further tends to be ethically subversive is shown not only by the *fin de siècle* Vice Lord Henry, but also by the idly decadent characters of *The Importance of Being Earnest*. The social institution of marriage in particular comes in for a buffeting at the hands of wit. Lady Bracknell, recounting a visit to dear Lady Harbury, comments: "I hadn't been there since her poor husband's death. I never saw a woman so altered; she looks quite twenty years younger" (1); and Algernon objects that the "amount of women in London who flirt with their own husbands is perfectly scandalous. It looks so bad. It is simply washing one's clean linen in public" (1). Cecily inverts and redefines the notion of hypocrisy: "I hope you have not been leading a double life, pretending to be wicked and being really good all the time. That would be hypocrisy" (2). Truthfulness itself becomes a negative quality, as Jack points out: "it is a terrible thing for a man to find out suddenly that all his life he has been speaking nothing but the truth" (3), and he asks Gwendolen for forgiveness for his inadvertent sincerity. Algernon debunks the Victorian work ethic by emphasizing the importance of *not* keeping business appointments, despises the shallowness of people who are *not* serious about meals, and demands an *im*probable explanation from Jack. It is clear from these examples that Wilde's wit is morally rather than politically subversive, mocking the sexual norm and the Protestant work ethic from above (with amused detachment) and not from below (with engagement and commitment to change). The man who asserted that "work is the ruin of the drinking classes" portrays, above all, indolently intellectual wits who can *afford* to be ethically unorthodox and play about with notions of truthfulness, but ignores the sphere of practical "wit" to be found in such figures as Figaro or Nestroy's Ultra (in *Freiheit in Krähwinkel*). Furthermore, Wilde confirms the tendency of subversion itself to become structured, ordered, and regular, the "shallow mask of manner" to which Cecily refers in *The Importance* (2), and it is often objected that the Wildean wit has a certain mechanical aspect that quickly lapses into predictability. On the other hand, however, his paradoxes thereby generate the paradoxical pleasure of expecting the unexpected. Joe Orton's lunatic psychiatrist Doctor Rance produces a tautological (or is it paradoxical?) piece of nonsense to describe his madhouse which possibly has a certain explanatory value in this context: "Just when one least expects it, the unexpected always happens" (2).

Yet Wilde's is not merely a case of willful recalcitrance or a purely playful love of nonsensical self-contradiction. If, on the one hand, paradox is a form of conceptual subversion (and, in *De Profundis*, Wilde says that what the paradox was for him in the realm of thought, sexual deviation was in the realm of conduct[65]), part of the comic effect also results from a recognition of the truth of the inversion or reversal. It is a similar principle that informs the reversals structuring the *Praise of Folly*, written by the Renaissance humanist Erasmus of Rotterdam. As with Erasmus, we are ultimately brought to acknowledge a wisdom in folly. The self-evident tautologies of Victorianism, unthinkingly churned out, are *not* the whole story, whatever rationality might say, for there is a sense in which an excessive regard for punctuality does waste time, appearances are telling, marriage is a bind, truthfulness boring, sincerity superficial, and feigned wickedness hypocritical. The arbitrary and distortive nature of our conceptual labeling and ordering of the world is unmasked by the truthfulness inherent in the reversal of the tautology or cliché. That this reversal is in turn only *half*-true does not invalidate it, but merely indicates the necessary imperfection of any conceptual mask. Wilde himself is reported as saying to Catulle Mendès that paradoxes, though half-truths, were the best to be had—there being no absolute truths.[66] Once again it is a question of a conceptual mask that at least has the integrity to admit that it is but a mask, its paradoxicality signaling its (half-)untruthfulness. A comparable message, although set against a religious backcloth, is proclaimed by Erasmus's figure Folly, whose eulogy on the wisdom of folly (and especially Christian folly) is a response to the folly of human wisdom. It is no coincidence that Lord Henry himself is a skilled praiser of folly firmly in the Erasmian tradition.

> "Yes," he continued, "that is one of the great secrets of life. Nowadays most people die of a sort of creeping common sense, and discover when it is too late that the only things one never regrets are one's mistakes."
> A laugh ran round the table.
> He played with the idea, and grew wilful; tossed it into the air and transformed it; let it escape and recaptured it; made it iridescent with fancy, and winged it with paradox. The praise of folly, as he went on, soared into a philosophy, and Philosophy herself became young, and catching the mad music of Pleasure, wearing, one might fancy, her wine-stained robe and wreath of ivy, danced like a Bacchante over the hills of life, and mocked the slow Silenus for being sober.... He was brilliant, fantastic, irresponsible....[67]

In the twentieth century, Joe Orton has shown himself equally drawn to the subversive epigram. In his diaries he records his appreciation of lines such as "No good deed ever goes unpunished,"[68] and his masterpiece *What the Butler Saw* portrays a topsy-turvy world where complacent ethical assumptions are turned on their head and linguistic expectations systematically exploded. After Mrs. Prentice has been assaulted by a page-boy at the Station Hotel, Rance's commentary inverts the notion of good service:

> *Rance.* What was the object of the assault?
> *Mrs. Prentice.* The youth wanted to rape me.
> *Rance.* He didn't succeed?
> *Mrs. Prentice.* No.
> *Rance.* (*shaking his head*) The service in these hotels is dreadful.
>
> (Act 1)

This rupture in the linguistic mask is simultaneously a breach in the social mask, a flaw in the normal facade of propriety that reveals a society motivated above all by sexual appetite:

> *Prentice.* A man exposed himself to you last summer.
> *Mrs. Prentice.* (*without looking at him*) I didn't see anything.
> *Prentice.* And your disappointment marred our holiday.
>
> (Act 1)

The schoolmistress of a party of holidaying schoolgirls is equally frustrated, when Nick the page-boy fails to misbehave with her:

> Nick.   Undeterred I took the lift to the third floor of the hotel where a party
>   of schoolgirls were staying. Oh, sir, what lonely and aimless lives they
>   lead!
> Prentice. (*with a frown*) Was there no mistress in attendance?
> Nick.   She occupied a room across the corridor.
> Prentice. Did you disturb her?
> Nick.   No. And she'll never forgive me for it.
>
>   (Act 1)

Simpson's *A Resounding Tinkle* also provides the epitome of a Wildean exchange amid its madness:

> Mrs. Paradock. You've never done anything to excess in your life. That's just
>   your trouble.
> Mr. Paradock. I happen to prefer moderation.
> Mrs. Paradock. You make a vice of it. You never know when not to stop.
>
>   (Act 1, scene 2)

Of course not all inversions and reversals are equally comic. Congreve's Witwoud, the would-be wit, again demonstrates how it is *not* done. A praise of insincerity in his hands forfeits its comic effect because it is presented in the shape of a dogmatic truth: "A wit should no more be sincere, than a woman constant" (1.6). Ignoring the paradoxicality of his position (whereas Wilde would perhaps have made a point to the effect that insincerity is sincere or sincerity insincere), Witwoud tries to compensate by spicing up his assertion with a not particularly inspiring analogy. The English poets Swinburne and Blake show for different reasons that reversals need not necessarily be comic—or need not exploit their comic potential. Just as Blake had produced such potentially subversive proverbs as "The road of excess leads to the palace of wisdom" in *The Marriage of Heaven and Hell,* Wilde's near-contemporary Swinburne exploited blasphemic inversions for poetic effect, creating a world where heaven is hell, where virtue is vice and vice versa. Blake's aphorisms in particular constitute radical ethical inversions of dominant contemporary ideals. If such poetic reversals are not comic, this can perhaps be attributed above all to the *serious* poetic context. Once ethical reversals start to take themselves seriously (as truth) and once they become a consistently represented perspective and thereby sacrifice the element of surprise— the unexpected or half-expected pleasure of seeing an unquestioned dogmatic mask being shed—the comic potential is necessarily lessened. Another contemporary of Oscar Wilde, George Bernard Shaw by contrast manifests how the heaven/hell inversion can be turned to more comic accoun´, playing with the paradoxes and absurdities of the reversal in his portrayal of hell as the place where all the fun is. The Statue (Roebuck Ramsden) condemned to heaven is bored stiff there, characterizing it as the "most angelically dull place in all creation" and hell as a "place where you have nothing to do but amuse yourself" (*Man and Superman*, act 3). Yet he admits his guilt and accepts responsibility for his fate in the hereafter: "I cant complain. I was a hypocrite; and it served me right to be sent to heaven."

When Brecht's Grusche Vachnadze is faced with the temptation to do good, when Martin Amis's John Self refers to his girlfriend as a "sicko" who sees nothing in him but himself, when Molière's Béralde interprets taking medicine and surviving as a sign of good health,[69] the comic effect derives from a recognized paradigmatic deviation from an unthinkingly accepted norm or cliché. Again, the acknowledgement of the deviation is coupled with an awareness of a degree of truth in the deviation—even if this *is* the product of the deviance inherent in the world itself! If indeed the world *is* sick and topsy-turvy, an inversion and perversion of the ideal, then we who share the sickness can appreciate the (half-)truthfulness of the upside-down perspective. Parodies of proverbs (a form of wisdom not far removed from the tautology and the cliché but with a better reputation), or "perverbs,"[70] similarly depend on the twin processes of recognition of deviation (from the source) and acknowledgement of a measure of applicability. Trevor Griffith's play *Comedians* provides a simple example: "A bad lover blames his tool" (3). The perverb is here supported by a slightly bawdy pun, but it is the same principle at work when the Duchess in *Alice in Wonderland* says: "Take care of the sense, and the sounds will take care of themselves,"[71] not only parodying the trite proverb about pennies and pounds, but also (perhaps) unwittingly making a philosophical claim about the primacy of thought in relation to language. The wit consists both in the difference from the source and the creation of a new meaning. But it is the youthful Gargantua, gleefully wallowing in a welter of his own piss, snot, and shit, who takes the perverbial cake, a cake that he of course both has and greedily consumes. His activity consists of a whole accumulation of nonsensical anticlichés, washing his hands in the soup, blowing fat farts and flaying the fox, ducking underwater to avoid the rain, striking while the iron is cold, putting the cart before the ox, always looking the gift-horse in the mouth....[72]

4
Cracking the Mask

Both Rabelais and Wilde in their different ways thwart our expectations, inverting or subverting the norm and fracturing the mask of linguistic predictability. In this they evidence a phenomenon that also applies at a more general level, for *any* sudden break in behavioral predictability may have a comic effect, as it were surprising the onlooker into laughter. It was to take account of this that the sixteenth-century scholar Madius, who in 1550 published a commentary on Aristotle's *Poetics*, went further than Aristotle in stressing not merely ugliness as the basis for laughter but also *admiratio*, meaning astonishment or surprise. Following in Madius's footsteps, Descartes too came to see mocking laughter as a consequence of the *sudden* perception of a weakness in the object of mockery ("When this happens unexpectedly, the surprise of admiration [*admiratio*] results in our bursting into laughter"[1]). In the light of Madius's and Descartes's use of the term *admiratio*, it is significant that a number of Renaissance commentators on the *cognitio* or recognition that clears up misunderstandings at the conclusion of the comic plot explicitly understand it as producing *admiratio* or *maraviglia* (wonder) in the spectator, while Aristotelian *anagnorisis* has frequently been associated with an unexpected turn, indeed with reversal or *peripeteia*.[2] If the happy ending's collective unmasking of the truth now tends to elicit at most an ironic smirk rather than shrieks of wonderment and surprise, however, perhaps it is because, as an age-old theatrical convention, it has ceased to astonish the audience and instead become fodder for parody.

This chapter is thus concerned less with the structurally predictable unmasking of the recognition scene—as everybody finds out who they really are—than with more sporadic comic suddenness, interpreted as a result of the *falling* or *cracking* of a mask when an actor (in whatever sense: trickster, social actor, or theatrical performer) proves herself unable or unwilling to keep up her role. The comedy here consequently consists in the momentary revelation, the instant of surprise, rather than in the continuous awareness of a discrepancy between appearance and lured us into complacent expectation of more of the same, the rupture of this mask constitutes an explosion of our complacency, and the comedy of the mask falling indeed often ensues when *we ourselves* have been taken in by a specific piece of role-playing. The shattering of a pattern retrospectively draws attention to the pattern that has been shattered (the automatism otherwise tending to be taken for granted by our perceptual automatism), just as the dropping of the actor's mask retrospectively rams home that we have been deceived by disguise, pretence, or imposture—that what we had assumed to be the face was in fact but a facade. Subliminally at least, such laughter might well, therefore, be directed at the *laugher himself* for having been fooled, duped by the acting, or lulled into a false sense of predictability. This is a point made by Cicero, who describes the effect of risibility "when we are expecting to hear one phrase and a different one is uttered. Here we are moved to laughter by our own mistake."[3] Under the influence of Cicero, the Roman rhetorician Quintilian also refers to the jest that creates its effect by deceiving expectations.[4] Yet the falling of the mask may of course equally work *in conjunction with* the spectator's or reader's prior awareness of the disparity between appearance and reality. Here the comic pleasure results from the superiority of the Olympian perspective, as the privileged observer is able to savor the sight of the bad actor trying (in vain) to keep a wobbly mask on. Gradations between the two aspects determine the extent to which the unpredictable becomes predictable and the unexpected is expected.

Comedy may accordingly be viewed in formalistic terms. Whether the mask is considered at the level of trickery and imposture, social role-playing, or theatrical performance, a certain kind of comedy can always ensue from the falling of the mask. In this respect, occurrences are not comic in themselves, but depend upon the prior expectations within the laughing subject. Francis Hutcheson points out in the second of his *Reflections on Laughter* (1728) that since laughter is provoked by a deviation from the normal, our conception of what is normal will have a radical bearing upon our conception of what is funny.[5] Our set of expectations, however, is a complex web of factors dictated not merely by social values, but also by rules pertaining to the aesthetic medium in general and to the genre in particular, as well as by the contextual immediacy of the text itself. There exists a corresponding formal parallelism between:

1. the slipping of the social mask: the social actor cannot keep up his social role but reveals his motivating anti-sociality, his aggressive sexuality or his selfish greed
2. the disruption of the theatrical illusion: the actors on stage draw attention to their acting *as* acting, mere show

3. the dropping of the mask of deception or self-deception *within* the play or novel itself: the fictive impostor or pretender fails to maintain his role but reveals his "true" feelings.

The next two chapters deal with these three closely intertwined branches of comic "surprise."

Of Molière's comedy it has been said that the mask worn by its deceivers and self-deceivers "is only affixed, and to a living organism. The point of interest for him, and for us, is the point when the mask slips or falls, when the underlying man appears."[6] This applies above all to his impostors, charlatans, schemers, and rogues, who impose a straitjacket upon their own behavior to which they are unable to conform, or who hide a "true" nature that nevertheless insists on revealing itself. Tartuffe's sexuality and his crookedness, Argan's healthiness, Alceste's desire for attention, Monsieur Jourdain's bourgeois background—all persistently manifest themselves in spite of the conscious or unconscious role-playing that seeks to mask the truth. So, while Bergson's explanation of Molière's comedy was certainly on target in its view of laughter as a response to the sight of man behaving like a machine and hiding his specifically human spontaneity behind the predictability of the mask, its incompleteness comes to light at those moments when the mask falls. This emerges particularly clearly (though in a very different context) from a twentieth-century parody of the Bergsonian theory in Simpson's *A Resounding Tinkle*. Mr. Paradock, having heard of Bergson's theory and decided to test it out by becoming an electronic computer in order to raise a laugh, does fine initially and produces some remarkable mathematical computations. He only really starts to become comic, however, when he short-circuits and lapses into a torrent of gibberish which doesn't subside until he is unplugged. If comedy is occasioned when man gives the impression of being a machine, the effect is doubled when the machine goes haywire.

Aristophanes's *Women at the Thesmophoria* offers a classical example of the comedy engendered by a wobbly mask or a perilously unconvincing imposture in its portrayal of Euripides's friend Mnesilochus trying his hand at deception at the exclusively female religious rite known as the *Thesmophoria*. Dressed as a woman, Mnesilochus has been persuaded by Euripides to take his turn on the orator's podium in order to try and defend Euripides's reputation with the women. Armed from the outset with the foreknowledge of the discrepancy between mask and face, the spectator is able to relish the sight of Mnesilochus's mask starting to slip as he overdoes his racy stories about female promiscuity and sexual ruses, and a decidedly male perspective emerges in blatant contradiction with his female appearance. As he gets carried away by his scurrilous sense of humor and lapses into anecdotes about pimps and loofahs, the women cotton on to his pretence, and the wobbliness of his metaphorical mask is complemented by the very real danger that his literal mask will be literally ripped off. As is so often the case, the comedy is compounded by the repeated deferral of the moment of revelation. When the women finally succeed in ripping off his robe, they do not immediately find his big floppy artificial stage penis for he has pushed it through to the back, and a bawdy bout of hide-and-seek-the-penis is played before his impressively multicolored dolichophallus is definitively brought to light.

This episode also reveals the importance of asides as a means of allowing the mask to slip. A character thus "plays along" in the fictive action, but divulges his or her "true" feelings and thoughts to the audience, thereby enabling them to see behind the mask as privileged observers and spawning a flattering sense of complicity. Faced with the disconcertingly imminent prospect of a disrobing at the hands of a mob of (more or less genuinely) phallophobic females, Mnesilochus rhetorically turns to the audience for advice, a move that brings the onlooker to share not only the knowledge but also the playful anxiety of the trickster. In Nestroy's *Der Talisman*, a play structured around the repeated deferral of the moment when Titus's imposture is exposed, Titus similarly establishes a degree of collusion with an audience privy to the wobbliness of his mask/disguise (i.e., his wig). After a skilled piece of salon banter on contemporary drama with Frau von Cypressenburg, for example, the entrance of the gardener's wife, who had been a sucker for his charms when he was on a lower rung of the social ladder and correspondingly coiffed with a different colored wig, elicits a bathetic "Verdammt!" from Titus audible only to the audience. Elsewhere, feigning moral indignation at Constantia's sexual advances, he winkingly whispers to the spectator that he prefers to be the one making the advances. Here we are granted access to a layer of specifically sexual truth beneath the appearance of celibacy, and the aside indeed has a special capacity for getting to the fleshly heart of the matter in a way that deflates the facade of moral continence. In Middleton's *A Mad World, My Masters* (1604), the comment whispered by Frank Gullman the Courtesan reveals to the audience a distinctly venereal subtext behind the mask of venerability worn by her mother:

Harebrain. And how does the virtuous matron, that good old gentlewoman thy mother? I persuade myself if modesty be in the world she has part on't. A woman of an excellent carriage all her lifetime, in court, city, and country.

Courtesan. Sh'as always carried it well in those places, sir. (*Aside*) Witness three bastards apiece.

(Act 1, scene 2)

If the comedy of deception results in part from the imperfection of the deception, inadvertent self-deception too can prove comic when exposed for what it is, a point corroborated by a brief passage from Martin Amis's novel *London Fields*, in which a mask of alcoholic self-deception (the perennial "I can take my liquor" maintained despite all circumstantial evidence to the contrary) is ripped down by retrospective revelation:

> Keith could hold his drink. No one knew the difference. He thought with all modesty of the times he had burst through Trish Shirt's plywood door and walked straight into the wall, and she never said a word. Keith just carried it off. "You're quite drunk already, aren't you, Keith," said Nicola.[7]

This principle applies not only to Molière's self-deluding monomaniacs who unwittingly manifest a well of human spontaneity that explodes the rigidity of the role they have imposed upon themselves, but also to those social self-deceivers who remain blind to the less obtrusive cultural role-playing into which they lapse, those who unsuspectingly allow some form of *mauvaise foi*, some behavioral pattern or conceptual cliché, to determine their conduct. Comedies accordingly have a capacity to unmask social self-deception, primarily either by debunking a particular cliché through the comic perspicacity or self-awareness of a fictive figure (just as Nicola deflates Keith's pretensions to sobriety) or by portraying the inadequacies of the social mask in concrete interactive situations. Two modes of comic mask-rupture thus emerge: it may be effected from *without*, through the acumen of a discerning observer (although this may also take the form of *self*-observation), or from *within*, owing to social incompetence, an ineptitude in wearing the mask on the part of the actor. At a certain level of course, we are all self-deceivers to the extent that we tend to ignore, suppress, or forget the theatricality of our social performance or to delude ourselves that we have a "true" inner self to which only *we* have access (via introspection). Yet comedy need not itself be informed by this awareness of the universality of role-playing; indeed it more often sets up an ideal of "genuine" behavior, of healthy self-identity, to act as an ethical yardstick in opposition to the acting of some deceiver or self-deceiver. The comic point lies above all either in the conflict between social mask and whatever is seen to be the "real self" or "real motivation," or in a deflating revelation of a specific social role in its hackneyed triteness.

The hero of Dürrenmatt's *Romulus der Große* is one such deflater of illusions, revealing all tragic heroism as a cliché. Neglecting his duties as the emperor of a dying empire, Romulus takes the wind out of any aura of historic or histrionic grandeur by buggering off to feed his hens at times of crisis, and he insults his military advisors by objecting to the style of their formulation when they momentously advocate total mobilization against the enemy. Indeed, on the arrival of Spurius Titus Mamma, who has ridden seven horses to death and braved three arrow wounds in the last two days and nights in his zeal to deliver a vital dispatch and thereby save the empire, Romulus apathetically responds by asking why all the fuss and pointing out that heroism is a pose. His heightened awareness that tragic posturing is but a role even prompts him to urge his dramatically orientated daughter, Rea, to turn to comedy rather than wallow in the self-pitying lamentations of Antigone: the comic mode has become an existential response to disillusionment in life.

Such comic deflation need not come from the external perspective of a perspicacious hero. Both Nestroy and, following in his tradition, Brecht regularly allow characters to step marginally outside their role in order to comment on their own conduct in such a way as to reveal its theatricality. Titus prefaces his exchange with the sophisticated Frau von Cypressenburg by self-consciously muttering (to himself and to the spectator): "Here I am face-to-face with an authoress; workaday words won't do any more, now it's time for my conversation to don its Sunday best" (2.17). When the small-town philistines in Nestroy's *Freiheit in Krähwinkel* decide to have a small-time revolution, the audience is constantly made aware of the element of cliché, imitation, and role-playing involved: the Krähwinklers have learned their insurrectionary scripts from the big-time revolutions. Even when the revolutionary turbulence has reached a climax, Ultra, the comic instigator of the move for freedom, debunks any sense of spontaneity by expressing a calculated realization that the time has come for an inspiring speech. Rousing political oratory is not an effusion of irrepressible political enthusiasm and genuine engagement from within, but tactical histrionics with a time, a place, and a rhetorical aim. The sight of Ui (alias Hitler) practising his speeches in front of a mirror has a similar effect in Brecht's *Der Aufhaltsame Aufstieg des Arturo Ui*.

Love is another pose in need of a healthy debunking from time to time. Sternheim's *Die Hose*, for example, consistently deflates the well-worn poetic clichés of amorous intrigue bandied about by Frau Reuter, Mandelstam, Scarron, and Frau Maske by juxtaposing their hackneyed rhetoric with the matter-of-fact philistinism of Herr Maske. Scarron's late-romantic idealization of his encounter with a prostitute, infused as it is with a tedious regurgitation of blasphemously inverted Marian imagery, is effectively punctured by Maske's (intentionally?) trite responses, his refusal to understand Scarron's rich and exotic vocabulary, and his pragmatic concern with how much it cost. Even more basic is the parody of the romantic death wish in *Leonce und Lena*: Valerio takes the wind out of Leonce's desire to consummate his love in suicide by bathetically saving his life. In Peter Nichols's *A Day in the Death of Joe Egg*, it is Bri's *self*-observations that burst the bubble of amorous theatricality: "I can't sustain a passion to the end of the sentence. I start to cry—aaaoooow! Then I think: are you mad?.... You must have felt like this—catching yourself in the mirror hamming away." (1). As in the case of Berowne, excessive self-awareness leads to a consciousness of oneself as a role-player, Bri's mirror here becoming a symbolic agent of the duality that splits the actor up into spectator *and* actor. Bri in this case exposes not only his own mask but also the audience's, bringing to light the way we all tend to ham our mimetically learned clichés, perhaps prompting us too to hold a mirror up to our everyday performances.

Martin Amis's Charles Highway typifies the actor who is always his own spectator, and, in *The Rachel Papers*, the narrative perspective grants the reader the privilege of being privy to this literary self-consciousness which constantly observes itself and marshalls the roles he plays. Before a meeting with Rachel, Charles mentally sketches his script(s) in advance:

> What clothes would I wear?... What persona would I wear? On the two occasions I had seen her last August I underwent several complete identity-reorganizations, settling finally somewhere between the pained, laconic, inscrutable type and the knowing, garrulous, cynical, laugh a minute, yet something demonic about him, something nihilistic, muted death–wish type. Revamp those, or start again?
>
> Why couldn't Rachel be a little more specific about the type of person *she* was? Goodness knew; if she were a hippie I'd talk to her about her drug experiences, the zodiac, tarot cards. If she were left-wing I'd look miserable, hate Greece, and eat baked beans straight from the tin.... No, don't tell me she's the very girl to show me what egotistical folly it is to compartmentalize people in this sad way; don't tell me she's going to sort me out, take me on, supply the *cognitio* and comic resolution. I couldn't bear it.[8]

Charles's behavior is necessarily patterned by literary and social clichés, but, as his own spectator, he not only "sees through" his role-playing, he also encourages it, planning it ahead and balking at the idea of ever finding out who he "really" is beneath his impressive sequence of masks. The first-person narrative itself becomes a reflection of this internalized script writing, directing, and producing. Not only does Charles anticipate, plan, and observe himself acting, but, in the act of narration, he watches himself watching himself, which is why the reader "shares" his perspective of perspicacity. Living his life as a character in a book, Charles's retrospective fictionalization of his life (what we read) duplicates the prospective one.

Theatre tends to lack the direct access to "inside" information characteristic of narrative, debunking the social mask either by monologues (as with Bri), by asides (as with Titus or Ultra), or by a bathetic juxtaposition of different viewpoints (as with Scarron). Yet the social mask may also betray itself by cracking because of pressure from underneath.

Central to the comedy of the social climber, for instance, is the moment when, forgetting his new status, the old (base or lowly) self pops out despite all attempts to hide it and counterfeit an elevated social standing. Molière's bourgeois Monsieur Jourdain, deluding himself that he is a gentleman, devotes considerable social energy to wearing a mask of gentlemanliness (calling his lackeys just to check whether they've heard him); yet his repeated gaucherie recurrently betrays his "real" bourgeois self. In his efforts to acquire a measure of musical sophistication, for example, his predilection for the trumpet would have been considered, by contemporary audiences at least, as a crass giveaway of his real class, and his clumsiness in bowing anticipates a later social climber, Nestroy's Titus (whose mask is equally wobbly though his skill and self-awareness greater). Shakespeare's "low" characters betray themselves by the malapropisms that slip out when they seek to speak a language above their station. Such comedy is clearly dependent upon an ultimately conservative sense that one's social standing is an essential, static aspect of identity (you *are* what you are born), and, if the baroque period saw social status as a mere role, this did not alter the fundamental conviction that one should not get too big for one's God-given boots. By the nineteenth century, however, Nestroy's Titus is much more flexible and successful in his attempts to adopt the register of his addressee, and he exhibits an altogether greater degree of social mobility. Indeed, *Der Talisman* uses echoes and parallels between the words and sentiments of the three classes portrayed to stress identity rather than difference, interchangeability rather than stasis. Nestroy's *Lumpazivagabundus*, by contrast, presents a more critical vision of the social climber in the figure of Zwirn, who is a tailor turned capitalist, an economic turncoat unable to hem his frayed edges. Zwirn's pretension is deflated both by the acuity of his colleagues and servants ("My master is a fool!" says one) and by his own blundering incompetence.

Restoration comedy makes great sport of the would-be, but here the social desideratum is repartee, and the chief butt of the joke is affected wit, not social standing. Congreve's Witwoud is ridiculous both directly through the failure of his attempts to be witty (his genuine dullness showing through his mask of wittiness) and indirectly through the incisively witty puncturing of his self-inflation by the external commentaries of the true wits. Mirabell points out his one good quality: "He so passionately affects the reputation of understanding raillery, that he will construe an affront into a jest, and call downright rudeness and ill language, satire and fire" (1.5). Wycherley's Sparkish is another would-be, an obtrusive wit who derives inordinate pleasure from his own bad jokes.

The appearance of moral decorum is the other social desideratum of Restoration comedy, which portrays a society where a mask of ethical conformity or chaste virtue is donned to conceal above all sexual motivation. This is a category of comedy recognized and described by Schopenhauer, whose metaphysical Reality (or Will) blurs into and becomes indistinguishable from psychological Reality, the Will that is the driving impulse behind human conduct. The human cognitive faculty can try as it might to hide this ultimately sexual force behind a mask (*Maya*'s veil) of rationalizing rationality, but the irrational and sexual dong-*an-sich* (a sort of transcendental Willy) will always rear its irrepressible head. In a passage permeated with the theatrical metaphor (portraying man as a puppet driven from within—or from above—by the priapic unknowable), Schopenhauer draws attention to the way we kid ourselves about sex, trying in vain to cloak its ubiquity through cognitive self-deception analogous to a theatrical mask. We may attempt to explain away our conduct with recourse to reasons and motivations (analogous to causality in the world of physics), but—whether we know it or not—the bottom line is always sexual: "Like all causality, the law of motivation is but a form of appearance [*Erscheinung*]. Incidentally, it is here that the origin of the comic, the burlesque, the grotesque, the caricatural side of life is to be found: for impelled forwards in spite of ourselves, we all do just what we can, and the ensuing pandemonium frequently assumes a farcical form, however serious the distress may be which lies behind."[9] Elsewhere Schopenhauer depicts the Will itself laughing at the vanity of human attempts to veil it, referring to the

> important role played by the sexual relation in the human world, where it strictly speaking forms the invisible hub of all doings and dealings and peeps forth everywhere in spite of all the veils which are thrown over it.... It is life's sportiveness and spice, however, that the main concern of all mankind is pursued on the sly and ostensibly ignored wherever possible. In fact, though, this selfsame concern is at every turn seen to be the hereditary and true sovereign of the world, on its own authority assuming its rightful place on the ancestral throne, whence it looks down with derision upon the provisions made by man to tame, incarcerate, or at least restrain it and if possible keep it completely concealed.[10]

Evidently Schopenhauer's musings apply not merely to the inadvertent dropping of the social mask, but also to the half-veiled sexual comedy of bawdy puns, allusions, innuendoes, and euphemisms. The main point is that the "amusement is to be found ... in the perpetual covering-up of the essentials,"[11] although it would perhaps be more accurate to speak of *unsuccessful* or *half*-concealment.

Once again, the social mask may be ripped off either because of pressure from within or as a result of the penetrating commentary of a true wit such as Mirabell or Horner. The laughter here ensues not so much from *identification* with a deliberate rejection of the social mask (see chapter 6) as from the sight of the mask *slipping* or being temporarily discarded when a piece of "china" is in the offing. Horner, who has seen through the disparity between appearance and reality from the outset, has his suspicions confirmed when the ladies enthusiastically drop their pretences of decorum once they've got him alone:

Lady Fidget.	Our reputation! Lord, why should you not think that we women make use of our reputation, as you men of yours, only to deceive the world with less suspicion? Our virtue is like the statesman's religion, the quaker's word, the gamester's oath, and the great man's honour; but to cheat those that trust us.
Mrs. Squeamish.	And that demureness, coyness, and modesty, that you see in our faces in the boxes at plays, is as much a sign of a kind woman as a vizard-mask in the pit.
Mrs. Dainty.	For, I assure you, women are least masked when they have the velvet vizard on.
Lady Fidget.	You would have found us modest women in our denials only.

(Act 5, scene 4)

Congreve's *The Way of the World* shows Lady Wishfort desperately struggling to deny her own sexual motivation as she is wooed by Waitwell playing the role of Sir Rowland. The negation here has the same function as Tristram Shandy's attempts to deny that he is being bawdy when he writes about ****s and ****s:

Lady Wishfort.	But as I am a person, Sir Rowland, you must not attribute my yielding to any sinister appetite, or indigestion of widowhood; nor impute my complacency to any lethargy of continence ... —
Waitwell.	Far be it from me—
	....
Lady Wishfort.	Or else you wrong my condescension—
Waitwell.	I do not, I do not—
Lady Wishfort.	Indeed you do.
Waitwell.	I do not, fair shrine of virtue.
Lady Wishfort.	If you think the least scruple of carnality was an ingredient—
Waitwell.	Dear Madam, no. You are all camphire and frankincense, all chastity and odour.
Lady Wishfort.	Or that—

(Act 4, scene 12)

Lady Wishfort indeed serves as a vehicle for the thematization of the mask and its habit of cracking. Leg of mutton that she is, she strives to deceive both herself and others in keeping up the appearance of lamb. Foible points out politely to her mistress: "Your ladyship has frowned a

little too rashly, indeed madam. There are some cracks discernable in the
white varnish" (3.5), but the comedy takes on a distinctly bittersweet dimension when Lady Wishfort then herself has the lucidity to respond:
"Let me see the glass—cracks, sayest thou? Why I am arrantly flayed—I
look like an old peeled wall. Thou must repair me, Foible." Sir Wilfull
Witwoud, who is wittier than his brother, comes up with a wickedly appropriate simile as he tells Mirabell not to fear her wrath: "She dare not
frown desperately, because her face is none of her own; 'sheart, and she
should, her forehead would wrinkle like the coat of a cream cheese"
(5.9).

Joe Orton's comedy of manners provides even more explicit evidence
of "essentially" amoral figures concealing their true motivation under
a mask of platitudinous morality. In *Entertaining Mr. Sloane* Kath's
"mask" consists of nothing but a see-through negation à la Lady Wishfort
(as she assures Sloane there is nothing behind her request that he take off
his trousers)—as defective a mask as the transparent negligee she later
dons: "I'm in the rude under this dress. I tell you because you're bound to
have noticed.... You can't see through this dress can you? I been worried
for fear of embarrassing you" (1).

Loot explores the insufficiency of the social mask from a different tack,
using above all moral *inconsistency* as a revelation of the arbitrary nature
of an ethical pose. The ultimate motivation is always patently sexual or
venal. Immediately after refusing to undress his mother's corpse on the
grounds that he's a Catholic, Hal blithely comes up with the suggestion
that he and Dennis pop out to a local brothel that offers a nice line in
crumpet. The exchange is echoed and varied in a later dialogue:

> *Hal.*   I shall accompany my father to Confession this evening. In order to
>   purge my soul of this afternoon's events.
> *Dennis.* It's at times like this that I regret not being a Catholic.
> *Hal.*   Afterwards I'll take you to a remarkable brothel I've found. Really
>   remarkable. Run by three Pakistanis aged between ten and fifteen.
>   They do it for sweets. Part of their religion. Meet me at seven. Stock
>   up with Mars bars.
>
> (Act 2)

Hal's second comment throws retrospective light on the first, exposing
the initial religious sentiment as a pose empty of any deeper conviction.
The ethical mask is as it were ripped down by hindsight, a stock comic
trick in Orton's repertoire. It is a similar principle that is at work in the
following snatch of narrative from Martin Amis's *Money*: "I have been
faithful to Selina Street for over a year, God damn it. Yes I have. I keep
trying not to be, but it never works out."[12] Such unexpected or half-
expected reversals support the Ciceronian idea that laughter may result

from a recognition in the laughing subject that he has been in error, been taken in, gulled, or duped. Amis peppers *Money* with comedy of this order, playing on our expectations regarding the big, boozy bulldozer of a protagonist. He first leads us up the garden path, then waggishly undeceives us: "After a while I thought of ringing down and having Felix bring me up some beers. I resisted the temptation.... Then I rang down and had Felix bring me up some beers."[13]

The examples so far show primarily sexual desire in various ways popping its megacephalic head out from beneath a mask of words that in vain endeavors to veil or negate it. Yet the same formal criterion comes to light in an even more concrete variation. In describing the laughter of the Middle Ages, E. R. Curtius cites the principle of *"unfreiwillige Entblöß- ung"* or involuntary exposure/denudation.[14] In this instance, it is the social mask in its most physical and substantial guise (namely clothing) that is shown to be imperfect, providing us with the jaunty "Carry On" comedy of over-filled bras bursting open under the pressure from within, the peeping-tom comedy of botties and titties, but not normally the nitty-gritties. Involuntary exposure is obviously liable to constitute a comic surprise in a culture where clothing is generally kept on with doggedly conscientious decorum. That figurative or literal nakedness may well do more than surprise us is a point to be considered later.

Sexuality is furthermore one of the chief weapons of bathos, the technique that derives its effect from a sudden plummeting in tone, register, or theme disclosing the preceding highflown pretension as an empty pose. Cliché may be parodied, therefore, not only by being repeated ad nauseam (as in Ionesco, etc.) but also by being superseded by a comic surprise, a jarring rupture of expectations that drags the hearer out of the passivity of nonreflective intercourse and focuses attention on the triteness or hollowness of that which has preceded it. The clichés that most readily lend themselves to such bathetic debunking are literary clichés, tending as they do to demarcate themselves by a "higher" style which can so easily be dragged down into the mud. Aristophanes's *Lysistrata* exemplifies how the sexual (as the "low") can be exploited to deflate the poetic (as the "high"), when Lysistrata gives vent to the difficulty the women on sex-strike are having in refraining from sex:

Chorus-leader. Queen of our great design and enterprise, tell me, why hast thou come so frowning forth?
Lysistrata. The female heart and deeds of evil women cause me to walk despondent up and down.
Chorus-leader. What say'st thou?
Lysistrata. Truth! Truth!
Chorus-leader. What is amiss? Tell it to us who love thee.
Lysistrata. 'Tis shame to speak and grievous to be silent.

Chorus-leader. Do not, I beg, conceal the ill we suffer.
Lysistrata.   We need a fuck....[15]

The veil of rhetoric in the end fails to mask the raw energy of sexual desire.

The downward motion of bathos need not, however, lead to the genitals. Any anticlimactic thwarting of expectations can be comic in effect, pointing up the vacuity and inappropriateness of the preceding bombast. In Fielding's *Tom Thumb*, the King debunks Noodle's histrionic lamentations after Tom Thumb's demise:

Noodle. Oh monstrous! dreadful! terrible! Oh! Oh!
           Deaf be my Ears, for ever blind my Eyes,
           Dumb be my Tongue, Feet lame, all Senses lost.
King.   What does the Blockhead mean?

(Act 2, scene 12)

Tom Thumb is himself bathos personified, exploding our expectations and presuppositions concerning a warrior-hero who has single-handedly rescued a whole land from the clutches of a mighty foe. His bathetic stature is underscored by his bathetic end: he is finally swallowed alive by a passing cow.

Bathos is but one of several techniques parody has at its disposal. If bathos works primarily by means of a temporally structured incongruity (a *syntagmatic* shift from exaltation to the poetic pits), parody operates equally frequently by a transferral of context, the deflating incongruity here working in *paradigmatic* simultaneity owing to a jarring juxtaposition of style and content. Rabelais's Panurge parodically takes the wind out of his master's rhetorical sails by repeating the structural pattern employed in Pantagruel's "serious" speech on the glories of war, but transferring it to the sphere of sex:

Then said Pantagruel:
"... there is no shade but that cast by banners, there is no smoke but that kicked up by horses, no clattering but the sound of harnesses."
At this Epistemon began to smile and said:
"There is no shade but that of the kitchen, no smoke but that of meat-pies, no clattering but the sound of cups."
To which Panurge replied:
"There is no shade but that of curtains, no smoke but that of steaming paps, no clattering but the sound of swinging ballocks."[16]

In Panurge's very capable parodic hands the clanking of harnesses is transformed into the jangling of gonads.

Literary parody may be broadly defined as the application of a particular literary style to a less "worthy" subject. Just as Panurge drags Pantagruel's style in the mud by zestfully applying it to the sphere of swinging cullions and steaming unchies, in Buckingham's *The Rehearsal* the foolish playwright Bayes applies the rhetoric of (courtly) love to the world of pigs, proudly reciting what he describes as "one of the most delicate dainty Simile's (sic) in the whole world":

> *Bayes.* 'Tis an allusion to love.
> So Boar and Sow, when any storm is nigh,
> Snuff up, and smell it gath'ring in the Sky;
> Boar beckons Sow to trot in Chestnut Groves,
> And there consummate their unfinish'd Loves:
> Pensive in mud they wallow all alone,
> And snore and gruntle to each others moan.
>
> (Act 1, scene 2)

The swollen diction deflates *itself*, for in its application to a "low" subject linguistic pretension reveals itself for what it is. The discrepancy between linguistic "surface" and the "reality" depicted constitutes a comic difference that draws attention to the language as a mask.

Whether the parody is specific (mocking the style of a particular work or author) or general (mocking a literary style or rhetorical pretension as such), it functions essentially by a surprising yoking together of incongruities. Travesty too, a genre exemplified by Scarron's *Virgile travesti* (1648), achieves its comic end in this way, juxtaposing its "high" subject with the familiar or "low" style in which it is presented. Heroes are exposed from their unheroic or human (i.e., unflattering) side—clumsy, crotchety in the morning, pestered by flies, sleepy, flustered, bewildered, and incompetent. Social stature and loftiness of sentiment and deed are grandiose poses that travesty deflates by narrating them in a completely "inappropriate" tone. In both parody and travesty, the procedure is bathetical to the extent that what is high is yanked downwards: rhetorical height in parody and social or moral height in travesty manifest themselves as airy illusions, masks with nothing substantial behind except the hot air of haughtiness that can so easily be punctured by a prick from below.

Not all parody is dependent upon the high/low opposition. Merely by being moved out of context, the words of the original betray their own hollowness or unsuitability. Quoting Shakespeare, who has the advantage of being recognized by almost everybody, is an easy comic trick, and the tragedies of Schiller or Goethe offer a similar target in German. Applying words that are several hundred years old to a modern or contemporary situation exploits incongruity of context and style, yet—especially in the case of second-rate literature—the original may be made even more ludicrous by itself being distorted. Here parody functions rather like satire, but in this case, it is a verbal not a physiognomic mask that is distorted by the twin means of synecdoche and hyperbole. *Tom Thumb* and *The Rehearsal* parody mediocre tragic poetry not just by bathos and incongruity, but also by exaggerating selected rhetorical features (similes and metaphors) to the point of grotesqueness.

Parody in general can be linked to a renewal of vision, a spring cleaning to combat the mustiness and dustiness of our conceptual mask. Hence the therapeutic qualities that permit Pantagruel to look upon the cheek of the court-fool Panurge not merely as negative or destructive mockery, but as a valid perspective complementary to his own. The radical ambivalence of parody is further intimated by its cheerfully indiscriminate choice of target: Shakespeare or Goethe will do as well as "bad" poetry or theatre. Not (necessarily) simply negating its butt, parody also *reuses* the language of its original text and is in a sense, therefore, dependent on it, repeating it while as it were invigorating it by employing it in a new context. In this respect it comes close to or coincides with the Brechtian concept of *Verfremdung* and the *ostranenie* (or defamiliarization) of the Russian Formalists. What counts here is that the startling incongruity prompts the listener or reader to *thought*, a movement beneath the superficiality of the conceptual or social mask. Descartes elucidates as follows the effects of the *admiratio* that, following Madius, he regards as generating laughter: "admiration [*admiratio*] is a sudden surprising of the soul, which moves it to pay attention in considering objects which strike it as rare and extraordinary."[17] Jolting us into laughter, a sudden incongruity or novelty seems to call for reflection and interpretation in a way that comfortably and predictably patterned occurrences and utterances clearly do not. The phenomenon of *Verfremdung*, which Brecht deemed central to the folk theatre and the Japanese Noh theatre as well as to comedy, has precisely this effect. By ripping an occurrence out of its context, the *Verfremdungseffekt* prevents it from being taken for granted (depriving it of *das Selbstverständliche*) and arouses critical interest that awakens us to the possibility of difference or change. Schlovsky's *ostranenie*, which he saw as the defining property of art, consists in the perception of objects divorced from their context, consequently what he termed a *seeing* as opposed to a mere recognition and likewise an antidote to the automatization of perception and behavior. If everyday usage tends to lapse into an unthinking taking-for-granted of the self-effacing language-mask, art (through *ostranenie*) combats this stultification by focusing attention on the signs themselves.

Parody, seen as the defamiliarization of a given style through transferring it to an incongruous context or through following it with a bathetic rupture in tone, is thus a function of the nature of our expectations. An incongruity in register is comic on account of its recognized deviation from the expected norm. This stress on expectations makes it feasible to reduce the joke, for example, to the product of a set of formal criteria (a buildup of expectations followed by a disruptive punch line) without paying any heed to what the joke is about. Schlovsky himself adopted this extreme formalist position, asserting that the blood spilt in anecdotes is not bloody. In the sphere of jokes, some might say, what counts is the way you tell 'em.

Yet jokes more than any other comic form illustrate the extent to which the unexpected is *expected*. The joke context ("Eh, did you hear the one about....") warns the hearer to get ready for a punch line in the same way that the theatrical/comic context prepares the spectator to expect behavior a little on the idiosyncratic or irrational side—or in the same way that the strangeness of the monomanic fool starts to become predictable after a while. This paradox arises because expectation is such a multilayered phenomenon. At one level, for example, everyday experience and external norms equip us with a core of expectations regarding both verbal and nonverbal behavior. Our perception of social conduct is necessarily colored by a notion of "normality," a yardstick against which deviations stand out, however liberally broad-minded we may like to think we are. Whence, of course, the cultural relativity of what is felt to be funny. At a second level, the aesthetic context influences what we anticipate, for genre and aesthetic medium inevitably generate a whole net of presuppositions: the fact we are sitting in a theatre or cinema or in front of a TV, or more specifically that we are watching a parody—or a tragicomedy or avant-garde gibberings—unfailingly supplies us with a second frame of expectations. At a third level, the specific aesthetic experience (the text, the play, the joke) in itself creates its own tangle of assumptions and patterns. Thus it comes about that even while parody can be seen as the result of a negation of the expectations engendered by serious theatre or by the extratheatrical social world,[18] the particular parodic piece itself functions by creating new patterns of expectations that allow the spectator to half-expect the bathetic and the incongruous.

This three-tiered categorization of expectations recalls to mind the three levels of comic mask-wearing and mask-discarding. Within the fiction itself, figures may adopt masks for the purpose of deception, and comedy ensues when they fail to keep up the role. To the extent that the fictive figures also embody our external expectations regarding the rules of the social game, it is comic to see their antisocial or asocial instincts well up from within and disrupt their social performance. The figures we watch on stage, however, are not "merely" fictive, they are also "real" people in the process of playing a theatrical part. Theatre is, after all, role-playing and illusion-creating in the most literal sense. Comedy can be further generated, therefore, when the theatrical figures focus attention on themselves in their capacity as actors, as fictive masks worn by a real person—when the theatrical illusion reminds us that it is but an illusion. This tends to coincide with a form of parody known as "romantic irony," in which it is the genre or aesthetic medium itself that becomes the butt of the mockery, and in which theatre (or literary text) defamiliarizes itself by focusing on its conventions as a medium. Just as the fictive trickster drops his mask to remind the audience that he is only role-playing, so the comic actor has a tendency to step outside his theatrical part in order to recall to mind that he too is only playing a part. Whereas tragic or real-istic drama is more inclined to take the spectator in, to pretend to be real, comic drama perpetually drops the mask of illusion and presents itself as play.

Comic anti-illusionism is examined more systematically in the next chapter: for a starter, however, one of the most common techniques for disrupting the theatrical illusion is the play-within-a-play, which frequently coincides with elements of deception or trickery (as in Aristophanes's *Women at the Thesmophoria*) or with unsuccessful social role-playing (as in Shakespeare's *Midsummer Night's Dream*). The play presented within the play may on the one hand be primarily parodic in nature; on the other hand, it may be so badly acted that it provides the comic spectacle of the mask slipping, of failed role-playing, while at the same time thematically highlighting that the "real" theatre itself is only acting and pretence. The fictional performance within the play brings to the fore that the outer play is likewise but a theatrical performance.

Aristophanes's *Women at the Thesmophoria*, which parodies the tragic theatre of Euripides, provides an explicit link between role-playing for the purpose of deception and theatrical role-playing, as Mnesilochus re-peatedly applies tricks gleaned from Euripides's plays in his attempts to flee the wrath of the gathering of rampant protofeminists. One melo-dramatically parodic imitation of Euripides's lost play *Telephus* has Mnesilochus kidnapping—and threatening to kill—the baby belonging to one of the leading women (although, as in *Don Quixote*, the human body turns out to be a skin full of wine), and he follows this up by writing a plea for assistance on votive tablets, an echo of the S.O.S. written on oar-blades in another of Euripides's plays. Mnesilochus's escape attempts then develop into a full-blooded burlesque of Euripides's tragedy *Helen*. When he starts acting the part of Helen, this serves as a cue for Euripides to enter in the guise of Menelaos come to rescue his "wife." Euripides and Mnesilochus act out a play-within-the-play that in the end seems to take over the outer play, as the boundaries between performance and real life become fuzzy and indeterminate: the histrionics culminate in an emotional recognition scene between "husband" and "wife," while the guardswomen remain outside the illusion and debunk the inflated rhetoric of the two men with their bathetically bemused commentaries. After a spectacularly unsuccessful endeavor by Euripides to operate the stage device normally used by the gods and goddesses for their dazzling descents from on high, Mnesilochus and Euripides launch into a burlesque of Euripides's *Andromeda*, parodying above all the tragic use of the Echo. Acting the part of Andromeda, Mnesilochus is supposed to lament his plight and Echo echo, but Echo overdoes his echoing and Mnesilochus drops his elegiac mask:[19]

Mnesilochus.	(*in a mournful wail*)
	O holy night,
	Long, long is the journey
	You take in your chariot,
	Crossing the ridges of the starry sky
	Over proud Olympus.
Echo.	(*nearly missing her cue*) Proud Olympus.
Mnesilochus.	Why should I, Andromeda,
	Of all maidens, have so great
	A share of woe?
Echo.	Share of woe.
Mnesilochus.	Ah, wretched me!
Echo.	Ah, wretched me!
Mnesilochus.	Oh, come off it!
Echo.	Oh, come off it.
Mnesilochus.	Stop it, you're coming in too often.
Echo.	Too often.
Mnesilochus.	I should be greatly obliged if you would kindly let me get on with my monologue. Shut up!
Echo.	Shut up!
Mnesilochus.	Go to hell!
Echo.	Go to hell!

(ll.1066–84)

Shakespeare's *Midsummer Night's Dream* similarly contains a play-within-a-play that (gently) parodies poetic pretension, and just over fifty years later the German baroque playwright Gryphius wrote *Herr Peter Squenz*, which is based above all on the theatrical performance of *Pyramus and Thisby* by the Mechanicals in Shakespeare's play. In the case of Shakespeare the parodic comedy is derived on the one hand from the material itself performed, which on occasion resorts to lavishing its alliterations with Swinburnean prodigality:

Quince (*as Prologue*)....
  Anon comes Pyramus, sweet youth and tall,
  And finds his trusty Thisby's mantle slain;
  Whereat with blade, with bloody blameful blade,
  He bravely broached his boiling bloody breast,
  And Thisby tarrying in mulberry shade,
  His dagger drew, and died....

(Act 5, scene 1)

On the other hand, the parody is augmented by the bad acting of the Mechanicals who, confusing illusion and reality, perpetually break the illusion (in order, for example, not to frighten the ladies with the sight of the lion) and whose sprinkling of malapropisms bathetically bring us back down to earth from the tragic heights.

Gryphius's play likewise shows its artisans unintentionally stepping outside their roles on a number of occasions, as well as intentionally breaking the illusion in order not to frighten the ladies. As in Shakespeare, the workmen themselves take the parts of the props (the lion, the moon, the wall), but Gryphius lays much greater emphasis on the bawdy potential of bathos, the imperfections of the theatrical performance coinciding with and complemented by imperfections in the mask of social propriety and decorum (which come to light by contrast with the dignity of the royal spectators). The comic attention is thus directed towards cupid's arrow, that bothersome love-shaft that proves such a hindrance to Piramus's gait and that Thisbe tries to pull out (through Wall's hole). Whereas Shakespeare's Thisby, in her attempts to kiss Pyramus through the wall, makes do with complaining "I kiss the wall's hole, not your lips at all," *Squenz* positively relishes the crass ambiguity of rods, shafts and orifices:

Thisbe.   Behold, behold! See him advance;
            Admire his weapon, yon lusty lance,
            ....
Piramus. 'Zounds! Could it be that Thisbe spake?
            This cranny I shall bigger break.
            ....
            Cupid plays a curious prank;
            Straight through my heart he's shot his shank.
            Oh, pluck me out the deadly dart,
            Else forthwith I'll this life depart.
Thisbe.   Quick! Come and stand before the crack
            And bravely raise your lower back.
            Now that's some shaft. Beloved, lo!
Piramus. Ouch, ouch! Efaith, it's throbbing so.
Thisbe.   Patience! We'll have it out anon.

(Act 3)

Squenz's Bulla-Butän, playing Wall, systematically bungles his lines, and he and Pickelhäring (who corresponds to Shakespeare's Bottom) forget their parts and get into a humdinger of a scrap, the first in a sequence of brawls among the artisans which end up virtually demolishing the stage. Shifting the Mechanicals' performance to the focal point of the play's interest, Gryphius explicitly devotes his attention to a consistent comic deflation of theatrical pretension in his portrayal of bad poetry and bad acting.

5
Rupturing the Illusion

Illusions-within-Illusions

Bungled theatrical performance is comic in the same way as is unsuccessful imposture, inadequate disguise, or any other form of botched role-playing. The attempt to create an illusion is thwarted by the moment(s) of weakness in which the mask falls to reveal the "true" face of the actor underneath. Both *A Midsummer Night's Dream* and *Herr Peter Squenz* incorporate comic plays-within-the-play acted by incompetent amateurs who confuse illusion and reality. Gryphius's Pickelhäring is typical in this. Although formally a tragedy, the play they are to perform is unequivocally designated a comedy by the muddleheaded clown for the simple reason that the actors survive it and are able to go and down a few jars afterwards: "The play will end in merriment, for the dead will come back to life, sit down together, and drink a rouse full heartily: for this reason it is a comedy" (1).

In Sheridan's brilliant burlesque *The Critic* (1779), in which, as with Buckingham, the play-within-the-play takes the form of a rehearsal, it is the playwright and the audience who jumble up levels of illusion and reality. At the outset of the mock-play *The Spanish Armada*, Sir Christopher Hatton asks Sir Walter Raleigh the reason for the military preparations currently being undertaken all around them. When the cynical spectator Sneer asks Puff the dramatist, "How came Sir Christopher Hatton never to ask that question before?" the foolish playwright responds: "What, before the Play began? how the plague could he?"—a retort that fully satisfies the credulous spectator Dangle, who muses "That's true efaith!" (2.2). In other instances it is neither the dramatist nor the actor who mixes up the play world and the real world, but only the audience, who as a consequence become the butt of the joke in a manner corresponding to the gull taken in by a rogue's trickery and role-playing. In Beaumont's *Knight of the Burning Pestle* (1613), the citizens, man and wife, consistently conduct themselves as if the events that occur within the fictional setting they are watching were real. They show themselves willing to act as witnesses to a theft committed within the dramatic action; the wife tends the wounds of a beaten character and gives advice on how to cure chilblains, and the husband contemplates joining in a scuffle on stage. When the fictive Knight, played by their servant Rafe, refuses to pay for his lodgings and fare at the inn he has mistaken for a castle (à la Don Quixote), the two of them benevolently step in to pay on Rafe's behalf and smooth things over. These fictive spectators even determine the course of the play, mercilessly depriving Mistress Merrythought of a monologue by dispatching her to the wings when they would rather see Rafe. Such comedy of course relies upon the overview of the "real" audience, who—as with imposture and deception—are tacitly assumed to be able to tell fiction and reality apart. In the bargain, the play-within-the-play unobtrusively (but surely) reminds us that the frame-play is likewise but a fictional creation: we would be just as silly as the objects of our mockery if we were to jump on stage and tell the citizen's wife that we know a better cure for chilblains or clasp the husband in a full nelson in order to restrain him from the fictive fight.

Mistaking desert for forest and inn for castle, Rafe, whom the stage transforms into a gallant knight willing to wield his burning pestle for any damsel in distress, is clearly modeled in part upon Don Quixote, and the comedy of the Spanish hidalgo is likewise structured around his chronic inability to keep illusion and reality apart. But whereas in part 1 Don Quixote's delusions are of his own creation, in part 2 (by which time his reputation has considerably spread) a number of the people he encounters take the initiative, "playing along" with his self-imposed role, humoring him—providing him with a maiden who pretends to be in love with him, a villain to do battle with (acted by a reluctant lackey), an isle for Sancho Panza to govern—and as it were setting up a whole sequence of minifictions within the fiction in order to gull Don Quixote and keep themselves entertained by the spectacle. In parallel fashion Molière has two of his most pig-headed self-deceivers, the social upstart M. Jourdain and the hypochondriac Argan, taken in by scenes of communal humoring, impromptu plays-within-the-plays initiating M. Jourdain as Mamamouchi and Argan as a doctor. Naturally, everybody except the two self-deceivers is alert to the fictionality of the proceedings. Whether the fictive "play" takes the form of official theatrical performance, impromptu entertainment, or mere role-playing and practical joking in a nontheatrical context, the potential for mockery of a credulous dope remains fundamentally the same.

One of the most farcically comic episodes within *Don Quixote*, however, comes to pass without such communal assistance, when the monomanic do-gooder attacks and annihilates a puppet show he is watching. The unfortunate puppet-showman makes the grave mistake of portraying a pack of Moors in pursuit of a pair of Christian lovers, the sight of which immediately spurs the Don to drastic intervention. Indeed, he rains blows upon the puppet heathenry with such frenzied force that they are mown down and the entire show demolished within a matter of minutes. The medium of the illusionism need not, therefore, be the theatrical in order to engender comic confusion: any "illusion" that pretends to be real can give rise to the same muddle. Pliny recounts an anecdote relating to the rivalry of two Greek painters: Zeuxis's trompe l'oeil painting of a bunch of grapes was so convincing that it deluded birds into coming and pecking at them, but Zeuxis was in his turn fooled and outdone by Parrhasios, who painted on the wall a curtain so lifelike that Zeuxis turned to him and asked what was painted behind it. This is illusionism in its most concrete or tangible form. At the house of the indolent prankster-slob Trimalchio in *The Satyricon*, Petronius's narrator becomes the target of derisive laughter for being momentarily deluded by a picture of a dog on a chain with "Beware of the Dog" inscribed above, just as the young German simpleton Simplicissimus arouses the mirth of his hermit-guardian by throwing water on the picture of a burning house.[1]

The confusion of illusion and reality is thus liable to be seen as a kind of folly or madness, a gullibility that is derisible in the delusions it produces. In his study of madness, Michel Foucault cites the French baroque play *La Comédie des comédiens* by Georges de Scudéry as capturing this association between illusion and madness. The play-within-the-play in this case is intended primarily as a vindication of the acting profession, the fictional performance convincing the initially philistine M. Blandimare that his son is leading a dignified and honorable life on the stage and in fact turning the sceptic into a thespian too. Yet it is not as simple as this: the *outer* play is preceded by a prologue spoken by Montdory, the leader of the troupe that actually performed the piece in seventeenth-century Paris and himself the actor about to play the part of Blandimare. This prologue is an ironic denunciation of the madness (*folie*) of the actors about to be seen in performance who, pretending that they are a real-life troupe of actors (in Lyon) and forgetting that they are in fact just actors acting the part of actors (in Paris), seem to him to be laboring under a dangerously fanciful set of delusions. Montdory insists on differentiating himself from the aberrancy of the actors:

> I have no wish to bear them company in madness, nor could I possibly purpose to deceive so many honest men and women as I see to be here. I do not know (Gentlemen) what extravagance it can be that has thralled my companions today, but it is indeed so great that I find myself forced to believe that some enchantment has stolen their reason; the worst of it being that they are also trying to deprive me of mine and you of yours as well. They seek to persuade me that I am not in the theatre; they say that this is the town of Lyons, that over there is

an inn and here is a tennis court where actors who are not us and yet who are ourselves as well are presenting a pastorale.... They say I am a certain Monsieur de Blandimare, though I'm really called Mondory. (Prologue)

For the sane philistine, the actor himself is a type of archetypal fool to the extent that he claims to be someone other than he really is and suspends disbelief in the illusions he is responsible for creating. Scudéry's play shows the sane philistine being converted to the folly of the stage.

Another dramatic product of the 1630s (a time when the French theatre was in the process of establishing itself as an accepted form of art), Corneille's *L'Illusion comique* is a somewhat subtler exploration of the relationship between illusion and reality, likewise presenting a play-within-a-play that ends up convincing a sceptical father that his son Clindor is leading a worthwhile life on the boards. In his endeavors to track down this son (who has fled from home), Pridamant consults the magician Alcandre, who—with skills analogous to those of a dramatist—conjures up in dramatic form the sequence of adventures undergone by Clindor. In other words, we (and Pridamant) magically witness Clindor *acting out* the incidents of his past life. The final act, intended to bring Pridamant up-to-date with Clindor's present situation, comes to a tragic climax with the latter's melodramatic demise, but then—surprise, surprise!—comes Corneille's comic coup de theatre: in a moment of dramatic dis-illusionment we are shown Clindor and his wife counting the receipts at the end of a theatrical production. The final act, it becomes clear, has only been acted. After the "real" but past adventures of acts 2 to 4, Clindor and Isabelle had become actors, and what we (and Pridamant) have just witnessed was simultaneously a representation of Clindor's present life as an actor *and* a purely fictive scene whose theatrical status is only retrospectively revealed by the sight of the actors unmasked. In Louis Jouvet's 1937 production of the play, this final act was distinguished from the rest by virtue of being presented on a stage-within-the-stage as if to stress its fictionality from the beginning. This is clearly in contradiction with Corneille's own aims, however, and is inconsistent with the "gullibility" shown by Pridamant who, convinced he is witnessing real-life events, manifests a genuine grief on seeing the "death" of his son. Corneille's play-within-a-play does not seem to be intended to mock the credulity of a foolish fictive audience who cannot tell fact from fiction as in *The Knight of the Burning Pestle*. Instead it is we, the real audience, who are gulled, believing we are viewing a slice of life whereas in fact we are being deluded by a theatrical spectacle. The moment of disillusionment, when we see Clindor as an actor, possibly generates—in conjunction with a sense of relief that the death is but a mock-death—that Ciceronian self-mockery which arises in response to the realization that we ourselves have been fooled or taken in. The Cornelian audience is prey to the same folly that Montdory pretends to condemn.

In Shakespeare, Cervantes, Beaumont, Scudéry, and Gryphius, the reader or spectator is able to laugh thanks to his superior knowledge, whereas this is patently not the case with Corneille. Indeed, a whole thicket of comedy shoots up from the fertile ground where it is not simply the actor or a fictive audience or playwright who confuses the theatrical levels within the play, but the "real" playwright doing so intentionally. In these cases actor and audience may move from one level of reality to another with evident ease, yet this is not a movement mocked as a sign of naivety or gullibility, but one apparently endorsed by the nonsensical logic of the play itself. The boundary between the playful and the serious, between appearance and reality, proves inherently ductile, bringing play and illusion to the thematic spotlight in a manner that may have either or both of two effects. On the one hand, attention is drawn to the play itself in its capacity as a play (as opposed to a mimetically convincing "slice of life"), exposing and undermining the aesthetic presuppositions (such as a stable, unilateral relationship between actor and audience) that conventional theatre tends to take for granted. On the other hand, the theatricality of life itself is more or less obtrusively brought to the fore. The overstepping of the footlights, by thematic implication at least, turns the audience too into actors.

In the twentieth century Tom Stoppard has gone further than most in exploring the comic potential of theatre-within-theatre. *The Real Inspector Hound* starts out sanely enough with two theatre critics, Moon and Birdboot, watching and commenting upon a corny country-house mystery, the cliché-sodden whodunnit parodying its genre just as the critics' cliché-sodden commentary parodies *its* genre. Yet at an early stage the theatrical levels begin to blur, as Moon claims to have seen Birdboot out on the town with Felicity, one of the fictional females. Midway through—when nobody else is onstage—Birdboot ventures to answer the persistently ringing stage-phone only to find it is his real wife who is speaking (possibly suspecting his fictive flirtations). Once "onstage," he gets caught up in an embarrassing barney with Felicity that turns into an almost verbatim reproduction of the clichés from an earlier (fictive) confrontation scene between Felicity and Simon Gascoyne. Birdboot has in a sense "become" Simon, adopting his dramatic role. Not surprisingly Birdboot is soon to bite the metatheatrical dust, and Moon, rushing onstage to the body of his fellow critic, finds himself playing the part of Inspector Hound—*but not the real one*, for it is wheel-chaired Magnus, alias long-lost lover Albert, alias third-string stand-in theatre critic Puckeridge, who is the *real* Inspector Hound.

It was the German romantic Ludwig Tieck who took this category of comedy to an extreme probably never to be surpassed. His *Gestiefelte Kater* (1797), known in English as *Puss-in-Boots*, is structured around the performance of a play-within-the-play that bears the same title as "our" play, interspersed with comments and speculations from a theatrical audience. Once again it is not until the second half of the play that the dramatic anarchy really sets in. At the end of act 2, the fictive play starts to go to pot when the King's rabbit (his favorite dish) is burnt: the King has a breakdown induced by this catastrophe, all the actors forget their roles, Puss climbs a pillar in the excitement, and the playwright intervenes—in vain—in order to try and calm things down. From here on, neither play ever really recovers its composure. Act 3 starts too soon, revealing the playwright still onstage, desperately struggling to restore order. The audience is of course unsure whether this belongs to the play or not. As the King refuses to reenter for fear of making an even bigger fool of himself, the Hanswurst (the German Harlequin or court-fool) "improvizes," asking leave to speak a few words, which, he insists, don't belong to the actual play, in order to clear up the controversy once and for all. This only increases the confusion of the audience:

Hanswurst. My dear fellow German countrymen—
Schlosser. I thought the play was set in Asia.
Hanswurst. Yes, but now I'm talking to you as actor to audience.
Schlosser. Men, I'm lost, I'm out of my wits now.
Hanswurst. May it please your Worships to mark that the previous scene, the one you just saw, is not actually part of the play.
Fischer. Not part of the play? Well how did it get into it then?
Hanswurst. The curtain was raised too soon. It was a private conversation which would not have taken place on stage at all if it hadn't been so frightfully crowded backstage. If you've been illuded, therefore, so much the worse: if you would please be so kind as to obliterate this illusion from your minds....

(Act 3)

Unlike in *The Knight of the Burning Pestle* where the naive citizens mistake illusion for reality, or at least behave as if they do, here the audience misconstrues the "real" as fictional—although, at a different theatrical level, there is in fact more than a modicum of truth in what they say. From "our" point of view, what is real within the fiction is ultimately no less fictional than the fiction-within-the-fiction. The metatheatrical permutations are to become even more convoluted yet, for the inner play further contains a disputation between court-fool and court scholar as to whether the play in which they are acting is a good one. Leander the court scholar argues that it is, because at least the audience is well portrayed. Hanswurst asks the audience what their opinion is, but they respond—justifiably—that there *is* no audience portrayed in the play! Play and play-within-play end up indistinguishable, rather like two mirrors facing one another, each of which seems to contain the other within its frame.

The anti-illusionistic impulse within the play-within-the-play in such comedy is thus so infectious that it may come to inform the whole play. We are never allowed to lose sight of the theatricality of the spectacle, for the depicted interplay of actor and audience draws attention to a variety of conventions that govern *our* relationship to what we see. Early on in the play, for example, when the King asks the exotic Prince from afar how come he can speak their language so fluently, the exotic Prince from afar urgently exhorts him to keep quiet, then explains why:

> *King.* But another thing, tell me, if you live so far away, how can you speak our language so fluently?
> *Nathanael.* Hush!
> *King.* Pardon?
> *Nathanael.* Hush! Hush!
> *King.* I do not understand.
> *Nathanael.* (*under his breath*) Pray hold your peace, for otherwise the public down there will end up noticing that it is indeed very implausible.
> *King.* That doesn't matter. It clapped just now....
> *Nathanael.* You see, it's simply for the sake of the drama that I talk in your language, for otherwise it is indeed inconceivable.
>
> (Act 1)

Tieck exposes and sabotages the convention conveniently dictating that theatrical dialogue take place in the language of the audience, rubbing in the point by having Leutner (one of the public) give voice to a demand for naturalism at all costs—in this case a Prince spouting gibberish in the presence of an interpreter. Later on, the protagonist Gottlieb, confusing theatrical levels, internalizes extratheatrical time within the fictive temporal system, asking Puss to be speedy with his help because it is half-past seven already and at eight the play is over. This reference to external time disrupts the normally unquestioned convention governing audience assumptions and expectations whereby an imaginary (flexible, artificial, and foreshortened) time continuum is created. By playing with the usages of verisimilitude, Tieck indirectly points the spotlight on them, defamiliarizing those tricks that are usually rendered invisible by the habitual delusions of naturalism (the illusion pretending to be nature). The "mask" of theatrical illusionism is exposed, as attention is drawn to its conventionality. One is reminded of the real time that continues to tick away "behind" the dramatic fiction, the truth behind the mask.

Tieck's relatively little-known *Die Verkehrte Welt* (1798) takes the metatheatrical joke, it has been claimed, to unplumbed depths of boredom. Rather unwieldy and long it may be—perhaps completely unperformable—but it at least has the virtue of consistency in its madness. Tieck takes the notion of a play-within-a-play beyond the bounds of realism by building into his play-within-a-play a play-within-a-play-within-a-play and by incorporating into this a play-within-a-play-within-a-play-within-a-play—these four theatrical levels of course refusing to remain clearly distinct from one another. This is indeed liable to prove tedious for the unsuspecting spectator brought up on a low-fiber diet of no-nonsense naturalism and desiring a ready-cut thin white slice of life with whose figures he can identify. Tieck's drama, however, merely takes to its extreme the tendency of comedy to generate the sort of intellectual distance that gives the consumer something to chew on rather than swallow whole. Like *Der Gestiefelte Kater*, the play is suffused with metatheatrical tricks and confusions. Right at the outset Pierrot, one of the actors, resolves to become a spectator, and Grünhelm, one of the audience, makes up his mind to try his hand at acting. After an Ubuesque ship battle between Pantaloon and Harlequin, the sailors "swimming" about in the stage-water suddenly stand upright and walk to shore, a stranded sailor laments that he is so isolated and alone that he cannot even make out what the prompter is telling him to say, and Neptune complains that there are loads of stage props floating about in the sea. Offended at not being recognized and acknowledged by Skaramuz (playing Apollo), Neptune drops his mask and reveals himself as Skaramuz's director Wageman, also harboring fears that the self-centred Skaramuz might seek to prolong the play indefinitely in order to prolong his reign. The final climactic battle scene includes a duel between playwright and stage technician, as well as the audience intervening to save Skaramuz, although unlike in *The Knight of the Burning Pestle* it is not the naive confusion of fiction and reality that is held up to ridicule, for the levels have been fused from the outset. Tieck's play itself is a nonsensical construction.

It is the figure of the innkeeper more than any other who typifies the befuddlement of the characters with regard to their own ontological status, for he is always *both* an innkeeper *and* an actor playing the role of an innkeeper, this metatheatrical muddle hiding the existential truth that we *are* always role-players in a certain sense, however spontaneous we may consider ourselves. His joy on receiving guests, for example, arises firstly in response to the anticipated benefits for his trade and secondly because the role of innkeeper was threatening to go out of theatrical fashion, yet he does not seem to feel any surprise or incongruity as a result of this juxtaposition of perspectives. One comic episode shows the innkeeper striving to behave in character as a solid uneducated publican, while the fictive playwright, intent on making ostentatious display of his erudition, cheekily inserts recondite mythological allusions into his speech. The innkeeper appears fundamentally aware of himself in his capacity as a role-player and is annoyed and upset by the dramatist's habit of making him play out of character. When his daughter asks him if he learned his part from the *ars poetica*, the innkeeper waxes theoretical:

> *Innkeeper.* Actually, no, for Horace does not mention innkeepers by name. But I've put together a kind of theory from all my experiences, so I don't easily go astray.
> *Anne.* How do you set about that?
> *Innkeeper.* My chief concern is not to turn all unnatural; the rest is more a matter of course. I must avoid all pomposity, all poetic figures, and not talk too intelligently either.
> *Anne.* Ah, that explains a lot. I never knew ...
> *Innkeeper.* Yes, yes, who are we to hold out against our destiny? It's just the way of the world. It's cost me effort enough to adapt to my part properly, and even so complaints have been lodged that the poet sometimes peeps out through my character. At times I've felt like Midas, who couldn't conceal his long ears.—Ha! there I go again, you see, falling completely out of character! How can an innkeeper make a witty and scholarly allusion to King Midas?... This Midas business was just the poet peeping out through my character again. It is a confounded failing of mine!
>
> (Act 4, scene 7)

When the innkeeper drops his mask, he explains (dropping his mask), it is the playwright's face that comes to light.

Such comedy is not restricted to a theatrical context. On the contrary, it adapts very easily to the cinema, as proved by both Buster Keaton's *Sherlock Jr.* and Woody Allen's *The Purple Rose of Cairo*. In the former, Buster, employed as a projectionist in a cinema, falls asleep on the job: when his girl and his rival turn up in the film he is projecting, Buster responds by jumping into the screen, and after initial difficulties (being burped back into reality at first), he is accepted into this fictive world, a realm that is at two removes from reality since it is both a dream and a film. In *The Purple Rose of Cairo*, the protagonist comes *out of* the film rather than going in, but once again comedy is extracted from the hiccups and turbulences that ensue: Allen exploits a duplication of identities generated by the spare fictive figure on the loose in the real world and the somewhat traumatic potential for the real-life actor of coming into contact with a doppelgänger of his own making. Cinema differs from theatre above all in that—by means of the close-up—the screen of the film-within-the-film can unobtrusively become identical with that of the frame-film, on the one hand truly obliterating the boundaries between fictive illusion and fictive reality, but also possibly tending to make the spectator forget the nonsensicality or logical implausibility of the situation he is witnessing.

The representation of a sort of unity of actor and audience in the plays of such dramatists as Beaumont and Tieck is a remnant of a basic theatrical impulse that has tended to be hidden or repressed by naturalistic and illusionistic theatre in its self-stylization as a *real* sequence of true-to-life events to be objectively observed by passive viewers. Its roots being traceable back to phallic ritual and communal celebration, comedy and theatre in general is indeed *originally* and essentially a collective experience and to this extent incompatible with the rationalistic, scientific distinction between subject and object that has come to hold sway in the sphere. Bakhtin's description of medieval carnival festivities clarifies the sense in which modern theatre may be seen as a dilution (and distortion) of this moment of communal celebration: "Carnival does not know footlights, in the sense that it does not acknowledge any distinction between actors and spectators.... Carnival is not a spectacle seen by the people; they live in it, and everyone participates because its very idea embraces all the people. While carnival lasts, there is no other life outside it."[2] The metatheatrical aspect of comedy may consequently be seen in part as a displacement of an original saturnalian or carnivalesque moment that links actor and audience, subject and object, viewer and viewed in the democracy of revelry—even if this linkage is normally now internalized or banished into the thematic innards of the play. Many of the German *Fastnachtspiele* which accompanied medieval carnival carousals ended in a dance in which the audience too participated, stressing not only that the play is just play but also that—for the festive period at least—the world in toto is play, a point reinforced by the "Doppelspiele,"[3] deception, role-playing, and disguise rife within the fiction itself. Shakespeare's celebratory comedies as well, permeated as they are both with song and dance *and* play-within-play, tended "to *be* a saturnalia, rather than to *represent* a Saturnalian experience."[4]

This is not to imply that the play-within-a-play, even in its most nonsensical and logic-defying manifestations, necessarily embodies such displaced Saturnalianism. Nor is it necessarily employed as a technique for thematizing theatrical conventions or drawing attention to the lusory or illusory nature of the proceedings. It is not even necessarily comic. Yet although theatrical performance may take place within (above all realistic) theatre with no comic or connotative strings attached, the festive and anti-illusionistic madness of shows-inside-shows is still a key comic moment. Within the history of theatre, moreover, the play-within-a-play has also had an additional function that, while not directly comic in itself, is fundamentally related to a comic (or tragicomic) perception of the world.

Whereas the examples so far have tended in their absurdity and madness to spotlight the fictionality and conventionality of the theatrical performance, the device may equally assume a more outward, allegorical significance, bringing to light the theatricality of the world. That the two impulses—the self-reflexive and the allegorical—may combine and complement one another will become apparent in particular in the comedies of Shakespeare, Büchner, and Grabbe.

Luigi Pirandello's *Sei Personaggi in cerca d'autore* is incontestably influenced by both of Tieck's plays, but the theatrical theme is here transferred to an area where identification with human suffering overrides the comic potential of the subject. Structurally built upon the performance of a rehearsal (like so many burlesques), Pirandello's play portrays its characters as painfully cut adrift from their author and, in their pain, transcending their theatrical limitations. In spite of the metatheatrical blurring of levels, which in a different context might have generated an aura of whimsical silliness, the audience is brought to associate with the characters as victims of a universal predicament: if acting is indeed an existential condition, as Pirandello seems to suggest, it is one that entails a tragic sense of self-difference, a loss of identity that condemns the existential actor to a life spent in bondage to a script anonymously imposed from outside. The play-within-the-play merges jarringly into the frame-play, openly hinting that the play we are watching is in turn but a play within the "play" of our life and that our life too is but a play within some grander scenario, another in an infinite set of Chinese boxes. The following dialogue between the father and the producer illustrates the thematic bond wrought by Pirandello between the illusory nature of the theatre and the illusory nature of the world. The rehearsal, the play-within-the-play, becomes a metaphor for life.

Father.   Now, just think that we (*briefly points to himself and to the other five characters*), as ourselves, have no other reality outside this illusion!
Producer. And what would you mean by that?
Father.   But don't you see? What other could there be? What for you is an illusion to be created is for us by contrast the only reality we have. Mind you, that doesn't only apply to us. Just think about it. Can you tell me who you are?
Producer. What do you mean, who I am? I'm me.
Father.   And what if I were to tell you that that weren't true? That you were me?
Producer. I should say you were mad!
             (*The actors laugh*)
Father.   You're right to laugh: because it's all a game here.... I only wanted to make you see that if we (*again points to himself and the other characters*) have no other reality outside of the illusion, then you too would do well to be suspicious of your own reality, the reality which

> you breathe and touch today, because—like yesterday's reality—it
> is destined to reveal itself as tomorrow's illusion.
>> (Certain stage directions omitted)[5]

With these musings, the fictional father disrupts the ontological complacency not only of the play's producer but also of the real-life audience
(i.e., "us"), or rather, the audience that had until then assumed it was real
life. Significantly, the producer regards the father as a madman for positing that the real is but a play or illusion: from the perspective of common sense, the confusion of the fictive and the real is a signal of folly.
Pirandello's play, however, brings the public to query this perspective, for
in this instance the fictive fool is absolutely right to point out that his
producer is himself but a fiction. In the end, it seems, Pirandello is
damning not only the actors but also producer and audience to a life of
acting, an existence spent not being oneself. Yet he intersperses these
heavy-weight metaphysical ponderings with moments of Tieckian levity.
When the father laments the fixity of his character, the producer responds
by making the sort of point originally raised by Tieck's innkeeper: "But
I'd like to know when anyone ever saw a character stepping out of his
role and launching into a long discussion on it, expounding and explaining it as you've just been doing. Can you tell me that? I've never seen it
happen before!"[6]

In the baroque hands of the Spanish playwright Calderón de la Barca,
the play-within-a-play also assumes a symbolic import, representing the
religious idea of the *theatrum mundi*. *El gran teatro del mundo*, as the title
suggests, portrays the world as a theatre and man as an actor, the theological framework in this case guaranteeing that the sequence of Chinese
boxes is ordered and finite: the transcendental gaffer in the gallery is the
final spectator. The man/God, actor/audience hierarchy within the play is
intended as an explicit and unambiguous reflection of the order structuring reality, an order that (given the pious context) brooks neither inversion nor any blurring of its boundaries, for His presence stifles the
possibility of frivolity or mirth.

It was Shakespeare who above all secularized the *theatrum mundi* motif, dispensing with the theocentricity that was to characterize Calderón's
drama. The Bard's use of the play-within-a-play and of the *theatrum
mundi* is of course as well-documented as Jaques's claim that "all the
world's a stage," yet it remains an extremely multilayered and subtle
phenomenon, defying summary. *A Midsummer Night's Dream*, one of
those holiday shows that not only represents a celebration, but also *constitutes* one, is perhaps one of the most complex of the dramas in the
permutations of its metatheatricality. For a start, it incorporates the rehearsal and performance of the Mechanicals, who are foolish for their

bad acting and their habit of mixing up illusion and reality and whose
malapropian bungling deflates both their own acting pretensions and the
amorous histrionics of the "elevated" figures of the "real" plot. The play
is indeed permeated by meditations on various forms of delusion, illusion
and folly: love, for example, is throughout seen as a symptom of folly and
delusion possessing transformative powers equal to those of the theatre,
transposing "things base and vile" into "form and dignity." While the
Mechanicals ham out their play *within* the human level of action, the human lovers are simultaneously acting out a farce dictated by the fairies
Puck and Oberon, and even Puck and Oberon are caught up in a play
written by a fool called Shakespeare. Theseus contemplates the folly of
lovers, madmen and poets:

> *Theseus.* The lunatic, the lover, and the poet,
>   Are of imagination all compact.
>   One sees more devils than vast hell can hold;
>   That is the madman. The lover, all as frantic,
>   Sees Helen's beauty in a brow of Egypt.
>   The poet's eye, in a fine frenzy rolling,
>   Doth glance from heaven to earth, from earth to heaven,
>   And as imagination bodies forth
>   The forms of things unknown, the poet's pen
>   Turns them to shapes, and gives to airy nothing
>   A local habitation and a name.

(Act 5, scene 1)

Identifying with and suspending disbelief in the fiction he is watching, the
real spectator proves himself as foolish as the Mechanicals, the lovers,
and anyone else who mistakes illusion for reality. But just as we laugh
both *at* and *with* the acting artisans, vicariously sharing and enjoying the
power of fantasy, so the play as a whole both mocks this power and celebrates it. It is as if Shakespeare is reminding us of the theatricality of the
play, while at the same time cheekily reveling in the capacity of theatre
and playfulness to exceed its bounds and surreptitiously pervade the do-
ings of the world.

Following Tieck, two German playwrights of the early nineteenth century also combined a comic predilection for metatheatrical devices with
an awareness of the *theatrum mundi*. Büchner's *Leonce und Lena* is permeated by an awareness both of the theatricality of the play and by a
corresponding consciousness of the theatricality of life. The portrayal of
the characters as puppets and role-players is complemented, however, by
a wistful awareness of sadistic spectators above, articulated when Valerio
likens the action in which they are involved to a game of cards played—
out of sheer boredom—between God and the Devil. This is admittedly
not in itself a comic idea, and similar imagery structures Büchner's trag-

edy *Dantons Tod*. The point is, perhaps, that in *Leonce und Lena* Büchner goes to greater lengths to turn to account the comedy of the situation, making the most of the ironic perspective, adding a measure of parody, and exploiting the repeatability and mechanical predictability of the figures. Grabbe's *Scherz, Satire, Ironie, und tiefere Bedeutung*, written in 1822 and anticipating and influencing Alfred Jarry's theatrical anarchy of seventy years later, makes an explicitly comic use of the *theatrum mundi* motif. The Devil, killing time on earth having been booted out of Hell while it is being spring-cleaned, explains the cosmic situation to the poet Rattengift:

Devil.   Do you even know what the world is?
Rattengift.   What a question! The world is the quintessence of everything that exists, from the tiniest worm to the vastest solar system.
Devil.   Well, let me tell you then that this quintessence of everything, which you honour with the name "world," is nothing more than a second-rate comedy scribbled down in the school holidays by a whipper-snapper of an angel still wet behind the ears....
Rattengift.   Sir, but this is madness! If the world's a comedy, what then is hell, which after all is just as much a part of the world?
Devil.   Hell is the ironical part of the play and—as is usual—it turned out better at the youngster's hands than heaven, which is simply the play's light-hearted part.

(Act 2, scene 2)

On the one hand reminding the real audience that it is watching a comedy, the Devil's words apply equally well to the second-rate comedy in which the audience is performing, i.e., to "our" world. The end of the play contains another metatheatrical coup when Grabbe himself turns up, seeking entrance to the hut where all the characters of his play have assembled. As in Tieck, the fictive figures feel decidedly lukewarm towards their maker: the churlish schoolmaster lets rip a stream of abuse, and it is only after a good deal of knocking that Grabbe is finally allowed in.

It would clearly be an oversimplification to regard the play-within-a-play as necessarily revealing or even implying the illusory status of the proceedings. Yet there is a large area of overlap where this frequently occurs, and this overlap often taps the comic energy of the phenomenon, as when the inner play is badly acted, badly written, or naively taken for reality by a fictive audience, and the break in the inner illusion implicitly spotlights the playfulness of the outer play. Just as the impostor is comic when he exposes himself to the audience as a role-player, the social actor is comic when he shows himself unable to keep up the social act, and the mask of language is comic when it draws attention to itself as a mask, so the theatrical illusion is comic when it focuses on its status as illusion. But there are many ways in which theatre can do this apart from the play-within-a-play.

Moments of Dis-Illusion

One of the most common and least subtle methods of drawing attention to the play in its capacity as a play is direct self-referential statement, although—as is the case with the play-within-a-play—this may have other functions as well or instead. The device whereby characters are presented as (half-)aware that they are inside a play likewise operates in two directions, both alluding to the theatricality of the world and the ubiquity of role-playing, puppetry, performance, and repeatability, while also, at a different level, implying an intuited realization in the figures that they really are in fact dramatic fictions. This dual impulse has already been demonstrated in the plays of Büchner and Beckett, one of the repeated clichés in Beckett's *Endgame*, for example, being "Why this farce, day after day?" a rhetorical question that is equally applicable on both levels. The technique most often takes the form of an explicit comparison by one of the characters (this is *like* a comedy, a farce, a skit; so-and-so is *like* a figure from the stage) or a question (are you all play-acting?). In *Volpone* Peregrine thus says of Sir Politic Would-be:

O, this knight,
Were he well known, would be a precious thing
To fit our English stage: he that should write
But such a fellow, should be thought to feign
Extremely, if not maliciously.

(Act 2, scene 1)

In *The Way of the World*, Witwoud exclaims towards the end of the last act, "Hey-day! what, are you all got together, like players at the end of the last act?" while Flora, in the first act of Eichendorff's extremely contrived romantic comedy *Die Freier*, gives voice to a hunch she has that she is taking part in the first act of a romantic comedy. The knavish Count of *Le Mariage de Figaro*, suspecting that he is being deceived left, right, and center, sardonically congratulates his wife, "You play comedy very well," and later on is led by his perplexity to ask "Are we all playing a comedy?" (2.19 and 4.6).

In using a comparative, interrogative, or conditional mode to allude to the fictionality of the fiction, the playwright may on the one hand be paradoxically asserting its verisimilitude. The claim that it is *like* a comedy may thus serve as an indirect affirmation of the mimetic notion that it is in fact *not* a comedy but a slice of life, just as exclamations drawing the improbability of a character or situation to our notice paradoxically work as signals of authenticity. On the other hand, however, the emphasis may be more on reminding the audience that the spectacle it is witnessing really *is* a comedy: either in the metaphorical sense that life itself—the world portrayed by the play—is a comedy, meaning a locus of unlikelihood and implausibility (as in Jonson), of contrived theatricality (in Congreve and Eichendorff), or of deception and role-playing (in Beaumarchais), or in the literal sense that it actually is a comic theatrical production. These three aspects—the mimetic factor which plays down the artificiality of the performance in order to appear real, the sense of the theatricality within the world, and the anti-illusionistic impulse that openly admits "this is play"—clearly coexist and interact in some sort of tension that varies according to context. Not merely alluding to the theatricality of the theatre or the world, the device of self-reference furthermore exploits an ambiguously open brand of comic dramatic irony, as the self-confidently real audience (unless they have been seeing too much Pirandello) enjoys the privilege of seeing the characters say more than they mean. Understandably enough, most fictive figures are normally prey to the delusion that they are real, but this is a delusion seen through by the "really" real audience, which "knows" they are but figments of an act of communal imagination. Comic self-reference shows the figures both in their subjection to the illusion of their own realness and coming ironically close to grasping their true (i.e., fictional) status.

The device may furthermore be employed as a form of mock-self-disparagement on the part of the playwright. In Aristophanes's *The Assemblywomen* for example, Blepyrus proclaims his aversion to providing the comedy's potty play, his reluctance to function as a sort of public chamber pot for the comic stage (line 370). In this case he is not testifying to the theatricality of the events nor to a heightened awareness of histrionics, however, but simply to the fact that he is constipated, a farcical contretemps that Aristophanes relishes turning to account while ironically making fun of himself for his scatological smirk. Similar self-irony is to be found in Grabbe's *Scherz*, where a minor incident of (relatively harmless) farce prompts the following exchange:

> *Mollfels.* Mr. Rattengift, you could without question put that scene into one of your comedies.
> *Rattengift.* Great heavens, no, Mr. Mollfels, have you taken leave of your senses? A scene of broad comedy like that? Nowadays comedy must be subtle, so subtle in fact that you don't notice it at all; ... the Germans are altogether much too cultivated and reasonable to be able to stomach any rude or indelicate foolery.
> *Mollfels.* That's true indeed; they're loath to laugh ere they're sure they can formally account for why they've laughed.
>
> (Act 3, scene 1)

Grabbe utilizes the occasion both ironically to deprecate his own coarseness and to indulge in bitingly satirical mockery of the "tasteful" German audience. Grabbe did not pander to his public (perhaps part of the reason why he never really had a public).

Of particular relevance to comedy's anti-illusionistic tendency is the way in which self-reference may function as a light-hearted defamiliarization of the clichés and stereotypes of the genre, simultaneously spotlighting the aesthetic conventions and thereby the structured artificiality of the theatrical illusion while wielding a heightened self-awareness to hoist itself above the level of the comedy it is mocking. In *La Lena*, for example, an Italian Renaissance comedy written by Ariosto, the stereotypical comic configuration of wily servant and dependent master is deflated *and* transcended by the perspicacity and wit of the servant Corbolo, who, called upon to show his skill, finds himself in need of a dose of the cunning he has observed in the servants of Roman comedies. Yet his plight is an unenviable one, for—as he complains to the audience— streetwise sixteenth-century Ferrarese society presents a different kettle of much less gullible fish than the doddering old dunderheads dreamt up by Plautus and Terence.

Self-reference occurs combined with a metatheatrical confusion of levels of reality when fictive figures mention or allude to the author who created them, a juxtaposition of perspectives that frequently produces a jarring absurdity when seen with the logic of the fictional point of view. In Molière's *Le Malade imaginaire* (3.3), Béralde recommends that Argan, the hypochondriac, should go and see one of Molière's plays, and the latter responds with grumbled fulminations against the "bon impertinent" who has the audacity to denigrate the medical profession. At a certain level, therefore, Argan is even railing against the play in which he is himself the protagonist. In Sternheim's *Die Hose* (3.2), Deuter goes to see a "dazzling" play by Sternheim. Martin Amis's novel *Money* takes this comic device still further, the author turning up in his own novel— but as a character among characters, not as narrator. The narrating protagonist, John Self, proves none too keen on the writer (the writer who in one sense has written *him*), an antipathy felt particularly acutely early on: "Oh yeah, and a *writer* lives round my way too.... He gives me the creeps. '*Know me again would you?*' I once shouted across the street, and gave him a V-sign and a warning fist. He stood his ground, and stared. This writer's name, they tell me, is *Martin Amis*. Never heard of him. Do *you* know his stuff at all?"[7] The relationship between narrating protagonist and author is characterized by a degree of latent and not so latent aggression that outdoes anything in Grabbe or Tieck, as well as by an ambivalence that comes to light in the fact that the narrator during one of his numerous visits to brothels adopts the name and identity of the author (possibly a clue that the two figures may be interpreted as existing in a relationship of symbiosis, as two sides of a single but split personality). This presents the reader with the curiously paradoxical situation of a fictive figure "pretending to be" his own creator, though it is his creator in a peculiarly fictionalized form. The irony is compounded when Martin Amis (i.e., "Martin Amis," the fictional one) explicitly theorizes about the relationship between author and narrator in a rather one-sided exchange with John Self:

> "The distance between author and narrator corresponds to the degree to which the author finds the narrator wicked, deluded, pitiful or ridiculous. I'm sorry, am I boring you?"
> "—Uh?"
> . . . .
> "The further down the scale he is, the more liberties you can take with him. You can do what the hell you like to him, really. This creates an appetite for punishment. The author is not free of sadistic impulses."[8]

The elaborate hoax that constitutes the backbone of the novel about John Self's downfall is a sort of theatrical illusion deluding both Self, the narrator-protagonist, and (in all likelihood) the reader, and while at one level it may be regarded as the creation of Lorne Guyland the crackpot out for revenge, at another level—as Self seems to suspect—it is the work of that more sophisticated authorial crackpot Martin Amis, the real-cum-fictional hybrid. It is no wonder that their final encounter ends with the narrator flailing about the room desperately trying to land his maker a punch—nor that he does not get anywhere near connecting. The symbiosis of knave and fool (which may be internalized within the creative subject—"Martin Amis" versus his other "Self") manifests itself both within the text and in the relationships of author to reader and—paradoxically—of author to fictive creation.

Such metafictional tricks explore the interaction of levels of reality not only within the fiction, but in the relationship of the fiction to the real world. Whereas fictive characters may refer *seemingly unwittingly* to the proceedings as a comedy or a farce (in the sense that anyone might equally justifiably describe a set of events as a fiasco or behavior as inauthentic and hackneyed), a parallel source of comedy thus arises when characters show themselves as *explicitly* conscious that they are performing in a theatrical production or leading their lives within a fictional creation. This consciousness, and the concomitant consciousness of the existence of the outside, the beyond, or the audience, is liable to annihilate the illusion that the events are real by openly conceding their fictionality. The illusionistic mask is pulled from the theatrical performance, preventing it from feigning realism, but showing it instead as a set of fictive roles played by actors who exist in the same "reality" as the audience and can consequently communicate with them. Rather than describing this as a fictional *con*fusion of levels of reality, it is perhaps less misleading to term it a *fusion*. Reality and play become indistinguishable, as in *Tristram Shandy* ("She listened to it with composed intelligence, and would have done so to the end of the chapter", "O Jenny! Jenny! replied I, and so went on with the twelfth chapter"),[9] in which the question whether it is narratorial fusion or fictive confusion is as irrelevant as it is unanswerable.

The anti-illusionistic and self-referential theatre of Brecht is in a line of dramatic descent—via Büchner and Wedekind—from the distance-generating drama of Tieck, as well as from the folk theatre of Nestroy, whose self-consciously histrionic figures such as Titus likewise blur the boundaries between art and life. In Brecht's *Trommeln in der Nacht*, for example, at a highpoint in the dramatic tension, Kragler deflates and destroys the illusion by pointing out the theatricality of the world and of the theatre: "It's routine theatre: boards, a paper moon, and behind it all the meat counter—that's the only thing that's real" (5). His *Mann ist Mann* shows Widow Begbick dropping her dramatic mask in order to reveal the didactic face of the dramatist who wrote her, rather like Tieck's innkeeper: "Mr. Bertolt Brecht says: man is man ...," she croons, telling the audience what is to be learned from the play. This break in the plot proper, intended as a means of generating distance to the action, gives us time to don our critical specs, to cogitate rather than vegetate, and thereby to combine work (learning) with play (theatre). In Grabbe's *Scherz* the mass-murderer Mordax, threatened with justice, steps out of his fictional role and escapes into the orchestra in order to save his (fictive or real?) skin:

> *Baron.*   I'll have you chained together like the commonest of criminals, I'll have you carted into town in broad daylight, I'll have you ...
>
> *Mordax.* (*losing his temper*) 'Sdeath, this is more than I can bear! Have me carted into town in chains!?! Ha! Is that the thanks I get for playing my role so splendidly? Do you imagine I don't know, Mr Theatre-Baron, that you are in truth the actor Mr V. and cannot do me any ill? Swiftly, Mr von Wernthal, let us repair to the musicians down in the pit; they're my bosom friends and will not lay a finger 'pon us.
>
> (Act 3, scene 6)

Like a badly disguised impostor, Mordax is unable to keep up his theatrical mask. Of course, the spontaneity of such an "unscripted" breakaway from the apparent authority of the playwright is itself an illusion, for it can only be feigned spontaneity, a scripted disruption of the script. Mordax's rejection of his theatrical role is paradoxically prescribed as part of his role.

The "spontaneity" comes closer to being genuine in the comedy of the commedia dell'arte, but even here it is planned spontaneity. Originating on the marketplace and influenced by the comedy of carnival, the commedia made a point of blurring the distinction between spectator and actor. As Goethe observed, "The audience take part in the play as well, and the crowd merges with the theatre in a single whole."[10] Unlike the "peep-show" naturalism and illusionism that were to replace it, the entertainment was akin to a dialogue with the public, spawning a communal bond of unity and festivity (although clearly the audience was more passive than in carnival celebration itself). Starting with the arrival of the troupe in town and the erection of the stage, the performance was characterized by a satirical immediacy that inspired the enthusiastic spectator Goethe to describe Pulcinella as a walking newspaper. It is in this context that Pulcinella would pretend to step outside his performing role in a manner comparable with Mordax's "extempore" escape from the stage. Goethe reports:

> One comic turn [*Hauptspaß*] sometimes performed onstage by this figure of low comedy ... consisted in him all of a sudden seeming completely to forget his role as an actor. He would pretend [*Er tat, als wäre*] that he were back home, and would talk intimately with his family, telling them about the play in which he was acting and about another in which he was due to perform; nor was he ashamed to take the liberty of answering nature's call. "But my dear husband," his wife would then cry out , "you seem to have completely forgotten yourself; think of the worthy public before which you now stand!"
> "E vero! E vero!" Pulcinella would then reply, remembering himself and returning into his former performance to the great applause of the audience.[11]

The theatrical mask here coincides with the social mask (which would have us piss in private), Pulcinella surprising the audience into laughter by dispensing with both. Two points, however, remind us that this is *planned* spontaneity. Goethe's depiction of the episode as a "Hauptspaß" pinpoints it unambiguously as an *established* comic routine in Pulcinella's repertoire, a repeated and infinitely repeatable aspect of his fixed mask that is as reassuringly recognizable as his sugar-loaf hat, his hunchback, or his conspicuous conk. Goethe's use of a subjunctive ("Er tat, als wäre") likewise signals that Pulcinella is still acting, performing, pretending. The "surprise" is a paradoxically predictable surprise based on the expectation of the unexpected. While seeming to leave his role, Pulcinella never ultimately ceases playing his part.

Improvization of this order has returned to the fore in the experimental theatre of the second half of this century, typified by the New York performance group "Squat" (see "Introduction"). Here the unscheduled entrance of the policemen into the performance area elicited laughter from the spectators, this "genuinely" spontaneous encroachment from outside fuzzing the borderlines between theatre and nontheatre. The sight of the "real" policemen as actors or players onstage may, moreover, be taken as implying that (at a certain level at least) *all* social interaction is theatrical, that performance pervades the outside world as much as the auditorium, that even the serious business of a policeman is just another role. While such experimental theatre may in one sense be spontaneous, therefore, it can only ever be as spontaneous as the real world, and that is about as spontaneous as a ham roll. Given this problematic gray area lying between (or swallowing up) notions of performance and spontaneity, context or frame again become the only *practical* criteria for distinguishing play and nonplay. In Schechner's words,

> The artists of Squat assert that what is 'art' depends on the frame surrounding the actions. When the cops walk into Squat's stage they have positioned themselves 'as art,' regardless of what they may intend to be doing or how they themselves feel about it. In an epoch of information media—I mean TV, movies, radio, the microchip, the satellite hookup—when 'authenticity' is often a highly edited, refined, idealized (or brutalized) version of 'raw' experience, people wonder exactly what is 'raw' and what is 'cooked.' Is there any such thing as 'human nature' understood as unmediated, direct, unrehearsed experience?[12]

If this awareness of the existential ubiquity of performance is often akin to a modern secularized version of the ancient *theatrum mundi* motif, it tends, like its ideological forefather, to function only indirectly as a comic moment or as a rupture in the theatrical illusion (through its fostering of comic or ironic distance and its smudging of boundaries between play and nonplay). In such cases, the performance or play may well only draw attention to its status as performance or play via the circuitous or circular route of implicitly showing that *all* is performance or play and thereby suspending every gesture of theatrical or social intercourse in paradoxical indeterminacy somewhere between play and reality, performance and authentic spontaneity.

Simpson's *A Resounding Tinkle* deals in characteristically whimsical fashion with the paradoxes of acted improvization. In the second scene, "the author" takes the stage in order to complain that what we have witnessed so far is not at all how he wrote the play, attributing this shoddiness to the inebriation of the actors. Later on, Mr. Paradock treats the matter more fully:

> *Mr. Paradock.* Let's put the case of someone forgetting his lines on the stage at the exact point where he's supposed in the play to pretend to have forgotten them.
> *1st Comedian.* I don't think I follow. You're a bit too drunk for me.
> *Mr. Paradock.* He has to give the illusion that he's forgotten his lines. As part of the play. All right?
> *1st Comedian.* Yes. I follow that.

Mr. Paradock. Now. At the precise moment when he's supposed to give the illusion of having forgotten his lines he quite forgets what it is he has to do. His mind goes blank. So what happens? There's a pause. The pause prolongs itself. But sooner or later he remembers what it is he ought to have been doing. He ought to have been giving the impression of having been at a loss for words. There's nothing he can do about it now. The audience will have to make do with the reality instead of the illusion—which would probably have been much better. They might well have had to do without both. He might well have forgotten not only that he was supposed to stumble for words, but that there was anything he was supposed to do at all. In that case he'd have gone straight on—word-perfect.

1st Comedian. Thus—the illusion of having remembered may be sustained only by forgetting, and the illusion of having forgotten only by remembering.

(Act 2)

The realization that they are taking part in a play is often accompanied in the fictive figures by a consciousness of the beyond, i.e., the spectators. Addressing the audience thus becomes a means of focusing attention on the actor-audience relationship, an aspect of theatrical performance that naturalistic drama takes for granted as an unsophisticated subject-object polarity: a subject is watching something that is the spitting image of objective reality. *A Resounding Tinkle*, in one of its periods of feigned spontaneity where the actors pretend to forget or deviate from their scripts, makes sport of this conventional subject-object duality, as the First Comedian decides to read a magazine with his back to the audience:

2nd Comedian. You're being a bit casual, aren't you? What about all these people?

1st Comedian. Well?

2nd Comedian. We can't sit down and read magazines.

1st Comedian. It's not my job to spoon-feed them.

2nd Comedian. They'll get restive.

1st Comedian. Let them talk among themselves for a time.

. . . .

2nd Comedian. Maybe it isn't your job to spoon-feed them. But it's not mine either.

1st Comedian. Then we can both stop worrying. If they don't want to amuse themselves they can make do with silence.

2nd Comedian. They'll never stand for it.

1st Comedian. We can break it up with dialogue from time to time if it would make you any easier. And silence isn't so easy to come by as all that, either, if it comes to that.

2nd Comedian. It's not what you go to a theatre for. You go to other places for silence. Not a theatre. They'll feel cheated.

(Act 1)

The paradox of feigned spontaneity is duplicated and echoed in the paradoxical fact that the silence that would result if they genuinely were to reject their theatrical role-playing is filled by their disquisition on silence. The First Comedian's wish to pass over to the audience the responsibility for their entertainment (in a sense a move back towards the communal origins of theatre) is thwarted by the articulation of this wish and by the ensuing discussion.

What in Simpson's hands is a thematic nonsensicality informing the play as a whole may also be employed somewhat more sporadically. Plautus uses the device to justify dramatic economy, metatheatrically pointing out the conventions of artistic expediency that noncomic drama would play down or paste over and, at the same time, spotlighting the theatrical convention almost universally taken for granted that the onus is on the actors to entertain the audience. When his liar Pseudolus is asked by Calidorus how he tricked Harpax, Pseudolus thus refuses to tell him on the grounds that the play is being performed for the benefit of the spectators and as they saw what happened it would be patently impractical to recap on events.

The fact that addressing the audience is itself a theatrical convention, however, means that it is liable to turn up in *naturalized* form—as a "natural" feature of the dramatized occurrences and one that does not attract attention to itself as being in any way disruptive of the fictional illusion. The aside, for example, is an important and conventionally established method of letting a slow audience in on the secret that a particular character is acting or hiding his feelings; it is a mode of access to "true" feelings, a way of showing what is behind the mask and hence a flattering sign of collusion for the spectator. Insofar as it involves addressing a body of people who from the strictly naturalistic point of view cannot be known by the character to be there, of course, the aside is a dropping not merely of the fictive mask within the fiction, but also of the theatrical illusion itself; but again—because of the conventionality of the device—this may tend to go unnoticed. Of a similar order is the "we hope you enjoyed our play" sort of statement so frequently appearing at the close of a comic performance as an aesthetic frame or as a vehicle for a didactic playwright's urge to moralize. A greater degree of surprise, absurdity, or paradoxicality is normally required before such devices become openly funny.

Within the novelistic tradition, the "dear reader" mode of address is even less related to an anti-illusionistic or nonrealistic impulse. On the contrary, it may be employed as a means of creating or reinforcing an illusion of orality, or at least generating a degree of narrative immediacy. Yet even as conventions, the aside as well as devices of narratorial intimacy hearken back to the prenaturalistic origins of theatre and story-telling, to dramatic modes in which the bond between actor-storyteller and audience was rooted in bilaterality. This interactive moment is evidenced by Rabelais's tales of Gargantua and Pantagruel, where the illusion of orality can be traced back to the emergence of the story-telling genre from a carnival tradition of communal creativity and festivity in which the spoken, not the written, word held sway. The prologue to Rabelais's *Gargantua* is pervaded by a mountebank's eloquence, a hyperbolical forcefulness that sells the book as a charlatan might sell a drug. Rabelais's narrator has to search for his spectacles in order to be able to see his audience properly, he exhorts his readers to read his words with booze to hand (himself having to curtail the first book owing to a hangover), and he bullies his victims into accepting the veracity of his accounts with a torrent of curses that would see intrepid doubters inflicted with, among other things, epilepsy, dysentry, and the same burning to a crispy noodle suffered by the inhabitants of Sodom and Gomorrah. In the prologue to the third book, those who dare to criticize his earlier work are likened to dogs who, snuffling and pissing around the narrator's Diogenic tub, are held at bay with the growled invective of a crapulent Cynic:

> As for those bonnet-brained nitpickers, pray do not talk to me of them, in the reverend name of the four buttocks which begot ye and the vivifying peg which coupled them. ... Down, curs! ... Gz, gzz, gzzzz. Off with ye! Off with ye! Will they not be gone? May ye ne'er shit but when lashed by stirrup leathers, ne'er piss but when strappadoed, ne'er be on heat save the heat of a good hiding!
>
> (Book 3, *Prologue*)

Martin Amis's *Money* perpetually plays with the illusion of orality, mocking the convention by using it in absurdly unorthodox ways. John Self is for a start somewhat more of a kamikaze toper than his beatifically bibulous Rabelaisian counterpart, and his protracted states of inebriety produce narrative gaps and unreliability of a sort not so patently present in Rabelais. The unreliable narrator, be he drunk, tripping, absent-minded, or simply mendacious, can function either as a signal of orality or as metafictional play with the conventions of narrative truthfulness, and John Self probably does both. He furthermore strikes up an intensely personal relationship with the reader, candidly exposing his weaknesses, secrets, and insecurity: "I love giving money away. If you were here now, I'd probably slip you some cash.... Would you put an arm round my shoulder and tell me I was your kind of guy? I'd pay. I'd give you good money for it." He asks the female readership for advice in sexual matters: "Hey, you, you chicks out there. How should I play it?" He asks us for a drink when in need and advice about what clothes to wear, and he proves to have pretty clear conceptions of his reader's masturbatory habits:

"Everybody does it. Girls do it. Vicars do it. I do it. You do it. (Yes, you do it, and *how* old are you?)"[13] Rather like alcoholic beverage in Rabelais (a great leveler and a *must* for good-natured sociability), the "deeply democratic" handjob in *Money* takes on a universal value linking narrator and reader. Amis applies an additional twist when John Self extends his paranoia to include a mistrust of the reader, sensing that we too are in on whatever hoax it is he is being subjected to. Once again, to the extent that the reader is in collusion with author and not narrator, he is not wrong.

Rabelais and Amis make it clear that the techniques of addressing the reader or spectator may include a healthy portion of audience abuse. This again betrays the origins of drama (and narrative) in communal ritual, which attributed to invective a magically salutary effect,[14] although in modern times it perhaps achieves its comic force more by disrupting dramatic and social convention, shocking the (mild and well-meaning) audience into laughter. The fictional mask and the social mask—and the rent produced in them by comedy—are in such cases clearly shown to be coterminous. Aristophanes was never one to squander an opportunity for verbally laying into his audience. In *The Frogs*, Xanthias begins by unenthusiastically surveying the public, wondering how best they are to be entertained, and later on, on the lookout for murderers and perjurers, it is in the auditorium that he and Dionysus spot them. Indeed the audience make ideal scapegoats and suspects. Molière's miser, Harpagon, over two millenia later harbors suspicions that the spectators are responsible for stealing his hoard of treasure, just as his Plautine ancestor, Euclio, had seen himself as exposed to the derisive laughter of an audience in on the plot when his pot of gold was pinched. In Aristophanes's *The Peace*, having ascended to Zeus in order to talk him into putting an end to the war ravaging Greece, Trygaeus tells us on his return: "Why, from above, you looked as bad as bad can be. But you didn't look half as bad as you do from down here" (ll.815–16). In David Barrett's translation of *The Birds*, Euelpides combines insulting the audience with mockingly drawing attention to illusionistic convention: "You do realize, by the way, that strictly speaking you aren't here at all" (line 30), a clever juxtaposition of comic procedure (addressing the audience) and the naturalistic or non-comic procedure of ignoring the audience and pretending they aren't there. Related to this abusive tendency is the Aristophanic—and presumably traditional—habit of insulting specific notables within the public, his chorus often being employed to jest and jeer at figures in the contemporary Athenian spotlight (as in *The Frogs*). Such malicious up-to-the-minute lampooning, suppressed by New Comedy, has never quite regained its footing on the mainstream comic stage, being displaced to marginal or plebeian comic culture and to carnivalistic caricature, but the same impulse is inherent in the television satire of *Spitting Images*, which lays into particular notables with Aristophanic gusto. New Comedy and, down the ages, the comedy of intrigue and farce has preferred to flatter its public by affirming a set of shared norms and exploiting the possibilities of an ironic perspective.

In recent times, the comedy of Samuel Beckett, influenced by the dialogic music-hall tradition, has also flouted the unilaterality of conventional theatre, whereby audience looks at actor and not vice versa. Vladimir and Estragon contemplate the spectators with revulsion in *Waiting for Godot*. Trying to escape from the stage and from the limitations of his dramatic/existential plight, Estragon makes two abortive attempts at departure into the wings, before seeking alternative possibilities:

> *Vladimir.* We're surrounded! (*Estragon makes a rush towards back.*) Imbecile! There's no way out there. (*He takes Estragon by the arm and drags him front. Gesture towards front.*) There! Not a soul in sight! Off you go. Quick! (*He pushes Estragon towards auditorium. Estragon recoils in horror*) You won't? (*He contemplates auditorium.*) Well, I can understand that.
>
> (Act 2)

In Stoppard's *Rosencrantz and Guildenstern Are Dead* contemplation of the audience (or is it the movement of the boat?) induces a bout of seasickness in Rosencrantz, whom Guildenstern sensibly advises to go and heave-ho on the other side of the boat (to take account of the wind). A subtle variation on the theme emerges in Beckett's *Happy Days* in which the "heroine," Winnie, has an intuition that she is being watched, an intuition that prompts her to recount an anecdote about a Mr. and Mrs. Shower or Cooker—a Mr. and Mrs. Piper in the French version[15]—who do little more than come and look at her, asking one another what she's doing "stuck up to her diddies in the bleeding ground" and what she's meant to mean. These curious parodies of the theatrical spectator (or *Schauer, Gucker*, or peeper) implicitly liken the real onlooker—"us"—to a sort of inquisitively detached voyeur.

Handke's *Publikumsbeschimpfung* violates the traditional relationship between performer and public from the very outset. It does so, indeed, with such consistency that the play never really creates an illusion to be broken in the first place, and if it is to be seen as comic, the comedy it generates is consequently of a different order. The audience are informed by the actors of the unity of actor and audience ("We and you gradually form a unity") and of the significance of their role ("You are the villains and heroes of this play"), as well as treated to a good deal of theorizing on the paradoxical nature of theatrical illusion and play, which after all is not what it is—but then again is what it is. The play ends with a bracing bout of abuse that starts by praising the snotfaced spectators for their part in the proceedings before getting into its stride. The vituperation is perhaps rather weak by today's standards, however, (for a lot of much fruitier insults have been hurled in the last twenty odd years), and it would be funnier if it were more sexual, scatological, anatomical, offensive, or verbally inventive. In the end Handke is too polite with his audience.

The comic habit of stepping outside the fictional action to address the public is inherently paradoxical. To the extent that the figure who does so is talking to a bank of strangers who from the naturalistic perspective (as Euelpides realizes) are "not there" or who exist on a different ontological plane, he might justifiably strike his fellow figures (who lack this awareness of an audience) as round the bend—just as in the real world the strictly rational perspective regards it as a sign of "madness" to talk to the anthropomorphically white-bearded celestial spectator known as God. Moreover, insofar as this "fool" may be implicitly (if not explicitly) drawing attention to the fictionality of the proceedings, he is generating a paradox akin to that of the Cretan who claims that all Cretans are liars. Rather like Simpson's actor feigning spontaneous forgetfulness, who only remembers his role by forgetting it and forgets it if he remembers to forget, the Cretan liar must necessarily be lying if he is telling the truth about Cretans. Seen from within the logic of the fictional system, the moment that reminds the spectator that what he is seeing is an illusion or play eludes semantic classification. "I'm an illusion," "I'm a fiction," or "I'm not real" are paradoxical assertions in a certain respect analogous to the celebrated "this statement is a lie," for in both cases the *act* of affirmation would seem to contradict the (implicit or explicit) *content* of the affirmation itself. In Scudéry's *Comédie des comédiens*, the appearance of Montdory as prologue hints at this semantic kinship. Feigning rationalistic scepticism with regard to the delusions of the actors who suspend disbelief in their own pretence and who try to delude us too, Montdory warns the audience: "In short, their mania compels me to go and visit St. Mathurin [saint invoked for the cure of folly] for their sake, which is what I'm going to do: in the mean time (Gentlemen), do not believe a word they may say, for I warrant there'll not be a jot of truth in it." Alerting us to the folly of confusing illusion and reality, Montdory of course fails to mention that his is a feigned or sham consternation. His reluctance to act is an acted reluctance, and in this he too typifies the semantic hypocrisy of the Cretan. Revealing that what we are about to see is a lie (admittedly a special sort of lie, an aesthetic lie, a fiction), he plays down the fact that he himself is a part of the lie.

Just as one could, however, (cheatingly) explain away the paradox by positing that the Cretan is in fact an occasional or unreliable liar *pretending* to be a Cretan (thus *not* entailing that he always lies) but *truthful* in his affirmation about the mendacity of Cretans, and just as the Simpsonian paradox can be clarified by remembering that the actor is in fact a real-life person *pretending* to be an actor who has forgotten his words, so the paradoxicality of the figure who addresses the audience inheres in his ambivalent status as one who stands both *within* the fictional system (as part of the play) and *external* to it (as a real, autonomous, living being). A mediator between the fictive and the real world, he exists both inside and outside the drama. It is no coincidence therefore that, traditionally at least, the great commentators on comedy from "within" the comic illusion have tended to be fools, clowns, and marginal characters teetering on the borderline between play and reality. Welsford writes: "As a dramatic character, the fool has a tendency to act as an intermediary between the stage and the auditorium."[16] Harlequin and Hanswurst are such figures, striking up intimate relationships with the audience, often mocking those dullards caught up in the illusion, and using their eccentric perspective to criticize and disparage the action, just as it tends to be Shakespeare's fools and clowns (such as Touchstone or Feste) who enjoy the closest rapport with the spectators and provide the most perspicacious commentary on the fictional events. This is a tendency going back to the German carnival play, to the French *sottie*,[17] and to French mysteries such as the mystery of "Saint Didier" in which the fool, who is invisible and not even contemporary with the fictive occurrences, relieves the religious tension by operating as a mouthpiece for the onlooker. In England, Nashe's pageant *Summer's Last Will and Testament* (1592) playfully assigned the role of Presenter or Chorus (meant to mediate between spectacle and spectator) to "Will Summers," the celebrated court-fool of Henry VIII. Hamlet, who took his theatre seriously, himself recognized and mistrusted the knack of the clown to drop his role, interrupt the illusion, and indulge in disruptive ad-libbing: "And let those that play your clowns speak no more than is set down for them," he warns the players, "for there be of them that will themselves laugh, to set on some quantity of barren spectators to laugh too, though in the meantime some necessary question of the play be then to be considered" (3.2). The fool's exclusion from the mainstream may be seen as accompanied by a degree of superiority in relation to the norm, enabling him to see the sort of social truth that can only be perceived from above and granting him the privilege of intercourse with us equally superior spectators. The fool, in other words, is situated both outside *and* above, at the limits of the theatrical as of the social drama.

An awareness within the fictive figures of the presence of the audience can function, therefore, as a means of disrupting the theatrical illusion. A consciousness of the theatrical props in their capacity as props (and not as items encountered within the reality of the fictional world) has the same effect, jarring the onlooker out of the comfort of an established illusion. Such "prop comedy" has already been observed at work in the meta-theatre of Tieck, and Aristophanes offers some more particularly illu-minating examples. The "machine" that enabled gods and goddesses to make their spectacular descents from heaven in contemporary tragedy turns up in his *Women at the Thesmophoria*, but of course such pomp is bathetically parodied, the machine malfunctions, and Euripides is whisked right across the stage and out of sight. The tragic Echo is sub-jected to a similar deflation in the same play. Aristophanic drama also derives a wealth of prop comedy from that perennial prop, the stage penis. This floppy phallic factotum comes to be used in a myriad of un-expected ways, an infinitely versatile practical pun rather like the word "it" in the verbal sphere. In *The Wasps* Procleon obligingly offers his penis to a flute girl as a handrope by which to hoist herself up onstage (after all, it can take a bit of friction—nudge nudge wink wink), while in *Peace*, flying up on a self-reared giant dung beetle to negotiate with Zeus, Trygaeus uses his all-purpose prick as a joystick to direct his beetle, this episode moreover parodying Euripides's *Bellerophon* in which Pegasus the flying horse had stolen the show. A fecal flavoring is added to the comedy, dragging Euripides's dramatic loftiness through the scatological sump with the downward motion characteristic of bathos: working on the age-old comic logic that fear entails an opening of the fundaments, Try-gaeus pleads with the stage crane-handler working the flying dung beetle to be more careful—or else the dung beetle will be getting an early meal.

In *Der Gute Mensch von Sezuan*, Brecht likewise derives comedy from the stage props, a device that, in his case, is explicitly designed to disrupt any easy illusionism and encourage a critical response. Deriding the idea of anthropomorphic divine intervention and the classical *deus ex machina*, Brecht shows his pathetic divinities descending onto the stage on a set of tasteless pink clouds. This tackily camp spectacle is the nearest they come to a moment of triumph, however, and, unable to cope with the hardships of earth, it is not long before they are sailing back home into the Nothingness from which they emerged—again transported by their fancy stage props. Equating religious and theatrical illusion, Brecht deflates both to reveal that the gods' biggest feat was tantamount to a low-budget theatrical illusion.

Playing with the conventions of the genre and the presuppositions of the aesthetic medium is another means of directing attention to the fictionality of the fiction as well as parodying traditional forms of the genre. Todorov describes the *vraisemblance* (or the verisimilitude) of a text or work as the extent to which it "attempts to make us believe that it conforms to reality and not to its own laws. In other words, the *vraisemblable* is the mask which conceals the text's own laws and which we are supposed to take for a relation with reality."[18] In terms of the metaphor, comedy arises when a text, be it theatrical or narrative, points out its own laws or when it breaks with them (since breaking with them is one of the most effective ways of retrospectively pointing them out): that is, when the mask falls. As in Tieck's *Gestiefelte Kater*, the play-within-the-play in Buckingham's *The Rehearsal* exemplifies this device: by consistently rupturing dramatic expectations, it simultaneously recalls to mind the conventions normally governing our response to theatrical performance. Like bad acting, bad theatre (i.e., bad play-writing) is comic for the imperfection of its illusion, but it thereby brings to light the ways in which "good" theatre strives to create illusion convincingly. In the play within Buckingham's play, important scenes are conducted entirely in whispers inaudible to anybody (doing away with the convention of theatrical audibility); Prince Pretty-man's response to the arrival of his loved one is to fall asleep on the spot (psychological plausibility going by the boards with anticlimactic abruptness); he on one occasion wakes up with the words "It is resolv'd" and promptly exits leaving everyone in the dark as to *what* is resolved; and characters are interrupted just as they are setting themselves up for long and centrally important speeches. Generic conventions—such as psychological motivation—are massacred with the same blithe oblivion to realistic coherence as the soldiers in this seemingly unprovoked slaughter scene:

> *Enter four men at one door, and four at another, with their swords drawn.*
> *1st Soldier.* Stand. Who goes there?
> *2nd Soldier.* A Friend.
> *1st Soldier.* What Friend?
> *2nd Soldier.* A Friend to the House.
> *1st Soldier.* Fall on. (*They all kill one another*).
>
> (Act 2, scene 5)

Sheridan's *The Critic* operates in a similar way, Puff's ludicrous drama unwittingly providing a parody of the stereotypical dramatic exposition in which one character gives another vital information concerning their situation and thereby surreptitiously supplies the spectator with the requisite details for an understanding of the plot. Puff's play, watched by Sneer and Dangle, defamiliarizes this convention by taking its psychological improbability to an absurd extreme, as Sir Walter attempts to "tell" Sir Christopher the necessary background information:

> *Sir Walter.* Philip, you know, is proud Iberia's king!
> *Sir Christopher.* He is.

Sir Walter. His subjects in base bigotry
              And Catholic oppression held,—while we,
              You know, the Protestant persuasion hold.
Sir Christ. We do.
Sir Walter. You know, beside, his boasted armament,
              The famed Armada, by the Pope baptized,
              With purpose to invade these realms—
Sir Christ.   —Is sailed.
              Our last advices so report.
Sir Walter. While the Iberian admiral's chief hope,
              His darling son—
Sir Christ. Ferolo Whiskerandos hight—
Sir Walter. The same—by chance a pris'ner hath been ta'en,
              And in this fort of Tilbury—
Sir Christ.   —Is now
              Confin'd,—'tis true, and oft from yon tall turrets top
              I've mark'd the youthful Spaniard's haughty mien
              Unconquer'd, tho' in chains;
Sir Walter.   You also know—
Dangle.   Mr Puff, as he *knows* all this, why does Sir Walter go on telling
              him?
Puff.   But the audience are not supposed to know anything of the matter,
              are they?
Sneer.   True, but I think you manage ill: for there certainly appears no
              reason why Sir Walter should be so communicative.
Puff.   Fore Gad, now, that is one of the most ungrateful observations I
              ever heard—for the less inducement he has to tell all this the more,
              I think, you ought to be obliged to him.

                                                              (Act 2, scene 2)

Puff's "star" Lord Burleigh likewise proves as enigmatic as Bayes's
Prince Pretty-man:

Puff.   But now for my principal character—Here he comes—Lord Burleigh
              in person! Pray, gentlemen, step this way—softly—I only hope the
              Lord High Treasurer is perfect—if he is but perfect!
              (*Enter Burleigh, goes slowly to a chair and sits.*)
Sneer.   Mr Puff!
Puff.   Hush! vastly well, Sir! vastly well! a most interesting gravity!
Dangle.   What, isn't he to speak at all?
Puff.   Egad, I thought you'd ask me that—yes, it is a very likely thing—that
              a Minister in his situation, with the whole affairs of the nation on his
              head, should have time to talk!—but hush! or you'll put him out.
Sneer.   Put him out! how the plague can that be, if he's not going to say any-
              thing?
Puff.   There's a reason! why his part is to *think*, and how the plague! do you
              imagine he can *think* if you keep talking?
Dangle.   That's very true upon my word!
              (*Burleigh comes forward, shakes his head, and exit.*)
Sneer.   He is very perfect, indeed—

                                                              (Act 3, scene 1)

In one sense, these plays operate against the yardstick of illusionism: "good" theatre should not show that it is theatre but convince us that what we are watching is real (or at least allow us to forget its fictionality). Puff's and Bayes's plays are "bad" theatre that obtrusively displays itself as theatre by ignoring or distorting and thereby spotlighting the conventions that can normally be taken for granted. Ironically, however (and this is the nature of parody), the plays *The Critic* and *The Rehearsal* do not merely *reject* "bad" theatre, they themselves incorporate it and turn it to account, indeed are constituted by it, and in this sense they can, therefore, be said likewise to draw attention to *themselves* as theatre.

It is Sterne's *Tristram Shandy* that goes furthest of all novels in its parodic play with narrative convention. Just as Tieck was to begin his *Verkehrte Welt* with an epilogue and conclude it with its prologue, Sterne's narrator, characteristically confusing his real and his fictive occupations, uses a "gap" in the narrative to write his preface in the middle of the third volume: "All my heroes are off my hands;—'tis the first time I have had a moment to spare,—and I'll make use of it, and write my preface."[19] The tendency of Sterne's narrator to get tangled up in digressions in the end approaches a kind of narrative comedy of (monomanic) character, becoming a predictable pattern repeated at intervals: "Imagine to yourself;—but this had better begin a new chapter," "My mother, you must know,—but I have fifty things more necessary to let you know first," and "I will not finish that sentence till I have made an observation."[20] As *Tristram Shandy* illustrates, breaking with convention may easily itself become a convention of its own, rather like the shaggy-dog story, a metajoke frustrating the hearer's expectation of a punch line, but which we come to *expect* to undermine our expectations in this way.

In Sterne's novel, the narrator is forever fooling the reader, having him on. He recurrently plays with expectations, leading one to expect a particular account, but deferring and deferring again: "If it was not necessary I should be born before I was christened, I would this moment give the reader an account of it."[21] Martin Amis's *Money* likewise—if in a different tone—makes the most of the comic potential of narrative to tease the reader, exploiting the fact that, like playwright (actor) and audience, author (narrator) and reader exist in a knave/fool configuration. The following passage (and remember the narrating protagonist is a big, boozy, sexist slob) exemplifies this treacherous trait:

> So, towards the end of dinner, as Martina stood at my side pouring out the last of the wine, I rammed my hand up her skirt and said, "Come on, darling, you know you love it" ... Relax. I didn't really. In fact I behaved doggedly well all evening.[22]

Illusion-breaking comedy not only surprises us, but also reminds us that, as the gull in the rogue-gull relationship, we ourselves have been taken in for as long as we allowed ourselves to be carried away by mimetic identification, to believe in the illusion. Metatheatre may, therefore, also generate the sort of laughter described by Cicero as arising from the realization of an error on our part. After initially catching us out, however, a theatre such as that of Tieck or Stoppard itself comes to create new patterns of nonillusionistic expectations, as we are able to anticipate and revel in new absurdities, enjoying the paradoxical status of self-referential play. Freed from the feigned honesty of naturalism, which claims to tell nothing but the truth, we are able to appreciate the illusionistic mask for what it is (a mask), and this can indeed ultimately be seen as the more candid alternative, for, like the Cretan liar, the metatheatrical actor by implication at least admits his histrionic untruthfulness.

6

Discarding the Social Mask

Comic Folly

Just as the enjoyment of language in its physicality as a mask serves as a release from language's representational responsibilities, so the appreciation of theatrical illusion *as illusion* provides a break from the functionality that would have theatrical performance standing in a straightforward mimetic relationship to some possible portion of the world. Precluding empathetic identification with its figures, such comedy also generates the aesthetic distance that allows the spectator to laugh rather than cry, fret or lose himself in admiration. It is slightly inaccurate to say point-blank that metatheatre simply "destroys" the illusion, however, for the dramatic spectacle remains at one remove from the outside world as well as a part of it. Play, by nature paradoxical and ambiguous, is both real and pretend: whereas illusionistic play hides or suppresses the element of pretence, self-aware play leaves the two aspects in suspension, transforming the illusion into a new kind of ironic or self-conscious illusion. A nonsensical ontological no-man's-land is created, a space in which the characters hover between reality and fiction.

It is the clown or the fool who embodies this state more than any other figure, hopping between play-within-play and frame-play ·and between play and reality with gay abandon and a subversive disrespect for the laws of logic. Traversing the boundary between fictional world and a contemporaneity shared with the viewing public, moreover, the forms of direct address employed by the fool reestablish the stage as a locus of communicative interaction and direct social contact. As such, the fool revitalizes elements of the popular entertainment and festivity that have so frequently informed the theatrical medium. The extent to which theatre is historically derivative from phallic rites or from carnival or saturnalian celebration is, of course, open to debate; what is clear is that theatre and plebeian festivity have frequently (especially in the late Middle Ages for example) been directly neighboring forms of social life, closely contiguous cultural institutions "with similar patterns of representation and similar orientations to political and economic practice."[1]

As both the proximity of carnival and theatre and the rampant illogicality of comic metatheatre suggest, this world of nonsense may simultaneously cross the footlights from actor to audience and thereby become a vicarious holiday from the drab reality of the nontheatrical world not merely for the lunatic performer but for the spectator himself. If the workaday world outside can be seen as imposing upon its social actors a (hot, sticky, and uncomfortable) mask of rationality and of social and ethical decorum, then the comic theatre is a place not merely where we *watch* bad social and theatrical acting, but also where we ourselves by identification *escape* from the sweaty discomfort of the ill-fitting vizard. Sexuality may be comic, therefore, not simply when observed as a natural phenomenon insistently poking out its tumescent head from beneath the Y-fronts of social propriety, but also insofar as the insistence of the observed sexuality at a certain level mirrors the insistence of the spectator's instincts. In the theatre, an audience can vicariously discard the mask of sexual restraint it normally wears, just as it can enjoy a temporary respite from rationality, politeness, and deference. Identifying with the fools onstage, the fool inside us is granted a two-hour parole from the prison-house of reason.

From the point of view of the spectator, the distinction can be rephrased as an active/passive one, the passive comic pleasure of watching the mask being dropped, doffed, or dislodged contrasting with the actively collusive rejection of the mask on the part of the identifying spectator. Whereas the passive component of laughter can be equated with it being directed *at* a butt (from the safety of the stalls), the active laughter of complicity by contrast corresponds to laughter *with* its object, as if we were to jump up on stage and muck in with the madness. From the perspective of the character, those cases where the comic figure involuntarily drops his mask can be distinguished from those where he consciously rejects it or simply does without it. In the former case the figure is more likely to be the target of ridicule, derided for the imperfection of his social or theatrical acting (although we might identify with his difficulties); in the latter instance, he is more likely to be admired for his openness and genuineness (although different historical circumstances might see him despised for his baseness).

These distinctions are patently problematic, however, insofar as all laughter implies a measure of activity, just as it would be misleading to envisage any form of spectatorship as the pure passivity of "objective" contemplation. Even the derisive mockery of a fool, laughter at a victim that seems purely passive in nature, may be interpreted as a channeling of currents of hostility that normal social intercourse generally requires to be subjugated and concealed, antisocial aggression that also comes to light in the mirth provoked by certain varieties of violent or sexual farce.

Conversely, even "active" laughter is only displaced action: we do not *actually* get up from our seats and fling ourselves into the folly. Identification is always ambivalent, coupled with distancing.

Laughter at folly is permeated by this intrinsic ambiguity. An audience may on the one hand laugh *with* an act of comic sexual frankness (performed, for example, by a child), celebrating its openness and unaffectedness. It may on the other hand laugh *at* a display of sexual unorthodoxy, disapproving of it, embarrassed by it, while still perhaps in some way enjoying the release provided by the laughter. It is an ambiguity that can be accounted for by the duality of our mask/face metaphor, which splits us into an unconscious and a conscious component, private and public, natural and cultural, and which thereby divides the social performer into a mask of normality and a hidden fool lurking beneath. To the extent that it is our asocial (or antisocial or presocial) self that is participating in the theatrical event, the comedy works as a ventilation for normally inhibited irrational impulses. Inasmuch as our vision is refracted and distorted by the social mask we wear, we are more likely to mock the abnormality, scorn and disparage it: alternatively we will go hot under our prudishly self-righteous collars, be outraged, shocked and dismayed, and lament the decline in standards of entertainment.

The comic may act as an escape from the social norm in diverse manners: its nonsensical irrationality may satisfy a playful sense of irrationality in the audience, the grotesqueness of comedy may function as a temporary release from the aesthetic mask requiring people to conceal their "ugliness," its aggression and sexuality may subvert moral standards, and the power relations depicted within the fictional performance may implicitly upend the political hierarchy structuring a particular society. Before turning to these specific aspects of comedy in the following chapters, the present chapter will be concerned with the way in which *identification* with some or all of the fictional fools may work as a vicarious holiday for the fool within us.

The at/with dichotomy has given rise to two major categories of comic theory, the first seeing the genre as a pillorying of some deficiency or error regarded as foolish, a normative social weapon (which consequently assumes the acceptance of the norm by the mocker), the second relating comedy to festive rejoicing, a joyful, convivial (and potentially subversive) context in which fooling is the order of the day.[2] The division is not an arbitrary interpretation of a single type of comedy, but corresponds to two impulses—distinct, if always latently copresent—within the comic canon itself. In the English tradition, for example, the classical corrective brand of comedy produced by Ben Jonson stands in opposition to the more romantic, conciliatory, and celebratory comedy of the early Shakespeare (even though Jonson's plays themselves can by no means be dissociated from a carnival context). One might further rephrase the distinction as one between a general suspension of the norm and a (more or less localized) distortion of the norm,[3] between an intentional discarding of the social mask and a faulty wearing of it. If we laugh *with* the licensed folly, unlicensed folly is something to be laughed *at*.

It is clear that central to the whole discussion is the notion of folly or madness, scorned by one comic moment, celebrated by the other. Joubert's *Traité du Ris* (1579), which among other things draws attention to the laughter provoked by a sudden revelation of the shameful parts and by the sight of someone taking a tumble, also depicts insanity as a cause of amusement. "Similarly, if a man who has become phrenetic or manic says and does anything foolish, then we cannot help but laugh, unless it be that we recall to mind the loss he has suffered of sense and understanding."[4] Madness is here recognized as the object of a normative mockery directed at what is seen to be a defect or deformity, even though pity may step in like a censorious party pooper to mar our mirth. In the same century, however, Rabelais and Erasmus had rejoiced in madness and folly in works permeated by the spirit of carnival.

A notoriously fluid notion, folly is inherently resistant to all attempts to contain, delimit, or control it by the rationalizing and beautifying eye of the beholder. The metaphor, therefore, offers a number of approaches to the phenomenon:

1. A fool is one who does not wear the social "mask" of decorum or normality, or who does so only intermittently. Naive people, child-like adults, people who in some way are unable or unwilling to play the social game, who say what they mean or who do what they want regardless of what is "done", all these are fools. Svejk, Candide, Justine, and young Simplicissimus stumble ingenuously into this category of folly. One of the most important criteria defining the image of the medieval court-fool, both natural and artificial, was that, because of a frankness uninhibited by social convention, he could be relied upon to *tell the truth*.[5] It is this cultural nakedness that generates a sense of the fool as someone different, abnormal, standing outside the order of the cultural system, yet that simultaneously engenders the notion of the wise fool. The other side of this coin is the classical association of madness with bestiality or animality.[6] Dispossessing him of that which is specifically human (his powers of reason and understanding), madness reduces man to the "zero degree of his own nature," to an untamed beast controllable (as classical thought would have it) only by incarceration and brutalization.

2. Related to the notion of a fool or madman ignorant of the mask of

social etiquette is the "fool" who self-consciously *rejects* the social mask: the anarchist, the glutton, the wastrel, and the rogue. Falstaff is the epitome of the roguishly amoral fool; less lovable is the shite-eating sadist Père Ubu. Fools of this order are sinners and devils when seen negatively, but are not far from the artificial court-fool, who was often equally self-conscious in his truthful folly, or from unfoolishly "admirable" individualists.

3. The mask of normality can furthermore be seen as coterminous with the cognitive mask that structures how we perceive both the world in general and our social interaction within that world. The capacity to play the social game, in other words, depends on a (dispositional, but not necessarily formulated or self-conscious) *knowledge* of how to play it. At a social level, therefore, the fool is someone who knows less than we do. By extension, fool may be synonymous with gull or dupe, i.e., someone who is *fooled* or deceived by a rogue, knave, or trickster and who is unable to tell fiction from reality. Madness has likewise frequently been interpreted as a vulnerability to delusion, classical thought seeing in both mania and melancholia a confusion of appearance and reality. Traditionally at least, lovers make ideal fools and madmen for—wandering around with most of their organs of sensory perception in the clouds—they are mono-manic prey to the distortive and transformative power of their pas-sion. Paranoia (in its common sense) is a particular sort of delusion that is a reversal of the above: instead of gullibly treating the fictional or illusory as if it were real, paranoia assumes that what is real is an illusion, seeing in every face a mask, in every person a persona. Laing describes the state of "ontological insecurity" that can engender chronic schizophrenia and other psychoses as a con-dition in which a person lacks "a sense of his presence in the world as a real, alive, whole, and in a temporal sense, a continuous per-son."[7] The schizophrenic has a heightened awareness of his own fictionality and of the theatricality of all social behavior.

4. A self-deceiver is a fool who deludes himself about himself, a form of folly frequently consisting in the monomanic self-imposition of a given role or behavioral straitjacket. This consequently manifests itself as an extension and perversion of patterns of behavior to which people normally conform less obtrusively, as when, for ex-ample, the need for monetary exchange is transmuted (by ag-gressive self-interest) into avarice, or when "normal" self-respect turns into vanity and pretension. The distortion of perspective im-plied by self-deception tends to mean that self-deceivers are not only their own fools, but—viewing society at large through warped lenses—are prey to all kinds of knavery and trickery. They are in-

clined either to gullibility (witness the misers outwitted by Volpone) or to paranoia (Harpagon suspecting that the whole world harbors a hidden desire to get their fingers on his hoard of treasure). The delusions of madness are likewise frequently compounded by a monomanic fixity that insists on attaching reality to the flow of images to which it is prey. The madman demonstrates a rational consistency in his irrationality. Foucault writes: "The man who imagines he is made of glass is not mad, for any sleeper can have this image in a dream; but he is mad if, believing he is made of glass, he thereby concludes that he is fragile, that he is in danger of breaking, that he must touch no object which might be too resistant, that he must in fact remain motionless.... Madness, then, is not altogether in the image, which of itself is neither true nor false, neither reasonable nor mad; nor is it, further, in the reasoning which is mere form, revealing nothing but the indubitable figures of logic. And yet madness is in one and in the other: in a special version or figure of their relationship."[8]

5. Corresponding to the proclivity of self-deceivers to be deceived by others is the comic truth that *rogues* are liable to meet their comeuppance in being transformed from deceivers of others into self-deceivers, the monomanic knave finding himself turned into a dupe during the course of an ironic plot, outdone by some wittier or more flexible knave, just as Volpone is outfoxed by Mosca. This comic tendency has its metaphysical echo in the medieval Christian truth that it is foolish to be a rogue anyway. Brant's *Narrenschiff* (1494) contains a cargo of such rogues and sinful fools. After all, come the glorious day, a particularly all-encompassing irony of events will prove Christian fools to have been a good deal wiser than the worldly-wise knaves whose knavery initially seemed to have been the cleverer choice.

6. The hidden wisdom of the fool is further hinted at by the contact often enjoyed by the comic clown with the audience. In this capacity the fool seems to be nothing less than a mediator between "worlds."

By these criteria everyone is a fool (several times over), and there is indeed a danger that if folly is universal it is also meaningless. Of course, in late medieval and Renaissance times especially, folly *was* seen as universal, and, via the influence of Cusanus and Erasmus, this perspective was to have a profound effect not only on the comedy of Rabelais but arguably also on the conciliatory comedy of Shakespeare. Like the French noun *folie* the term *folly* assumed an enormous breadth, incorporating:

1. madness, mental derangement, and insanity
2. behavior regarded as vain, improvident, and frivolous
3. sin and satanic pride
4. the natural human condition affecting man as indiscriminately as death
5. sexual excitement and love
6. Christian (or Socratic) wise folly, not to mention
7. the artificial or acted folly of the court-fool.[9]

Two distinctions have been of particular import, however. First, even within a context of universal folly, it has generally been considered possible to differentiate "natural" folly from evil or wicked folly, where the former gives rise to collusive mirth and the latter corrective scorn. Clearly, if nature is wicked, the distinction collapses. Second, within the pantheon of fools exist subcategories considered wiser than the rest: namely, the self-aware Socratic or Christian fool whose knowledgeable ignorance has a practical analogue in the feigned folly of the court-fool, the tactical madness that (on occasion) allowed the expression of wisdom.

When the empathetic laughter at or with folly is seen in terms of the absence or discarding of the social mask (as is primarily the case in this chapter), it presupposes a self that is split into private and public (sub-) selves. The private part struggles for personal sensual satisfaction, egoistically removing any constraints and obstacles to its own short-term hedonistic happiness. The social persona by contrast is governed by moral and cultural norms, by long-term considerations of prudence, and by a concern for the approval of fellow human beings; in a sense it has the status of a mask hiding "the way we really are." In watching an anarchic or hedonistic "fool" on stage, it is argued, we give vicarious vent to our private self. This theory poses problems, however, that require brief consideration before turning to the fools themselves.

Role theorists (amongst others) maintain that the idea of a private core within a person is a fiction: the inner, "true" self, they claim, cannot be separated from the rest of our role-playing, for the human being is a social actor not by choice but by definition. It would be misguided, therefore, to regard (for instance) the act of coition as a pure, presocial expression of an entity called human nature, both partners baring their true selves and shedding all social artifice. Even sex, which seems the most natural of acts, is itself necessarily ritualized and institutionalized and is radically histrionic. It is not an escape to the private(s), nor a salubrious regression to our precultural birthday suits, but always some sort of role or act. Angela Carter gets to the point with polemical bite: "We may believe we fuck stripped of social artifice; in bed, we even feel we touch the

bedrock of human nature itself. But we are deceived. Flesh is not an ir-
reducible human universal. Although the erotic relationship may seem to
exist freely, on its own terms, among the distorted social relationships of
a bourgeois society, it is, in fact, the most self-conscious of all human relationships, a direct confrontation of two beings whose actions in the bed
are wholly determined by their acts when they are out of it."[10]

A number of comic authors have depicted the inevitable theatricality of
spontaneity and naturalness, but it is Wilde's Lord Henry who phrases
this awareness as lucidly as any: "Being natural is simply a pose, and the
most irritating pose I know."[11] Amis's figure Charles Highway (who on
one occasion congratulates himself that an encounter "couldn't have
been more spontaneous if I had planned it") self-consciously *feigns*
spontaneity in his conduct with the opposite sex, the conjunction of intention and involuntariness creating a tension that runs through the
novel. One intimate meeting with Rachel, for example, "seemed totally
spontaneous. I moved closer, intending to seize her hand with involuntary
earnestness." When his mate Geoffrey advocates "being yourself" he
rejoins: "Who ever acts naturally with a girl? Do you think you do? How
much of the time isn't it lovable vague Mandied Geoffrey, or big-cock
groover Geoffrey, or just plain old honest-to-goodness *Geoffrey*, who
doesn't put on any acts or play any games?"[12] If everyday delusions of
spontaneity correspond to the sort of (illusionistic) acting that hides or
forgets its theatricality, Charles Highway's self-aware, planned im-
pulsiveness is its metatheatrical development, for he is too conscious of
his own nature as an actor (social and literary) to be able to lead his life
as anything other than a self-referential comedy.

McFadden's parody of psychobabble, *The Serial*, satirizes the outlook
so prevalent in the United States of the seventies which espoused a return
to being natural, to being oneself. The very formulation of naturalness as
a creed plunges it into a yawning paradox: "Everybody knew, in these
days of heightened consciousness, that the rational mind was a screw-up;
the really authentic thing to do was to act on your impulses."[13] A twentieth-century Lord Henry would have countered that being authentic is a
screw-up too, and a particularly irritating one at that. McFadden's figures
wish to strip themselves of all social artifice, but become ridiculous in so
doing because—self-deceivers that they are—they ignore that their being
natural is but an act. They are taken in by their own role-playing, lacking
the ironic self-distance to notice how histrionic they are.

Acting can thus be understood to permeate even our most genuine and
private moments. If the theatrical actor who feigns spontaneity or pretends to deviate from his script does not ultimately escape from his
theatrical part and even genuine improvization remains framed within the
defining context of theatrical performance, then this—so the role theorist

might claim—reflects the existential fact that any apparent escape from social role-playing can never be more than just another kind of role. Doing what seems natural is no gesture of self-unmasking that reveals the "truth" about ourselves any more than Pulcinella pissing in public was a genuine respite from his theatrical role. Yet the role theorist's perspective is of course not the whole story, for it is the product of just one level of analysis. Just as the theatrical actor participates simultaneously both in a real and a pretend world and illusion-breaking self-reference and improvization in particular show him both as an actor and as a character, so the social actor embodies an essential duality. Not only is he a role-player within the social drama, therefore, he is also (seen from a different level) an autonomous subject endowed with the capacity to query, to negate, as it were to stand "outside" the social system—even if without finally being able to leave his own performance behind.

The mask metaphor should not, therefore, necessarily imply a single "natural" face behind the social mask. This is clearly a myth, albeit a useful one for explaining how we tend to see comedy: the comic fool is being "himself," behaving "naturally," airing his "true" instincts. What the metaphor can equally be used to suggest is that any social mask comprises a homogenizing restriction and patterning of behavior and that, in presenting itself as a normal identity, it hides the infinite potential for deviation and difference, the possibilities for saying *no* and denying the norm. Behaving foolishly is in these terms not so much doing what comes naturally as negating the social order or breaking taboo: folly is a manifestation of social negativity. Sex itself is neither comic nor foolish when unthinkingly performed within the orthodoxy of the system (which is not to say that it is not a laugh for those having it); yet it enters the realm of folly when it rears its head out of place or in unusual fashion, as when the naughty Winnebago Trickster—in fact more of a fool than a trickster—breaks with custom by cohabiting with a woman *before* going on a warpath. Correspondingly, as puns and verbal inversions have shown, *speaking* foolishly consists in uttering profanities, speaking the unspeakable, saying what cannot be said, negating the "truth," contradicting the tautological.

Structuralism has consequently seen in madness a kind of cultural unconscious comprising the discourse deemed irrelevant and unmentionable within the terms of the set of linguistic practices constitutive of social and cultural activity. Foucault's study of madness indeed implicitly raises the question whether madness can be understood even in principle, since all that rational discourse has access to is images and descriptions useful essentially for its suppression or marginalization. If the attempt to translate the unintelligible merely reproduces the discourse of the dominant and domineering sanity, the excluded "other" remains fundamentally silent, a silence figured by the classical confinement that sought to conceal lunatics from the public eye (and manifested in such pronouncements as Mirabeau the Younger's "those who have lost the use of reason must be hidden from society"). *Pure* madness is indeed as unknowable as the Freudian unconscious or the Kantian thing-in-itself, because it can only ever be seen through the lenses of rational understanding. Negativity thus falls foul of the same paradox that confronts the notion of the natural. In its self-realization, it might be argued, the negative is necessarily "positivized" into an affirmative act: that which is not done *is* done. Foucault writes: "The paradox of this *nothing* [madness] is to *manifest* itself, to explode in signs, in words, in gestures.... For madness, if it is nothing, can manifest itself only by departing from itself, by assuming an appearance in the order of reason and thus becoming the contrary of itself. Which illuminates the paradoxes of the classical experience: madness is always absent, in a perpetual retreat where it is inaccessible, without phenomenal or positive character; and yet it is present and perfectly visible in the singular evidence of the madman.... All that madness can say of itself is merely reason, though it is itself the negation of reason."[14]

Seen as negativity, madness is a signal of a radical otherness or difference phenomenally present only as an absence, a nothing. It is perhaps partly for this reason that medieval comic fools regularly had names denoting their negativity, names such as Nought in *Mankind*, Monsieur Rien in the *Sottie pour le cry de la Bazoche*, while Rien, in *La Farce Nouvelle de Tout, Rien, Chascun*, represents Folly in the guise of Death, its conceptual sibling in unknowability. The fool is a nothing, as windily empty as the bellows from which he is etymologically descended. His name points to the absence of sense he incorporates, the nothingness of nonsense. For Foucault, it is specifically the classical confinement of madness that relegates it out of existence,[15] but it may equally well be seen as an essential characteristic of reason in general to strive to reduce its opposite to nothing. In this case, confinement becomes an overt symbol of the more insidiously authoritarian activity necessarily constitutive of reason's very structure.

Yet *pure* folly—as *pure* otherness or nothingness—is a theoretical fiction and, as such, has a tendency to be as misleading as Kant's unknowable thing-in-itself or as the word "nothing" when hypostatized by philosophers and theologians, the denotations creating the verbal delusion of a type of something. Instead of the inference that madness simply cannot be comprehended in its purity, it seems more profitable to suggest that—for all the endeavors of reason to reduce its other to silence—madness in practice necessarily coexists in a relationship of mutual interaction with the sanity that would gag it. Reciprocal mimicry is the primary point of intersection, folly imitating the language of normality and vice versa in a world permeated not by the single autocratic voice of reason but by a medley of heterogeneous discursive types. Rationality is "infected" by what it purports to exclude, just as madness apes the discourse that seeks to master and exclude it. Thus, while comedy is on the one hand characterizable as a disruption of social role-playing that reveals an antisocial core, it is equally permissible to speak of an interplay of different *sorts* of role if even madness is an act.

This is exemplified by the monomanic method inherent in much madness. Gogol's "Diary of a Madman" brilliantly portrays the logic of the insane perspective in the figure of the "madman" Poprishchin, who deludes himself he is the King of Spain. When the sight of his signature (as Ferdinand VIII) stuns his (former) work colleagues into a bewildered silence, he merely waves his hand and makes a regal exit with the comment "There's really no need for this show of loyalty," and, with like fixity, he interprets his transportation to the asylum as a flight to Spain and the farcical beatings he receives for his recalcitrance as some sort of initiation test for a future king:

> A strange country, Spain: in the first room I entered there were a lot of people with shaven heads.... But the way one of the government chancellors treated me was strange in the extreme. He took me by the arm and pushed me into a small room, saying: "Sit there, and if you call yourself King Ferdinand once more, I'll thrash that nonsense out of you." But as I knew that this was just some sort of test I refused, for which the chancellor struck me twice on the back, so painfully that I nearly cried out.[16]

Madness and self-deception of this order is based on the donning of a monomanic mask and the obsessively consistent logic of this identity. Don Quixote's delusion that he is a chivalric hero is likewise only relinquished at the point of his death. Indeed, playing along with the delusions of madness in the way that the good-natured Spanish nobles humor the Don even came to be employed as a cure for insanity, the logic of the position ironically leading the victim back to the ways of common sense. Foucault cites the case, also recounted in more exhaustive detail in the eighteenth-century comedy *Jeppe from the Hill* by the Danish playwright Ludvig Holberg, of the patient who—in the belief that he was dead—really was dying from not eating:

> A group of people who had made themselves pale and were dressed like the dead entered his room, set up a table, brought food, and began to eat and drink before the bed. The starving "dead man" looked at them; they were astonished that he stayed in bed; they persuaded him that dead people eat at least as much as living ones. He readily accommodated himself to this idea.[17]

Madness is indeed often so patently histrionic that the bounds between mimicry and madness are blurred if not completely indistinct. R. D. Laing's phenomenology of schizophrenia, for example, sees the original schizoid condition from which the ensuing psychosis may develop as the consequence of a self-division on the part of the schizoid person into a true and a false self, which differentiates the "persona" put on for social performance (in order to appear in compliance with the expectations or intentions of others) from the hidden noncorporeal self. Interestingly, the development from a schizoid condition to schizophrenia illustrates the inadequacy of an understanding of the self based upon a duality of truth and falseness, inner and outer. With time, the pure potential of the true self comes to be experienced increasingly as an absence, as anyone in fantasy but nobody in reality, and the concomitant schizophrenic sense of being "no-one" or of having no identity may then be literalized into the psychotic "death" of catatonia:

> If all the individual's behaviour comes to be compulsively alienated from the secret self so that it is given over entirely to compulsive mimicry, impersonating, caricaturing, and to ... transitory behavioural foreign bodies as well, he may then try to strip himself of all his behaviour. This is one form of catatonic withdrawal.[18]

Spending his life just pretending, the schizoid person is inclined to become more and more obsessively parodic until he finds he has no "real" self that is doing the pretending or parodying; this is when psychosis may set in.

The histrionic nature of schizophrenia extends above all to the psychiatric clinic where schizophrenics often *play at being schizophrenic* as a mask to hide the privacy of their true self, as a preservation of that inner secrecy. "The schizophrenic is not going to reveal himself for casual inspection and examination to any philandering passer-by. If the self is not known it is safe."[19] In *Self and Others*, Laing puts it from the point of view of the psychiatrist: "We are not convinced that all people who act in a psychotic way are 'true' schizophrenics, or 'true' manics, or 'true' melancholics, although the 'true' schizophrenic is not always easily distinguishable from the person we feel can dramatize himself into a counterfeit madness, because we tend to impute psychosis to the man who pretends to be psychotic. The act of pretence itself, if carried to extremes in that direction, tends to be regarded as mad in itself."[20] Once again, acting and madness reveal their proximity.

Just as madness has a tendency to mime the logic and speech of sanity, sanity in its turn has often been compelled to don the mantle of madness in order to articulate the home truths that could not otherwise be said with impunity. But, whereas the French medieval tradition frequently distinguished between the *fou* and the *sot*—the former referring to mental illness, the latter to one who feigns *folie* in order to enjoy the immunity enjoyed by the *fou*[21]—the English word "fool" denotes both the natural and the artificial varieties, as a result of which historians of folly are hard pressed to ascertain whether specific court-fools were *fous* or *sots*. This difficulty poignantly comes to light in Angela Carter's novel *Nights at the Circus*, in which she self-consciously develops the association between clowning and folly in a description of the clowns' quarters:

> Clown Alley, the generic name of all lodgings of all clowns, ... was a place where reigned the lugubrious atmosphere of a prison or a mad-house; amongst themselves, the clowns distilled the same kind of mutilated patience one finds among inmates of closed institutions, a willed and terrible suspension of being. At dinner time, the white faces gathered round the table ... possessed the formal lifelessness of death masks, as if, in some essential sense, they themselves were absent from the repast and left untenanted replicas behind.[22]

The clowns' sustained feigning of folly seems to mask a tragic absence or lack that is evident only to the privileged reader who witnesses them being "themselves" among themselves. It has its dangers too: Buffo the Clown's real fit of madness goes unnoticed amidst the merriness of the other clowns' acted madness. During the euphoria of performance, genuine folly generates the same mirth as the standard antics of circus foolery, the audience remaining oblivious to the pathos of an identity in the throes of chronic dissolution.

The difficulties that arise in the attempt to differentiate "acted" from "genuine" folly are made more acute by the perspective that universalizes role-playing, a perspective that, in practical terms, gets us no further than the corresponding universalization of folly. If we are not careful, we are likely to end up with the claim that human beings are always necessarily actors (i.e., always "performing") and are always necessarily fools, which may be part of the truth about our existential condition, but is also a rather vacuous assertion and not particularly helpful. In practical terms, two main criteria are of especial use in ascertaining "degrees" of folly. On the one hand, the putative level of "self-awareness" underlying the folly is of import in judging how "deep" it goes. The "sinful" folly resulting from a "defect of character" or the insanity arising from a "mental defect" is thus regarded in a different light from the self-conscious lunacy of a comic hero. If naive folly is viewed as the product of ignorance, moreover, and the deviation from normality as fortuitous rather than intentional, tactical folly is a dramatic ploy arising from precisely the opposite, and may be employed as an explicit critique of that norm (not merely an implicit one as with naivety). Even within the sphere of celebratory folly, sociologists have distinguished "liminal" festive observances (such as rites of separation, transition, or incorporation), which may often comprise reversals of secular reality or inversions in the social structure, from "liminoid" phenomena typified by the carnival of industrial and postindustrial societies, which are fragmentary and decentred rather than collective and in which the inversion is more likely to be potentially subversive in nature.[23] While the relatively nonreflective perpetuation of a tradition of folly offers a welcome release from bondage to reason and order, it is clearly of a different order from the more purposive and self-conscious variants, which, parodying or deflating the *excesses* of reason, are likely to be motivated by a rationality of their own. If uncritical folly may be enjoyed on its own account as a holiday from sanity while simultaneously being disparaged or mocked (from the perspective of rational thought) for its unthinking simplicity, critical foolery likewise performs a precarious balancing act between the impulse to escape from reason and the sort of rationality, perspicacity, or truthfulness that may well arouse applause or admiration.

A second point of relevance here is the *context* in which the folly rears its bauble, for, in a world where all social intercourse may be interpreted as performance, *practical* determinations of play amount above all to a way of looking at or appraising a phenomenon within a situational framework, not an attribute inherent in the phenomenon itself. Consequently, categories of folly may be classified in the light of whether they are viewed as constituting a threat or not (be it to the individual or to the social whole), or alternatively according to whether they are in some way cordoned off from the sanity of reality by means of a play-frame. Ritual folly is correspondingly to be held apart from those "outbursts" of folly which have not been framed off or allocated a specific duration and location and thus tamed or rendered harmless (in theory at least). In this, it amounts to a socialization of the antisocial, an institutionalization of that which resists institutions, an acting out of the unrepresentable.

The folly and madness that takes place on the theatrical stage is an act in an even more fundamental sense. More so than ritual, comedy constitutes a form of ordered disorder, structured anarchy. It is a mimicry of madness, even if the act of miming (and the accompanying "confusion" of appearance and reality) may become a kind of madness of its own, a point that again spotlights the inextricability—or perhaps the kinship—of madness and theatre. The vicarious theatrical folly that appeals to the anarchist and the fool in us is always very much a *displaced* folly, a displacement that works on three levels at least.

First, like carnival and popular festivity, comedy is folly transposed to an overtly ludic context. Just as carnival is (or used to be) a temporary release from the pressures of the socio-political order, a licensed but brief period of disorder, so comedy too is temporally (and locally) defined and delimited. A spectacle of comic folly lasts no longer than the play in which it occurs and is restricted to the locality of the theatre. If the play itself occurs within a celebratory context, as was the case with Shakespearean and Aristophanic drama, the boundaries of the folly are blurred but still unlikely to exceed the duration of the festivity of which it forms a part. This comic/festive context creates a set of expectations that allow the spectators/participants to order or align the folly and abnormality within the system of rational normality. Deviation is thereby recognized as deviation and given a significance as such with the aid of criteria imported from the real world. Madness is seen either as a flight from staid sanity or as a mirror to the folly of a corrupt, sinful, or frivolous world. Just as a certain type of bad acting yields the paradoxical gratification of expecting the unexpected (when the wobbly mask slips), the ordered disorder of communal festivity generates the same paradoxical anticipation of the surprising. Carnival is a time when we *expect* the badly fitting and itchy social mask to go for a burton: the eccentric conduct of the comic rogue-fool likewise reassures us by being classifiable as play. Even that ubiquitous mininarrative the joke—with its bawdy or seditious irreverence—works along the same lines, the punch line being the most self-evident case of expecting the unexpected. "I say, I say, I say" for a long time served as the most common metasignal, and nudges in the ribs as well as collusive winks are perennial play-signs indicating the joke context and immediately transposing what is said into the ambivalent realm of fun and jesting. Clearly some of the "this is play" metasignals are subject to the same semantic ambiguity as the Cretan's claim that Cretans are liars, and not all of them are equally successful or credible. If the initial play-signs are absent or should happen to be overlooked or ignored, the tactically clumsy joketeller is normally forced to backpedal with a retrospective play-signal such as "I was only joking ..." in order to avoid being taken for a real fool or being bopped on the nose by the dullard who took the joke literally. Like carnival play, jokes and humor stand in a metaphorical relationship to reality, as a "suspension of being" where folly can have its say.

Second, and unlike carnival and plebeian culture, the comic theatre depends upon a displacement from active and universal madness to a more passive observation of it that generates mirth by empathetic identification rather than by firsthand activity. The violence of farce, for example, does not yield the immediate gratification obtained by thuggishly working someone over whom we don't like; instead, it confers the pleasure of seeing someone else doing the hitting (as well as the security of not being hit back). It is likewise this aesthetic distance that allows for the perception of the temporal and local delimitation of the context, imparting meaning to the disorder on account of its difference from the order outside. The participatory nature of active celebration, by contrast, tends more often to swallow its revelers up in the intoxication of folly, discouraging detached spectatorship. For its duration, as Bakhtin put it, carnival *is* reality. Art necessarily implies a compromise between order and chaos as soon as it defines itself as art, for definition entails a localization within a wider context, and pure disorder can assume significance within the framework of order constituted by the outside social world. Even the most radical of antidrama (for instance, Ionesco's *La Cantatrice chauve*), indeed even such rampantly nonsensical drivelings as *Vaseline Symphonique* by the Dadaist Tristan Tzara ("a cacophony of inarticulate sounds, performed by an ensemble advertised as twenty strong"[24]) can therefore—from the distance of the spectator's seat—be framed as an aesthetic happening and thereby ordered and given a meaning, albeit only the minimal meaning of anti-art. The literary theorist Culler, who explains comedy in terms of a set of generic expectations,[25] defines the expectation-generating conventions of a genre as "ways of naturalizing the text and giving it a place in the world which our culture defines"; in other words, "the strange or deviant is brought within a discursive order and thus made to seem natural."[26] If the acausal and illogical events of Ionesco's play, typified by the random striking of the cuckoo clock, were to occur in the real world, our lack of distance (i.e., our "participation" in the real world) would be likely to hinder our ordering of the experience: we should be afraid and not amused, doubt our senses, seek supernatural causes, or perhaps retrospectively (i.e., with temporal distance) try to explain it away. Watching a comedy, and especially an avant-garde one, we expect the unexpected, and the possibility of discomfiture caused by novelty and surprise is nipped in the bud. Even the raving gibberish of Dada is not without sense: its meaning is the opposition in which it stands to all conventional and traditional (i.e., above all naturalistic and mimetic) art and communication. Aesthetic distance thus ensures that the madness remain unthreatening, and, should human folly turn up in its wicked, malevolent, or sinful guise, comedy has a habit of intervening to remind us that it is only a play and thereby preventing the malice from becoming frightening rather than funny.

Third, folly is structured and regulated within the aesthetic event itself. Once again, the analogy with carnival is enlightening, for such festivity, being institutionalized madness, is also ordered, ritualized madness. The upturning of the social order brings with it a special kind of order (not pure anarchy or chaos), incorporating the king of carnival and a new inverted hierarchy. While parodying the old order and relativizing the status of order in general, the reversed structure still depends for its comic effect upon the recognition of patterns and ironic shifts. Bakhtin's description of medieval carnival emphasizes this "reversal of the hierarchic levels: the jester was proclaimed king, a clownish abbot, bishop or archbishop was elected at the 'feast of fools,' and in the churches directly under the pope's jurisdiction a mock pontiff was even chosen.... From the wearing of clothes inside out and trousers slipped over the head to the election of mock kings and popes the same topographical logic is at work: shifting from top to bottom, casting the high and the old, the finished and completed into the material bodily lower stratum for death and rebirth."[27] The topsy-turvy world or world upside-down (*die verkehrte Welt*) is indeed an age-old symbol of universal folly, while individual fools have regularly demonstrated their craft by turning things on their heads, inverting values, reversing relationships and orders. Erasmus's celebrated fool by the name of Stultitia or Folly advocates folly instead of wisdom. The fool Panurge displays his not inconsiderable sleight of tongue in praising debt as opposed to solvency, and Falstaff eulogizes wine at the expense of sobriety. Schelling indeed saw reversal as central to the comic moment ("the upturning of every possible relationship based upon opposition"[28]), while A. W. Schlegel perceived an inversion in the normal master-slave relationship holding between reason and the passions to be essential to comedy. *A Midsummer Night's Dream* portrays the folly of love as possessing a power of reversal that could equally apply to carnival—"Things base and vile, holding no quantity, / Love can transpose to form and dignity" (1.1)—and Sancho Panza describes the madness of that archfool Don Quixote as being the sort of state of mind that "thinks white black and black white."[29] The world of folly, where folly is wise and wisdom foolish, is a realm in which illusion is real and the real is illusory: these two fundamental reversals lie at the heart of the topsy-turviness of comedy.

Comedy also displaces the anarchy it internalizes by transposing its sexuality, irreverence, and irrationality into their verbal equivalents (bawdy puns, aggressive wit, verbal euphoria). This does not amount merely to the truism that actions speak louder than words or that sublimating our sexuality in jokes about sex is a poor second-best for the real two-backed McCoy and the verbal aggression of theatrical satire a rather tame surrogate for the immediacy of actual G. B. H. Briefly stated, the point is perhaps also that articulation is itself a mode of ordering the disorderly, of enclosing the antisocial, the chaotic, or the unintelligible within the structures of verbal signification, just as the word "nothing" is liable to reify nothing into a sort of something. The comic dramatist Dürrenmatt makes a similar point in drawing an analogy between comic drama and the dirty joke:

We can see how comedy works even in the most primitive form of the joke, the dirty joke [*die Zote*], a dubious affair to be sure, which I only mention because it most clearly illustrates what I call the creating of distance. The dirty joke takes as its object the purely sexual, which—because it is the purely sexual—is also formless, distanceless and, if it is to assume shape, turns into nothing other than the dirty joke. The dirty joke is therefore an archetypal comedy, a transposition of the sexual onto the level of the comic.... The dirty joke makes it clear that the comic consists in the shaping of the shapeless, the fashioning of the chaotic.[30]

The comic emerges from a chiaroscuro of order and chaos, a *domestication* of folly or madness typified in the habit even madness has of becoming predictable and thereby reassuringly classifiable. Jouvet described Molière's fools as "des déraisonnables qui raisonnent dans la déraison"[31]—unreasoning fools "who reason in their unreason"—but the point is illustrated even more graphically by the measured symmetry of the tit for tat logic informing Laurel and Hardy's systematic trashing of James Finlayson's house in *Big Business*. Whereas Kant had certainly recognized part of the truth in his formulation that "in anything which is to make one shake with vigorous laughter, there must be an element of nonsense (something which does not meet with the approval of the Understanding [*der Verstand*] in itself),"[32] the philosopher von Hartmann was justified in complementing this with the stipulation that "the dissolution of nonsense must leave some sense intact or allow some to remain in evidence"[33] if the effect is to be truly comic. Comic folly always has a wisdom of its own; there is a logic inherent in comic madness.

A Mad World

Comedy may either concentrate its folly in a single character or group of characters or create a context of universal folly. It is the latter that serves as the greater incitement to vicarious celebration, but a number of moments may be discerned here, not all of which are equally celebratory.

Most obviously revelrous are comedies such as those of Aristophanes, which cannot be seen as separate from the Dionysian festivals at which they were performed, the German *Fastnachtspiele* or carnival plays, and Shakespeare's early comedies, which formed a part of the native English equivalents of saturnalian celebration, May games, and feasts of misrule. Such comedies were themselves constitutive of a holiday humor in which licensed folly was the order of the day, showing their debt to their context in a variety of ways. Aristophanic comedy, for example, regularly integrates festive song and dance performed by the chorus *within* the comedy itself, as well as making metatheatrical references to the judges at the festival. (In *The Birds*, the Chorus promises not to attack Euelpides and Peisthetaerus but only on condition that the play win first prize unanimously.) This metatheatrical moment is related to the carnival blurring of the distinction between art and life, and in Beaumont's *Knight of the Burning Pestle*, a revelry that is presumed to have been written for May Day, it is juxtaposed with the inversion of hierarchical order characteristic of carnival as Rafe—one of the lowlier members of the audience—takes the stage and steals the show. Inversions in the social order, boisterous sexuality, and ritual abuse (sometimes) are all features common in varying degrees to both carnival and festive comedy, where communal celebration functions as a collective unmasking of social artifice or restraint. The verbal accumulation of the French medieval *sottie* and of Rabelais can likewise be seen equally well as a verbal analogue to the processions of carnival and as an ecstatic reenactment of the euphoric folly of merry-making. This is especially the case when the verbal deluge is located somewhere in the gastronomical or anatomical sphere, for carnival and festive comedy represent reversals not merely in the social order (as fools become kings and masters servants), but also in the relation between reason and nature, the rational faculty finding itself transformed by folly into the slave of the senses. The comic novels of Rabelais and Cervantes indeed prove to be directly influenced by and suffused with the carnival folklore out of which they sprung.[34] In Rabelais's case, this is exemplified by the sausage war, the battle-cum-banquet taking place in the *Quart Livre* (chs. 35–42) harking back to the cheerfully excremental foodfights in such carnival plays as *La bataille de Sainct Pensard* (1485). *Don Quixote* too contains scenes modeled on carnival festivities, above all the episodes occurring at the inn and at the castle of the Duke and Duchess, where disguises, deceptions, confusions, inversions, and beatings are characteristically coupled with ceremony and show.

Shakespeare's Forest of Arden in *As You Like It* is the locus of a gentler folly than the raucously abusive and phallic anarchy of Dionysian ritual, recalling a saturnalian utopia of harmony and happiness, prosperity and plenitude. It is a place where the Duke and his merry men "live like the old Robin Hood of England" and are said to "fleet the time carelessly, as they did in the golden world" (1.1). Characterized by the same liberty from the briars of workaday inhibitions and limitations, it is primarily a folly of romance that calls the tune in Shakespeare's Green World, generating an aura of unreality that can house the magic of fairies no less than the silliness of lovers, poets, and madmen. Suspending disbelief in such a world, we may even see in it a symbol of that joy which Joyce described as the feeling proper to comic art: "A comedy ... which does not urge us to seek anything beyond itself excites in us the feeling of joy."[35] The folly is an end in itself, a release from the drudgery of ordered reality, and desirable for its own sake. It may be queried whether the context of universal folly is itself laughter-provoking, just as the point has frequently been made that Shakespeare's comedies tend (for the modern audience at least) not to be particularly *funny*. Indeed, laughter is more typically produced by an episodic or "paradigmatic" deviation from a norm than by the distance-creating framework as a whole, the "syntagmatic" plot that is its precondition.[36] Even so, when folly is universalized within a context, the contextual and the specific deviation tend to become indistinguishable. The whole setting of licensed madness is a temporally delimited deviation from the external norm, from the relentless logic and implacably dull sanity of the outside world. The world of folly in its entirety exists at one metaphoric remove from the noncomic real world.

Love is the archetype of joyful folly. *A Midsummer Night's Dream* is pervaded by universal folly, situating the fatuous blindness of the infatuated in the midst of the theatrical and social naivety of the Mechanicals and the misguided roguishness of the fairies who themselves forget that they are but "airy nothings" penned by a madman called Shakespeare (or was he???). A form of monomanic myopia, love has a transformative power similar to madness and poetry, as well as the carnival tendency to stand things on their head, embodied in the Fairy Queen's deluded passion for the asinine figure of Bottom, who himself has the insight to point out that "reason and love keep little company together nowadays" (3.1). The audience—exempt from the delusions of love and benefiting from the superiority of the theatrical perspective—is able to see through Queen Titania's self-deceptions, just as it maintains the overview during the course of the amorous fiasco caused by Puck and enacted between Helena, Hermia, Lysander, and Demetrius. *Twelfth Night* is likewise structured by universal folly, juxtaposing and playing off the folly of Malvolio's proud vanity, the confusions of the lovers, the vacuity of the fop Sir Andrew Aguecheek, the rumbustious excesses of the beer-swilling rake Sir Toby Belch, and the wise lunacy of the Clown Feste—a fellow "wise enough to play the fool" (as Viola recognizes) and who uses his fool's licence to mock the rest of the fools. Illyria, the play's setting, is "a country permeated with the spirit of the Feast of Fools, where identities are confused, 'uncivil rule' applauded, cakes and ale defended against virtue, and no harm done."[37] In *As You Like It*, another festive comedy informed by amorous folly, Rosalind expresses the lunacy of love in unambiguous terms: "Love is merely a madness, and I tell you, deserves as well a dark house and a whip as madmen do; and the reason why they are not so punish'd and cur'd is, that the lunacy is so ordinary, that the whippers are in love too" (3.2). The comedy is in a similar vein when, in a commedia dell'arte scenario called the *Enchanted Arcadia*,[38]

Pollicinella dons a magic garland that causes all those who see him to mistake him for their beloved. Like the spectator enjoying the disparity between appearance and reality, Pollicinella sits back and derides the derangement of the sequence of unfortunates who come and fall for him.

Just as self-deception often assumes the form of role-playing and cliché that is not aware of its own histrionic nature, love too becomes risible when it turns into trite and self-inflated sentimentality, as well as when its monomanic tunnel vision proves conducive to fancy and delusion. That love may be envisaged as a sort of theatrical performance not very successfully concealing the ulterior motivation of sex further reduces it to a tatty emotional G-string (barely) hiding what we all know to be at the back of everybody's mind anyway, a point seized upon by Shakespeare's old cynic Mercutio as he makes fun of Romeo's lolloping love-sickness: "For this drivelling love is like a great natural that runs lolling up and down to hide his bauble in a hole" (2.4). Considered as a mere front to fornication, love is comic not in its capacity as a hallucinogen but for the insistently bouncing bauble that inadvertently betrays itself.

The tradition of amorous folly, in evidence as much as eighteen centuries before Shakespeare (Plautus's crafty servant Pseudolus telling his infatuated master that a "lover must behave like a fool or there's no fun in it"), was perpetuated and modified after Shakespeare in the romantic comedies of Marivaux who, influenced by the commedia dell'arte, dropped the commedia's Pantalone and il Dottore and replaced them in the limelight by the lovers who had generally served as pallidly "normal" foils in the improvized Italian lunacy. The comic conflict became one of *raison* and *coeur*. The German Eichendorff, in his turn synthesizing the influences of Shakespeare and Marivaux, exploited a comic setting of role-playing, disguise, and universal folly to show the madness of love in a self-consciously theatrical world in which deluded figures fall in love with masks and illusions.

The intellectual heritage for the idea of the folly or madness of love can be traced back to Erasmus, whose character Folly claimed that "the propagator of the human race is that part which is so foolish and absurd that it can't be named without raising a laugh,"[39] and ultimately—transmitted via the Italian humanist Ficino—to Plato's *Phaedrus* and *Symposium*. Indeed, the spirit of Erasmus and his humanist predecessors seems to pervade Shakespeare's conciliatory awareness of man's natural imperfection. As in Rabelais and Cervantes, the festive impulse is thereby conjoined with the late medieval sense of the universality of folly, not merely in the context of merry-making but as an intrinsic aspect of the human condition. During the Renaissance, this conjunction of ideas meant that the words "Stultorum numerus infinitus" found their place in serious sermons and the mock-sermons of the fools' societies alike. This awareness need not, however, be conciliatory in nature: it may easily merge with a pessimistic sense of worldwide wickedness, of sin, malice, and deception. Such a bias does not necessarily exclude the folly from the realm of comedy. Even when watching an all-embracing network of knavery, we are still likely to identify with some rogues more than others, and the likeable or charismatic rogue may well appeal to the likeable rogue (we like to imagine) within us.

Developing from the French fools' societies, which reached a relatively high level of literate bourgeois organization, the French medieval *sottie* was based upon the same consciousness of ubiquitous unreason. These were short plays acted by a group of performers either dressed openly as fools or hiding their fool's costume until a moment of revelation, and they could combine both satirically critical comment on contemporary events and the verbal folly and celebratory clowning of festive comedy.[40] Dealing with the universal sway of Mother Folly (the star), the plays reduced the whole gamut of human types to a lowest common denominator of folly, with time becoming more and more bitterly satirical in response to a world they saw as mercenary and ruttish. The *Farce Nouvelle nommée la Folie des Gorriers* typifies the ethos of the plays, portraying two wastrels and would-be dandies who fall in love with a female figure—later to unveil herself as Folly—whose sway over them sends them both round the bend. Blurring the boundary between actor and audience, the *sots* also took pleasure in insulting the spectators, implicating them in the *sottise* of the world: during one play performed by the *Enfants de Bontemps* in Geneva in 1523, for example, a number of Mother Folly's attendant fools responded to a summons from their mistress by springing up from the audience and leaping onstage.[41] Just as the carnival plays influenced Rabelais's *Quart Livre*, it seems likely that the *sottie* was of substantial import for his *Tiers Livre*, which shares both its verbal exhileration and the theme of universal folly with these short bouts of dramatic lunacy.

The morality play or moral interlude was, in theory at least, significantly less comic than the *sottie*: an afterlife was seen to depend upon the good behavior of the protagonist whose pilgrimage through life's temptations was being depicted—even though the conventional guarantee of a happy ending did prevent the play from becoming too harrowingly pessimistic. As Sandra Billington has argued, however, the funniest of the English morality plays, *Mankind*, can itself be regarded as a type of "metaphysical *sottie*," an indication of the complexity of the phenomenon of folly.[42] Founded on the one hand on the medieval conviction that the sin of satanic pride is the archetype of folly while on the other hand presumably developing from the English tradition of fool activity (which in contrast to France remained mainly—surprise, surprise!—at the less sophisticated level of dance and riot), this play additionally seems to incorporate a figure of Christian folly in the figure of Mercy. The Vices (New-gyse, Nought, and Now-a-days) are clearly presented as rumbustious clodpates to be derided and scorned, but the goody-goody Mercy, come to save Mankind's spiritual skin, is likewise an object of ridicule, mocked by the Vices for his pompous Latinisms ("yowr body ys full of Englysch Laten," [line 124]), which they imitate and exaggerate. Condemning equally and without discrimination both sinful folly and festive folly, Mercy indeed becomes an *agroikos* figure,[43] a spoilsport possibly anticipating Shakespeare's Puritan fool Malvolio, and he exposes himself to the raillery of the fun-loving dunderheads by refusing to join in the merry-making and dancing ("Men have lytyll deynte of [pleasure in] yowr pley," they tell him, "Be-cause ye make no sporte" [ll.267–68]). Credit where credit's due, however, his Pauline folly does succeed in rescuing Mankind from sin and thereby procuring the happy ending.

The sway of universal folly is portrayed in a particularly sombre light in Sebastian Brant's *Narrenschiff* (1494), a systematic and not exceptionally funny catalogue of the world's madness, moralistic in tone and founded upon a basic equation of sin and folly. As in the *Hundert Ausbündigen Narren* written by the Viennese court chaplain Abraham a Santa Clara over two centuries later in 1709, all folly is pilloried as ungodly and wrong and in need, moreover, of a stiff measure of corporal correction: wastrels and beggars should be taught the meaning of a hard day's work, just as children should have the foolery beaten out of them. *Agroikos* that he is, Brant not only warns us not to be voluptuaries, sluggards, and gluttons, he also decries festive folly and proclaims the diabolical origins of dancing. Yet a certain sort of tension is perhaps present even within Brant's apparently unambiguous didacticism, suspended as this is between mockery (as he derisively distributes his caps and bells) and unsmiling sternness (for it is foolish, as he points out, even to mock folly). The fact that he throws *all* folly—flagrant vice and simple ignorance alike—into the same *Narrenbrei* can indeed be taken as signaling a development from the medieval fear of sin to a humanistic or rationalistic belief in possibilities of improvement. Significantly, Brant deemed the fool's cardinal sin not to be his sinfulness in itself (which is unavoidable anyway) but his refusal to *recognize* his folly, to *see* his sinfulness. Self-ignorance and self-deception lie at folly's heart (just as Socrates had judged them central to comedy), and self-knowledge is accordingly elevated to the work's primary ideal. Self-aware folly is wise folly, a timely repentance being the way to assure ourselves of our own private happy ending: "The man that deems himself a fool / Ends up the wise man as a rule" (*Introduction*, ll.41–42).

Depicting a society dominated by roguery and sin rather than frivolity

and levity, Middleton's *A Mad World, My Masters* is from a moral perspective an equally pessimistic picture of universal folly. Corruption and
knavery give rise to the laughter, yet the tone is lighter, less didactic, and
more amusing, and, because of the ubiquity of the madness, it is comedy
of a different order from satirical portrayals of vice measured reassuringly
against a yardstick of normality from which the evil stands out as a manifest aberration (as in Jonson). Deprived of an internal moral measure, it
becomes possible to view the spectacle with an amused tolerance that
may at times border on the celebratory—as we come to admire the role-
playing and the machinations of the Protean hero/rogue/fool Follywit and
the courtesan Frank Gullman and to revel in the gullible munificence of
the lecherous *senex* Sir Bounteous. The Tudor tradition of the comedy of
evil permitted both vicarious release from social inhibitions *and* moral
indignation at man's fallen state—a combination that could be modulated
and modified according to taste and circumstance. The German carnival
play *Von eim thumherrn und einer kupplerin* likewise presents universal
deviation from a sexual norm absent in the play itself but presumably
brought along (like a ball and chain) by the audience—if only for the
purpose of basking in its transgression. All four main figures attempt to
contravene the sanctioned form of sexual conduct, but any possibility of
censure is forestalled by the overtly playful nature of the proceedings.
The dramatic illusion is ruptured by having a single actor performing the
roles of the two male protagonists (necessitating crass role-swapping on
stage), and, just as the husband is on the point of giving a good pasting to
the bawd who has fixed him up with his own wife, the servant intervenes
with an invocation to dance which presumably extends to the audience.[44]
Sexual or "vicious" folly and festive folly merge into a playful potpourri
that transgresses rational attempts at restraint as it transgresses the theatrical footlights.

Two comedies of madness above all exemplify the way in which universal folly leads to an (often festive or conciliatory) moral relativity.
Cervantes's Don Quixote is a fool in almost all the senses in which the
word has been defined. He regularly mistakes his own delusions for reality (interpreting inn as castle, windmill as giant) and, under the paranoid
conviction that he is the victim of a malevolent enchanter, he misguidedly
interprets reality as an illusion: the inn, he claims, only *seems* to be an inn
because of the tricks of an illusionist. He is self-deceived by his own perpetual role-playing, his monomanic pose as a knight-errant distorting his
vision of the world and turning him into a gull to other knaves and
pranksters. A foolish naivety is embodied in his romantic yearning for the
Golden Age, and his text-book chivalry is an anachronism rendering him
fundamentally different from his contemporaries, an idealistic but well
battered fish out of water. Yet as the novel develops, it emerges that his

folly contains a certain wisdom. His comic paranoia, for example, implies a subliminal awareness in him of his own fictionality, just as his self-stylization as the hero of a chronicle echoes the fact that this is what he in a sense is. Aware of his status as a figure in a narrative and of his subjection to the whims of some sort of transcendental trickster, he is also shown in part 2 as having to fight off a pirate Don Quixote, such episodes on the one hand asserting the authenticity of *our* Don Quixote, yet simultaneously alerting us to his fictionality (and once again evoking the paradox of the Cretan liar). The Don himself draws attention to the possibility that his narrator may be an evil enchanter distorting the truth about his beloved Lady Dulcinea and "changing and turning everything which might give (him) pleasure into shapes other than their true ones"[45]—and perhaps he is.

More strikingly, Don Quixote's folly proves so contagious that it transcends all limitations imposed upon it. The Duke and Duchess, intending merely to have some fun at the dupe's expense, stage a huge performance in order to humor his fantastic whims, playing along with his delusive world of chivalry by providing him with a villain to do battle with and a maiden to test his constancy, and all the while looking on as the "show" unfurls. Indeed, the whole farce, culminating with the maiden melodramatically passing away for unrequited love, was

> so well and convincingly contrived that the play was but little removed from reality. In fact Cide Hamete says that he considers the mockers were as mad as their victims, and the Duke and Duchess within a hair's breadth of appearing fools themselves for taking such pains to play tricks on a pair of fools.[46]

As Brant had pointed out, only fools make fun of fools. On the Don's arrival in Barcelona, the locals "feign" such a rapturous welcome and are so plausible in their "pretence" of hero-adulation that the simulation seems to become reality, and Don Quixote ironically ends up genuinely fulfilling the function of a hero. Forever exceeding its limits, play takes over and in itself turns into a cause for celebration. By the end of the novel Don Quixote's folly—initially viewed as morally reprehensible—has festively infected an entire shipload of fools and taken on the status of a wise and healthy madness, whose passing is lamented as a loss to all and brings the narrative to a muted end.

The epigraph to Joe Orton's *What the Butler Saw* (taken from *The Revenger's Tragedy*) articulates a similar comic feeling: "Surely we're all mad people, and they / Whom we think are, are not." If the social order in its entirety is mad, then any judgement on madness is necessarily a function of where one is situated within that order, and madness only exists in relationships of reciprocality or mutuality: I may seem loopy to

my psychiatrist but, believe me, he's the one who's the real frother. Orton
transposes his playground for licensed lunacy indoors into a private clinic
where it is not the patients but the doctors who are maddest of all. Rance
is a parody of the certifiable shrink (whose symptoms include—briefly
put—a monomanic tendency to psychoanalyze everything), and he justifies his unorthodox treatment of his patients by recourse to his intellectual background in madness:

> *Rance.*   You'll have no trouble recognizing the patient, Prentice. I've clipped
> her hair to within an inch of the scalp.
> *Prentice.* (*shocked*) Was it quite wise to do that, sir? Is it in accord with the
> present enlightened approach to the mentally sick?
> *Rance.*   Perfectly in accord. I've published a monograph on the subject. I
> wrote it at University. On the advice of my tutor. A remarkable man.
> Having failed to achieve madness himself he took to teaching it to
> others.
> *Prentice.* And you were his prize pupil?
> *Rance.*   There were some more able than I.
> *Prentice.* Where are they now?
> *Rance.*   In mental institutions.
> *Prentice.* Running them?
> *Rance.*   For the most part.
>
> (Act 1)

The topsy-turvy world in which the mad are sane and the sane mad is
depicted with such satiric bite that the madness we witness is less to be
seen as an escape from the "sanity" of the world than as a caricatural
exaggeration of the "madness" already inherent *within* the "sanity." The
sense of systematic silliness is underscored by a series of self-referential
comments by Rance, however, which confer a spirit of carnivalesque liberation upon the proceedings. As he tells Sergeant Match, who has come
to impose law and order upon the madness:

> *Rance.* Afterwards I'll take a look at you.
> *Match.* (*stunned*) At me?
> *Rance.* Yes. We can't be too careful.
> *Match.* It seems a bit unusual, sir.
> *Rance.* (*with a bray of laughter*) You're in a madhouse. Unusual behaviour is
> the order of the day.
> *Match.* Only for patients.
> *Rance.* We've no privileged class here. It's democratic lunacy we practise.
>
> (Act 2)

Satirically topsy-turvy the madhouse may be, but the anarchy is pervasive
enough for anyone to have a go if they want. As humanity's lowest common denominator, madness is as egalitarian as masturbation, and all-

comers are welcome to try their hand at it. As in carnival the specific satire remains enclosed within a framework of universal pandemonium. Ultimately all distinctions between sanity and madness become untenable, as the figures wallow in a quagmire of all-embracing lunacy where even the two psychiatrists are on the point of certifying one another.

Geraldine.	Help me! I'm suffering untold anguish. Untie me.
Nick.	Why are you tied up?
Geraldine.	Dr. Rance did it. He says I'm mad.
Nick.	He's a psychiatrist, he must know. He wouldn't put you in a straitjacket if you were sane. He'd have to be mad.
Geraldine.	He is mad!
	Nick supports himself on the desk and stares at the sobbing Mrs. Prentice.
Nick.	(*to Geraldine*) Is she mad?
Geraldine.	She thinks she is. She imagines you're a figment of her imagination.
Nick.	(*to Mrs. Prentice, nodding to Geraldine*) She can see me. Doesn't that prove I'm real?
Mrs. Prentice.	No. She's mad.
Nick.	If you think I'm a phantom of your subconscious you must be mad.
Mrs. Prentice.	(*with a hysterical shriek*) I am mad!

(Act 2)

Rance furthermore assumes the role of a carnival praiser of folly, espousing madness as the only sane response to a mad world: "You can't be a rationalist in an irrational world. It isn't rational" (2); "His belief in normality is quite abnormal" (2); "His behaviour is so ridiculous one might almost suspect him of being sane" (2); "Your mind has given way. You'll find the experience invaluable in your efforts to come to terms with twentieth century living" (2); and "No madman ever accepts madness. Only the sane do that" (2). Rance is a less sophisticated twentieth-century version of Wilde's Lord Henry, transposed into a madhouse.

Given such a relativistic context, it is evident that the comedy as a whole may easily turn into a celebration of folly, a praise of madness and abnormality, and a critique of normality. The Hegelian view of the comic takes account of this aspect of the phenomenon. Apparently with the Aristophanic or Shakespearean comic hero in mind, Hegel sees in comedy an affirmation of subjectivity, which he here equates with a triumph of folly (in defeat)—"die sich durch sich selbst auflösende Torheit" (the dissolution of folly through itself). In comedy, he writes, "the laughter of those individuals who cause the dissolution of everything in and through themselves graphically demonstrates the triumph of their subjectivity,

which for all this remains secure in itself." It is a kind of self-aware folly
that necessarily comes a cropper but stands in conciliatory and self-
assured geniality *above* its failure. Indeed, this tone of joyful reconciliation
is what distinguishes comedy, according to Hegel, from the lesser genre
of satire. "Comedy on the other hand generally incorporates the infinite
cheerfulness and self-assurance which come of being well and truly above
one's own contradiction and not as one might expect bitter and unhappy
in it; the felicity and wellbeing of a subjectivity which, being sure of itself,
can put up with the dissolution of its goals and achievements." To the
comic fool belongs a certain element of buoyant resilience that keeps him
jesting even when his folly is thwarted and that enables him to transcend
the self-contradiction necessarily implicit in any individual subjectivity. It
is a resilience that means that, at a certain level at least, the folly or subjectivity has carried the day: "In other words, subjectivity is in general
comic when it of itself brings its activities into contradiction and causes
their dissolution, while at the same time remaining every bit as im-
perturbable and sure of itself."[47] Hegel had himself already produced
something akin to a philosophical *sottie* in the shape of the *Phänomenologie des Geistes*.

Another influential German theorist, Joachim Ritter, has similarly interpreted comedy as a celebration of that which is normally excluded by
(and from) the social order, or—more awkwardly phrased—as a pos-
itivization of the negative.[48] His point is that the socially "null" (*das
Nichtige*, or that which from a social perspective is nonexistent or invalid)
necessarily stands in a relationship of mutual interdependency with the
order that does the invalidating or annulling—or, in other words, that the
positive presupposes its negative quite as much as the negative its positive. We can indeed have no conception of order, normality, and sense,
without also conceiving of disorder, abnormality, and nonsense. Ritter
posits that laughter constitutes a shining of the spotlight on the *Nichtige*
that sense and seriousness normally hush over and outlaw from existence:
"What is grasped and played out in the case of laughter is the fact that
nullity [*das Nichtige*] secretly belongs to existence; it is grasped and
played out not in the manner of the exclusionary seriousness which can
only ever keep it at a distance and treat it as null, but in such a way that it
becomes visible and audible within the exclusionary order itself, as it
were a part of the order."[49] Just as the fool has been envisaged as a
paradoxical manifestation of "non-being," the negative coming to light
as a positive phenomenon, comedy is understood by Ritter as validating
the existence of the nonexistent. The *Nichtige*, the irrational, and the deviant are of course "normally" only defined negatively, but laughter
stresses that this radical otherness or difference is also at a certain level
identical with its opposite. Like the Hegelian comic hero who stands

above the internalized self-contradiction that the folly of his subjectivity inevitably entails, laughter transcends the contradiction (whether seen as internalized within a self or not) between identity and difference, sense and nonsense, the rational and the irrational. Emphasizing "that in other words comedy is a matter of establishing the identity between the proscribed and excluded and the exclusionary," Ritter asserts that the function of laughter is to bring to the fore "what is not accessible to seriousness—the affiliation of the Other to the existential reality which excludes it."[50]

Peter Barnes's comedy *The Ruling Class* gives an exemplary demonstration of the way in which abnormality may be "positivized," simultaneously showing the insidious violence of the so-called normal. While the Earl of Gurney is undoubtedly well round the bend (for he is convinced he is God), his self-delusion is an initially benevolent one (for at least he is the God of Love) that involves stripping British society of its fusty, musty coatings of decorum, decency, and hierarchical pomp—that is, a healthy ripping down of the social mask to expose our natural nakedness.

> *Earl of Gurney.* The axe must be laid to the root. Pomp and riches, pride and property will have to be lopped off. All men are brothers. Love makes all equal. The mighty must bow down before the pricks of the louse-ridden rogues.
> (*Suddenly warmly embraces Sir Charles*) I love you dearly, Uncle Charles.... Enjoy yourself while I'm gone. Relax. Have sex.
> *He exits with Tucker. Claire and Sir Charles look after him.*
> *Sir Charles.* (*exploding*) My God!
> *Earl of Gurney.* (*popping his head back*) Yes?
>
> (Act 1, scene 4)

Like a drivelling fool looking to hide his bauble in a hole, the Earl displays a sexual frankness that intimidates prim old women. This naively optimistic God of Love advocates a sexual and a political open house clearly against the interests of the "normal" people who benefit by the hierarchical, traditional, sexually inhibited order in existence, and, from their perspective, the God of Love stands in obvious need of normalization. The sinister second act of the comedy shows the Earl shorn of his delusions, a completely sane archconservative with a rampant sense of decorum. "Let's have no talk of bestial orgasms," he reprimands Mrs. Piggot-Jones. In fact, the God of Love has been transformed into a God of Vengeance (in the guise of Jack the Ripper) and, in a scene that recalls Wedekind's *Büchse der Pandora*, his new, repressed, distorted sexuality manifests itself in a grotesque murder scene.

The absurd nonsense of Simpson's *A Resounding Tinkle* exalts madness with a much more frivolous force. One passage in particular illustrates the topsy-turvy world of madness:

> *Prayer.*   Let us laugh with those we tickle.
> *Response.* Let us laugh with those we tickle.
> *Prayer.*   Let us weep with those we expose to tear-gas.
> *Response.* Let us weep with those we expose to tear-gas.
> *Prayer.*   Let us throw back our heads and laugh at reality:
> *Response.* Which is an illusion caused by mescalin deficiency.
> *Prayer.*   At sanity:
> *Response.* Which is an illusion caused by alcohol deficiency.
> *Prayer.*   At knowledge which is an illusion caused by certain biochemical changes in the human brain structure during the course of human evolution, which had it followed another course would have produced other biochemical changes in the human brain structure, by reason of which knowledge as we now experience it would have been beyond the reach of our wildest imaginings; and by reason of which, what is now beyond the reach of our wildest imaginings would have been familiar and common-place. Let us laugh at these things. Let us laugh at thought:
> *Response.* Which is a phenomenon like any other.
> *Prayer.*   At illusion:
> *Response.* Which is an illusion, which is a phenomenon like any other....
>
> (Act 1, scene 2)

The carnivalesque mock-thanksgiving on the one hand reverses our normal conceptual hierarchy, giving ontological priority to the contingent and attributing contingency to what is ordinarily regarded as absolute: reality is a hallucination, and tripping is the real thing; sanity and sobriety are phantasms, for alcoholic intoxication is the prior condition. Incorporating a relativization of *all* human cognition, however, it also ends up undermining itself in a move typical of the foolish perspective: if illusion as well as reality is an illusion, then all is illusory, and the mock-thanksgiving has—with democratic fairness—razed all concepts equally to the ground, just as the carnival world upside-down ultimately shears all social actors with equal vigor down to the lowest common denominator of folly. Yet the "mad" perspective does not merely do the negative work of destroying hierarchies; what it ends up also producing is an aura of festive relativism, a cheerful awareness of the reciprocality, interdependence, and even identity of madness and sanity, illusion and reality.

If Ritter's theory, like Bakhtin's contention that laughter is a sportive subversion of the existing social order, is slightly one-sided in ignoring the way derisive, scornful, and satiric mockery can fawn upon the existent order by *negating* the negative and helping to exclude and banish what is foolish, mad, or irrational, the two aspects in conjunction draw attention to the fundamental ambiguity of laughter, with its potential simultaneously to mock and celebrate, deride and collude. The ambiguity of the fool, who may be vicious or festive, cynical or naive, has its counterpart in the ambiguous folly of the laughing spectator, who is himself split between sanity and madness, a divided identity whose private core does perpetual battle with its public face. This ambivalence is present not merely in the mirth generated by festive and saturnalian folly as a context, but also when the folly is displaced into and concentrated within a single fool (the "comic hero"), the equivocality of our laughter frequently reflecting an essential equivocality in the comic heroes themselves. As Shakespeare's Falstaff is arguably the most subtle and complex of all such figures, a brief glance in his direction will perhaps shed some light on the rest of the gallery of rogues-cum-fools.

Nobody's Business

That old white-bearded Satan by the name of Falstaff seems above all to be derived from the Vice of the medieval morality play. There are indeed striking structural similarities between the two parts of *Henry IV* and moralities such as *Everyman* and *The Castle of Perseverance* as well as moral interludes like *Lusty Juventus*. The plot, for instance, leads the protagonist (Lusty Juventus in the play of that name corresponding to Hal in *Henry IV*) on a path from virtue, via temptation and a period of vice, thieving, and revelry, to final repentance and the concomitant rejection of the Vice figure (Hypocrisy in *Lusty Juventus* corresponding to Falstaff in *Henry IV*). In this capacity, the folly of Falstaff manifests itself in his role as tempter, an overweight embodiment of the satanic pride that has him quote Scripture for his own unholy ends. The tavern scenes interspersed throughout the action symbolize the life of dissolution into which the protagonists of morality plays are wont to lapse, and, as a huge bombard of sack, a stuffed cloak-bag of guts, a roasted Manningtree ox with pudding in his belly, Falstaff echoes the Vice as Glutton or Gula, a figure who turns up in *The Castle of Perseverance*. The Vice here incarnates the image of psychomachia,[51] the soul struggle or agonizing choice Mankind must make between Gluttony and Good Deeds, disorder and order, anarchy and government. Overcoming (on the surface at least) his internal duality, Hal rejects Falstaff and chooses order: as external onlookers we are in a position to suspend judgement and enjoy the ambivalence.

Falstaff may equally be seen as descended from the Lord of Misrule who presided over the English tradition of saturnalian revelry, and from this standpoint the folly he represents is less the folly of sin than of festive fun. His parodying of biblical texts and his feigned piety thus need not stem so much from the satanic pride of the Vice as from the licensed parodic irreverence of the Feast of Fools. Falstaff has been compared to the figure of Bacchus in Nashe's pageant *Summer's Last Will and Testament*,[52] another festival lord who serves as a focal center to his show. This character, himself a fusion of the classical deity (the god of wine and generator of ecstasy akin to Dionysus), the traditional Elizabethan toper, and the round-bellied carnival king of Shrove Tuesday games,[53] shares with Falstaff (and the Vice) his gargantuan girth and directly anticipates him in his erudite praise of wine: "Give a scholar wine, going to his book, or being about to invent, it sets a new point on his wit, it glazeth it, it scours it, it gives him *acumen*.... There is no excellent knowledge without mixture of madness. And what makes a man more mad in the head than wine?" (ll.976–995). Falstaff's encomium is no less bacchanalian:

> A good sherris-sack hath a two-fold operation in it. It ascends me into the brain, dries me there all the foolish and dull and crudy vapours which environ it, makes it apprehensive, quick, forgetive, full of nimble, fiery and delectable shapes, which delivered o'er to the voice, the tongue, which is the birth, becomes excellent wit. The second property of your excellent sherris is the warming of the blood, which before, cold and settled, left the liver white and pale, which is the badge of pusillanimity and cowardice.... If I had a thousand sons, the first human principle I would teach them would be to forswear thin potations, and to addict themselves to sack.
>
> *(2 Henry IV*, act 4, scene 3)

Turning the world on its head, Falstaff would doubtless concur that sanity is an illusion caused by a lack of sack. In this capacity, Falstaff signifies a release from the order that takes such pains to keep its hierarchies the right way up, and our identification with him becomes a vicarious release for us. Auden has made the point that we were all Falstaffs once, and then we became social beings with superegos.[54]

Falstaff also incorporates and transcends stock figures from within the comic tradition. He has something of the *miles gloriosus*, the cowardly military braggart, for a start, and his lies are as thoroughly translucent as those of Plautus's Pyrgopolynices, even if his cowardice—as when he plays possum in battle—does show a measure of self-preserving craftiness not normally associated with more farcical variants of the blubbering lily-liver. Especially in part 2, moreover, he is shown in his capacity as a *senex*, a dirty old man whose desire—as Poins malevolently puts it—has outlived performance (by a number of years). Yet Falstaff does differ from the traditional *senex* in important aspects, for never does he seek to marry and monopolize some buxom young wench against her will, which would disturb the "natural" order and expose him to the comedy of cuckoldry; his desire is simply to go a-riding with a like-minded night-errant. Certain episodes do indeed reveal in the ageing fool an *awareness* that he is no longer in his prime ("I am old, I am old," he tells Doll, "Thou't forget me when I am gone" [*2 Henry IV*, 2.4]), while others show him cheerfully and self-consciously *pretending* to be young, playing down and masking over his self-deception while also hinting at the spiritual youth that makes him such a lovable old bugger. He cheekily tells the Lord Chief Justice: "You that are old consider not the capacities of us that are young; you do measure the heat of our livers with the bitterness of your galls; and we that are in the vaward of our youth, I must confess, are wags too" (*2 Henry IV*, 1.2).

Falstaff is historical as well as literary in origin, and, while he may incorporate elements of the *miles gloriosus*, he may with equal justification be seen as a satire on the corrupt Elizabethan military officer in his treatment of his recruits (or is he just having us on when he claims to have led his ragamuffins to where they are peppered—i.e., to their death in order to be entitled to their "dead pay?"). Falstaff at the same time embodies traits of the historical Prince Henry, whose reputed wild youth is transposed by Shakespeare to that of his partner in folly, as well as of the historical personage Sir John Oldcastle, the immediate prototype of Falstaff, who, having fought for Henry IV in France and Wales, was eventually hanged for Wycliffite beliefs and apparent involvement in treasonous conspiracy. By a peculiar irony, the ambiguity in the reception of Falstaff is echoed by the diversity of pronouncements upon Oldcastle. Originally seen as a wicked traitor, he came to be regarded as a Protestant hero, scholar, and philosopher,[55] although it is primarily the "wicked" Oldcastle on whom Falstaff is based.

Both Oldcastle and Falstaff thus appear to incarnate the ambiguity characteristic of the scapegoat or *pharmakos* figuring in the fertility ritual from which comedy is said to descend. According to descriptions by anthropologists such as Frazer, the *pharmakos* is a figure in whom the evils potential in a social organization are embodied, acknowledged, and enjoyed, before in turn being mocked and laughingly expelled. Of particular significance is that, during the period of licence, the scapegoat enjoys the freedom to pronounce *alternative* truths, to say and do that which is normally disallowed. In Tibet, where the Buddhist scapegoat is known as the "King of the Years," he not only spends his ten-day spell of licence on the marketplace helping himself to whatever he likes, he also ridicules the authority of the Jalno (who stands in lieu of the Grand Lama) by pronouncing such heresies as "What we perceive through the five senses is no illusion. All you teach is untrue."[56] For his pains he is hootingly driven out of the city and into isolation. The ritual clown of various American Indian tribes of the southwest (such as the Zuñi Katcinas) performs a similar function in a somewhat more overtly shocking manner, masturbating in public, making passes at married women and virgins, besmearing himself with turds, breaking religious taboo, and deriding the gods. Yet it is all a performance, restricted to a temporally limited period. It is a histrionic excess of jesting and sacred folly that allows the spectators vicarious release from the order they are normally required to maintain.[57] Like the fool, the scapegoat, and the sacred clown, all of whom do what is not done and say what is not said, Falstaff too abuses his prince, praises the wisdom of wine, and mocks the abstract truths, ideals, and theories of his society. It is with the perspicacity of a truth-speaking fool that he pricks the self-inflated bubble of "honour":

> Can honour set to a leg? No. Or an arm? No. Or take away the grief of a wound? No. Honour hath no skill in surgery, then? No. What is honour? A word. What is in that word honour? What is that honour? Air. A trim reckoning. Who hath it? He that died o' Wednesday. Doth he feel it? No. Doth he hear it? No. 'Tis insensible, then? Yea, to the dead. But will it not live with the living? No. Why? Detraction will not suffer it. Therefore I'll none of it. Honour is a mere scutcheon. And so ends my catechism.
>
> (*1 Henry IV*, act 5, scene 1)

Essential to the scapegoat and the sacred clown is that they are both derided and celebrated, again implying an ambivalence both in the laugher's attitude towards transgression (playful transgression at least) and in the figures themselves.

The ambivalence of Falstaff is further manifested by his histrionic nature. Falstaff has been interpreted both as a true liar and poltroon and as one who seeks to entertain the prince by *acting* the roles of coward and liar. A strong case may be made for both points, but Falstaff's lies are so transparent and so exaggerated that they seem to become ends in themselves, accompanied by a sort of self-awareness that generally accompanies performance. At one stage he even turns into a Cretan liar, soliloquizing: "Lord, how subject we old men are to this vice of lying!" (2, 3.2). His role as Monsieur Remorse does not fool anyone, nor do his acted youthfulness and tales of bravery, but they are not ultimately intended to. As Hazlitt describes him: "he is an actor in himself almost as much as upon the stage,"[58] and another critic makes the point that insofar as he is a liar, "Falstaff surely comes under Sir Philip Sidney's defence of the poet who 'though he recount things not true, yet, because hee telleth them not for true, he lyeth not.' "[59] This view of Falstaff has tended to be the product of a romantic idealization of the swollen parcel of dropsies in the literary imagination and hides the fact that from a dramatic point of view pretending to be a liar is virtually indistinguishable from actually being one. Perhaps the point is rather that, as a self-aware existential role-player, Falstaff symbolizes the *unity* of mask and face: in other words, he becomes his role, he lives his act, for his identity is essentially fluid. Rather like the great Hindu god Siva, who is a creative/destructive god of fertility, king of the dance , and a mercurial figure one of whose roles is "the great ascetic," Falstaff can be Monsieur Remorse as easily as Sir John Falstaff or again as easily as Sack-and-Sugar Jack, the Lord of Misrule and father of lies. The Protean self emerges as one of the stamps of traditional folly.

In his mercuriality Falstaff indeed echoes his creator, of whom Hazlitt was to write that his "genius consisted in the faculty of transforming himself at will into whatever he chose: his originality was the power of seeing every object from the exact point of view in which others would see it. He was the Proteus of human intellect."[60] As in *A Midsummer Night's Dream*, therefore, the fictional folly is a duplication of the folly of the poet, and, in his perpetual process of entertaining self-dramatization, Falstaff himself is a sort of "poetical character" in the sense defined by Keats: a character that is "not itself—it has no self—it is everything and nothing."[61] Rejecting the fictional mask of self-identity we normally impose upon ourselves, the fool gives vent to his potential to be anybody, a potential recognized in the claim of the Irish mystic A. E. that the "inner being is Protean."[62] As the schizophrenic is painfully aware, however, this pure potential may also be felt as a pure absence, for being anybody is tantamount to being nobody and can lead to the existential emptiness of being a jack (or jill) of all roles (an every man jack, a clowning Jack-a-Lent, a sweet, kind, true, and valiant Jack Falstaff), but master of none. This is not, of course, how the self-conscious jackasses of comedy—the Hegelian fools who stand above their self-difference—tend to experience their versatility. Monsieur Rien, medieval fool and nobody, boasts of his "negative capability"[63] with suitably foolish pride:

> All things can I do and can undo,
> I can transmute an aye into a nay ...
>
> Naught I am and long have been a naught,
> And then turned into one and all ...
>
> A fool I can transform into a sage,
> Or so at least will he appear ...
>
> (*Sottie pour le cry de la Bazoche*, lines 223ff.)

Falstaff is incessantly performing both for the spectator and for the prince, and, as such, he assumes a role analogous to that of the court-fool, as an entertainer whose licence allows him the privilege of irreverence and parodic mockery. He is a type of wise fool, indeed, whose unorthodox vision stands the conventional order on its head (by praising the folly of wine and mocking the wisdom of honor) and whose Cretan lying attests to a truth in untruth. He himself draws attention to the duality of his madness by contending that he is not only witty in himself, "but the cause that wit is in other men" (2, 1.2). Like the court-fool or the court dwarf (stature aside), he is both wit and butt, mocker and mocked.

Rabelais's Panurge is histrionic in the same way Falstaff is, if not more openly so, a trait that explains the radical character transformations to which he is subject and that otherwise would render him psychologically incoherent. Characterized by relative courage in *Pantagruel* and by sheer cowardice in the *Quart Livre*, sacrilegious blasphemy in the earlier book and fearful zeal later on, it is his self-difference that holds his identity together. A natural actor, he slips from one role into another and remains throughout a performer, entertaining Pantagruel just as Falstaff was to entertain Hal. Stamped furthermore by a comparably anarchic cruelty (witness the drowning of the sheep together with their owner Dindenault and all his followers in the *Quart Livre* and his grim practical jokes in *Pantagruel*), by a liking for bawdy and subversive puns, by the parodic relationship in which he stands to his master, and by a verbal virtuosity that permits him to ask Pantagruel for food in thirteen different (real or nonsense) languages, he also represents, amidst the universal folly of the *Tiers Livre*, a kind of particularly foolish wise fool. Like Falstaff, the wise fool who learnedly praises wine, Panurge the wise fool turns normal reasoning on its head with an erudite eulogy to improvidence and debt. At the end of the book, during the course of which nobody has been able to answer the question whether Panurge ought to marry or not, he concludes:

> All is folly. Solomon says that infinite is the number of fools. Naught can be subtracted from infinity, nor can aught be added to it, as Aristotle proves. And I should be a mad fool if, being a fool, I did not count myself one. This is equally what makes the number of maniacs and madmen infinite. Avicenna says that there are infinite brands of mania.[64]

If folly is universal, Panurge really would be a fool not to opt for the wise folly of admitting his folly.

Panurge the actor comes to light in typical fashion in the episode in which he fails to woo the Parisian lady. The reason for his failure cannot possibly be anything to do with sexual insufficiency—after all, he is the man with the tireless tadger. Rather, it is the manner of his courting that lets him down, for he consciously rejects the mask of social civility and explicitly negates or breaches the accepted code of sexual conduct. A true fool indeed, he subverts all amorous convention by asking her how she fancies mating with him, indulging in a fit of femoral frottage, dancing a jig with Master John Thursday, providing a nest for Master John Owl; he even prays to the gods that he might be granted a bit of houghmagandy with her, concluding his prayer with a jaunty "let's get a-figfirkfuttering!" Offering himself at the service of her body, goods, tripe, and bowels, he solemnly proclaims that he can neither piss nor shit for love. Panurge thus debunks the hackneyed rhetorical pretension of love by getting straight to the point. Above all, however, it is a *performance* milked for its comic potential; at the end of it, Panurge is described as turning his mask round ("Adoncques Panurge tourna son faulx visaige").[65] For want of fictive spectators (Pantagruel is not present at that moment), it can only be assumed that Panurge has acted his farce for *us*, the readers, or for the sake of acting itself. The fool's awareness of the extrafictional spectators or readers, and thus implicitly of his own fictionality, lends him a self-conscious theatricality that structures his existence.

The two *zanni* or servants of the commedia dell'arte are further agents of folly, who similarly exist in a special relation to their audience, rupturing the dramatic illusion and generating links between performance and reality through the introduction of contemporary and local references. Arlecchino, who underwent countless modifications through the centuries, also came to be seen as the quintessential actor, subject to permanent changes of identity.[66] Starting his commedia career as a lazy, happy-go-lucky, credulous, ever-hungry porter from Bergamo, he developed increasing acrobatic expertise, a higher level of cunning, and mimetic skills that meant that, by the time he had reached Germany (in the guise of Hanswurst) and France (as Arlequin), role-playing was regarded as his dominant trait. He would in fact impersonate *anything*, male or female, and then be flabbergasted to find himself as a "a bride, a goddess, or a mother surrounded by dozens of baby Harlequins."[67] Brighella, the descendant of Plautus's Pseudolus and ancestor of Molière's Scapin and even Beaumarchais's Figaro, was an intriguer, an organizer, and a plot-weaver from the word go, controlling the play and cynically and unscrupulously manipulating people as if they were puppets. A liar with similar powers to those of the poet and playwright himself, Brighella too is intrinsically flexible: "He does not merely play the role of servant but can also adapt himself to the most diverse professions: soldier, tavern-keeper, hangman, fortune-teller, professional thief."[68] Like Falstaff and Panurge, both the *zanni* are Protean figures, natural actors who *are* their masks. The potential ambiguity inherent in laughter is reflected in the ambivalence of these archetypal comic figures: if the laughing individual necessarily comprises a dissonant identity of mask and face, public and private, sanity and madness, then the special significance of Falstaff, Panurge, and the *zanni* is that—in their different ways—they *symbolize* this identity, even while enacting its difference. The mutable identity of the natural actor bodies forth the necessary theatricality of all social performance and, fusing social "act" and antisocial "instinct" within a single figure, betokens the naturalness of acting. While laughter itself often depends upon a binary opposition created by the *difference* of mask and face, the symbolic nature of the comic hero allows for him to transcend this duality. His folly is but a mask, but his mask is his face; his madness is a role, but his role coincides with his real self.

It is no surprise that in the Christian tradition in particular, which always requires a morally healthy binary opposition between genuineness and imposture, the natural actor is often associated with the Devil. The Devil is, after all, the archetypal fool, the negator incarnate who says no to the truth of God. Just as Falstaff can be derived from the Vice of the morality play, and perhaps ultimately from the Devil of the miracle play, so too is Harlequin diabolical in origin, apparently going back to the clown-devils of the early Middle Ages, a demon called Alichino making a brief appearance in Dante's *Inferno*. By the time of the commedia, Harlequin is more of a clown than a devil, but his diabolical derivation continues to betray itself in his ugly black half-mask, the carbuncle on his forehead presumably the remnant of a horn. Lucifer had been a figure of gross comic fun since the late Middle Ages, after his fall becoming a parody of his former archangelic self, a simple target for crass derision with his unbecoming hooves, claws, and fangs. Two of the English mystery cycles (York and Chester) mock Satan by showing him as an actor, a deceiver, and an impostor, and, in the Temptation of Eve, he appears in drag wearing a woman's face-mask and a pair of falsies and addressing Eve in a falsetto voice. The audience is evidently meant to scorn such an undignified avatar of duplicity, yet although satanic folly is particularly closely associated with acting and the loss of self-identity entailed by this, Lucifer is not the only one to have taken a theological tumble: the fallenness of man in general implies that self-difference and "inauthenticity" is essential to the *human* condition. Perhaps, therefore, even apparently unequivocal Christian contempt for the Devil also contained a measure of clandestine collusion with a hidden aspect of the self, a (half-)recognition of one's own lapsarian sinfulness.

Symbolic significance apart, Falstaff, Panurge, and the *zanni* are comic because they appeal to the anarchist in us. They create the sort of havoc we (more or less consciously) would also like to have a hand in. This is made clear by the example of one of Harlequin's descendants, Pierrot. One of the masks akin to Harlequin in the commedia had been Pedrolino, a dreamy and merry servant who in eighteenth-century France was sentimentalized into the subtle, graceful and melancholy character of Pierrot. The poetic fantasy of the French creation, however, was metamorphosed by the choppy trip across the Channel into the complete anarchist of nineteenth-century English pantomime. Discarding his poetic pallor and moonlit mystery, he turned into a hyperbolic hurricane, a violent representative of our unconscious desires who captured the imagination of the French poet Baudelaire as well as appealing to a peculiarly English taste in comic thuggery:

> The English Pierrot arrived on the scene like a typhoon, fell to the ground like a bale, and when he laughed, his laughter made the whole hall ring; this laughter was like a jovial clap of thunder.... it was the giddiness of hyperbole.
> Pierrot walks past a woman cleaning her doorstep. Having picked her pockets, he attempts to cram into his own the sponge, the broom, the bucket, and even the water. As for the manner in which he ventures to declare his love, it can be pictured by recalling to mind one's memories of time spent studying the phanerogamic conduct of the monkeys in their well-known cage at the Jardin-des-Plantes.[69]

The Clown of the first part of the nineteenth century is equally amoral, indiscriminately brushing aside all the dictates of manners, authority or property:

> If Clown had fixed traits, they were all ones that mocked convention and exposed social habits pretending to morality or self-conscious graciousness. He rebelled against stuffiness and tradition and did what others wished to do but never dared. If Clown encountered another's property he would break it if fragile, wear it if portable, paint it or deface it if immovable. If there was a woman, old or young, he would make advances, if there was food he would eat it gluttonously; if the food were someone else's he would first steal it. The law held terror for him only when he was in danger of being caught.[70]

Like his Italian forefathers and like Panurge, this Clown is also a natural actor, an impostor and mimic in perpetual performance, and as with the *zanni* of the commedia, Clown's accomplishments offer occasion for the spectators to associate with his breezy disregard for the law, deriving vicarious satisfaction from seeing the fool with whom they identify carry out the sort of misdemeanor they themselves would love to commit—if only they could. This includes the perennial pummelling of the police, an anti-authoritarian gesture that goes back to the bailiff-bashing of the Middle Ages. In this respect pantomime represents illegality and lawlessness transposed into the safety of a ludic context and a passive mode. "No single harlequinade dramatizes a complete roster of crimes, but few pantomimes are without a capital crime committed in the course of the harlequinade.... One may find rioting, destruction of property, theft and destruction of the mail, attempted murder, refusal or inability to pay for large meals and quantities of drink consumed at restaurants, assaults on watchmen, and most common of all, every kind of theft."[71]

Alfred Jarry's creation Père Ubu is a figure of thunderingly anarchic disposition, incorporating aspects of Falstaff and Panurge in particular, but also an undiluted nastiness that anticipates the totalitarian despots of the twentieth century. His phallic gorbelly outdoes even Falstaff's (for he eats some twelve meals a day); he is every bit as cowardly as the Panurge of the *Quart Livre* (and with the same laxative consequences); he feigns repentance about as convincingly as Falstaff ("I am on the point of becoming a holy man," he burbles unimpressively, in the belief that his wife is an apparition); he takes a Panurgian pleasure in invective and displays a comparable sexual and scatological inventiveness in this sphere; and he loves massacring people. The carnage is indeed of a Rabelaisian order, yet, as in Rabelais, nobody is any the worse for being debrained, cleaved down the middle, or exploded. In his capacity as a fool-cum-carnival-king he also—in *Ubu Enchainé*—generates a topsy-turvy world, a social and logical inversion of the existing order.

In the context of such big-bellied behemoths, an additional analogy comes to light, namely the "Trickster" figure central to the legends and myth-culture of the North American Indians, China, Japan, and Greece. The American ethnologist Paul Radin has described the Winnebago Trickster as follows: "Basically he possesses no well-defined and fixed form.... he is primarily an inchoate being of undeterminate proportions, a figure foreshadowing the shape of man.... he possesses intestines wrapped around his body, and an equally long penis, likewise wrapped around his body with his scrotum on top of it."[72] This *Ur*-monster is again essentially fluid in form and identity, follows his impulses, seems to know neither good nor evil, and breaks taboo by cohabiting with a woman prior to going on the warpath. The Trickster is above all a fool, and the callous trickery he attempts to perpetrate in his endeavors to obtain food almost always results in *him* being the one who is deceived— and normally by himself at that. After one particular act of exemplary goofiness, he exclaims with bewilderment: "My, my! Correctly indeed am I named Foolish One, Trickster!" He may consequently be interpreted as appealing to that rabid, slobbering, stupid beast located in the depths of our psyche (the unconscious), and Jung correspondingly describes him as "a faithful copy of an undifferentiated human consciousness."[73] Alternatively, he can be viewed simply as an embodiment of the human potential to break taboo, to negate the order (by word or deed), and to be disorderly.

His flexible identity manifests itself in his capacity, like Harlequin, to undergo sex changes without ill effects, using an elk's liver as his vulva, and the trials of the housewife are not unbeknown to him. Like the comic hero, the ritual clown, and the scapegoat (and Siva), he is also *radically* ambiguous: hovering between buffoon, deity, and culture-hero, he embodies in equal measure creative and destructive tendencies, trickery and folly, cunning and imbecility. This unity of order and chaos, identity and difference—as with the natural actors—seems to symbolize or represent the self-difference (public and private, social and asocial) we internalize within *our* identity, a paradoxicality that echoes and reflects the paradox of the fool, who—in Foucault's terms—manifests the being of nonbeing, the positivity of the negative. Incorporating bestiality and divinity alike (not unlike human beings in general), the Trickster's fluid identity means he is a kind of every-man-jackass thoroughly resistant to theological classification. Radin writes: "No generation understands (the Trickster) fully but no generation can do without him. Each had to include him in all its theologies, in all its cosmogonies, despite the fact that it realized that he did not properly fit into any of them.... And so he became and remained everything to every man—god, animal, human being, hero, buffoon, he who was before good and evil, denier, affirmer, destroyer and creator. If we laugh at him, he grins at us. What happens to him, happens to us."[74]

Not all anarchic and disorderly figures are equally amusing, however. Camus's Caligula and Brecht's Arturo Ui (a parody of Hitler) both incorporate the social irresponsibility and the histrionics of the trickster-fool (although Ui does have to take lessons in acting) yet are fundamentally fearsome because the artistic creation remains indissociable from the historical prototype, as well as being associated with a position of tyrannical power. Brecht's Baal—anarchic poet, homosexual, and joker—is an interesting case. A self-consciously "Dionysian" individual, he seeks to fuse his identity in an ecstatic union with nature and displays utter ethical indifference in his systematic disregard for the discrete identities of the anonymous faces with whom he comes into contact. He embodies a creative/destructive duality that celebrates nature and scorns the hardened abstractions of social thought. He inverts the conventional perspective and pronounces topsy-turvily "outrageous" truths: "I see the world in a mild light; it is the excrement of our dear God," "love is ... like a coconut, which is good so long as it's fresh, but which must be spat out as soon as the juice has been crushed from it."[75] Yet he is never really very funny. Two possible reasons for this come to mind. First, he is a murderer. This is not noncomic in itself, as proved by such comic hooligans and butchers as Ubu and Grabbe's Mordax, yet when the play operates at a certain level of illusionism, the grotesqueness of murder and murderers becomes frightening or repulsive rather than killingly funny. A second possible reason is that Baal takes himself too seriously, lacking both the levity of wit and a sense of self-distancing humor. Hegel was perhaps right thus to draw a distinction as to "whether the characters in question are comic in their own eyes [*für sich selbst*] or only in the eyes of the spectators," defining the truly *comic* fool as one who is both aware of his own comedy and joyfully indifferent to his personal (mis)fortunes.[76] Baal's post-Nietzschean anti-individualism fuses with an expressionistic sense that he is *being himself*, with the result that his subversiveness seems to have solidified into a pose without him knowing. His anti-individualism is the expression of an individual who never stops taking himself seriously as an individual, and Baal remains very much a child of his time—a time in which being the cosmos was a particularly hip thing for an individual to do.

Azdak, the "good-bad judge" from *Der Kaukasische Kreidekreis*, is a more comic Brechtian anarchist, who, while seeming to be corrupt and hedonistic, in fact ends up paradoxically upholding justice. Merry toper that he is, he inverts conventional legal practice by using the lawbook—but only for sitting on—by impudently suggesting that the victim of a rape accompany him to the scene of the crime (a barn) so he can check things out for himself, and by "condemning" one (unjustly accused) defendant to share a bottle of wine with him and the public prosecutor. Using feigned inattention to wangle the happy ending for Simon and Grusche ("accidentally" divorcing Grusche from her former husband), he invites all the accused to a dance that lends his topsy-turvy reign the aura of saturnalian festive folly, a utopianism that underscores the ludic irreality of the happy ending. In a world whose values are themselves inverted, the inversions of the fool-cum-judge turn things back up the way they should be. But Azdak's is only a *temporary* reign, a holiday humor.

As a "corrupt" judge, Azdak is in the tradition of Kleist's Adam (from *Der zerbrochne Krug*). Adam however is less of the festive fool and more of the *senex*-scapegoat, finally forced to beat a hasty retreat for having done whatever it was he did with Eve and thus thwarted the path of young love. Another gulous guzzler, Adam indeed bears a certain resemblance to Falstaff (who at one stage himself says: "Thou knowest in the state of innocency Adam fell and what should poor Jack Falstaff do in the days of villainy? Thou seest I have more flesh than another man and therefore more frailty" [*1 Henry IV*, 3.3]), and Adam's name as well as the "fall" that sparks off the whole comic action both contribute to turn him into a more general symbol of man's imperfection. Kleist additionally integrates parallels with the Devil to hint at Adam's origin: he has a lame foot and smells of tar and sulphur, and Frau Brigitte, witnessing his escape from the scene of the misdeed, implies that it *was* the Devil she saw. Yet Adam is not the butt of unambivalent scorn. Feigning innocence, he is from the outset wearing an extremely wobbly mask symbolized by his judicial wig, but although *we* know he is lying, the comedy consists in a repeated deferral of the moment of revelation to the rest of the characters, the communal unmasking. Adam's imposture is the motor that keeps the comedy running, and his wit in keeping up the role prolongs the comic enjoyment.

Almost all of the rogues and fools so far have been boozers, which implies some sort of connection between alcohol and comic anarchy. Of course, excessive drinking in itself can be seen as an aspect of the vice known as gluttony or intemperance, or—more positively—as a symbol of conviviality, communal festivity, and abundance. In this capacity, it either constitutes a contravention of the aesthetic and ethical code or signifies a saturnalian plenitude in which the code proves unnecessary. Drink, however, may also become comic in a more specific sense, for the moment of drunkenness itself tends to entail a dropping of the social mask. Using the model of a nasty private self pasted over with the flowery wallpaper of sociability, Hobbes describes the madness of alcoholic intoxication in revealing terms:

> That Madnesse is nothing else, but too much appearing Passion, may be gathered out of the effects of Wine, which are the same with those of the evill disposition of the organs. For the variety of behaviour in men that have drunk too much, is the same with that of Mad-men: some of them Raging, others Loving, others Laughing, all extravagantly, but according to their severall domineering Passions: For the effect of the wine, does but remove Dissimulation; and take from them the sight of the deformity of their Passions. For, (I believe) the most sober men, when they walk alone without care and employment of the mind, would be unwilling the vanity and Extravagance of their thoughts at that time should be publiquely seen: which is a confession, that Passions unguided, are for the most part meere Madnesse.[77]

Indeed, much of the comedy of a night on the town undoubtedly consists in the dubious pleasure of seeing people behave like complete fruitcakes, being loud and raucous, lusty and playful ("Laughing"), chatting up muff with the slavering subtlety of Panurge at his best ("Loving"), and, turfed out onto the streets at eleven o'clock having manically supped four pints in the mad half-hour before closing time, cheerfully launching into a series of mass brawls ("Raging"). Using an analogous model, Freud interprets drunkenness similarly, pointing out that "a jovial atmosphere, whether produced endogenously or toxically, reduces the inhibitory forces, criticism among them, and thereby makes sources of pleasure accessible again which have been under the weight of suppression."[78] Of course, the cheery drunkenness of carnival celebration is difficult to transpose convincingly into the aesthetic context of a comic drama. Inebriation is notoriously difficult to act well for a start, and the playwright has the problem of lending dramatic form to the sort of scene to which order and form is a natural anathema. Grabbe ambitiously attempts to do just this in *Scherz*, introducing an appropriately gratuitous scene of paralytic revelry in which the characters rant and rave, bellow and bluster, and flop all over the shop, before waking up next morning distributed randomly in unusual places across the village. But such scenes are rarities.

Freud attributes a primarily regressive nature to such drunken folly: "Under the influence of alcohol the adult becomes a child again, enjoying the pleasure of having the course of his thoughts freely at his disposal without regard for the constraints of logic."[79] This thematic link suggests that the comic moment informing the spectacle of drunkenness is akin to the comedy of naivety, and the descriptions of the latter by philosophers corroborate this view. In the *Kritik der Urteilskraft*, Kant defines naivety as "an outburst of the openness originally natural to mankind in the face of the art of dissimulation which has now become second nature," emphasizing (unlike Hobbes) not the nastiness but the honesty of the private self. Kant also grasps the equivocacy of the laughter prompted by naivety: "We laugh at the simplicity [*Einfalt*] which has not yet learnt how to dissemble; and yet also rejoice in the simplicity of nature here nipping that artifice in the bud."[80] Laughter *at* ignorance converges into laughter *with* innocence. Kant brings his comments into line with his general theory of laughter as the product of a rupturing of expectations (here the expectations of social role-playing) by drawing attention to the way this comic impulse unmasks the rogue in *us* and pointing out "that the beautiful but false appearances [*Schein*] which are normally of great weight in our judgements are here suddenly transformed into nothing; and the rascal within ourselves is as it were exposed."[81] Five years later in 1795, Schiller was likewise to stress the ambivalence of naivety and the ensuing doubt "whether we should laugh at the simple-mindedness [*Einfältigkeit*] or venerate the noble simplicity [*Einfalt*]."[82] Freud, also working in a Kantian tradition, views the comic ingenuousness characteristic of children and uneducated adults as resulting from the absence of a social inhibition normally present in members of a society.

Several comic innocents have already been encountered. Candide and Justine both possess an incorrigible optimism that subjects them to misfortune after misfortune, the figure of fool here coming to coincide with that of *victim*, whose best-known incarnation is Chaplin's Tramp. In an evil world, the innocence of the artless fool is easy prey for the legions of sadists and rogues. Svejk's naivety, by contrast, turns out to be a more profitable folly, protecting him as it does from the destructive madness of a sick society. It is because society is so insane that Svejk shows such appreciation of the sanity of the madhouse:

There's a freedom there which not even Socialists have ever dreamed of. A chap can pass himself off as God Almighty, the Virgin Mary, the Pope, the King of England, His Imperial Majesty or St Wenceslas....

Everyone there could say exactly what he pleased and what was on the tip of his tongue, just as if he was in parliament.... It was really like living in paradise there. You could kick up a row, fight, sing, cry, bleat, yell, jump, say your prayers, turn somersaults, crawl on all fours, hop, run about, dance, skip, squat all day on your haunches and climb up the walls. No one would come to you and tell you: "You mustn't do that, sir. It's not decent."[83]

A wise fool in a foolish world, Svejk turns the "normal" conception of madness and sanity on its head (back the right way up), eulogizing the madhouse as a place of fluid identities, truth-speaking, and absolute freedom. His praise of folly could almost have come from the mouth of Erasmus's Folly.

Grimmelshausen's Simplicissimus is an extremely complex fool figure, undergoing different categories of folly at different stages in his development. It is primarily in the first two books that he is the most naive and the most comic fool, as he progresses from a poor "natural" fool, a Christian innocent unaware of his folly and regarded as a no-hoper even by the narrator, into a "wise" or self-aware fool, a court-fool who consciously and critically exploits the freedom of speech granted to him. His initial naivety is shown above all in the lack of rectal restraint generally taken for granted in social intercourse, as Simplicissimus on one public occasion produces a sequence of overpowering pumps that put the reveling guests completely out of countenance and on another is prompted by his fear on seeing the bizarre cavortings of the guests at a dance to stink the whole room to a standstill. Yet Simplicissimus the simple fool serves as a foil to the corruption of a decadent society, his innocently noisome flatulence throwing into relief the more noxious dissolution of the guests. Having taken a hiding for his toe-curling crepitations, he muses: "Their entire behaviour was so farcical, so foolish, so singular and at the same time so wicked and ungodly that the foul smell which I had allowed to escape and for which I had nonetheless taken such a fearful thrashing seemed but a jest by comparison."[84] Like Svejk, the eponymous hero is derided as a fool by the fictional world, yet he is indisputably presented to the reader as possessing qualities lacking in the rest of his society. The folly of Simplicissimus, mocked for his Christian beliefs and his ignorance of the way of the world, is also a type of wisdom that shows up the *sinful* folly of that world.

Having been officially appointed as the court-fool by his master, however, he actively inverts the rogue-fool configuration by resolving only to *pretend* to be foolish: it is now Simplicissimus who does the laughing ("I

... laughed up my sleeve that those who would make a fool of me were now to become my fools").[85] Acting the ass, he exploits his fool's licence in order to mock, deride, and criticize society, feigning the ingenuous frankness that is brazen enough to speak such home truths:

> I had resolved to censure all folly and chastize all vanity, an occupation for which my station at that time was most excellently suited. No table companion was too good for me to pluck out and upbraid his depravity, and if any of them were unwilling to put up with this, they were in addition either made a laughing-stock by the others or admonished by my master that no wise man be given to quarrelling with a fool.[86]

It is his "wise" folly that moreover enables him to turn the established order of truths on its head, as he does in his eloquent disquisition on the wisdom of animals by comparison with humans (he himself "officially" being a calf). Simplicissimus has become a foolishly truth-speaking inverter of values.

Folly is never allowed to relinquish its problematic status in Grimmelshausen, however, and at no stage is Simplicissimus portrayed as unambiguously wise in his foolishness. His early Christian folly is that of an ignorant simpleton and therefore useless, while his later wise, critical folly—being shammed—signals the start of his descent into a career as a *rogue*. Himself now a trickster, he has lost the innocence through which he served so effectively as a foil to the depravity of the world. The picaresque element in the novel shows Simplicissimus playing folly at its own game as he moves from adventure to adventure, and it thwarts the moral-satirical thrust by depriving it of a yardstick of "pure" wisdom against which to measure the madness.

The naive fool thus evidently embodies a necessary tension between wisdom and folly, innocence (to be laughed with) and ignorance (to be mocked). Given that the most unworldly-wise of children may be considered able to articulate a kind of truth, their perspective undistorted by the conceptual clutter accumulated on the road to maturity, even the least reflective naivety is, in a certain sense at least, wise folly. This tension is homologous to the radical tension structuring the chaotic folly of the trickster, the scapegoat, the sacred clown, and the comic hero, who—"acting" their "instincts"—represent the identity of order and chaos, mask and face. The medieval institutionalization of the fool in the form of the court-fool reproduces the same ambivalence. In the Mohammedan world, for example, there is reason to believe that the court-fool was a close relation of the court poet.[87] The madman and the inspired seer were frequently indistinguishable (as in the case of Buhlul-al-Madjnun, a poet-saint-cum-court-fool at the court of Haroun-ar-Rashid at Baghdad in the ninth century), just as in Ireland the clairvoyant poet and the dwarf-fool often merged into a single figure, wisdom and folly again in convergence. Once more, this ambiguity corresponds to the duality in the laughing spectator, who may mock or celebrate, but perhaps normally does a bit of both. It is well-nigh impossible to draw hard and fast distinctions in this regard, for the European court-fool was a post influenced to varying degrees in various places by Celtic and Mohammedan inspired madmen, Roman dwarf-fools, and medieval court jesters, buffoons, and parasites. While many early *natural* court-fools in European courts were little more than chattels or domestic animals and subject to cruel practical pranks, some "wise" court-fools attained a protected position of power akin to that of a confidant (invaluable in a world of imposture, and political and domestic scheming), also becoming a symbol of the king's or queen's political magnanimity. Even so, although the laughter of the monarch and his or her entourage could indeed be festive, it seems unlikely that it ever freed itself entirely from the moral and intellectual self-applause that denigrates and mocks the imperfect, the powerless and the negative.

The empathetic identification with folly observed presumably works in various manners according to the type of folly concerned. Most obviously, it may consist in a vicarious *release*, the spectator as it were living the anarchy at one remove. Aristophanic comedy is thus an expression of ebullient sexuality to be shared and participated in by the audience, just as Shakespearean foolery is an infectiously festive escape from the brambly reality of workaday life and, as such, meant to pervade both sides of the footlights. Restoration drama, in which the universal folly takes the form of acting, imposture, and mask-wearing, has similarly been described (by the English essayist and critic Charles Lamb in the early part of the nineteenth century) as a moral respite—"that happy breathing-place from the burthen of a perpetual moral questioning"—with the spectator returning to the social order all the healthier and more content for having had a two- or three-hour saturnalian breather. The characters we meet in the comic world of Wycherley and Congreve, writes Lamb, "are profligates and strumpets—the business of their brief existence, the undivided pursuit of lawless gallantry. No other spring of action, or possible motive of conduct, is recognised; principles which, universally acted upon, must reduce this frame of things to a chaos. But we do them wrong in so translating them. No such effects are produced in *their* world. When we are among them, we are amongst a chaotic people. We are not to judge them by our usages. No reverend institutions are insulted by their proceedings,—for they have none among them."[88]

Lamb is here anticipating those twentieth-century anthropologists who ascribe to carnival release the function of a periodic "ventilation" for our subversive and playful instincts, and it is but a small step from this communal letting of wind to the notion of tension-management attributed to humor by sociologists (who point out the way a stand-up comedian, for example, can help his audience to cope with otherwise distressful social situations by articulating the sort of irreverent or antisocial sentiment that they may feel but are prevented by conventional norms from voicing).[89] Such ventilation theories are not new. The Theological Faculty of Paris in 1444 used a telling metaphor to justify the Feast of Fools in the same way: "Wine-casks would burst if one didn't open their bung-holes and vent them now and again. Now, we are all ill-coopered barrels and casks which the wine of wisdom would burst asunder if—through perpetual devotion and piety—we let it keep on fermenting; it must be vented, so as not to spoil. For this reason we play the fool for a few days, so that we may afterwards return to worship with all the more fervour."[90] Fifty-five years after Lamb, however, another English critic, George Meredith, was to espouse a less favorable view of the comic anarchy of the Restoration, seeing in it a moral relapse to (and even below) the depths of Greek comedy. Linking the truly comic spirit to the flow of "harmless wine," he would doubtless also have preferred his phallic rites without any genitals. The laughter of comedy, he indeed writes, "is impersonal and of unrivalled politeness, nearer a smile."[91] Peter Barnes's *The Ruling Class* portrays how the Victorianism which did not even allow its comic madness to let rip found the ventilation for *its* pent-up folly in the grotesque guise of an every-man-Jack-the Ripper.

The release that the audience enjoys through the fictional figures may also—but need not—coincide with degrees of *admiration* for them. In a mad world, where all are knaves and rogues, comic drama often creates complicity with the wittiest, the most self-aware, or the most charismatic of the rogues—especially when he or she emerges from a position as social underdog. In the Italian comedy of the Renaissance, the *beffatore*, the witty and skilful practitioner of the *beffa* typified by Machiavelli's Ligurio, constitutes the positive pole of the play. Roguery is here an absolutely natural response to the ubiquitous stupidity of the dupes and gulls, a comic principle that lives on in Lesage's Frontin and Wycherley's Horner among many others. The natural or naive fool, by contrast, has frequently kindled *moral* admiration for his truthfulness, fulfilling a sentimental yearning for childhood "innocence." Individuality, abnormality, eccentricity, and unorthodoxy are all concepts whose reception over the years has necessarily been a function of socio-cultural variables. Greek thought, for example, seemingly had little but scorn for personal idiosyncrasy, the *idio* of which—signifying the private or separate individual—has a mainly pejorative etymological history, as the word "idiot" suggests. Since the romantic era in particular, however, individuality has taken on heroic connotations that may even push the protagonist out of the sphere of comedy altogether (as happens with Baal), the idiotic hero seen as taking a stance against an idiotic world. A further complication is that there are different *types* of norm-infringement. What is seen as a bouncing, healthy (especially male) sexuality—with a celebratory tendency to satyriasis—has tended to provoke a laughter to be distinguished from the derision frequently directed at eccentric forms of sexuality. (More on this later.)

Even when the abnormality is not openly judged to be admirable, the comic moment may still work in a third way, namely through a process of self-recognition. This may simply consist in the fact that, at a purely superficial level, even the most unsympathetic rogue may show some sympathetic traits that we condescendingly consider him to share with us. No one is a complete bastard, surely (??). Elder Olson makes the point that "the victim (is) viewed as unlike ourselves ... but he must also be *like* in some respects, or we should never find him ridiculous.... it is the likeness which supplies the standard with which we must compare him."[92] This may be an important logical point about the nature of the comic rogue, but the fact that no rogue can be utterly different from us and that even Mr. Nasty must needs contain a dash of Mr. Nice does not necessarily make him more comic. What seems just as likely is that the self-recognition is a recognition not of the Mr. Nice in us but of the Mr. Nasty. The sight of the anarchist wreaking his havoc may thus unmask *us*, reveal the anarchist in *us*. This is indeed an aspect latent in all folly, whether positively and festively presented or scornfully portrayed as sin, vice, and roguery. If we all contain the capacity for evil, anarchy, and chaos, then even the most outrageous of fools may be interpreted as exorcizing the potential antisociability that we recognize (perhaps only subliminally) within ourselves. As the nineteenth-century German theorist Ruge contests, the laughing subject and the object of laughter are one and the same person.[93] When we laugh at the miser or hypochondriac, therefore, we are not mocking something fundamentally different from ourselves, but rather a consciously or unconsciously recognized aspect of ourselves: we all contain the seeds of avarice and hypochondria. This internalization of the subject-object relation within the individual self is but another outcome of the mask-face duality within the spectator, which in turn echoes that of the comic hero. At once both anarchist and social actor, we recognize within our identity the potential for (self-) difference, the latent abnormality nestling at the heart of our normality. Jean Paul had made a point not dissimilar to Ruge's two decades earlier, but primarily with regard to the conciliatory comedy of the humorist: "For [humor] there are no fools, but just folly and a mad world"[94], the humorist making fun of mankind and self in the most general of terms.

Given that we are *all* potential fools, humor, according to Jean Paul, involves the recognition of the fool, the knave, the glutton, and coward in every one of us. Our relatively overt identification with a lovable rapscallion like Falstaff is therefore parallel in structure to our covert self-recognition in the unequivocally nasty character, the mean bastard.

One of the most unambiguously obnoxious figures in the history of the comic rogue is Aristophanes's Philocleon, who appears in *The Wasps*. He is sadistically malicious, cowardly, venal, and kleptomanic and allegedly has an incestuous relationship with his daughter. He assaults and insults passersby at random, firstly a breadwoman (a common object of Greek derision, for some reason) and secondly a perfectly "reasonable" person, for whom we ought (in theory) to feel outraged. Veteran yob and rampant *senex* he may be, but he survives the play as self-assuredly ebullient as ever, ending the proceedings with a dancing competition as if to prove his vitality. One critic writes of him: "Philokleon ... is noteworthy for the readiness with which he inflicts on others drunken violence and insults to a degree which incurs threats of prosecution for *hybris*. Recent commentators have remarked on the sympathy and affection which he evokes in the spectator and the reader. I admit that he evokes mine; and yet I remain astonished at the hidden strength of antinomian sentiment which that sympathy and affection imply."[95]

Nearly twenty-four centuries later (in the early sixties of this century), John Kennedy Toole's creation Ignatius J. Reilly dominates *A Confederacy of Dunces* with his equally antisocial, if somewhat more complex, personality. Novels indeed have a fundamental advantage over drama in this area, for selective omniscience and narrative techniques such as free indirect style can lend the narration a degree of immediacy that creates the illusion that the protagonist's inner (i.e., private or *idio-syncratic*) life is being represented. While employing the tense and the pronoun of a third-person narrative (he *did* this, she *did* that), free indirect discourse corresponds to the character's and not the narrator's perspective in its use of deictics (now, this, here).[96] In *A Confederacy of Dunces* the ambiguous status of the narrative, which leaves it open whether it is an omniscient narrator or the protagonist who is narrating, is complemented by a quirky viewpoint that can be taken as marginally deviant from "ours," as well as from that of an "objectively" omniscient narrator. The initial description of Ignatius's appearance typifies this tendency:

> Ignatius himself was dressed comfortably and sensibly. The hunting cap prevented head colds. The voluminous tweed trousers were durable and permitted unusually free locomotion. Their pleats and nooks contained pockets of warm, stale air that soothed Ignatius. The plaid flannel shirt made a jacket un-

necessary while the muffler guarded exposed Reilly skin between earflap and collar. The outfit was acceptable by any theological and geometrical standards, however abstruse, and suggested a rich inner life.[97]

If the narrative spectacles are colored by its protagonist's point of view (and who else but Ignatius would deduce a rich inner life from his wacky appearance?), then we too are brought to view the confederacy of dunces with his eyes, associating with his "private" life to the extent that it corresponds to ours. The narrative technique indeed grants us access to those extravagant thoughts that—as Hobbes puts it—most people would not want to be publicly exposed. A later passage shows how the deictic "this" functions to confirm the sentiment in question as Ignatius's, during a traumatic encounter with some bad breath.

> Some halitosis filtered through his moustache. He ripped the scarf from his cap and shielded his nostrils with it.
>
> . . . .
>
> Again the breath wafted toward Ignatius, who pressed the scarf to his nose so tightly that he felt he would suffocate. He would catch some germ from this woman that would speed to his brain and transform him into a mongoloid.[98]

Ignatius is radically misanthropic and antisocially hate-filled. He hates the twentieth century, he hates television, he hates kids ("the children on that program should all be gassed," he muses cantankerously),[99] and he hates his girlfriend. He is a hypochondriac, a glutton, a borborygmic behemoth with a problematic pyloric valve, and, like John Self and Alexander Portnoy, he comes into his own in the sphere of self-gratification. "At one time he had almost developed it into an art form, practicing the hobby with the skill and fervor of an artist and philosopher, a scholar and gentleman."[100] The comic abuse he dispatches with self-assured gusto consistently breaks taboo ground in the spheres of miscarriages, abortions, zoophilia, mongolism, and rape and is also characterized both by hyperbolic excess ("Your total ignorance of that which you profess to teach merits the death penalty," as he tells a lecturer) and by originality and imagination ("This liberal doxy must be impaled upon the member of a particularly large stallion").[101] Offensive he may be, but his invective has roughly the status of Panurge's vituperative wit, characterizing his correspondence even with his only "friend":[102]

Beloved Myrna:
  I have received your offensive communication. Do you seriously think that I am interested in your tawdry encounters with such sub-humans as folk singers? In every letter of yours I seem to find some reference to the sleaziness of your personal life....

... my personal life has undergone a metamorphosis: I am currently connected in a most vital manner with the food merchandising industry, and
therefore I doubt quite seriously whether I shall have much time in the future
to correspond with you.

Busily,
Ignatius

Ignatius's manner is a parody of normal communicative convention.

If we are not too busy being shocked and repelled, we may therefore
enjoy Ignatius's odiousness, as well as coming to respect his resistance to
the social forces of normalization. When his mother suggests that he allow himself to be "treated," Ignatius asserts his autonomy with a passion
that comes across more heroically than Baal's literary pose:

> "They would try to make me into a moron who liked television and new cars
> and frozen food. Don't you understand? Psychiatry is worse than communism. I
> refuse to be brainwashed. I won't be a robot!"
> "But, Ignatius, they help out a lot of people got problems."
> "Do you think that I have a problem?" Ignatius bellowed. "The only pro-
> blem that those people have anyway is that they don't like new cars and hair
> sprays. That's why they are put away. They make the other members of the
> society fearful. Every asylum in this nation is filled with poor souls who simply
> cannot stand lanolin, cellophane, plastic, television, and subdivisions."[103]

A true fool, Ignatius relativizes folly ("Most fools don't comprehend my
worldview at all") and, for all his nastiness, becomes a type of wise fool
standing in opposition to the confederacy of dunces.

The inherent ambiguity characteristic of all folly echoes the ambiguity
at the heart of comedy's tendency towards metatheatre and anti-illusionism. Just as we simultaneously believe and disbelieve the fiction, identifying with while distancing ourselves from the "illusion," so we
simultaneously identify with and reject or dissociate ourselves from the
scapegoat, the clown, the idiosyncratic comic hero. The failure or the rejection of the social mask is comic for the same reason, but also paradoxical for the same reason, as the failure or the rejection of the
theatrical illusion. The liar's paradox ("I am a liar") is structurally analogous to the paradox of the fool, "I am a fool" being the words of a wise
fool who is acting or self-conscious in his folly.

7
The Political Mask

Master-Servant Reversal

Describing carnival, Bakhtin makes two assertions that at first sight seem to contradict one another. On the one hand, the "suspension of all hierarchical precedence during carnival time was of particular significance ... and ... all were considered equal during carnival."[1] On the other hand, "another essential element was a *reversal* of the hierarchical levels"[2] (my emphasis). Yet the contradiction between reversal and universal leveling is only apparent. The topsy-turvy world of festivity may indeed proclaim an inverted order in which the jester is king, but this new order is a parody not merely of the official order in existence but of order in general. As an act of communal unmasking, carnival is a removal of the facades and costumes bestowed by arbitrary rank and social privilege, to reveal that underneath we are *all* fools—master and servant, sage and ass alike. It is the same principle that is at work in the praise of folly. Having a personified Folly eulogize folly does indeed stand the relation of folly and wisdom on its noddle, but, by exposing the folly within what is judged to be wisdom, it ultimately razes wisdom and folly alike to a lowest common denominator, that of folly.

The medieval motif of the *danse macabre* or dance of death is equally all-encompassing in its leveling function and, as such, betrays the deep-seated kinship of folly and death in traditional systems of popular imagery. Frequently appearing in frescoes and wallpaintings of the time (as well as rearing its cranium on board Brant's Ship of Fools and in actual celebratory entertainments during the fifteenth century), the motif presents its dancing skeletons, often sporting carnival masks, as taunting the living with the vanity of their worldly achievements. Mundane honors and distinctions, ranks and riches are mocked as impotent and foolish in the face of Death, and, stripped of these, man is reduced to the Nought so closely associated with Folly in medieval thought. Death is less a communal than a universal unmasking and as undiscriminatingly egalitarian as wine and wanking. Like the perennial banana skin and like the folly of carnival, it is one of the great levelers.

Folly has been inextricably bonded with falling and downward movement ever since Lucifer fell and became a ludicrous self-parody and since
Adam's tumble set the human comedy in motion. The fall is indeed the
archetypal bathetic motion, a sudden, surprising downward rush degrad-
ing the pretensions of posture and man's bipedal pride. It is comic not
merely for the suddenness that jolts expectation, however, but as a gesture that may be identified with and enjoyed. Pride is not just debunked
by the ensuing fall, it is punished by a satisfying irony of events that
transforms what is high into what is low. Joubert's *Traité du Ris* (1579)
takes account both of the formal element of surprise and of a social element of *Schadenfreude* which allows us to take greater pleasure in the
tumble of a figure of authority than in the drunkard's lurch. "On seeing
somebody fall over in the mud we are moved to laughter, for this is very
unsightly, and without any danger which would incline us to commisera-
tion.... Children and drunkards habitually fall over and so make us
laugh, but we laugh incomparably more when a great and notable personage ... suddenly falls in a bog.... But there is nothing so gross and
which arouses less pity than when this same personage is unworthy of the
rank he holds and the honour he is paid."[3]

Central to the comedy of carnival is that moment of bathetic travesty
that thus mimics the getup and garb of authority for the express purpose
of dragging it downwards and traipsing it through mirth's muddy puddles,
rethinking and redefining the elevated in terms of lowly material existence and bodily gunk. "The orientation of plebeian culture, both to itself and to the elites that hold political and economic power, is expressed
in the form of travesty.... These forms facilitate the disclosure of contingency and arbitrariness in the allocation of social identity. The noisy
and colourful masquerades of Carnival represent all of social reality, even
its most powerful and majestic aspects, as changing and transitory. Political reality is brought into familiar contact with everyday life; its pretensions to grandeur are uncrowned."[4] Just as the rhetorical device known
as bathos takes the wind out of literary pretension, carnivalesque travesty
deflates the hot air balloon of political power with a timely prick from
beneath. Such celebration might consequently seem to be unambivalently
seditious, as a political expression of communal solidarity and a radical
critique of privilege and hierarchy. In practice, however, this collective
harmony need be neither as progressive nor as benevolent as it sounds.
The critical resistance to arbitrary domination is frequently complemented by a conservative impulse through which the community seeks
to maintain and preserve its own identity and authority—an impulse that
may be realized at the expense not only of the privileged but also of
outsiders, foreigners, and surrogate victims such as prostitutes or actors.
The laughter of carnival folly may be bullying as well as bathetic, totalitarian as well as egalitarian.

Schopenhauer gives a particularly apposite depiction of what might be called the political mask:

> On stage one person plays the prince, another the counsellor, a third the servant or soldier or general etc. But these differences are only present on the outside. Inside, at the heart of all such appearances [*Erscheinung*] the same thing lies hidden: a poor player with all his trials and tribulations. It is the same in real life. The differences of rank and wealth give to each his role to play, but by no means does this correspond to any inner differences in happiness or contentment, for here too we find hidden within everyone the same poor wretch with all his trials and tribulations.[5]

Political status is a role or mask, therefore, concealing the wretched, naked fool to which we are all in the end reducible. Carnival and carnivalistic comedy unmask this whole political performance not simply through their underlying assumption of universal folly and their revealing satire of the powerful, but also by concretely demonstrating the contingency of the social personae we play within the *theatrum mundi*—and in particular by turning master into slave (or servant) and slave into master, swapping the arbitrarily distributed masks around in a topsy-turvy reversal of the social hierarchy. Rotating the social ladder 180 degrees exposes its fictional nature by defamiliarizing it and reveals its wobbliness as a human construction "hiding" either natural equality or the formless negativity of pure human potential. While neither carnival nor theatrical comedy need *articulate* any such awareness (just as other forms of ritual inversion and festivity may show a greater or a lesser degree of self-consciousness in their political orientation), this social upturning seems likely in some sense at least to function as a surrogate release from the restrictions of the socio-political straitjacket. Nonetheless, the nature and extent of this release is crucially dependent upon the type of comic context in question.

In the case of plebeian counter-culture, for example, the radical potential of theatre has at times been felt to be exacerbated by the fluid identity of the actor, who is defined by the fact that his public utterances fail to correspond to what his "real" feelings are.[6] The discarding of the political mask is here incorporated within a more general rejection of identity, a mercurial self-difference that has a tendency to escape or evade the claims of jurisdiction and the calls of responsibility. The freedom not to be oneself grants the actor (or carnivalist) the liberty to do and say things he or she would not normally dare. The late sixteenth-century polemic against the English theatre was indeed occasioned by the ambiguous relationship of the player to all authority, and it was as a response to the concomitant call for abolition that theatre became limited and controlled by the introduction of a well-defined "author" function, which developed the ownership of "texts" and speeded the transformation from the anarchic freedom of improvization to the accountability of dramatic literature. Consequently, even comedy found itself obliged to legitimize itself by the adoption of pedagogic responsibility typified by Jonson's whip-wielding comedy of correction. The author—in his capacity as an individual with legal liability—becomes the proprietor of a finished and integrated comic text, and this master text holds sway over a dominion of servant-actors. Although the comedy of Tieck and Grabbe has playfully subverted even this convention by having its characters (pretend to) improvize or rebel against their playwright, by and large modern theatre—unquestioningly based as it is on the authority of the author—is constituted by a fundamental master-servant relationship that itself normally goes unchallenged. Not only in this sense is the moment of political reversal offered by comic theatre diluted by comparison with the extempore immediacy of carnival, for it is also displaced to a passive mode whereby it is but the *sight* of the mastery of servants or the bondage of masters that yields vicarious satisfaction. Nor does all comedy spend equal energy on inverting the social order. The Old Comedy of ancient Greece for a long time took malicious pleasure in beating, tormenting, and molesting its slaves, effectively confirming the power structures within society, just as laughter and self-disparagement have themselves so frequently had to function as strategies of appeasement used by servants as deferential gestures.[7] The comic tradition has a lineage of servile or subordinate slaves and servants who feel no desire to outwit their master or sabotage the social ladder. The question of servant-master reversal may simply not arise.

Even so, the upturning of the hierarchy of power constitutes one of the most important aspects of comedy's topsy-turvy world, and it is in accordance with this socio-political bias that comedy, like the frank and free marketplace speech of carnival revelry, has traditionally expressed itself in the vernacular, employing what Dante described as a "low and unstudied" style by comparison with the elevation and sublimity of tragedy.[8] The manifestations of such comic role-swapping sublimate the subversive potential of the device to varying degrees:

1. the servant may prove himself intellectually superior to his master, yet without any exploitation of this superiority or questioning of the social order.
2. the servant and master may act out a role-reversal within the scope of the comic fiction.
3. a subordinate or underdog may outwit his master by actively turning his intellectual ascendancy and wit to account.
4. a servant or underdog may enjoy a period of temporary mastery by chance or accident, or as part of a festive or in some way licensed reversal.

The first part of this chapter is concerned with examining these variations in turn.

The theatre òf Molière exemplifies the comedy of the cheeky or spirited servant. Argan's servant Toinette in *Le Malade imaginaire* is a paragon of well-meaning impertinence who takes pleasure in needling and nettling her master, refusing to pander his hypochondriacal whims or to let herself be tyrannized by him. Her "power" over her master consists in the fact that his imagined physical incapacity prevents him from meting out brute force, a fact she exploits by aggravating him to the point where he drops his mask of illness and chases her round the room. Her good sense constantly exposes and unmasks the cantankerous old geezer's self-deception (to everyone except himself), and, like virtually all the other characters in the play, she makes sport of the fool's gullibility, playing the part of a doctor in order to disenamour him of his other doctors and steer the action towards its happy ending. Yet her insubordination never assumes an overtly political or subversive dimension: while deceiving her master, she never stops serving him (it is simply that she has a better idea what is good for him than he does), nor does she ever question her social status. Rather, by thwarting and baffling the foolish old *senex* insofar as he represents an obstacle in the path of "young love," it is in fact her master's daughter whom she more loyally serves. The cheeky wit of the stock "wily servant" works as an agent of young love and, helping to avert the daughter's betrothal to the jibbering jerk from the medical profession, is indispensable in propelling the plot towards the celebratory happy ending.

In *Le Tartuffe*, Orgon's self-deluded monomania manifests itself in his desire to marry his daughter off to the scheming hypocrite Tartuffe, again standing in the way of what seems to us "reasonable people" to be the "natural" marriage. It is the saucy servant Dorine who this time puts up resistance to the folly of the *senex*, for her disrespectful lucidity enables her to see through and debunk Tartuffe's shammed piety, just as Toinette's perspicacity deflates Argan's pose and Nicole's unchecked hilarity (in *Le Bourgeois gentilhomme*) undermines the hopeless efforts of her bourgeois master to play the part of a *gentilhomme*. To achieve her ends, Dorine indeed uses the same tactics as those later to be employed by Toinette, such as insistent interruption, the claim to be working for his sake, and the technique of reminding the master of the principles of his own obsession (piety, illness) when he loses his temper. Like Toinette she succeeds in bringing her master virtually to admit his folly inspite of himself (Orgon: "I don't want to be liked" [*Le Tartuffe*, 2.2]; Argan: "I'm not good, I'm bad when I want to be" [*Le Malade imaginaire*, 1.5]), and like Toinette she almost, but not quite, takes a beating for her troubles.

The awkwardness and unhelpfulness may of course equally be involuntary, with the subordinate unwittingly thwarting the master's designs, as well as probably provoking a drubbing into the bargain. While appealing to a spirit of seditious release, the sight of the slave or servant being awkward, stubborn, or a pain in the neck—especially when unintentionally so—need not thus imply greater wit, wisdom, or intelligence, nor entail any basic role-reversal. Indeed, the social hierarchy is frequently endorsed by the pasting meted out for such inadvertent recalcitrance. In spite of remaining structured by the existent order, however, what this vicarious contumacy does illustrate is the interdependence of master and slave or servant. As Hegel pointed out, the master is as reliant on the slave for assistance, recognition, and confirmation of identity as the slave is on the master—if not more so.

Plautus's figure Pseudolus had been one of the first comic slaves explicitly to prove himself craftier than his master, prompting Nietzsche to take the New Comedy to task for its inherently proslave stance. Pseudolus is a plot-weaver comparable to the playwright, a liar who like the poet spends his time creating fictions out of airy nothings, and at the outset he establishes his complicity with the audience by playing the Cretan liar, warning them to be on their guard against him and not to trust a word from his lips. Helping his master Calidorus to win his loved one (by overcoming the malevolent pimp Ballio about to sell her as a slave), Pseudolus's wile places him firmly in the emotional driving seat and permits him to boss his master about ("Orders is orders. Do as I tell you"), to express his displeasure with him, and to overcome any resistance with his considerable powers of persuasion. Yet he never ceases to serve his master. The cerebral pecking order is independent from the social order, but also seems to serve as a compensation for it. In Plautus's *The Pot of Gold*, however, Lyconides's crafty and refractory slave, likewise working in the name of young love, wins his manumission to boot. The Italian comedy of the Renaissance was to resort with striking frequency to this stock Plautine situation in which a young man relies on the guile of his servant to win the girl denied him by his filial dependence. Again we are witness to the mastery of the servants.

The moment of festive inversion is evidently diluted to the nth degree in the motif of the cheeky or wily servant, which can equally be seen as a mimetic reflection of the real-life fact that some servants *are* cheeky and many *are* brighter or more practical than their social superiors. Nevertheless, there is a sense of irreality and release in seeing the underdog intellectually on top. Indeed, given political impotence and economic dependency, all the characters in question are substantially reliant on *luck* in establishing the reign of their wit. Toinette, for example, only enjoys her impunity thanks to the influence of Argan's second wife, Béline, who prevents him from discharging her, and Plautus's Calidorus is too much of a lovesick looby to have any control over his slave. Pseudolus complicates the issue by claiming to the audience that he was born of noble stock anyway (although are we to believe an inveterate liar?).

The comedy of Plautus further provides an example of the second category of master-slave reversal. *The Prisoners* presents the spectacle of master acting slave and slave acting master, once again the inversion qualified by the fact that the slave never stops serving his master. Such comedy complements the sense of topsy-turviness with the comic potential of role-swapping, disguise, and acting, and the prologue heavy-handedly makes sure the spectator understands what is going on: "Thus, they have exchanged their clothes and names. Tyndarus is now calling himself Philocrates, and Philocrates Tyndarus: each is posing as the other" (ll.37–39). Master and slave further labor the joke: "Now, you are pretending to be my master, and I am pretending to be your slave" (l.225). Again, Plautus ends up weakening the subversive potential of the situation by revealing that the slave is in fact noble anyway.

The device of acted reversal by mutual consent was especially popular in French comedy of the seventeenth and eighteenth centuries, yet it remains ultimately conservative, deriving its comedy primarily from the sight of the servant (and master) *failing* to act their adopted role convincingly. The wobbly mask is funny because the servant is viewed at heart as a servant and cannot genuinely hide his "true" status. This is not universally so. The little-known plays of Hauteroche and Dancourt have their servants adopt the part of master perfectly, both in dress and speech. But here a rich source of comedy goes begging, and Scarron, Lesage, and Marivaux all turn shaky social masks to comic account by showing the servant's attempts to imitate the master marred by lapses into boastfulness or indecorum as well as hyperbolic excess in courtly love-making. While generating an irreal reversal of the immutable social ladder in the play-filled leisure time of the aristocracy, the topsy-turvy motif turns against its underdog by confirming the existent order in its very presuppositions. In Marivaux's *Le Jeu de l'amour et du hasard*, where the intricacies of the plot involve two sets of role-swapping (master-servant and mistress-maid), the inability to play the role in question functions as a dramatic device cleverly bringing the two couples together in accordance with the dictates of rank and, after a goodly measure of humming and hawing about amour propre, producing the happy ending. The master, pretending to be the servant, is—contrary to his own expectations—attracted to the maid, acted unbeknown to him by the mistress, while the servant, playing the master, gets on much better with the mistress, played by the maid. Underlying this web of confusion is the essentialist principle that you are what you are born (once a servant always a servant): master and mistress are made for one another as much as servant and maid. A similar principle informs Goldsmith's *She Stoops to*

Conquer, in which Charles Marlow falls in love with a "chamber maid" (in spite of all class barriers), only to have this chamber maid reveal at the denouement that she is really the girl he had been supposed to court all along.

Although such acted role-swapping tends to presuppose and reinforce an essentially conservative sense of stable social identity underpinning the acted deviation, it may at the same time perform other dramatic functions. Seeing the servant *play* the master may stress that the servant *is* the servant at bottom, but the spectacle also presents a disrespectfully parodic double or caricature of nobility. The lowly figure's travesty of his superiors need not resemble the actual conduct of those being imitated or emulated any more than do the struttings and posturings of Shakespeare's lowly Bottom, who lords it with the subtlety of an ass, yet it does bring to light the image of the socially elevated in the eyes of their inferiors. The situation may additionally be used to explore the relationship between master and servant, characterized as this may be by mutual dependence and reciprocal affection or disaffection, just as the obstinacy or obstreperousness of the slave exposes the symbiotic interdependence of social opposites.

The role-swapping of slave and master is to be found as early as the Old Comedy of Aristophanes, whose figure Dionysus exchanges places with his slave Xanthias in *The Frogs*. Dionysus, on his way to the underworld to bring Euripides back to life, has (unconvincingly) disguised himself as Heracles in order to cope with the dangers of the trip, but, when things threaten to become violent, he persuades Xanthias to take over the imposture while Dionysus pretends to be the slave. Xanthias of course starts to relish the role when the attentions of one of Persephone's pretty flute-playing girls are promised for his entertainment, and Dionysus (of course) immediately wants his lion-skin disguise back. Yet he gets the raw deal again (at the hands of a band of irate landladies), and so the mask passes to and fro between master and slave. When the two of them are eventually faced with the prospect of an immediate and unavoidable mauling, Xanthias wittily tries to wangle his way out of trouble ("Tell you what: how about you torturing this slave of mine" ll.615–16), but in the end they both take a thrashing. Again, however, it emerges that it is only enlightened or weak masters who permit such role-swapping. Pluto's slave, who goes in more for backbiting and eavesdropping, later expresses his surprise that Xanthias should be treated so leniently:

> *Pluto's slave.* By Zeus, he's quite a gentleman, your master.
> *Xanthias.*   Indeed he is, for he's a master at the arts of swigging and frigging.
> *Pluto's slave.* Yes, but not beating you for making out that you were the master and him the slave ...

Xanthias.   He'd have regretted it if he'd tried.
Pluto's slave. Ah, that's spoken like a true slave. I like that.
Xanthias.   Like it, eh?
Pluto's slave. Why, there's no greater pleasure than cursing the master behind
his back.

(ll.739–47)

Xanthias may indeed be taken as Pseudolus's ancestor and, by extension, as the prototype of the crafty servant or slave. He constitutes a crucial step in the development of Old Comedy, for, up until his appearance, Aristophanes had treated slaves primarily as *butts* to be scorned and (in *The Wasps*, *Lysistrata*, and *The Birds*) derived callous and brutal comedy from the maltreatment of lowly figures. Perhaps a consequence of the intellectual scrutiny under which the institution of slavery was to come from the late fifth century B.C. onwards, Xanthias marks a turning point that was to be followed up in Aristophanes's last extant comedy, *Wealth*, in which Carion behaves more like a friend than a slave to his master Chremylus. This play in turn seems to set the tone for the New Comedy, by which time the young man's dependence on the cunning slave has become an established motif that arguably reaches its apogee in Pseudolus.

The canny *zanni* of the commedia dell'arte are a continuation of the tradition, generally operating in the service of young love (as well as for their own ends) and in opposition to the doltish old lechers Pantalone and il Dottore. Brighella is insubordinate and impudent and as fervent a liar as Pseudolus. Under his French name Scapin (the Italian equivalent Scapino or "The Escaper" hinting that we are dealing with a comic Houdini), he takes on definitive literary form in Molière's *Les Fourberies de Scapin*, where he works for two sets of young lovers against two mean and stubborn old fathers. A *valet fourbe* with a natural tendency to take the side of youth in the never-ending generation conflict, Scapin emerges as a jack of all roles and master of intrigue, creating comedies within the comedy to trick the gulls and bring about the happy ending. Yet not only does he zestfully mete out a farcical whacking to the irascibly senescent Géronte (his young master's father), he also has his young master himself completely under his thumb. This comes to light in one of Molière's characteristic reversal scenes, where the comedy consists in an ironic turning of the conversational tables. At the outset of this exchange Léandre would seem to be on top of his subordinate, whom he angrily accuses of "betraying" him to his father—although it is noticeable that even at this stage Scapin retains a certain superiority through his tactical ploy of admitting to a number of minor faults as a diversionary trick. News of the abduction of Léandre's sweetheart, Zerbinette, however, turns the servant-master relationship emphatically upside-down, for when wile and wit are in demand, the sly servant has absolute power over his master. Now it is Scapin's turn to be haughty and proud and make his master grovel:

> *Léandre.* Would you abandon me, Scapin, to the cruel extremity in which my love finds itself?
> *Scapin.* Suddenly coming up and insulting me so!
> *Léandre.* I was wrong, I do concede it.
> *Scapin.* Treating me as a rascal, a scoundrel, a blackguard and a knave!
> *Léandre.* I am all penitence.
> *Scapin.* Making to run me through with your sword.
> *Léandre.* I crave your pardon with all my heart; and if you would have me throw myself at your knees, here I am, Scapin, imploring you once more not to abandon me.
> *Octave.* Faith, Scapin, to this you must yield.
> *Scapin.* Arise. Another time, be not so swift.
>
> (Act 2, scene 4)

Natural actor that he is, Scapin milks the reversed situation for its full comic potential, playing with his master's servitude. Despite consistently outwitting his superiors, however, he shows no awareness of any disparity at all between his wit and his wages. It is as a servant that he exerts his domination, as though the hierarchy of wit renders the hierarchy of rank and fortune irrelevant—an irrealistic escape from the social actuality in which it is the hierarchy of wit that is rendered irrelevant by power. Motivated neither by a desire for wealth and status nor a sense of social justice, Scapin's playfulness is playfulness for its own sake. He exploits his intellectual ascendancy over his masters, but—a performer through and through—it is for "our" entertainment that he does it.

This was soon to change. In Lesage's figure Frontin, the trickster-servant acquires a previously unheard-of self-assurance and actively pursues his intellectual domination with a view to its long-term substantiation in real terms. Whereas Scapin does his deceiving out of a primeval love of fun and mischief coupled with an impishly benevolent urge to serve the cause of young love, Frontin is motivated exclusively by a craving for wealth and the aspiration to improve his social standing. He is a skilled trickster in his feigning of naivety and shows flashes of wit, yet he lacks Scapin's timeless and self-perpetuating vitality and the charm that was to characterize Figaro. The comedy's "happy" ending incorporates Frontin's proposal to the equally cynical maid, Lisette, whose acceptance cannot be seen as entirely unrelated to the success of Frontin's financial schemings. Having ruined their superiors, the servants end in the ascendant, and their fictional reign continues "after" the final curtain: "And thus ends the reign of Monsieur Turcaret; now for mine to begin," gloats Frontin as the curtain falls. Elsewhere, Lesage has his "Diable boiteux" make the point that the public "like laughing at the expense of those who make them cry."[9] *Turcaret* is a vicarious turning of the tables on those who normally have the last laugh in the social comedy.

One critic has interpreted the increasing tendency of comedy to portray a *permanent* reversal in the servant-master configuration as being the result of the passing of the baroque period.[10] Although such historical claims are bound to be contentious in their habit of lumping cultural phenomena together like slabs of ideological concrete and thereby flattening out all difference, dissent, and diversity, the stabler world order of Elizabethan England, for example, where everyone played a God-given role, would indeed have been less likely to be conducive to the social mobility of Lesage's figures, who embody instead an Enlightenment belief in the power of the rational individual characteristic of the spreading sway of bourgeois liberalism. Not that social movement was impossible in baroque culture, but where the dominant ideology purports to constitute a "ladder of degree" accounting for all hierarchy, the mobility is more liable to generate the comic friction of farcical incongruity and flawed role-playing than the subversive sight of the successful social climber. The "permanent" reversals of Beaumarchais and Nestroy by contrast are inextricably bound up with the spirit of revolutionary turbulence sweeping across Europe at the end of the eighteenth and beginning of the nineteenth centuries.

Beaumarchais's *Le Barbier de Séville* (1775) is relatively conventional in structure, consisting as it does of Figaro, the clever servant, helping two young lovers to overcome an importunate old man. Cheekily insubordinate and lovably lazy this Figaro may be, but he does little more than claim the freedom to speak one's mind, wittily exposing the weaknesses of his superiors without ever questioning the underlying order. *Le Mariage de Figaro* (1784) was justifiably seen as much more dangerous. Not only does Figaro continue to outshine the Count at the level of conversational wit and repartee, he also out-tricks his roguish master and is shown moreover as thoroughly vindicated in doing so. Since being helped by Figaro to win the hand of Rosine at the end of *Le Barbier*, the Count has grown bored with the earlier play's happy ending and is now in hot pursuit of Figaro's fiancée, Suzanne. Two comic moments, therefore, converge in Figaro's resolve to strike back: the servant carries the day over the master, and the potential fool-cum-cuckold outwits the dastardly knave. Figaro wins the conflict hands down. Admirable for his schemings and plot-weaving and the mental alacrity with which he improvizes lie after lie, he also embarrasses his master with witty barbs ("You are in command of everything here except yourself" [5.12]) and ironic references to his virtue, constancy, and wisdom. The play turns "dangerous," however, with the interspersal of a number of noncomic

moments in which Figaro *seriously* defends his conduct ("Take vengeance on those who spoil our plans by upsetting theirs—anyone would do
it" [2.2]) and gives articulate vent to his political dissatisfaction, as in the
following more or less completely unfunny apostrophe:

> Because you are a great nobleman, you deem yourself a great genius! ... no-
> bility, fortune, rank, honours: all this makes you so proud! What have you done
> to deserve so many benefits! You took the trouble of being born, no more. A
> common enough man otherwise!
>
> (Act 5, scene 3)

In another passage, Figaro describes the world of power and politics in
terms that could just as well apply to the realm of comic intrigue: "pretending not to know the things one does know, to know all the things one
doesn't know ... playing a role well or badly" (3.5). Although Figaro is
here associating intrigue with such rogues as the Count, he also—in testifying to the power of the true *esprit* to outwit the rogue—himself embodies wit's capacity to subvert or topple the political order: "Wit alone
shifts everything." Unlike Frontin, Figaro ends up exploiting his wit out
of a hankering for justice.

It is notable that Figaro ceases to be funny when he has a guillotine to
grind. The political hero and the comic hero are two different aspects of
the same person or, viewed more cynically, the political hero is only one
of the roles played by the Protean comic hero. Nestroy's Ultra, in *Freiheit
in Krähwinkel*, likewise typifies the divergence of the two facets. The play
as a whole indeed offers an interesting contrast with *Le Mariage*, for
whereas the latter preceded the French revolution, Nestroy's came in the
eight months of relative freedom following the 1848 revolution in Austria
(and before its capitulation in November). While Beaumarchais justifies
and anticipates the French Revolution, Nestroy, though unambiguously
ridiculing the reactionaries, also pokes gentle fun at the Austrian Revolution, Krähwinkel serving as a symbol of small-town bourgeois pettiness
and at the same time holding up a critical mirror to its Viennese public.
Ultra may not strictly speaking be a servant in the sense encountered so
far, but he is a "revolutionary": more importantly, however, he shows
himself to be in that comic tradition of natural actors of the Pseudolus-
Brighella-Scapin mold. In this capacity, he transcends his revolutionary
role.

Nestroy mocks the political reaction by representing his chief reactionary, Klaus, in the comic guise of the *senex* who constitutes an obstacle to the course of young love, the happy ending thus involving the
gulling or outwitting of an old fool who is right-wing in the bargain, a
political as well as a domestic tyrant. That Nestroy is also proffering a

critique of the revolution, however, is clear from his portrayal of the Krähwinklers' distortion and parody of the ideal, suggesting that the play may even have been meant as a prognostication or warning in the face of the imminent quashing of the real-life insurrection. For the people of Krähwinkel, the revolution is little more than an opportunity to pursue their own vocational or amorous ends: Willibald, for example, wins the hand of the nightwatchman's daughter by becoming a rebel, while the furrier is shown speculating on the consequences of revolution for his trade. The insurgency is not depicted as glorious and great but small and comic, a revolt in miniature echoed by the parody of Viennese diminutives in Ultra's characterization of the situation. "All the elements of revolution, everything conducive to revolt, elsewhere found on a large scale, we Krähwinklers have on a small scale. We have an absolute despotlet, we have an irresponsible cabinetlet, a bureaucratic systemlet, a censorshiplet, public debtlets substantially beyond our meanlets, and we therefore need to have a revolutionlet, and through the revolutionlet a new constitutionlet, and in the end—freedomlet" (1.8).

Ultra himself can on the one hand be taken as Nestroy's mouthpiece, as when he lays into the censorship(let) of the time, every playwright's bête noire: "Censorship is the living confession of those in power that they can *trample* all over the slaves they've knocked senseless but cannot *govern* free peoples" (1.14). On the other hand, though, he is also a trickster, if a benevolent and likeable one, and, as such, perpetually in performance. Even the "spontaneous" ardor of his revolutionary speeches is histrionic, and his self-distance permits him to debunk his pose in a way that passion would have tended to preclude. He turns up in a sequence of disguises as a Ligorian, a Russian, the new European Commissioner for Liberty and Equality, the politician Metternich, and a proletarian. He is as Protean as such comic heroes as Falstaff, Panurge, and Harlequin, but fluid identity and permanent self-difference stand in direct opposition to the unequivocal self-identity requisite for ethical and political consistency and commitment. Whereas Figaro implicitly renounces his origins in chaotically benign trickery in order to turn serious and adopt an ethical position at key moments, Ultra reveals himself above all as a crafty bugger. Dramatically fusing the sexual happy ending (the union of the three pairs of lovers, including Ultra and Frau Frankenfrey) and the political happy ending (the overcoming of the senescent reactionaries), Nestroy has his protagonist—still togged up as a working-class hero—getting married to an extremely rich widow. The political happy ending is placed in the shadow of a parodic question mark, for just as Mother Folly's praise of folly ends up reducing both wisdom and folly to the level of folly, social reversal tends to have to undermine *itself* in order to stay truly comic. As soon as the politically radical moment hardens into doctrine and then into dogma, it has a habit of forking away from the comic impulse and rejoining it only inadvertently—as an object of ridicule.

The ambivalence of a revolutionary utopia is symbolized by the play of the light-dark motif running through the comedy. Right at the outset, the tinsmith's retort to the claim of the nightwatchman that the days of darkness are numbered is that, once the darkness goes, so will the night-watchman's job, the pun metaphorically yoking together literal darkness with the spiritual darkness of an age of oppression. As the play progresses, however, it becomes evident that the comedy itself depends upon a certain *use* of darkness. The final comedy of disguise and resolution of the happy ending (in which the women dress up as revolutionaries) is intentionally carried out at night to exploit the ignorance of the reactionaries, the fact that they—unlike the spectators—are *in the dark*, and throughout the play Ultra has been toying with disguise in order to turn their lack of enlightenment to account as well as punish it. It is Ultra who, acting the part of the real-life autocrat Metternich, orders the deferral of the reactionaries' quashing of the uprising until nighttime, in turn giving the revolutionaries the time they need to carry out their deception. In a particularly ambiguous passage he claims:

> Night has always been the element of my effectiveness. The great people on earth are stars, and so can only shine when it's dark. In the sun of freedom the twinkling of the stars is obliterated, and therefore it should not be allowed to shine too long. Besides, night never fails to return. The universal confusion I foster is the darkness of dusk, a bloodred sunset. The starsparkling night of the Reaction will triumph in the political firmament.
>
> (Act 3, scene 14)

In the guise of Metternich, then, Ultra is explicitly drawing attention to the metaphorical proximity of nighttime and political repression, daytime and the enlightenment of freedom: clearly night is—from "our" point of view at least—something to be banished. Circumspection, however, is due: it is not Metternich saying this, but Ultra-disguised-as-Metternich, and there is a sense in which the words can, in part, also be read as applying to Ultra, whose success as an intriguant equally depends upon the unenlightenment of his gulls and who can only shine at the expense of their dullness. The comic wit needed to procure the happy ending is a well-placed shaft of illumination that mockingly outmaneuvers the agents of darkness. Were the happy ending as a reign of *pure* enlightenment ever to be definitively secure, however, Ultra—like the nightwatchman and like Nestroy himself—would be out of a job. The opening wish of the chorus of Krähwinkel to trap freedom and make it compulsory ("Freiheit muß sein") signals the paradox of freedom that, analogous to the paradoxes of spontaneity and of folly, ensures that comedy is always chiaroscuro.

The fourth category of master-servant reversal shows the servant or underdog enjoying a period of licence or freedom, but only a temporary one, which (though not mere acting) is internalized *within* the fiction and does not pretend to continue after the final curtain. The underdog has his day, albeit a brief one. It may simply take the form of a few moments of vigorous invective or vilification when the master's back is turned, as Pluto's slave goes in for in *The Frogs* and Molière's Sganarelle when Don Juan is presumed to be out of earshot. Alternatively, it may constitute the focal point of the drama. Again it is difficult to make generalizations about the political implications of the device. In *Jeppe from the Hill*, written in 1722 by the Dane Ludvig Holberg, the slothful peasant Jeppe—after a drunken binge—wakes up to find himself dressed in fine linen in the bed of the local aristocrat, who has stumbled upon him lying on a dung-heap and decided to see what happens when the peasant assumes his position in society. Jeppe abuses his newfound freedom to the full by among other things being gluttonous and socially irresponsible and taking advantage of an encounter with the bailiff's wife to fondle her mammets. The moral of the story is unambiguously conservative: admit the baseborn yokel to a position of power and he will misuse this authority to the detriment of society as a whole. Sanctioning the absolutist structure of the social order and the essentialist belief that a peasant is a peasant is a peasant ..., Holberg's play propounds—in its didactic frame at least—an *opposition* to the spread of liberal individualism. The period of temporary folly may be fun to watch, but it is ultimately to be castigated and corrected, and as the Baron's lackey points out, if the change had been permanent the comedy would have turned into a frightful tragedy. Yet in the hands of a less moralistic playwright and given a little more emphasis on Jeppe's sexual cheekiness and his gluttony and less on his tyrannical selfishness, the folly could equally well have assumed an explicitly positive, festive, or utopian character. This is the case, for example, in *Don Quixote*, where Sancho Panza the goatherd enjoys a temporary reign as the governor of his "isle." As with Jeppe, it is all a setup, but more carnivalesque in tone, a celebratory world upside-down (and the final beating Sancho Panza takes is very much in the tradition of the carnival king). Here the reign of the rustic dolt turns out to be a reign of common sense, fairness, and simple wisdom, as even Don Quixote is forced to concede: "Where I expected, friend Sancho, to hear news of your negligence and folly, I have had accounts of your wise actions, for which I return especial thanks to Heaven, which can raise the poor from the dunghill and make wise men of fools."[11]

The temporary ascendancy of the underdog in Gogol's *The Govern-*

ment Inspector is a result not of a playful reversal but a chance mis-understanding, Hlestakov the junior official being mistaken for a figure of power. Although only short-lived, Hlestakov's social rise is less intended to confirm the existing order by showing Hlestakov's behavior as deviant than to mock and satirize the Tsarist bureaucracy, which cannot tell the real thing apart from the imposture, blinkered as it is by its own corruption. Zuckmayer's *Der Hauptmann von Köpenick* is in the same spirit. The play is permeated by social criticism, for Voigt is a down-and-out in the tradition of Büchner's Woyzeck, articulate and sensitive, but a victim of unjust officialdom who is seemingly unable to escape from the vicious bureaucratic circle excluding him from a job. When he dons a military uniform as a way of deceiving people and holding his own in the community, it is not Voigt who is being derided: his mask fits him well enough, even if it does chafe. Instead, Zuckmayer is scoffing at the pedantic Prussianism which, apotheosizing the military mask, is blinded by its obsessive reverence for the uniform. A militaristic society deserves to be hoist by its own petard.

The Woman on Top

Voigt is described by an admiring chauffeur as the sort of person to turn the world upside down—"der stellt noch die janze Welt uffn Kopp!" (3.20)—again drawing attention to the link between comedy and the topsy-turvy world. The servant-master reversal is in fact just one among a whole series of inversions to be found in the broadsheets depicting the world upside-down (*mundus perversus, verkehrte Welt, il mondo alla riversa*, etc.) in evidence in so many cultures—above all in the sixteenth and following centuries. These broadsheets also focused with even greater frequency upon a second category of inversion in the social order, that between man and wife, regularly presenting the husband as sitting and holding a baby or a distaff while the wife stands upright and armed. In the world of comic drama, what Wilde was to call "the tyranny of the weak over the strong"[12] could manifest itself in a whole variety of more or less subtle ways.

One of the old favorites is pure brute physical superiority. *The Mumming at Hertford* (ca. 1425), the oldest extant English text of a completely secular drama, introduces the audience to six battered husbands who have forlornly come to complain to the king about their "wyfly purgatorye" and implore him to restore them to mastery in their own homes. The principle seems to be that the tougher and brawnier the husband is, the greater the comic pleasure in seeing him utterly routed. The stout and bold butcher, for example, who "killéd hathe bulles and boores olde," is thoroughly cowed by his wife ("for al his broode knyff" and his belly "rounded lyche an ooke"), and we learn that the uxorial fist "ful offt made his cheekis bleed" (ll.92–108). The pleasurable inversion of the everyday conjugal hierarchy is furthermore vindicated by one of the wives' citation of Chaucer's Wife of Bath. Chaucer's figure supports her claims to domestic mastery with a devastating, tripartite strategy of sheer force, deception, and good old-fashioned griping and grousing. She lays down her conditions with authoritarian self-assurance:

> An housbonde I wol have, I wol nat lette,
> Which shal be bothe my dettour and my thral,
> And have his tribulacion withal
> Upon his flessh, whil that I am his wyf.
> I have the power durynge al my lyf
> Upon his propre body, and noght he.
>
> (*Canterbury Tales*, 3.154–59)

What's more, she broadens these stipulations into universal principles concerning female mastery in general, for

> Wommen desiren to have sovereynetee
> As wel over hir housbond as hir love,
> And for to been in maistrie hym above.
>
> (*Canterbury Tales*, 3.1038–40)

Is this vicarious release, or a warning of the dangers when the pecking order is reversed and the hen is allowed to rule the roost(er)? The topsy-turvy world can function either as a festive-utopian social inversion or as a caricatural representation of what is considered an actually existing perversion of the way society *ought* to be. Incontestable is that (Christian) theory—the product of Christian males—envisaged man wearing the pants. Given that we can never really know whether woman wore them merely in comic fiction and, if not, how often she was able to appropriate them in real life, it seems reasonable to conjecture that the comedy of the time hovered between satirical castigation of male wimpishness and female shrewishness and the celebratory moment of vicarious release. The ambivalence of the topsy-turvy world echoes the ambivalence of folly, which may be identified with or dissociated from.

The motif of matrimonial conflict even comes to extend its reach over certain of the mystery cycles, in particular in the episode of Noah and his wife. In the biblical account, Noah had been the only actor directly mentioned except God, and, while the Coventry version of the tale imitates this in its piety, its absence of characterization, and its lack of conflict, the Chester *Deluge* and the York equivalent add to the skeletal situation the stubbornness of Noah's wife in her refusal to board the ark, coupled with Noah's ensuing irritation. When Noah welcomes his wife on board after she has finally changed her mind, he "gets a clowte" for his pains, and she subsides into sulky silence for the remainder of the play. The brief fragment of Newcastle's *Noah's Ark* portrays Uxor getting on the nerves of a rather colorless Noah, but in the Towneley cycle the conflict of henpecked husband and cantankerous wife moves into the center of the dramatic attention. The fact that—unlike in Chester and York—Noah does not accept Uxor's insubordination ("I shall make the still as stone, begynnar of blunder," he rants uxoricidally, "I shall bete the bak and bone, and breke all in sonder" [ll.406–7]) results in two bitterly fought bouts of connubial combat, which leave both participants severely mauled, although if anyone it is Gyll, giving Noah "thre for two," who ends up on top. French medieval drama too is never far from the conjugular vein. *Le Chauldronnier* shows husband and wife indulging in a jovially abusive slanging match before laying into one another with batons, the wife unequivocally coming out on top. It is a victory won for her sex as a whole: "Victory and domination!" she cries in her moment of triumph, "And power to the women!" (ll.56–57).

As Chaucer's Wife of Bath makes clear, the battle of the sexes is carried out not merely at the physical level, but also in the domain of ruse, trickery, and guile. Cuckoldry is one of the timeless comic themes, derision aimed at the tricked *cornuto* coexisting with a sense of comic release enjoyed by the woman. If the Christian marriage is the institutional yoke that holds woman in her subordinate position within the man-wife hierarchy, then exploding the marital bonds constitutes a (temporary) escape from the tyranny of this domestic order. As Wilde's Mrs. Allonby puts it, cleverly explaining why women have all the fun: "There are far more things forbidden to us than are forbidden to them."[13] In the *Decameron*, Boccaccio shows himself to be explicitly on the side of extramarital clipping, or at least the *right* of women to have a bit on the side if their aged husbands are too busy practising religious abstention. In this he is a welcome antidote to the radically dualistic, medieval stylization of woman on the one hand as Sin or Folly (the agent of man's fall) and on the other as unattainable perfection, a tradition stemming—via European imitation—from the love songs of the Arabs whose ladies, immured within veil and harem, really were unattainable.[14] Accepting women on a much more flexible basis, Boccaccio is consistently supportive of what he considers to be "natural" (which explains why homosexuality does not fare quite so well in his hands). In the many stories devoted to tricks played by wives upon husbands, Boccaccio combines the dual comic pleasure of deception (the reader of course sharing the narrator's omniscient perspective and thereby knowing better than the gull) with that of cocking a snook at the marital yoke. Reversal here coincides with revenge.

In the world of the *Decameron*, female wile is matched by female wit. Of course wit need not be the domain of exclusively female supremacy. It is, however, an important weapon for justifying and asserting oneself in a man's world. The first story of the sixth day indeed focuses on the shaft of epigrammatic brilliance—as opposed to long-winded male repetitiousness—as a specifically female gift, even if this does arise from a belief in a "natural" order that decrees that it is unseemly for women to make long speeches. In the commedia dell'arte, the rise of female wit, verve, and craftiness came to be personified in the figure of the maid. A later development than Arlecchino, Brighella, and Pulcinella, Columbine's appearance constituted a significant chink in the social chastity belt that strove to keep the sinful and foolish parts of humanity tucked away out of sight. Unlike Arlecchino, moreover, there is no *zagna* known to have been lazy or stupid, while, in comparison to Brighella, she proves substantially more capable of deep affection, a contrast also with the pallid posturings of the "official" lovers. Even in love, Columbine retains her wit and vivacity, never descending to the level of lovesick ninny (as most male characters do).

The war of the sexes is contested particularly fervently on the conversational battleground in the comedy of Shakespeare. Benedick and Beatrice, for example, fight it out hammer and tongue at the conclusion to *Much Ado About Nothing*:

Benedick. Do not you love me?
Beatrice. Why, no; no more than reason.
Benedick. Why, then, your uncle, and the prince, and Claudio,
Have been deceived: they swore you did.
Beatrice. Do not you love me?
Benedick. Troth, no; no more than reason.
Beatrice. Why, then my cousin, Margaret, and Ursula
Are much deceiv'd; for they did swear you did.
Benedick. They swore that you were almost sick for me.
Beatrice. They swore that you were will-nigh dead for me.
Benedick. 'Tis no such matter.
. . . .
Come, I will have thee; but, by this light, I take thee for pity.
Beatrice. I would not deny you;—but, by this good day, I yield upon great persuasion, and, partly, to save your life, for I was told you were in a consumption.
Benedick. Peace! I will stop your mouth.

(Act 5, scene 4)

Highly stylized and patterned by repetitions and symmetries, the exchange brings to light a love not so much hidden by the sophisticated mask of witty banter as itself constituted by the game of wit—and it is Benedick who capitulates. As Beatrice has an answer for everything he says in the form of playful modulations of his own words, Benedick si-

lences her in a less subtle way—a sign of love perhaps, but also an appeal
for a truce in the (feigned) verbal antagonism.

Love's Labour's Lost is an equally stylized game of courtship, "a set of
wit well played," and one that emerges as a love game for the women,
who are the more sensitive, sensible, and wittier, love having turned the
men into fools. Echoing the Princess's words ("None are so surely
caught, when they are catched, / As wit turned fool"), Maria explains the
phenomenon:

> Folly in fools bears not so strong a note
> As foolery in the wise when wit doth dote,
> Since all the power thereof it doth apply
> To prove, by wit, worth in simplicity.

> (Act 5, scene 2)

One particular exchange of punning wit creates and exploits a whole web
of associations between wit, sex, and archery, as if playfully to underline
that wit is not only inherently sexual in nature, but also a courtly game
(like archery) of martial origin. Responding to a bout of wit played between Rosaline and Boyet, Maria applauds it using the metaphor of the
"mark," meaning a shot at target. Boyet warns her to be careful in her
use of the word "mark," which can also mean pudendum, himself playing
on the double meaning of "prick":

> *Maria.*   A mark marvellous well shot, for they both did hit it.
> *Boyet.*   A mark! O, mark but that mark! "A mark," says my lady!
>   Let the mark have a prick in't, to mete at if it may be.
> *Maria.*   Wide o' the bow hand! I'faith, your hand is out.
> *Costard.* Indeed, 'a must shoot nearer, or he'll ne'er hit the clout.
> *Boyet.*   An if my hand be out, then belike your hand is in.
> *Costard.* Then will she get the upshoot by cleaving the pin.
> *Maria.*   Come, come, you talk greasily; your lips grow foul.
> *Costard.* She's too hard for you at pricks, sir. Challenge her to bowl.
> *Boyet.*   I fear too much rubbing. Good night, my good owl.

> (Act 4, scene 1)

Like sex and archery, wit is a matter of hitting a target with a timely
prick. This particular bout of "meta-wit" (being witty about wit) shows
the female participant doing more than hold her own. In fact she seems to
have the male pricks well in hand, prompting Costard to suggest bowls
(masturbation) instead of archery; Boyet's Parthian shot (referring to her
as a "good owl"—to rhyme with "bowl") is distinctly below the belt.

Shakespeare's comedies—influenced by the theatre of the Italian Renaissance—frequently feature episodes in which young women (such as
Portia, Nerissa, Jessica, Rosalind, Viola ...) disguise themselves as men.

Just as acted master-servant reversals tend to derive their comedy from the imperfection of the acting, however, male-female disguise too normally structures itself around the presupposition that the role-playing is but a superficial mask to an essential or natural gender. In *As You Like It*, for example, Rosalind, though wearing the garb of a man, betrays herself by swooning and wanting to cry and doing the sort of sissy thing that real men (i.e.,"Real Men") just don't do. Shakespeare utilizes the device additionally by creating situations of dramatic irony dependent for their success upon the shared knowledge of the spectator that things are not as they seem: fainting at the sight of her lover's blood, she mumbles that she "should have been a woman by right." Even more subtle are her encounters with the man she loves, in which she "pretends" to be herself, or rather she pretends to be a lad acting the part of Rosalind, her double-pretence permitting her to say "I am your Rosalind" in the knowledge that this will not be taken at face value by Orlando. Orlando has access to only one "layer" of acting (boy pretending to be girl), whereas the spectator has access to two (girl acting the part of boy pretending to be girl). Although such comedy may be seen as conservative in its assumptions that, ultimately, a Rosalind is a Rosalind is a Rosalind (i.e., a girl is a girl is a girl) and that women cannot hide their female characteristics when it comes to the crunch, the adoption of male clothing by women can also have more progressive implications, allowing women to wear the pants for a while and see life from the elevated perspective of the male. It can also (whether intentionally or not) have the effect of highlighting the artifice and conventionality structuring social intercourse between the sexes. "Male-female disguise serves therefore to break down the barriers between the sexes, to expose the power of social conventions and prejudices, and to question the significance of superficial sexual distinctions. And at a more general level it exposes the strong element of role-playing in all human relationships, and perhaps a deep yearning among men and women type-cast by themselves or their fellows to break free of the costume that symbolizes that constraint."[15]

Rosalind's male disguise gives her a temporary freedom of speech and thereby casts a thematic side-glance at the social order that normally silences her wit. Part of the pleasure arises from what has been described as the "daring abnormality"[16] of such vivacious and captivating heroines, a daringly abnormal insubordination that—as with Figaro—couples liberty of expression with an actual or an acted reversal in social power relations. Restoration comedy continues the tradition established by Rosalind and Beatrice, Congreve's Millamant displaying equal self-assurance as she fights in advance for her rights in marriage and gives vent to her mistrust of the odious marital yoke: "Ah! I'll never marry, unless I am first made sure of my will and pleasure" (4.5). Although her defiance

may have remained an enactment of the wishful thinking of most women
of the time, it can be speculated that such comic impertinence ("if I continue to endure you a little longer, I may by degrees dwindle into a wife")
at least had the potential to prove infectious in its illumination of the
equal footing on which any relationship ought to be based. Meredith describes the heroines of comedy as being "like women of the world, not
necessarily heartless from being clear-sighted: they seem so to the senti-
mentally-reared only for the reason that they use their wits, and are not
wandering vessels crying out for a captain or a pilot. Comedy is an ex-
hibition of their battle with men, and that of men with them."[17] He regards this moreover as only possible when "women are on the road to an
equal footing with men," for "where they have no social freedom, Comedy is absent: where they are household drudges, the form of Comedy is
primitive."[18] For Meredith, then, the battle of wits is a reflection of social
progress *already made*. This overlooks that, even in eras when women
have enjoyed roughly the same status as chattels (in ancient Greece),
they have proved capable of outwitting their owner in comic fiction,
women having in a sense spent the whole of history since the Neolithic
period *on the road* to equality—i.e., not there yet. Nonetheless, Meredith
does also seem to hint that the Comic Idea may itself act as an agent of
change, propelling women along that interminable road. Cultivated
women, he argues, should "recognise that the Comic Muse is one of their
best friends."[19] Especially when presented as festive, the "folly" of the
world-upside-down may concretize the utopian ideal to be moved towards.

In France, Molière's theatre provides a variation on the theme of conversational combat, his *scènes de dépit amoureux* working on the same
table-turning principle as the servant-master reversal acted out by Scapin
and Léandre. More significantly, in both *Turcaret* and *Le Mariage de
Figaro*, where crafty servants end the play in the ascendant, female ruse
and female wit are very much in evidence. Lesage's Frontin is matched
both in cynicism and guile by Lisette—a sign of compatibility maybe, but
who is to say that the ricochet of knaveries has come to a standstill? In *Le
Mariage*, Figaro's plot-weaving and role-playing is complemented by the
intriguing of the Countess and Suzanne (Figaro's fiancée), who decide to
deceive the unfaithful Count without telling Figaro, the mistress playing
the part of her lady-in-waiting and the lady-in-waiting that of her mistress. Under the delusion that he is being deceived by his fiancée, Figaro
is thus brought to lament the deceitfulness of women, the irony here
being that the deception is a deception—it is the Countess, dressed
as Suzanne, whose rendezvous with the Count Figaro witnesses, not
Suzanne herself. The wit of the women, therefore, turns even Figaro the
archtrickster into a jealous fool, albeit only momentarily so. Trickery and

guile, especially when coupled with feminine solidarity, are a necessary form of female self-assertion in the face of the domineering but foolish masculine sex, a point made clear by Figaro's mother, Marceline: "Ah! when personal interest is not arming us against one another, we women are all given to sticking up for our poor, oppressed sex against this proud, this fearful ... and yet rather half-witted male sex" (4.16).

At the beginning of the twentieth century, the male-female reversal assumes a particularly silly form in the surreal world of Apollinaire's *Les Mamelles de Tirésias* where Thérèse, a feminist, resolves to become a man, growing a beard, bursting her breasts (one red and one blue balloon), and physically overcoming and swapping clothes with her husband. In his turn, the husband, choosing to conform to his new role, succeeds in giving birth to 40,049 babies in one day simply by a strenuous act of volition. In Apollinaire's case, it is evident that the reversal is linked to a topsy-turvy world of fantasy, a nonsensical *escape* from the reliability of the real. This element of fantasy is traceable back to the two plays of Aristophanes in which sexual reversal is central to the action. Here again, the borderline between satiric vision of a conservative ilk and (potentially subversive) festive-utopian irrealism is impossible to discern, for the "folly" of sexual reversal is as fundamentally ambivalent as folly's other manifestations.

In *The Assemblywomen*, the women disguise themselves as men in order to monopolize the assembly and win genuine mastery for their sex, female wile and wit generating the power reversal. The comedy initially lies in the *bad* acting of the women as they rehearse for their political "performance" at the assembly but keep allowing their femaleness to show through. The comic heroine Praxagora, by contrast, performs thoroughly convincingly and makes the most of her disguise to proffer a critique of Athenian society and propose that power be handed over to the fair sex. Once in a position of authority, Praxagora outlines her plans for the utopian society under female control in a blueprint that bears a not inconsiderable resemblance to that put forward by Plato in *The Republic* (a work that is nevertheless believed not to have circulated in its published form until some years later). It is a society governed not merely by feminine intuition and trust, but run on principles of economic and sexual communism: all land, money, and private possessions will be common property, Praxagora claims, as will girls—although the phrasing, here as in Plato, does betray that the communistic wet dream is still ultimately phallocentric. The topsy-turvy reign of the female further becomes even more specifically festive-utopian in spirit when this communist blueprint adopts cornucopian imagery of material and sexual plenitude ("There'll be plenty of everything for everybody"), imagery corroborated by the final scene of merry-making and revelry. Aware of Plato's ideas, Aristophanes may well have been poking fun at them in advance of their publication and using the utopia as an object of derision. Yet it does seem that the mockery is benevolent rather than biting, most of the comedy arising from a rather gratuitous clause that stipulates a form of positive discrimination in the matter of sex by granting senior citizens first bash. Barring this troublesome clause, the implications throughout are that, under the sway of women, things would be better—no more informing, slander, harrying for debt, court cases, dicing.... At this time in Athens, of course, women had no more political or legal rights than slaves or than their contemporaries in Egypt or Babylon, so there was no practical possibility of a world ruled by women: the subversive potential of such fantasy remained well and truly concealed by the conservatism of the social order. Nevertheless the thematic association of the woman-on-top motif and cornucopian carousing implies at the very least that, although not openly advocating the sovereignty of women, Aristophanes is half-laughing *at* and half-laughing *with* the utopian impossible, the paradisical folly.

The same balance is present in *Lysistrata*, written at a military low-point in Athens's ancient history. Hardly likely to have been championing an unduly hasty end to the war with the Spartans, the comedy is more a work of sheer fantasy, a dream about peace, a surrogate or temporary harmony to be appreciated in the safety of the theatrical/festival context. The play yields the gratifying sight of the power reversal being brought about by the brute strength of the women, who physically overcome the men and thereby deflate male authority by outplaying it at its own game, before going on an ultimately successful sex-strike as a protest against the war. As in *The Assemblywomen*, the female protagonist, later to be celebrated as a "paragon of common sense," exploits her position of domination to indulge in criticism of the male-run social order and the perpetual blunders made by men in the realm of politics. Once more, the reign of woman is shown as justifiable, even if it is in the end regarded as a pie-in-the-sky fantasy.

No less pie-in-the-sky is the reversal enacted in *The Birds*, where the feathered protagonists build a city in the sky (Cloud Cuckoo City) that will enable them to exercize power over the gods by cutting off their supply of sacrifices. The inversive impulse is manifested both by Peisthetaerus, who indulges in a flight of fancy to prove the sovereignty of birds over man and gods, and by the Chorus leader, who sings of the birds' revenge on those who have mistreated them. But this topsy-turvy world also incorporates a utopian vision of youth, laughter, dancing, peace, happiness, and wealth.... The set of reversals even includes a striking degree of irreverence regarding Zeus: Peisthetaerus threatens to burn down his palace if given any more trouble and to give his daughter Iris a "very big surprise." This power reversal is fictionally permanent as well: marrying Basileia ("Sovereign"), keeper of Zeus's thunderbolts, Peisthetaerus keeps the balance of power tipped very much in his favor.

Hegel viewed Aristophanic irreverence as the signal of a change in the way of seeing the world. It was the expression of a historical development in the understanding of the gods, who now came to be regarded as the creation of a histrionic human subject, and, as with the Sophists, Hegel felt, Aristophanes's unmasking and illusion-destroying vision led to the rise of the individual subject and the demise of the gods.[20] Hegel's conjectures only hit part of the truth. First, although Zeus is treated disrespectfully, he is never openly ridiculed in person in the same way as Poseidon, Hermes, or Dionysus, who in ungodlike manner beshits himself for fear in *The Frogs*. Second, Aristophanes never denies the existence of the gods, he merely plays with the absurdities in the traditional conceptions of them. Third, Hegel ignores the frequency with which ritual mockery of the gods has been a part of the moment of saturnalian release, which can invert or raze the god-man hierarchy without necessarily having to throw the existence of the hierarchy's components into explicit discredit. Aristophanes's cosmological inversion was not so much innovatory as ventilatory. Dover describes the phenomenon as follows: "The Greek's relation with one of his gods was essentially the relation between subject and ruler ... and a prudent subject will pay his tribute, obey the rules, and keep out of the ruler's way. But a subject needs something else: the opportunity to assert himself by ridiculing the ruler. Fifth-century comedy provided a notable outlet for this kind of self-assertion by depicting deities not only as worsted by aggressive humans, as in *Birds*, but also as stupid, greedy and cowardly."[21] It is anachronistic to treat Aristophanes as an iconoclast, a pacifist, or a feminist and extremely difficult to read a consistent political or philosophical point of view out of his comedies. What does seem to be the case is that Aristophanes's topsyturvy visions are works of comic fantasy, festive in nature, and above all a *release* from the socio-political straitjacket. Any subversively political import is but a dormant potentiality.

Anthropologists have posited two alternative views of carnival release, corresponding to which the two discrete—if intersecting—impulses within the phenomenon of comic inversion (the negating and the affirming, the satiric and the celebratory) emerge in even clearer form. The "ventilation" theory views ritual reversal and disorder as guardians of order and social stability within a hierarchical community, strengthening, clarifying, and renewing this order by allowing a period of temporary departure from it. The medieval theologians of Paris hit the spigot on the head with their simile of a wine cask, which for its own good requires its bunghole to be vented now and again. A modern day critic uses an

equally graphic image, that of collective exhaustion: "By depleting re-
serves and leaving everyone bruised and sore, a collective binge brings on
a collective hangover and sets the stage for vows of sobriety and getting
back to work."[22] Preferring the metaphor of a "counterpoint"[23] to that
of "ventilation", the Dutch sociologist Zijderveld represents the view
that, while saturnalian humor doubtless serves as a temporary liberation
from cultural constraint and perhaps even as a medium of protest, the
bottom line of the festive transgression is a *confirmation* of the necessity
of the norms, values, and hierarchies as protection from the "*Ur*-chaos"
that would reduce us to blathering idiots or poo-eating freaks with
twenty-foot penises wrapped around our waist. Not merely serving as a
periodic release (like a steam valve) for antisocial energies, carnivalesque
comedy also, it is argued, shows anarchy to be inviable as a long-term
alternative. The deviation from the norm makes the norm under-
standable—and even desirable.

Generating emotional and intellectual distance, moreover, the disorder
works by a contrast with the norm. Like a sort of universalized irony of
events, the world-upside-down requires the recognition of the patterns of
inversion (as illustrated by the structured irony of the reversal scene between Léandre and Scapin, where Scapin's authority repeats but upturns
that of his master). Just as the irony of events involves a knave becoming
the object or victim of an act of knavery, the world-upside-down shows
the angry master transformed into the victim of anger, the cringeing servant. Bergson likewise depicts the "monde renversé" in terms of *ironic*
reversal: "You get a comic scene by turning the situation on its head and
inverting the roles.... It is thus that we laugh at the sight of the accused
giving the judge a ticking off, or the child purporting to teach his parents
a lesson.... Often we are presented with a character preparing the net in
which he will himself end up getting caught. The tale of the persecutor
who becomes the one being persecuted, of the trickster tricked, lies at the
heart of a good many comedies."[24] Distance is a prerequisite for the
perception and enjoyment of such ironic reversal, and humor, indeed,
often works as a means of *creating* distance, the intellectual dissociation
from a situation perhaps convergent with an emotional overcoming of
difficult or traumatic circumstances and relationships. Laughter is a type
of anaesthetic, therefore, conservative in its effects because it discourages
action, whether by functioning as a substitute anarchy that channels our
potentially destructive energies off into the harmlessness of laughter, by
showing disorder to be ultimately unacceptable, or by generating palliative distance between the laugher and the source of his social woe. Society may be unjust, that is, but you've got to laugh about it. Analogously,
the topsy-turvy world of carnival serves as a replacement for actually

altering the order, as licensed or playful disorder reduces the need for serious disorder. Unlike Marx, Trotsky regarded seasonal folk rebellions as steam valves *hindering* the development of revolutionary consciousness.[25]

Yet this is not the whole story. Ritual reversal may be interpreted not merely as self-regulating control, but also as wishful thinking, if not explicitly articulated criticism and protest, a movement from within society tending to explode its own limits rather than secure the self-regulation of the social order. Anthropologists have shown how comic and festive inversion can *undermine* as well as reinforce the structure: "Rather than expending itself primarily during the privileged duration of the joke, the story, the comedy or the Carnival, topsy-turvy play had much spillover into everyday 'serious' life and the effects were sometimes disturbing and even novel."[26] Just as carnival riots have been known to get out of hand and develop into full-fledged revolution, especially in the slave communities of the New World at Christmas and carnival time, so too may comedy be seen as (potentially at least—or perhaps involuntarily) sowing the seeds of dissent. Similarly, irony of events may be linked not simply to an anaesthetizing generation of distance, but also to a dissident spirit of vengeance typified by Poe's Hop-Frog, whose power reversal combines the knave-fool with the master-servant configuration: here we applaud the "foolish" underdog who eventually outwits the knave and overcomes the master. In other words, the antisocial energies may explode their bounds, festive disorder may portray chaos in a flattering light, and even ironic distance may mean an intellectualization rather than an anaesthetization of the bubbling seditious impulse within us. Just as carnival folly may be castigated or celebrated, therefore, so its world-upside-down hovers between conservatism and rebellion. Incorporating both a social and an antisocial tendency, it may both renew collective harmony through ritualized solidarity and effect an anarchic social protest and a critique of order. This tension between communal solidarity and anti-authoritarian dissent is echoed even in the Janus-faced nature of its utopian vision, which looks both forwards and backwards. Images of material plenitude seem to fuse a visionary anticipation of an ideal future with a conservative hankering after a recently past "Golden Age" (manifest in an unhealthily whingeing retrospection and a regressive "Things ain't what they used to be" mentality).

The satiric songs of the *Carmina burana* exemplify the *verkehrte Welt* in its least festive mood.[27] Here it is the existing world that is portrayed as upside-down, a reprehensible reversal of the "natural" order. It is a world in which the rich are poor, the truth is false, and virtue is vicious, a transposition caused above all by the corrupting sway of money:

The freeman is a slave	The slave is honored	The parasite holds forth	The dandy gives orders	The rascal lords it

(no. 5)

If the servants are shown to be masters, this is not idealized as an escape from the real, but lamented as the symptom of a society gone to the dogs, misused and abused by the underdogs. These satirical songs are not conservative in the same way as Holberg, therefore, who derided (the possibility of) reversal for the sake of preserving the status quo. Instead, contemporary society itself is comprehensively taken to task as a deviation from the "good ol' days," and the conservatism is a yearning for the order of the past rather than a confirming of the order of the present, a conservatism that may indeed be a more explicit and ethically engaged advocation of change than much festive inversion with its cheerfully mercurial amorality.

The politics of comic and carnival reversal are thus inherently ambiguous. Placing the social world on its head may—implicitly or explicitly—espouse a retention of the status quo, champion progressive or retrogressive change, or exist in sublime indifference to any specific ethical or political position. It may—implicitly or explicitly—criticize a specific order (or disorder) with an eye to a new order, or it may simply proffer a critique of order in general. While *acted* reversals tend to be comic owing to a "conservative" tendency to recognize the acting as mere acting, for example, festive reversals *may* prove infectious, given the right circumstances. When the reversal is displaced to the sphere of wit, in particular, the freedom of speech may be viewed as preparing the ground for more deep-seated change. All reversal, indeed, *can* be seen as implying the fictional nature of the political mask, but whether this unmasking potential is ever realized is another matter. Moreover, as laughter may be directed at the powerless every bit as easily as at the powerful (if not more so), it seems that the lowest common denominator to all such mockery is some form of vicarious self-assertion. Political potential notwithstanding, laughter has its roots above all in aggressive urges that the social mask generally requires to be hidden.

8

The Ethical Mask

If You Can't Join 'em, Beat 'em

Political order in a hierarchical culture is but one aspect of a whole code of ethical norms structuring social behavior. Englishmen, as Shaw's Devil observes in *Man and Superman*, "never will be slaves: they are free to do whatever the Government and public opinion allow them to do."[1] Political slavery is thus merely a subcategory of the (legal and) ethical slavery that binds us with more insidious pervasiveness. The "mask" metaphor would have it that, were it not for this cultural straitjacket, man in all his asocial nakedness would be in a state of perpetual internecine warfare. Thomas Hobbes has given one of the most lucid accounts of such naturally egalitarian anarchy: "During the time men live without a common Power to keep them all in awe, they are in that condition which is called Warre; and such a warre, as is of every man, against every man." Nature having made men "apt to invade, and destroy one another," the life of human beings in this uncivilized state of warre is "solitary, poore, nasty, brutish and short."[2] Communal existence requires a mutual curbing of our natural desire to beat everybody else's brains out and grab their possessions.

The verbal aggression of satire—or so our model might have it—is a vicarious outlet for our natural hostility, the "original" need for self-assertion that social interaction has compelled us to repress, hide, or sublimate. This may apply equally well to the playwright whose satirical belligerence is a form of personal axe-grinding or to the spectator whose laughter presumably testifies to some degree of complicity with the aggressive intent, just as successful joke telling relies on collusion between teller and hearer.

The malice that may be present in mirth is a feature recurrently acknowledged by philosophers down the centuries. In Plato's *Philebus*, Socrates draws attention to the duality within comedy as a *mixed* state of pleasure and pain, for it is a "painful" malice that results in us being *pleased* by the misfortunes of our friends: "When we laugh at the ridiculous qualities of our friends [i.e., their lack of self-knowledge], we mix pleasure with pain, since we mix it with malice; ... malice is a pain of the soul, and ... laughter is a pleasure, yet these two are present at the same time on such occasions."[3] Descartes, who perceived in mockery an amalgam of joy and hatred, inferred from his own experience that "in all encounters capable of producing that burst of laughter from the lungs, there is always some small element of hatred or at least admiration [admiratio],"[4] while Meredith was to describe satire as "a blow in the back or the face,"[5] although, in the ungentlemanly twentieth century, a knee to the groin would probably be nearer the mark. It is but a tiny typographical step from man's laughter to manslaughter.

Satire indeed seems to have its origins in tribal aggression. In the pre-Islamic Middle East, the poet-seer or *shā'ir* was the most powerful member of his tribe, for it was thought that the lampoons (*hijà*) with which he denigrated his enemies possessed magical qualities fatal to the foe, and the rhymes of his satiric accompaniment to the feud were often likened to arrows.[6] In Ireland too there is evidence that satire was a war weapon (the handling of which was an official function of a skilled poet) intended to weaken the opposition through its magical power. As the druidic wizard turned into the bard, injurious spells were transformed over the years into the malice of satire, a Gaelic *aer* (whose meaning followed this transformation from "curse" to "satire") having originally been believed capable of causing facial disfigurement, and even death.[7] That the target of such verbal missiles need not be external to the society (an enemy), but might just as easily be internal (an individual scapegoat to be punished for his "abnormality"), does not ultimately impair the *institutional* nature of such attacks. It is as if (antisocial) aggressions are being sublimated or channeled into social functionality, utilized for a "good cause"—the welfare of the community as a whole. Nonetheless, the terroristic implications of such derision have at various times resulted in legal restrictions on the degree to which lampoon might be explicitly directed at specific individuals. Considering the significance of satire in the Gaelic tradition, it is appropriate that the Irish satirist Swift should give expression to the sublimated violence contained within the genre. In his "Epistle to a Lady" he writes:

> Like the ever-laughing sage
> In a jest I spend my Rage
> (Tho' it must be understood
> I would hang them if I cou'd).

(lines 167–70)

This is laughter in its most clearly ventilatory function. Mocking somebody is the next-best alternative to stringing him up.

Ever since the days of Aristophanes, who had no qualms about naming names, theatrical satire has tended to be diluted into the form of a car-icatural portrayal of a *type*. The selective simplification and exaggeration characteristic of caricature turns the butt into a mask to be derided either for predictability, norm deviation, or both, allowing self-congratulation at the expense of the depicted "mental" or "moral" abnormality. The victim is scorned either for knowing less than we do (being a dupe or gull) or for not knowing "how to behave." The inherent cruelty of such laughter becomes manifest by analogy with the mockery of *physical* abnormality or deformity, from which the commedia (for example) derived so much amusement and which was still common currency in Tudor and Stuart England. In modern times, the sick joke, which makes no secret of its tastelessness and as such constitutes an explicit and intentional rejection of the mask of decorum, can perhaps be viewed as a more blatant parallel to the cruelty latent in all satire.

Even though the celebratory aspect of norm deviance or folly is apparently suppressed by the brown-shirted bludgeoning of satire, ambivalence is still present within the satiric mode, as implied by the enjoyment that such laughter yields. At one level affirming ourselves as moral representatives of the social order in the face of deviations from that order, the act of laughing—an act that always has the potential to get out of hand and turn subversive—may at another level be regarded as a release from the order, an expression of the body transcending social control. Natural nastiness wells up from within as we put in the gelastic boot. What this may ultimately be taken to indicate is the inextricability of social order and asocial instinct (or the development of the former out of the latter): the energies that hold the structure intact are but sublimations of original, disorderly drives. Even the mask is thus but a modality of the face. This was one of Nietzsche's major insights: "All instincts which do not find outward expression *turn inwards*: this is what I would term the *introversion* of man. It is only then that man develops what is later known as his 'soul'.... Animosity, cruelty, the delight taken in pursuit, assault, change and destruction—when all these instincts turn against their owner, *that* is the origin of the 'guilty conscience.' "[8] If the soul is a product of man's or woman's instinctive cruelty being internalized and directed against himself or herself, mockery gives one a welcome opportunity to reexternalize one's target, yet without openly infringing the rigorous dictates of this illusory moral master. The violence of scornful satire deludes itself that it is all perpetrated in a good cause.

Within the classical corrective tradition of comedy, Ben Jonson exemplifies this very violence both in his life (by all accounts) and his work, which at times fuses the universality of moral castigation with caricatural public pillorying in the service of his own personal feuds and enmities. In the prologue to *Everyman Out of His Humour*, Asper is speaking as a mouthpiece for his author when he claims:

... with an armed and resolved hand,
I'll strip the ragged follies of the time
Naked as at their birth ... and with a whip of steel
Print wounding lashes in their iron ribs.

(ll. 16–20)

Fine. Morality itself has here become a pretext, a mask hiding the latent (or not so latent) aggression of the moralist. In his *Divine Comedy*, Dante enjoys the satisfaction of putting all his enemies in Hell (as well as those of his friends who happened to be sodomites).

If satire thus tends to assume the guise of an archconservative public flagellant, it is conservatism of an ethical, not (necessarily) a political order. Even politically radical satire attacks its adversaries by turning them into risible figures, transforming those in power into objects of mockery (normally with a view to undermining their power). In Brecht's *Der Aufhaltsame Aufstieg des Arturo Ui*, the author ridicules Hitler (thinly disguised as Ui) by presenting him as a histrionic, wheedling, ultimately ludicrous gangster straight out of the world of movies. The demythologization of the Führer and such figures as Goebbels, Göring and Röhm demands that the masks in question (Ui, Givola, Giri, and Roma) be both recognizable and grotesquely distorted or exaggerated, although in this instance not much distortion was required. The political intent of the play notwithstanding, the satiric import exploits "moral" standards from which the protagonists are seen as deviating, turning to account Goebbels's physical deformity and Röhm's homosexuality, just as in the sixties Lenny Bruce was to make fun of Göring's transvestism and effeminacy. Even pillorying the powerful in the name of progress and change relies upon a common core of socially accepted ethical standards. Programmatically using his laughter as a weapon for the weak against the powerful, Dario Fo likewise satirizes the police in *Morte accidentale di un anarchico* by presenting them as a set of utter dunderheads, just as Nestroy had mocked his reactionaries (in *Freiheit in Krähwinkel*) by showing their adversaries repeatedly outwit them. Presenting the powerful as stupid is indeed the perennial form of the political joke, and, as such, it has proved an absolutely invaluable weapon for the oppressed or powerless in totalitarian states around the world. In its technique, however, it is often not all that different from the racial joke, which likewise frequently portrays its victims as dull, irrational or inferior.

The invective characteristic of satire may furthermore be internalized within the comic fiction, taking the form of a slanging-match between two (or more) characters. Although a displacement of the original satiric malice, there still seems to be a vicarious pleasure-through-identification in watching somebody really let rip with a torrent of abuse, annihilating all standards of decorum and propriety. The relationship between mocking spectator and mocked fictive figure may even be reversed, as when the abuse is aimed at the audience, this trick serving as a handy meta-theatrical joke at the same time. From the world of the nightclub and the American burlesque, forthright comedians of the Lenny Bruce stamp generate much of their comedy not merely by shocking the audience but also by *abusing* them, probing their comic proboscis into society's most sensitive spots. Yet this device redirects attention to the other side of the coin of ritual abuse, which, while functioning as a lexical Exocet in some cultures, in others came to be associated with magical properties of a more benevolent order. The anthropologist Frazer amassed a number of examples from as far apart as Greece, Rome, and India to demonstrate how vituperation often became the object of deliberate courting as a means to good luck (working on the principle that its opposite, praise, might be likely to incite cosmic disapproval), while Cornford, claiming that "the element of invective and personal satire ... is directly descended from the magical abuse of the phallic procession,"[9] saw the hurling of abuse operating as a type of fertility charm. If invective constitutes a falling of the social mask, it can indeed be surmised that it is this periodic mask-dropping that exercizes a sort of communally therapeutic effect. That Lenny Bruce was repeatedly arrested for obscenity in the United States and in 1963 refused entry to Britain (for being rude) illustrates the extent to which the salutary properties of vituperation—officially at least—have been lost from sight. The tradition of flyting or ritual insulting, however, does still appear able to flourish at a subcultural level—as at present in Black ghetto culture.[10]

Invective has frequently reared its (war-)head within the comic canon. Medieval German carnival plays took special pleasure in litanies of abuse known as *Schimpfreden.* In the *Spil von eim thumherrn und einer kupplerin,* for example, the farcical beatings are accompanied by a chain of invective as the wife verbally lays into her husband and the husband into the bawd. The *hubsch vasnachtspil* contains a competitive *Schimpfrede* that does not even necessitate translation:

Der man dicit:
. . . .
Du kumet, rosfeil und uberlast,
Du fegenteufel, rollfaß, du schimelkast,
Du leschtrog, harmkrug, lochrete tasch,
Du stinkender eimer, du kunige flasch,
Du anhank, du schelmigs aß,
Du kiteltuch, teufelsslucht und rollfas,
Du merwunder, ungelucksnest, du falldubel,
Du mürfeltier, du herhur, du lasterschubel,
Du kupplerin, geitiger schlunt und nasenrimpf,
Du spulnapf, hebenstreit, wentenschimpf,

Du fiper, nater, du weter, donder und plitz,
Du wulfin, preckin, unhuld, pilbitz!

(lines 37–48)

The comedy of vituperation is here conjoined with an exuberant verbal accumulation as the stream of words, impelled by rhyme and meter, seems to gain a momentum of its own. In this sphere, Rabelais's Frère Jan perhaps takes the (rock)cake for his apostrophe to his bollocky friend Panurge, while the cake bakers of book 1 start the Picrocholine War by heaping a more maliciously meant cartload of verbal dung upon the farmers of Grandgousier's country, whom they address as "diteulx, breschedens, plaisans rousseaulx, galliers, chienlictz, averlans, limes sourdes, faictnéans, friandeaulx, bustarins, talvassiers, riennevaulx, rustres, challans, hapelopins, trainne-guainnes, gentilz flocquetz, copieux, landores, malotruz, dendins, baugears, tézez, gaubregeux, gogueluz, claquedans, boyers d'étrons, bergiers de merde,"[11] and other such defamatory epithets. The farmers respond by giving the cake bakers a good trouncing.

The encounters between Hal and Falstaff in *Henry IV* are also characterized by bouts of flyting, in which Falstaff is not simply enjoying the licence of a privileged court-fool figure, but also serving as opposition in a playful battle of wits. Unconvinced by the lies of Falstaff the *miles gloriosus*, Hal resorts to the sort of abuse to which Falstaff the fool is only too willing to respond:

> *Prince Henry.* These lies are like their father that begets them, gross as a mountain, open, palpable. Why, thou clay-brained guts, thou knotty-pated fool, thou whoreson, obscene, greasy tallow-keech—
> ....
> This sanguine coward, this bed-presser, this horse-backbreaker, this huge hill of flesh—
>
> *Falstaff.* 'Sblood, you starveling, you eel-skin, you dried neat's tongue, you bull's pizzle, you stockfish! O for breath to utter what is like thee, you tailor's yard, you sheath, you bow-case, you vile standing tuck—
>
> (Part 1, act 2, scene 4)

Just as Frère Jan calls Panurge's sexuality into question by apostrophizing his bollocks as blighted, shriveled, all in all rather unimpressive appendages, so too Falstaff's imagery makes a point of implying genital emaciation or impotence in his ruler's yard.

If the tradition of flyting went under for a number of centuries of verbal decorum, Jarry's anarchic creation Ubu revivified the carnivalesque spirit of invective inventiveness at the end of the last century. His figures glee-

fully trade insults as they slash one another to pieces, Ubu himself in-
carnating a particularly Rabelaisian admixture of gore and verbal creativity. More recently John Barth's *The Sot-Weed Factor* has provided an
even more hyperbolical, excessive, vituperative inventory as two whores
prove their lexical prowess (in their own specific field):

"A quail!" the woman named Grace shrieked. "You call me a quail, you—
you *gaullefretière!*"
"Whore!" shouted the first.
"*Bas-cul!*" retorted the other.
"Frisker!"
"*Consoeur!*"
"Trull!"
"*Friquenelle!*"
"Sow!"
"*Usagère!*"
"Bawd!"
"*Viagère!*"
"Strawgirl!"
"*Sérane!*"
"Tumbler!"
"*Poupinette!*"
"Mattressback!"
"*Brimballeuse!*"
"Nannygoat!"
"*Chouette!*"
"Windowgirl!"
"*Wauve!*"
"Lowgap!"
"*Peaultre!*"
"Galleywench!"
"*Baque!*"
"Drab!"
"*Villotière!*"
"Fastfanny!"
"*Gaure!*"
"Ringer!"
"*Bringue!*"
"Capercock!"
"*Ancelle!*"
"Nellie!"
"*Gallière!*"
"Chubcheeker!"
"*Chèvre!*"
"Nightbird!"
"*Paillasse!*"
"Rawhide!"
"*Capre!*"
"Shortheels!"
"*Paillarde!*"

"Bumbessie!"
"Image!"
"Furrowbutt!"
"Voyagère!"
"Pinkpot!"
"Femme de vie!"
"Rum-and-rut!"
"Fellatrice!"[12]

By this time the two hookers (or conycatchers, fluters, sallydallies, hip-flippers, hamhockers, pisspallets, codhoppers, bumpbacons ...) are enjoying their game so much that they have no difficulty unearthing another 175 terms for one another and are still going strong when the focus of narrative attention shifts elsewhere.

As an extension of the verbal violence of vituperation into the realm of actual physical brutality, the gore characteristic of Rabelais and Jarry draws on the same untapped sources of aggression or cruelty in reader or spectator, serving as a vicarious release from the restraint normally necessary in social conduct. Unable to go about indiscriminately pulping people, we watch people being pulped—but transposed to the harmless sphere of play, it being play (as Frye put it) that separates art from savagery. Farcical beatings on stage of course rarely reach the level of those meted out by Frère Jan to an army several hundred strong in *Gargantua* ("He beat the brains out of some of them, he broke the arms and legs of others, he dislocated the vertebrae of others, he pulverized the kidneys, gouged out the noses, blackened the eyes, smashed the jaws, knocked the teeth down the throats, staved in the shoulder-blades, shattered the fibulas, dislodged the femurs, and levigated the limbs of yet others")[13] or the sort of sadistically fantastic tortures applied by Père Ubu ("twisting of the nose, tearing out of the hair, insertion of the little wooden stick into the nearoles, extraction of the brain via the heels, laceration of the posterior" [*Ubu Roi*, 5.1]). Yet it was clearly the Ubuesque brand of comic anarchy that Antonin Artaud had in mind when advocating his influential Theatre of Cruelty. Regarding the comedy of cruelty as a revelation of man's hidden brutality ("a base of latent cruelty"), he further interpreted this revelation as the dropping of a mask: "Bringing men to see themselves as they really are, it causes the mask to fall." Artaud's ideal theatre constitutes a return both to man's and the theatre's roots, an embodiment of the original chaos, for "theatre will only be able to become itself again ... by providing the spectator with the authentic precipitates of dreams, in which his taste for crime, his erotic obsessions, his savagery, his fantasies, his utopian sense of life and the world, indeed his cannibalism burst forth in a setting not fictitious and illusory, but interior."[14] Utopianism, violence, and cannibalism coexist in heady poetic harmony in Artaud's myth of original plenitude. Artaud indeed intended his *Théâtre Alfred Jarry* to do actual damage to the spectator. It was to be an experience comparable to a visit to the dentist or surgeon, the farcical brutality *so intense* that it swallowed the spectator up in its giddy gore. His miniplay *La Pierre philosophale*, a parody of the commedia, was an attempt to put this aesthetic into practice. The traditional theme of cuckoldry is assimilated into the proceedings as the horner Harlequin enters the service of a sadistic *dottore* now transformed into the guise of a mad scientist, le docteur Pale. The beatings typical of the commedia have accordingly developed into mutilations and sinister experiments, even Harlequin finding himself the victim of the butchery. Fortunately, however, showing the resilience that is a prerequisite for the world of puppetry, he is none the worse for wear and, gathering up his arms, legs and head, he tups the doctor's wife as if to prove his point. Also in the Artaudian tradition is the playwright Ionesco who, rejecting realism and psychological subtlety, sought to renew the theatre with a welter of furious exaggeration (to be found in such plays as *La Lecon* or *Les Chaises*). Ionesco urged the dramatist to "push everything to the point of paroxysm, to the point where the tragic has its origins. Create a theatre of violence: violently comic, violently dramatic."[15]

The farcical ferocity of the commedia dell'arte, taken to such a gruesome extreme by Artaud, was developed in a somewhat more boisterous spirit in the English pantomime of the early nineteenth century, where the violence was coupled with a socially retributive (or topsy-turvy) impulse embodied in Clown that channeled the blows and beatings in particular in the direction of Pantaloon, the central figure of authority and patriarchal power. Yet it was not only Pantaloon who was singled out for a bad time. His chief partner in suffering tended to be the Dandy Lover, who regularly had to endure being dismembered, fired from mortars, bedaubed with mud, exploded by new contraptions for manufacturing illuminating gas, as well as mocked and ridiculed for being the character with the slowest wits. A *Times* review from 1832 reports on the satisfaction yielded by seeing someone being given such a hammering: "It does one good to see how heartily the clowns and pantaloons ... cuff and bang each other; indeed, as naturalists, we marvel much touching the organization of their joints and sinews, and, as moralists, with respect to those idiosyncrasies of disposition which make the annoyance of a fellow-creature the only business and comfort of existence. Hobbes must have been deep in the philosophy of pantomimes."[16] Pantomime is *warre* indeed, but it is comic *warre* and has a happy outcome—wit and ruse and youthful versatility carrying the day over the tyranny of established authority.

Within the farcical tradition itself, which extends back not only to the frenetic chaos of the commedia but ultimately to the tough Old Comedy of ancient Greece, batterings, pummellings, and thrashings have not normally proved fatal for the unfortunate recipients. Aristophanes's comedy is peppered with (nonfatal) physical horseplay and chastisements. *The Birds* especially goes in for this brand of comedy, not only portraying a cruel episode of slave maltreatment but also demonstrating what is to be done with charlatans and pseudointellectuals such as the innovator Meton: clobber them out of town (the more Ubuesque variety of grotesque farce would of course extract their brains via their heels or do nasty things to their nearoles). At a time when Athenian law rigorously punished physical violence (if interpreted as a sign of *hybris*—a crime not against the individual but against the community as a whole in that it signaled an attempt to establish moral or social domination), the sight of beatings onstage must have assumed all the greater significance as a release for pent-up aggression.

Shakespeare's *Comedy of Errors* brings to light an extremely common link between farcical beatings (in this case nonfatal slave-bashing) and the comedy of misunderstandings. The whole comedy of errors is a consequence of the unwitting convergence of two long-lost twin brothers—both called Antipholus—on one town, together with their servants, two long-lost twin brothers both called Dromio. As the wrong Dromio repeatedly bumps into the wrong Antipholus at the wrong time, an entire web of confusions is spun, resulting in both Dromios taking a drubbing for (in the eyes of their masters) getting things muddled and failing to carry out orders in fact given to somebody else. The pleasurably inversive comedy of witnessing the servant cross the master, albeit unwittingly, is thus juxtaposed with a series of cantankerous reassertions of authority by bewildered masters. Beating itself develops into a comic leitmotif, a focus of patterned predictability, its serious implications thematically underlined by the bitterly witty remonstrances with which the servants defuse the tension and come to terms with the discomfort of their physical subordination:

Dromio of Syracuse.	Was there ever any man thus beaten out of season, When in the why and the wherefore is neither rhyme nor reason. Well, sir, I thank you.
Antipholus of Syracuse.	Thank me, sir, for what?
Dromio of Syracuse.	Marry, sir, for this something that you gave me for nothing.
Antipholus of Syracuse.	I'll make you amends next, to give you nothing for something.

(Act 2, scene 2)

Dromio of Ephesus states his case with an even more sorely felt rancor:

Dromio of Ephesus.   I would I were senseless, sir, that I might not feel your blows.
Antipholus of Ephesus. Thou art sensible in nothing but blows, and so is an ass.
Dromio of Ephesus.   I am an ass indeed; you may prove it by my long ears. I have served him from the hour of my nativity to this instant, and have nothing at his hands for my service but blows. When I am cold, he heats me with beating; when I am warm he cools me with beating; I am waked with it when I sleep, raised with it when I sit, driven out of doors with it when I go from home, welcomed home with it when I return, nay, I bear it on my shoulders as a beggar wont her brat; and I think when he hath lamed me, I shall beg with it from door to door.
(Act 4, scene 4)

Bearing in mind the genuine grievance underlying Dromio's eloquent litany and his clever quibble on donkey's years of service and the donkey's ears of an ass (both being long and in a thankless position), the comedy produced by the network of convoluted mix-ups ends up being more excruciating than joyful or festive. Moreover, the vertical distance enjoyed by the audience not only enables it—unlike the fictive characters—to distinguish appearance and reality, but also yields the distinctly painful pleasure of anticipating *future* pain. The ambiguity of such an emotion concurs with Socrates's notion of laughter as a fusion of painful malice and pleasure. Again, it is distance that can be regarded as transforming the harrowing into the hilarious. Hazlitt writes: "What is sport to one, is death to another. It is only very sensible or very honest people, who laugh as freely at their own absurdities as at those of their neighbours. In general the contrary rule holds, and we laugh only at those misfortunes in which we are spectators, not sharers."[17]

The farce of Feydeau works on similar principles, its characters chasing about in a pandemonium of confusion, mistaking identities, and dishing out drubbings to bemused innocents. In *La Puce à l'oreille* Feydeau exploits the comic potential of bringing together the dignified figure of Chandebise and his lowly "double," Poche, by having the former end up on the receiving end of the stylized pastings normally part of Poche's daily wages. The sight of the gentleman subject to the same physical humiliations as the hotel porter adds an element of social reversal to the vicarious violence, which is perhaps what Bentley has in mind when he claims that farce "offers the one simple pleasure: the pleasure of hitting one's enemy in the jaw without getting hit back.... In farce we hit back at our oppressor."[18] Yet farce in itself seems ultimately just as apolitical as the other forms of comedy encountered so far: it can no less easily derive its laughs from the blatant maltreatment of the slaves (as in Aristophanes) and is not prevented from doing so even when this social injustice is simultaneously exposed to serious or semiserious thematic scrutiny (as in Shakespeare) or when the master is himself derided for his own lack of self-control.

Hitting the wrong person, often through clumsiness or as a result of the actual target fortuitously bending over at precisely the moment in question, is indeed a stock device in the comic repertoire, and its repercussions may branch in any number of directions. Quite apart from the gratuitous satisfaction of hitting an often completely innocent or unsuspecting bystander, the basic situation is also likely to generate the self-perpetuating snowball effect, which may in turn degenerate into the anarchy of a mass brawl. The slapstick comedy of the nineteenth-century music hall has constant recourse to such farcical turbulence. The original "slapstick" was a wooden bat with a split in the blade designed for walloping people with the maximum amount of din, the search for ever more spectacular effects seeing gunpowder inserted in the slapstick's cleft as a means of amplifying the noise.[19] In the early days of the cinema, the custard pie became a particularly popular missile, starting with the one Fatty Arbuckle received in his face in *Mabel and Fatty's Married Life* (1916) and reaching an apotheosis with Laurel and Hardy's *Battle of the Century* with its record of 3,000 dispatched pies. The foodfight is nothing new of course, for it handily sublimates aggressive or chaotic impulses while remaining utterly painless. The fecal foodstuffs ("a bowl full of ordure and dung") propelled through the air at the climax of the carnival play *La Bataille de Sainct Pensard* in 1485 and also contributing to the excremental merriment of the medieval Feast of Fools[20] were presumably just as harmless as the shaving foam of the twentieth century.

The hostile urges present in such farce may alternatively be tempered by being directed at objects rather than people, as in Laurel and Hardy's *Big Business*. Similar destruction is wreaked by the blind man (Mr. Muckle) in W. C. Fields's movie *It's a Gift*[21] when he "involuntarily" razes an entire grocery store to the ground by a few minutes' resolute stomping around in his sturdy boots and the nimbly indiscriminate application of his cane. That it is a blind man who should generate such systematic havoc again signals the recurrent—although not necessary—association of farce and topsy-turvy reversal: witness also the reign of terror exercized by Hell's Grannies, those bovver-booted wrinklies from *Monty Python's Flying Circus*. It is especially satisfying to see the physically weak or disadvantaged trash things up a little.

Taboo or not Taboo

Joubert's treatise on laughter, written in 1579, directs attention to the comic effect of a sudden exposure of the pudenda in terms that remind us that, etymologically speaking at least, the pudenda are something to be ashamed of: "If we happen to uncover the shameful parts, which by nature or public propriety we are accustomed to keep concealed, the sight of this—being ugly, while unworthy of pity—incites those present to laughter." More specifically, the unmentionables down below provoke laughter when the mask that normally covers them so diligently is seen to fall, slip, or rip. "This should happen unthinkingly, as when they are glimpsed through some tear in the person's breeches."[22] The comic surprise of spotting the mask fall is here conjoined with the subversive pleasure of seeing that which is forbidden. What is more, just as postlapsarian society dictates that we should at least have the decency to don a fig leaf to hide our shameful organs, the social mask in general constrains us to conceal our shameful *urges* (both aggressive and sexual), thus making sure that our private parts stay in the dark corner to which we have confined them, without getting any ideas of their own. Hidden even from ourselves, our instinctual drives (as Freud claimed) are refused entry to the conscious and forced to remain at the level of the unconscious.

Accordingly, Freud perceived two primary *Tendenzen* in the purposive joke: sex and aggression. While the aggressive joke serves as a surrogate for our "natural" pugnacity ("By making the enemy small, abject, despicable or comic, we indirectly procure ourselves the pleasure of overcoming him"[23]), the bawdy quip provides a release for hidden desires, making possible "the satisfaction of a drive (the lustful or the hostile drive) in the face of an obstacle which stands in the way" and drawing "pleasure from a source rendered inaccessible by the obstacle."[24] The hindrance that is thereby circumvented, writes Freud, is the culturally determined repression or *Verdrängung* which forbids the enjoyment of unveiled obscenity and deprives us of potential sources of sexual pleasure. By analogy, it can be conjectured—although Freud never made the connection—that in the world of theatre it is satire and farce that correspond to the destructive joke and sexual comedy that performs a similar function to the dirty joke. Affording a moment of release for the asocial urges deep down inside, for the "real self" that we normally reveal neither to ourselves nor to society at large, comedy (like the joke, the dream, and the parapraxis) thus becomes a link between the conscious and the unconscious, the knowable and the unknowable.[25]

The boundary between the sexual and the aggressive in Freud always remains problematic, this theoretical blur reflecting the obvious possibilities of sexual aggressivity and aggressive sexuality. In comedy, the two components correspondingly fuse in the tendency, for example, of invective to resort to the sphere of sexual imagery (Hal being a bull's pizzle or a tailor's yard, Panurge a moldy old bollock) and satire to make sport of the sexuality of its victims, while the whirlwind turbulence of farce often takes the form of a sexual merry-go-round. The complications in Freud's work on the subject arise in part because he himself employs different topographical models at different times to illustrate his conception of the psyche. The first model (used in *Witz*) involves an unequivocal logical differentiation between the unconscious on the one hand and the conscious and preconscious on the other—or, in terms of the mask metaphor, between the underlying body and the culturally imposed mask. The second topographical model replaces these terms by the id, the ego (which strives to control the instinctual drives of the id), and the superego (the representative of parental and social forces, mercilessly upbraiding the ego for its sexuality). The fundamental difference between the two models is that, whereas the unconscious was logically separate from the preconscious and the conscious, the energies of the id are seen as *creating* the ego and are also operative in the superego, as is manifest in the tyrannical violence this wreaks upon the ego. Coming to recognize an essential interdependency of law and desire, Freud now sees the law as itself grounded in desire: the superego is less an external agency than a transmutation of the id's bodily drives. Just as Nietzsche had interpreted the "soul" or "conscience" as a displacement or internalization of our natural cruelty, so Freud writes in *Das Ich und das Es* (1923), "The id is completely amoral, the ego is at pains to be moral, and the super-ego can be hypermoral and in this case every bit as cruel as the id."[26] The cruelty of comic sexuality becomes an opportunity to practise on others the cruelty we normally practise on ourselves.

In this light, comedy emerges as a gratification for our not very nice sexual instincts. Freud indeed sees the *Zote* or bawdy joke, told by a male in male company at the expense of a woman, as the frolicsome equivalent of *rape* (by the teller) and *voyeurism* (by the listener), leaving the woman embarrassed and exposed by verbal obscenity with which she cannot cope.

> A person who laughs at the bawdy joke he hears is laughing in the same way as a spectator to an act of sexual aggression.... The bawdy joke is like a denudation of the sexually different person at which it is directed. By the utterance of the obscene words it forces the person being assailed to imagine the part of the body or the act in question and shows her that the assailant is himself imagining the same thing. There can be no doubt that the desire to see what is sexual exposed is the original motive behind the bawdy joke.[27]

Considering this interpretation of male malice in the *Zote*, it is a rather sobering thought that Dürrenmatt judged the *Zote* to be the *Urkomödie*, or archetypal comedy.[28]

Theatre is consequently a form of voyeurism, a point implied by Robert Pinget's play *Abel et Bela*. This is a self-conscious dramatic exploration into the nature of theatre, where the protagonists' plans for a play display an insistent preference for the idea of an orgy, the essence of theatre apparently being the sight of men and women "revealing themselves." It is indeed with the act of undressing that the play itself ends, yet—tantalizingly enough—the curtain comes down too soon and the *pure* nakedness of orgy remains an absent ideal. Having stayed at the level of mere intention during the course of the play, as well as being transposed into the discursive nudity of the protagonists' (fictive?) soul-searching, the orgiastic nakedness is finally displaced behind the final curtain. If spectatorship is voyeurism, it is a peephole voyeurism that is never fully satisfactory.

The whole notion of the theatre as an agent of unmasking and of penetration to the truth supports this sense of the scopophilia inherent in spectatorship. The rent in the moral mask, like the breach in Joubert's breeches, reveals the "real" motivation attempting to assert itself like a disobedient body that insistently bulges out at embarrassing moments. The facade of moral rationalization with which we mask the underlying amorality of our *body* is as flawed and fissured as a flimsy bra that, at the flick of a finger, goes flying across the room. The comedy of manners specializes in this revelation of true motivation, stripping its characters down to the core of their egoistic venality and lustfulness, as in Orton's *Entertaining Mr. Sloane*, where Kath's negations of her sexuality ("I wonder, Mr. Sloane, if you'd take your trousers off? I hope you don't think there's anything behind the request" [1]) are as transparent as the (Freudian?) slip she is wearing ("They make garments so thin nowadays you'd think they intended to provoke a rape" [1]). In similar vein, Aristophanes's *Lysistrata* exploits the comic possibilities of a sex-strike in a community where everyone—men and women alike—is absolutely fixated on the same (temporarily unavailable) commodity. Not only do we see Lysistrata's own ranks reduced to blacklegs, tiptoeing out of the Acropolis with the most implausible of excuses (suddenly remembered household chores that require attention), but the men too are soon confined to a state of permanent erection. Again the comedy arises from their utter failure to hide this importunate priapism. Walking about bent double, they become easy prey for cheeky allusions to the "spear" they seem to be concealing under their cloaks.

What Barthes says about the erotic can perhaps, therefore, be taken as applying equally to this sort of comedy: "Isn't the most erotic part of a body the part where the garment gapes?"[29] It is not the blinding light of absolute (carnal) knowledge, the complete nakedness of orgy, which is comic/erotic, but the inevitable chiaroscuro, the interaction of lightness and dark, bareness and dress. The difference between the comic and the erotic is that, whereas eroticism is an (often nauseatingly) cool and controlled half-exposure, comedy's revelation tends to be involuntary and decidedly uncool.

Theatrical voyeurism is a product of the *distance* enjoyed by the spectators, who know more than the fictive figures and whose superiority allows them a flatteringly godlike transcendence, the ironic perspective. Freud himself explicitly associated knowledge with voyeurism, seeing the *Wißtrieb* or thirst for knowledge both as a sublimated form of mastery and as a channeling of the energies of the *Schaulust*, the little child's desire to see other people's genitals.[30] The German word *Wissen* indeed, like wit, is an etymological descendant of the Latin *videre* (to see). As theatrical voyeurs, seeing but not being seen, we exploit our privileged position of knowledgeability, while the poor fools down below inadvertently make exhibitionists of themselves. That such voyeurism further borders on covert sadism is illustrated by the inherent cruelty of dramatic irony. Watching from above with divine self-satisfaction, we laugh at (or with?) the discomfiture of the fictive dunderheads onstage whose ignorance impels them—with consummate predictability—into ever more painful situations.

The element of voyeurism, being a function of the *passivity* of the audience, has not always been equally in evidence. The originally participatory nature of, say, the commedia—or of the celebratory plays of carnival, indeed of the phallic rites from which comedy arguably derived—would imply a different stance on the part of the audience. It is above all the psychological theatre of the nineteenth century that assumed the form of a theatrical peep show, an all-revealing (and admittedly not very comic) exposure of the whole sordid truth. Reacting against such illusionism, Brecht was to describe it as giving the audience the illusion of sitting in front of a keyhole,[31] the moral implications of which had been made clear by Tristram Shandy: "Key-holes are the occasions of more sin and wickedness, than all other holes in this world put together."[32] Metatheatre, with its habit of calling into question the relationship between actor and audience, has implicitly focused upon such theatrical scopophilia, mocking the passivity of the onlooker. Beckett's *Happy Days*, Genet's *Le Balcon* (where Irma's final comment implies that we too are perverts every bit as much as the fantasy-enacting visitors to her brothel), and Simpson's *One Way Pendulum* all touch upon the theme. In Simpson's play, Barnes, who has periodically served as a mediator between actor and audience, sheepishly takes his leave of the fictive characters at the end of the play and "takes" us (the audience) with him:

Mrs Groomkirby.	Just off, are you?
Barnes.	Yes—they've had a good look round and ...
	....
Mrs Groomkirby.	Seen all they want, have they?
Barnes.	I think they have, yes. More or less. *(Edging off)*.
Mrs Groomkirby.	*(half to herself)*. Day in day out. Gawping. The place isn't your own.
Barnes.	*(escaping)*. Back tomorrow about half past seven then, Mrs Groomkirby—if that's all right.
Mrs Groomkirby.	They won't have to come expecting anything.

(Act 2)

Sylvia (the one who is obsessed by the length of her arms) even wonders why "we" don't go and gawk at Buckingham Palace instead. The presence of the audience is a crass intrusion into the privacy of fictional people who would prefer to keep themselves to themselves.

Theatrical productions may furthermore be seen as intrinsically sexual, not merely in origin or content but also in form. Modern theatre in particular has imitated this sexuality by building up to *climaxes* that are blatantly coital in character, and the proliferation and general acceleration of pace into the fury of farce (which are taken as simulating the sexual frenzy) may be reinforced by overt verbal references or allusions. Towards the end of the ever more hectic orgy of misunderstanding and misdemeanor in Orton's *What the Butler Saw*, for example, Rance comments: "We're approaching what our racier novelists term 'the climax.'" Of course, the fact that this is said by Rance, a walking parody of psychiatry at its most psychotic, should serve as reason for caution. Indeed, it is all too easy to go blithely trotting off on a pansexualist hobbyhorse and, in the words of Karl Kraus, to turn psychoanalysis into the illness for which it is supposed to be the therapy. Moreover, sublimated sexuality—if that indeed is what we are dealing with in frenetic theatrical climaxes—is only likely to become comic when, as with Orton, it draws attention to itself or parodies itself as such. Even overtly sexual climaxes may in fact be employed primarily for sinister ends. Following Jack the Ripper's emphatically unfunny stabbing of Lulu at the conclusion to Wedekind's grotesque *Büchse der Pandora*, Ionesco's *La Leçon* reaches an orgastic crescendo as the (female) pupil is stabbed by the (male) teacher's verbal/phallic knife, a symbol both of mental and sexual domination. Peter Barnes's *The Ruling Class* turns into a "hysteric hubbub" when the sexually "normalized" Earl of Gurney (in the guise of Jack) commits a comparable sex murder, likewise a signal of perverted sexual or ideological power. Again, if the theatre is sexual in nature, it appears to be a basically frustrated or impaired form of sexuality.

In *Le Balcon*, Jean Genet, who viewed acting itself as masturbatory,[33] thematically follows up the consequences of the link between sex and theatre: the brothel in which the play is set symbolizes this fusion of acting and desire, for its customers can here act out their sexual fantasies of domination and subordination, beating and being beaten, riding and being ridden. These acted power configurations within the brothel are an explicit counterpoint to the histrionic sexual politics hammered out in the "real" world—and, by implication, in the world of the spectator too. An interesting extension of the metatheatrical principles informing Genet's drama is Belle de Jour, a sadomasochistic theatre in modern-day New York,[34] where a salmagundi of comic and S & M sketches is followed by allowing spectators on stage so that they can themselves have a go at being spanked or doing some spanking, a few being worked over with more painstaking attention. In this case, the breach in the boundary separating actor and audience permits theatrical voyeurism to be developed in the direction of active sadism or masochism and, as Schechner points out,[35] Belle's theatre—together with many other such establishments—is advertised not on the theatrical pages of New York's *Village Voice*, but under "adult entertainment."

Recent literary theorists have even used sexuality as a metaphor for a variety of narrative forces involved in getting to grips with a text. The text is erotic in that it draws its reader into it, tantalizing and teasing him: in the end, it indeed escapes his desire, for the written word is ultimately a symbol of lack, indicating the *absence* of what it means. Roland Barthes sees in this resistance to "possession" (a function of the text's openness, ambivalence, its capacity to undermine its own meaning, etc.) the source not only of the text's subversive potential but also of blissful (orgasmic) enjoyment or *jouissance* in the reader. Lustful bibliophile that he is (or strictly speaking isn't, for in his own words "the author is dead"[36]), Barthes boldly claims that "the text is a fetish, and *this fetish desires me*."[37] (On this note, however, it is perhaps wise to give our pansexualist hobbyhorse a tug on the reins before it becomes too unclear whether we are riding it or ourselves being ridden....)

Theatrical comedy may also incorporate sexuality in more obviously positive ways. Descended as it (arguably) is from phallic ritual, it has frequently functioned as the expression of an ebulliently festive sexuality. Aristophanes's *The Acharnians*, to take but one example, is openly phallic in intent, unambivalently associating the celebration of peace to the celebration of sex in a song addressed to Phales (a minor deity personifying the phallus) in which peace is anticipated with unconcealed relish as allowing more time for swiving one's neighbor's pretty Thracian slavegirl.

It was this spirit of moral "freedom" that was the appeal of Aristophanic drama to the German romantic Schlegel as well as to following generations of above all German critics: the removal of all social barriers signaled an unparallelled autonomy and individual liberty in their eyes, the Old Comedy of Greece coming to be seen as the paragon of "delightful gaiety, sublime liberty and comic vigour."[38] This is clearly an oversimplifying idealization of a phenomenon that could be sordid, aggressive, and "macho" in its own way. The very idea of a phallic rite indeed presupposes a phallocentric perspective blind to the nicety of whether one's neighbor's pretty Thracian slavegirl actually wants to have "her cherry stoned." (For Aristophanes the question simply does not arise: everybody—male or female—always wants as much sex as he or she can possibly get.) Nevertheless, it is clear that this brand of openly saturnalian comedy, like the medieval carnival plays and Shakespeare's festive drama, is primarily intended as an *affirmation* of sexuality.

The Oedipal pattern characteristic above all of the Roman New Comedy can also be regarded in this light, analogous in structure to the joke in that both constitute the satisfaction of a (sexual) instinct or desire despite the opposition of a parental or cultural obstacle. Frye thus speculates that the "New Comedy unfolds from what may be described as a comic Oedipus situation. Its main theme is the successful effort of a young man to outwit an opponent and possess the girl of his choice. The opponent is usually the father (*senex*), and the psychological descent of the heroine from the mother is also sometimes hinted at. The father frequently wants the same girl, and is cheated out of her by the son, the mother thus becoming the son's ally."[39] The phallocentric bias is implied not only in Frye's account, according to which it is through the *action* of the young man that the latter comes to possess the purely *passive* woman, but also in Freud's own version of the Oedipus complex, which is fundamentally *boy*-orientated. Freud's adaptation of the myth has it that, initially wanting to possess his mother and seeing in his father a rival, the antisocial little boy is socialized by the threat of castration from the father: it is the warning voice of the father—with whom the boy comes to identify—that is internalized in the form of the superego. Little girls, never truly socializable, fit uneasily into this myth. Sexual politics aside, however, the important point is that the comic overcoming of the *senex* represents a vicarious triumph over the social constraints embodied in the father figure and internalized in that savage spoilsport the superego. The happy ending is an assertion of the sexual moment and a symbol of an (imaginary) state of plenitude: having dispatched his superego, the ego can devote a bit of long-overdue attention to his id.

The influential German philosopher Schopenhauer, whose concept of the *Wille* or Will in so many ways anticipates Freud's unconscious, likewise understood comedy as an affirmation of sexuality (in the form of the *Wille*). A rather vaguely formulated notion, the *Wille* is on the one hand a thing-in-itself ("the Will as thing-in-itself is completely distinct from its appearances"[40]), and, as such, it partakes of the radical otherness characterizing not only Freud's unconscious but also Kant's *Ding an sich*. On the other hand, Schopenhauer, like Freud, takes the audacious step of describing the indescribable: it is a blind force, a dark and gloomily impenetrable power, the incomprehensible motor that propels us through life. It is, moreover, intrinsically sexual in nature (and here Schopenhauer's terminology subtly switches from *Wille* to the *Wille zum Leben* or Will to Life), and the act of copulation is its ultimate concretization. "The world," writes Schopenhauer, "is vast in space and ancient in time and inexhaustibly manifold in its forms. All this however is but the appearance (*Erscheinung*) of the Will to Life; and the hub or focus of this Will is the act of procreation. It is thus in this act that the inner essence of the world is most clearly expressed."[41] Sex is a manifestation of the essence, the hidden face of the world, the omnifutuant unknowable; the genitals are its focal point. The comedy Schopenhauer perceives in our attempts to suppress this metaphysical unconscious beneath the illusions of rationality and sexual decorum has already been encountered. Our efforts to explain away our perpetual rut (as love, for example) are ludicrously pathetic undertakings, doomed to comic failure. But not only does Schopenhauer, anticipating Freud, recognize that sex is "the target of the jest, the inexhaustible wellspring of the joke, the key to all innuendoes and the sense of all insinuations,"[42] he also, unlike Freud, interprets comedy as a *celebration* of the sexual impulse, and thereby a corroboration of the Will to Life, an "incitement to the continued affirmation of the Will."[43] Comedy both draws back Maya's veil, revealing things as they really are, and—through the happy ending with its triumph of hope and harmony—celebrates what is unveiled. Yet Schopenhauer is quick to emphasize that this happy ending is itself illusory, a utopian mythologization of the Will's amoral sordidity: "Admittedly, however, (the comedy) must hasten to drop the curtain while the joy lasts, so we do not see what comes afterwards."[44] The play's audience must be hurriedly ushered home before the newly united lovers start bickering and the celebratory wine turns back into sour grapes.

Yet the sexual exuberance of comedy may equally move in a quite different direction. Instead of rejoicing in marriage, sexual farce tends to be radically antimarital in character. By way of analogy, Freud's third category of tendentious joke (along with the obscene and the hostile) is what he termed the *cynical*. This in fact could be construed as a subcategory of the hostile, with an insistent habit of drawing upon the sphere of sexuality as well, but in this case it is not individuals who are pilloried but institutions or beliefs—and the most frequently pilloried institution is the marital one. Freud writes: "Of the institutions which the cynical joke is given to attack, there is none more important or more stringently protected by moral precepts but at the same time more inviting to attack than the institution of marriage, which for this reason is the target of most cynical jokes."[45] Laying into monogamy or associating with its infringement reveals itself as another form of release for pent-up pugnacity and sexual frustration. One of the unfailing comic themes is cuckoldry, abundantly present in the comedies of the Italian Renaissance (following Boccaccio's lead) and the English Restoration, as well as the bourgeois boulevard farces of the nineteenth century. The underlying assumption of such farce is that marriage does not yield sexual satisfaction, and adultery functions as the comic carrot dangling teasingly in front of the characters' noses, luring them inevitably into roguery, folly, or both. Wycherley's Horner is perhaps the archetypal horner, the Restoration rapscallion evading the traps of matrimony by means of carefully concealed promiscuity. The rakes of Congreve and Farquhar, by contrast, are less vigorously polygamous than those of Wycherley and Etherege thirty years earlier, owing to both moral pressures (such as Collier's diatribe "A Short View of the Immorality and Profaneness of the English Stage," [1698]) and the fact that, under the Protestant monarchs William and Mary, divorce had become a viable alternative for relieving the perennial itch beneath the marital chastity belt.

The English comedy of manners in particular, whose chief subjects have always been the venal and the venereal, attacks the mercenary institutionalization of sex not merely through its positive portrayal of cuckoldry but also by explicit, often wittily formulated disparagement. Congreve's Millamant, for example, voices her fear that marriage will mean an infringement of her personal freedom: "My dear liberty," she laments, "shall I leave thee? My faithful solitude, my darling contemplation, must I bid you then adieu? Ay-h adieu—my morning thoughts, agreeable wakings, indolent slumbers, all ye *douceurs, ye sommeils du matin*, adieu—I can't do it, 'tis more than impossible" (4.5). But she does. Wilde's Lord Henry views marriage more positively, acknowledging that "the one charm of marriage is that it makes a life of deception absolutely necessary,"[46] while, in *The Importance of Being Earnest*, Algernon ("If ever I get married, I'll certainly try to forget the fact" [1]) points out to Jack the ubiquity of marital deceit:

Algernon. ... in married life three is company and two is none.
Jack.   (*sententiously*). That, my dear young friend, is the theory that the corrupt French drama has been propounding for the last fifty years.
Algernon. Yes; and that the happy English home has proved in half the time.
Jack.   For heaven's sake, don't try to be cynical.

(Act 1)

The post-Freudian sexologist Wilhelm Reich expressly connected the liberation of the "true self" to the abandonment of the marital institution, just as R. D. Laing's antipsychiatry was to be based upon the assumption of an inherently healthy being that would emerge if only freed from the distortive familial straitjacket (of which society as a whole is but an extension). Reich thus differs at heart from Freud in that he posits a *naturally* "healthy" sexuality, our asocial or disorderly impulses being the product of the patriarchal organization of society and of the morality that developed as an oppressive ploy of the politically (domestically) powerful. The social mask arose, says Reich, as a weapon of economic and social control, a political show of strength. Whereas Freud, in the tradition of Hobbes, sees the naturalness of our nastiness, Reich embodies a Rousseauistic spirit of optimism, perceiving in sadism and sexual aggression the legacy of a basically sick social structure and claiming "that the moral regulation of human drives creates the very thing it professes to be able to keep under control: asocial drives."[47] In other words, the mask itself brings into existence that which needs to be masked. Reich's model accordingly establishes a direct correlation between the sexual and the political mask, the *family* being the root of all evil in that it buttresses both, churning out sexual "cripples"[48] and generating a disposition of subservience and submission in a movement of self-perpetuating circularity. The sight of cuckoldry in the theatre may therefore be assumed to serve both as a political release from the tyranny of the family (thanks to the subversive pleasure of seeing the male representative of the patriarchal order being outwitted and hoodwinked) and a sexual flight from the moral coercion that normally holds sway over our bodies.

Reich consequently advocates a brand of sexual and economic communism not entirely different from the Platonic utopia mocked by Aristophanes—but of course without that troublesome small writing ordaining positive discrimination for the old and ugly in the matter of the sexual pecking order. The only ethical rule in this collectivistic *Urgesellschaft* (*Ur* signaling that such a state is the *original* state) would be that there are no rules, for "he who is satisfied in his life neither rapes nor therefore needs a moral code prohibiting it."[49] (He would presumably not even feel the pull of the peep-show theatre or cinema.) Communism of this order is a perpetualization of the comic happy ending (and just as imaginary)—but without the marital yoke: Jack gets not only Jill but any other woman he fancies—and Jill any man. Such a utopian vision of society is the offshoot of a utopian vision of the "true self" as a nucleus of natural sexuality from which "perversion" is a contingent deviation. What it ignores, however, is that this real self, this copulatory core hidden by the structures of patriarchal capitalism and a repressive morality, is also a fundamentally unknown quantity and, in a certain sense, unknowable. As such, it partakes of a radical ambiguity—analogous to the ambivalence of folly—that goes deeper than Reich's one-sided analysis would allow, for the unknown (like the madness of the topsy-turvy world) may either be idealized into a cornucopian utopia *or* conceived as a dystopian realm of atavistic anarchy. A society without law may be a Rousseauistic haven or a Hobbesian hell. While Reich's version of Freudianism is committed to a virile heterosexuality as the "natural" thing, therefore, who is to say that the state of nature is not in fact a domain of rape, buggery, masturbation, and zoophilia, all the things now swept under the cultural carpet and condemned to a sort of discursive nonexistence? In this case, the human being is not judged to have a single, essential human nature; instead, our "hidden" face consists in an absolutely protean essence incorporating our potential to negate the order, to behave as "irrationally" as the Zuni Katcinas' ritual clown who masturbates in public and bedaubs himself with excrement or as the naughty Winnebago trickster who cohabits before going to war.

Two broad versions of the model therefore emerge. The one sees the social mask as hiding *natural* sexuality. The other regards the social mask as silencing or concealing the subject's *negativity*, the infinite potential to deviate or be different, to do what is not done. This mask may be envisioned as consisting either of a passively unquestioning acceptance of the (moral/social) order as it is or of an active enforcement of the norm by social institutions that suppress transgression by condemning its perpetrators to the nonexistence of prisons or psychiatric establishments.

Alternatively, however, one can free the mask metaphor from its bondage to such "repression" hypotheses and view it instead as existential in nature. Given that transgression itself is a sort of role and that we can never simply doff our social mask and behave absolutely spontaneously, free from the determinants, influences, and compulsions of social intercourse, what at one level seems to be a rejection of the mask is at another level interpretable as just a different category of mask-wearing. The pure negativity hidden behind the mask is nothing other than nothing, as much of a gap in our epistemological framework as Freud's unconscious or Kant's thing-in-itself, which is likewise only definable in negative terms— as that which can*not* be known. Like madness and sanity, like reason and folly, sex and its cultural appropriation always in practice exist in dynamic interaction. While ritual clowns and comic fools may thus symbolize this fiction of radical social otherness through their institutionalized taboo-breaking, the paradoxical manifestation of what is not can also be understood as implying that the negative is not simply to be banished to a different ontological plane (nonbeing), but exists in perpetual symbiosis with the positive: social order depends upon its other just as law is meaningless without the possibility of transgression.

This is something that becomes clear in Foucault's later work. Calling into question the notion that sexuality is "natural," Foucault shows how discursive power in its infinite manifestations itself invents sexuality, regulating it while also creating the resistance to such regulation. Foucault refuses to accept either that the law merely represses sexuality or that it merely creates desire or is created by it, emphasizing instead that social power is polymorphous, ambivalent, and in constant flux. Power is never simply oppressive, Foucault would have it, for it is the precondition for resistance, itself a form of power. Static positions of domination and subordination necessarily give rise to possibilities of subversion: "Discourse can be both an instrument and an effect of power, but also a hindrance, a stumbling-block, a point of resistance and a starting point for an opposing strategy. Discourse transmits and produces power; it reinforces it, but also undermines and exposes it, renders it fragile and makes it possible to thwart it."[50] Consequently, Foucault writes, sexuality "must not be described as a stubborn drive, by nature alien and of necessity disobedient to a power which exhausts itself trying to subdue it and often fails to control it entirely. It appears rather as an especially dense transfer point for relations of power: between men and women, young people and old people, parents and offspring, teachers and students, priests and laity, an administration and a population."[51] Sexuality in its myriad manifestations, he might have claimed, is a part of the social mask (in *its* myriad manifestations). It is a perpetual theme of the social discourse that creates it and forms it, represses it and resists this repression, be it in the confessional, in the psychiatrist's clinic, or in school, no less than in the theatre, the strip club, or during plebeian festivities.

Freud himself regarded the *original* sexuality (both in evolutionary and in developmental terms) as polymorphous in character, suggesting "that the predisposition towards the perversions is the original general predisposition of the human sexual drive, from which normal sexual conduct has developed in the course of maturation as a result of organic changes and psychic inhibitions."[52] Originally, we are all (or *were* all) constitutionally bisexual, our heterosexuality a social fabrication impressed, imposed, or stamped upon the protean potential of our bodies. In fact—why not admit it?—we are all latent zoophiliacs too. Zoophilia was indeed frequent practice in the pastoral societies of the Neolithic period, only being banned when the nomads settled down.[53] At a certain level, it is a question of taking whatever comes to hand, animal, vegetable, or mineral. As Lenny Bruce points out to his audience:

Like all of us: me, you, you—put us on a desert island for five years, no chicks, you'll ball mud.... *Knotholes.*

"Are you kidding?—What are you doing next to that tree, you slob you? What are you doing? *Schtupping* a tree!"
"It's *my* tree."[54]

Whereas Freud did in fact posit a time (as children and "primitives") in which we really were hermaphroditic (and anthropologists have indeed discerned in tribalistic communities a more laid-back attitude to sexual variation as against the uniformity traditionally insisted upon by authoritarian civilizations), our model need not do this. It is not necessary to attribute chronological primacy to polymorphous sexuality: logical priority will do. The point is, however, that—despite the absolute polymorphism of logical possibility and the fact that my sexuality *could* manifest itself in any way—sexuality in practice is always interior to a social framework and therefore in some way structured or conditioned. The human self, necessarily an embodied subject, is the product of a matrix of socio-cultural determinants that shape what we are and tend to veil the possibility that we might have been different.

Corresponding to the models that have come to light (which see the sexual mask as a concealment either of "nature" or of "negativity"), the mask is thus perceived by the wearer, if perceived at all, either as an unnatural restraint upon what is natural or a normal suppression of what is abnormal. It is according to this rough schema that the comic presentation of sexuality provokes mirth that is (at a conscious level at least) either more or less collusive with respect to its object. While sexual deviance has since time immemorial been the target of mockery, "natural" sexuality, bursting forth like a fountain of lost innocence, is liable to be laughed *with*.

The mask thus exists in different forms and at different levels, one mask superimposing itself upon another in the manner of a Russian doll. Deeply ingrained and ancient cultural habits and ethical norms, which have perhaps developed as a response to climatological or geographical factors, are more likely to be "naturalized" (to pass themselves off as natural, or remain unquestioned), their infringement consequently being an incitement to corrective mockery, if not more drastic measures. Other legal and religious codes, perhaps imposed from without upon a specific culture or as part of a system of political control, have, by contrast, a greater tendency to go against the grain. The dictates of discursive decorum too—determining what is permitted to be *spoken*—are more openly conventional in nature. With its concomitant suppression of "unseemly" speech, this mask has likewise helped modify sexuality into a terrain of unknowability, of literal and metaphorical darkness.

Sexual comedy and the sexual joke may accordingly operate with varying degrees of intensity. The taboo-breaking shock of unmasked verbal obscenity in spheres of sexual deviation explodes all notions both of what is (morally) right and what is (socially) seemly, but in a society where even talking candidly about sex was until recently considered unforgivably indecorous, the very act of joking explicitness—simply mentioning those unmentionables normally hushed out of sight—may be a gesture of comic subversion even when the tone of the joke is relatively conventional and norm affirmative. The innuendo goes as far as to hide its naughtiness behind a facade of verbal decorum. Taboo-breaking Lenny Bruce makes no bones about where he stands within the comic tradition:

> One thing I'd like to tell the people who are leaving, is that you're very genteel. This is the first time I've had an audience that walk out, but *nicely*.
> In Milwaukee, *Phew*! They used to walk out and walk *towards* me.... But the only thing that confuses me, I used to lie in bed and think "What do those guys come in for? What kind of humor is *their* humor? Is it the Joe E. Lewis, the Sophie Tucker, the *double-entendre*, the naughty-but-nice, the spicy-haha-you-know-what-that-means wedding-night jokes...?"[55]

The irony is that in mocking and parodying the tradition of saucy nudge-nudge-wink-wink-say-no-more humor, he is also exploiting it. Disparaging a joke is a good way of telling it without having to accept the responsibility for its success or failure, and at the same time it gives him the opportunity to mock not the deviant individuals (which he does do as well on other occasions) but a repressive and unhealthily decent society that—through typical topsy-turvy lenses—can itself be viewed as deviant. This is confirmed by Bruce's anecdote of the "flasher" who keeps getting arrested for flashing his bunch of lilacs. Nobody ever actually gets to see what he is flashing (for his shameful thing-in-itself must be hidden, hushed up, and bundled away); instead people simply punch him up and drag him off as soon as he says "Hallo there." Bruce's point? "That the society is perverse."[56] Rapping old ladies in the chops is less severely punished.

Dr. Jonathan Miller, who together with Peter Cook, Dudley Moore, and Alan Bennett had produced *Beyond the Fringe* for the 1960 Edinburgh Festival, makes a similar distinction to Lenny Bruce's (and for similar reasons): jokes about bottoms, breasts, bedpots, and bras, he maintains, are "a psychological decoy which gives a false impression of relief so that the more dangerous issues can fester undisturbed. For when it comes down to it the items mentioned above ... are no more than the second eleven of sexuality. The first eleven, the central sexual issues, are never allowed to get out to the wicket." This effect, moreover, "falls in quite happily with the intentions of the Lord Chamberlain, who will blithely license this routine at the same time that he bars an honest treatment of the crucial themes. In this way the Lord Chamberlain is exploiting the immaturity of English humour in order to preserve that very immaturity."[57] Although such naughtiness permits a glimpse of taboo areas, our indecency remains veiled in a cloak of harmlessness (which obscures its subversive potential), by this means evading the censorial scissors of the cultural superego.

Freud too describes the *Witz* as a mask or facade (half-)hiding its tendentiousness, its forbidden belligerence or obscene sexuality,[58] and here he clearly has in mind the innuendo, the saucy allusion, and the pun. These forms of verbal comedy draw attention to themselves in their capacity as masks and thereby implicitly disclose what is being masked. The metaphor is less fitting where the comedy works (as with Lenny Bruce) through outrageously exhibitionistic overstatement rather than nictating understatement, yet here too the sexuality is displaced or masked in a sense. Even screamed obscenities, when intended and taken as a joke, are both verbal (a mask of words as opposed to actual physical activity) and ludic (defined as play by their context and thus only as half-serious, half-real). In the theatre, the cinema, or the club, the sexuality is framed in its aesthetic context as illusory or "just pretend."

As with folly and inversion, the inherent ambivalence of sexual comedy comes to light, vacillating as it does between playful escape and positively or negatively envisioned subversiveness. Freud's explanation of the *Zote* illustrates this: "The process can be described thus: when the first person finds his libidinous impulse inhibited by the woman, he develops an antagonistic tendency towards this second person [the woman] and appeals to the originally interfering third person as an ally. Through the smutty talk of the first person the woman is denuded in front of this third person, who as a listener is now bribed by the effortless satisfaction of his own libido."[59] The third person is initially felt to be a hindrance to the gratification of the joketeller's libidinous tendencies and in this respect assumes the disapproving locus of what Freud was later to call the superego. In a displacement of aggression, however, the joketeller attacks the woman (the second person) by verbally denuding her and seeks the complicity of the third person, bribing him into approval by appealing to *his* libidinous drives through this jocular "rape" of the woman. Despite the rather contrived bent of Freud's speculation, what can be gleaned from it is that the laugher (the third person)—like the teller—is both a superego (a cultural mask-wearer) and an id (a body with drives to be satisfied). Laughter is both a "spontaneous" breakthrough of the id in an uncontrollable somatic movement and a cultural act with a communicative import. Ego-psychologists in particular have stressed that laughter is a mark of collusion between teller and listener, author and reader, playwright and spectator, a social act that manages and regulates our instinctual drives. In this respect, one might see the formational principles of wordplay, patterning, and repetition as bolstering the listener's sense of identity by flattering his power of recognition and giving him cause for self-applause. Yet even when the comedy or the joke is apparently noncollusive, as in the case of "shocking" obscenity and acted deviance, a degree of unacknowledged collusion may be presumed. What would be unceremoniously frowned upon or oppressed in real life may be not only mocked but temporarily celebrated under the condition that it is only "play." The moral ambivalence of playful abnormality (as abnormality) is complemented by its ontological ambivalence (as play). When we watch the comic fool (Falstaff or Lenny Bruce), therefore, his ludic status, hovering between the real and the nonreal, the literal and the nonliteral, the serious and the nonserious, corresponds to the mixture of distance and identification with which our dual nature, as superego and id, mask and face, allows us to treat him. Superegoistic vertical distance—permitting us to mock, to know better, to recognize a deviation—may thus coexist with the identification that grants us vicarious release from our hang-ups.

In the absence of the play context, by contrast, the obscenity or deviance is much more likely to produce either indignation, unambiguous derision (purely scornful laughter), or the laughter of embarrassment. Such disconcerted giggling has indeed been equated with a feeling of having been undressed, exposed, unmasked, seen through.[60] It is rather like the position of the second person in Freud's joke-telling configuration (the "raped" woman), for whom the joke is not really very much of a joke. Forced on the defensive by the man's penetrating, aggressively phallic sense of humor, the best the unmasked female can do is a "silent bared teeth display" signaling appeasement. The less Victorian option is to turn the tables on the man by using her feminine wit (or by learning jujitsu or its Hertford equivalent).

Just as the distinction between so-called "natural" forms of sexuality and "unnatural" or "abnormal" practices is an arbitrary, social construction, it is evident that the boundary between more displaced and more openly shocking forms of comedy is a necessarily fluid one and can serve at best as a rough classification. In a repressively Victorian society *any* reference to sex, however oblique or veiled, may appear outrageous and breach accepted norms. Conversely, the most offensively taboo-breaking comedy is always in some way structured, "licensed," and thereby appropriated by the social order, even if only on account of its play context, just as the antisocial promiscuity and the masturbation of the ritual clown assumes a social significance through its institutionalization. Comic sexuality has a variety of possibilities at its disposal as regards modes of displacement or semi-concealment. It may be displaced, for example

1. spatio-temporally, by chase and deferral
2. metaphorically, through puns and wordplay
3. histrionically and imaginatively, into the realms of fantasy and acting
4. verbally, into the realm of wit.

Feydeau's *La Puce à l'oreille* typifies the way in which farce exploits the comic potential of the chase. In frantic pursuit of their sexual ends, the characters are condemned by the mechanisms of the plot to repeated frustration, as sequences of misunderstandings, mistaken identities, and chance encounters all prevent sexual gratification. The sexuality thus manifests itself in the structure of the play, a series of frenetic climaxes, followed by breathers, followed by even more frenetic climaxes, while verbally remaining at the level of the saucy innuendo, the "nudge-nudge-wink-wink, say no more, we know what you mean" derided by Lenny Bruce. A product of the sexual repression of Victorianism (in its gallic manifestation), Feydeau's comedy, which is among the best of its sort, is symptomatic of comedy's metamorphosis into a peep-show fusion of frustration and (semi-)gratification. Sternheim's *Die Hose*, though not a farce, demonstrates how the sexual frustration characteristic of the era may indeed turn into an explicit comic theme, as sexual *anti*climax both structures the play and generates repeated bathos. Scarron's "love" for Luise is so histrionically hackneyed that, at the very moment when Luise is hoping to consummate it, he deflates our sexual expectations by insisting on transforming his experience into poetry:

Scarron. Do you see, Luise, I love you fervently. Let there be no doubt about this.
Luise. I am yours!
Scarron. How classical the gesture! In these three words a destiny is embraced. What humanity! Could I but capture it on the page—I should count among the Greats.
Luise. (*Inclining*) Let me be yours!
Scarron. Table, quill, let me draw near her essence. Nearing nature's simplicity, the work of art must succeed.
Luise. Yours!
Scarron. Let it be!.... Suspended in rhythms, I feel blissfully removed from the world. Turned towards you on my knees, my desire is to capture your image for humanity and—presenting it to you—claim your favour as my requital.
   (*Runs into his room*)
Luise. Why? What?

(Act 2, scene 4)

The plenitude of the real McCoy is mockingly transposed into the emptiness and clichéd windiness of the poetic McCoy.

In the England of the sixties, Peter Nichols's *A Day in the Death of Joe Egg* similarly thematizes sexual insecurity and disappointment, another sign of the transformation undergone by phallic rites in a society in which the natural juddering buoyancy of the phallus has been weighed down by moral millstones. Bri openly admits that the pleasure he derives from smutty talk is a consequence of the sexual failings of his marriage and the sense he has of getting his hug "somewhere between the budgerigar and the stick-insect" (1). Having originally intended, he claims, to keep the school class he was teaching in detention, Bri rushes home impulsively to test the defences of his indifferent wife:

Bri.   I came home early specially.
Sheila. The usual time.
Bri.   Yeah, but I was *going* to keep them in.
Sheila. Who?
Bri.   Four D.
Sheila. Did you *say* you would?
Bri.   Yes.
Sheila. To them?
Bri.   Yes.
Sheila. Then why didn't you?
Bri.   I kept imagining our bed, our room, your legs thrashing about—
Sheila. When *are* you going to learn?
Bri.   My tongue half-way down your throat—
Sheila. You must carry out your threats.
Bri.   —train screaming into tunnel—
Sheila. They'll never listen to you if you don't—
Bri.   —waves breaking on rocky shore.
           (*She moves out of his reach. Pause. He sips tea, winces.*) Sugar. (*He helps himself.*)
Sheila. You want bromide.
Bri.   I want you. It's you I want.
           (*Turns, makes a joke of it, pointing to her like the advert.*) I want you. Kitchener, look. I want you.

                                                                        (Act 1)

Intentionally talking at cross-purposes to her husband, Sheila staves off his verbal advances and keeps her physical and emotional distance from him. As he moves from pornographic semi-explicitness to cheap cliché to jocular role-playing, it becomes clear that *play* is the means by which he sublimates his sexual frustration, the ludic impulse not merely serving as verbal foreplay but even replacing any "genuine" gratification (as was the case with Panurge's histrionic antiwooing of the Parisian lady). In spite of his oral bravado, Bri proves to be fundamentally afraid of marital sex, prey to self-doubt and insecurity. When, at the end of the play, Sheila comes to suggest a second honeymoon, a twentieth-century version of the

traditional bourgeois happy ending (and of course implying a reinvigora-
tion of their flagging sex life), Bri—still smothered by his mother and in
awe of his wife's sexuality—runs away from the possibility of a copulatory cornucopia. Where love is a pose and passion a role that can
scarcely be kept up till the end of the sentence, the chase culminates in
the anticlimactic parody of a climax as the chaser beats a hasty retreat.

It would be wrong, however, to associate such sexual frustration exclusively with the repressive sexual regime of Victorianism and post-
Victorianism. In the ebulliently farcical medieval play *Un Amoureux*, the
audience is tantalized with the possibility of actually witnessing an extramarital scrogging on stage. When the wife suggests a precoital swig of
wine, the curate bluntly tells her of his more immediate preoccupation:

> The drink we'll have anon, my sweet:
> Let's make haste to lie us down.
> I'm burning with desire to meet
> Thee 'twixt the sheets, my pretty coun.
>
> (ll.82–85)

The deferral in this instance takes the form of the curate's inability to get
his trousers undone, and he spends agonizing moments clumsily fumbling
about with his "esguillette" while we, the audience, get hot under our
vicarious dog collars in anticipation of the husband's imminent return.
After the husband has eventually been and departed a second time, the
two of them are left to get down to business, and the sexual miniplot
can be counted as over, the bed moving offstage and the plot cheerfully
nosediving into the excremental.

In the utopian sexual plenitude of Aristophanes's *The Assemblywomen*, the catch that generates the comedy of the second half of the play
is the positive discrimination granting senior citizens first whack. This
stipulation gets completely out of hand and reveals the farcical spectacle
of swarms of liquorish old ladies chasing around in hot pursuit of one
particularly handsome young man. The cause of young love is utterly
overridden as the youth is dragged away from his young sweetheart and
into the den of the hoary hags (to be heard of no more?), while the
audience returns to the celebratory festivity framing this carnal contretemps. *Lysistrata* derives amusement from a specific variety of sexual
frustration, that of intentional tantalization, or cock-teasing, as the
Athenian wives on sex-strike seek to make the predicament of the walking erections to whom they are married as painful—and as comic—as
they possibly can. Myrrhine teases and torments her husband for almost
100 lines, reluctantly agreeing to have sex with him, then insisting on
fetching a campbed, then a mattress, then a pillow, all the while repeating

her condition for yielding (that the men make peace with the Spartans), all the while getting undressed at a painfully ponderous pace, then fetching a blanket, then insisting on anointing her husband—but oh! she's brought the wrong bottle and has to pop in to fetch the proper unguents—before eventually skipping off for good back into the Acropolis. Yet the excruciating deferral of satisfaction is all in a good cause. Priapic pain unites the warring forces of Greece, for sex is more important than territorial bickering, and, as in *The Acharnians*, a truly happy ending will allow the peace-loving Greek peasants to return to the pleasures of husbandry and tilling the land. *Lysistrata* is a topsy-turvy dream about a (feminine) world in which people really can make love and not war.

In the novelistic sphere, it is *Tristram Shandy* that epitomizes the art of comic deferral. Such deferral need not always be of an explicitly sexual nature. The narrator-protagonist repeatedly promises to reveal some particular detail or description, only to delay the "revelation" and allow an infinitely self-perpetuating mass of digressive narrative to accumulate on the way. The first volume, for example, concludes with this interesting piece of noninformation regarding Uncle Toby's peculiar problems:

> What these perplexities of my uncle Toby were—'tis impossible for you to guess;—if you could,—I should blush; not as a relation,—not as a man,—nor even as a woman,—but I should blush as an author; inasmuch as I set no small store by myself upon this very account, that my reader has never yet been able to guess at any thing. And in this, Sir, I am of so nice and singular a humour, that if I thought you was able to form the least judgment or probable conjecture to yourself, of what was to come in the next page,—I would tear it out of my book.[61]

The narrator is playing a game with the reader analogous to that played by Myrrhine upon her painfully tumescent husband, a tantalizing mixture of (half-)revelation and refusal. Sterne's text refuses to be "possessed," but continually fools the (tumescent?) reader into hoping for narrative satisfaction and thereby keeps him interested. For those riding, or being ridden by, a pansexualist hobbyhorse (and who is to say that the comic novel is not the great-grandnephew of the phallic rites of ancient times?), *Tristram Shandy* may in this sense become a paradigm of the erotic text. What is common to Myrrhine and the narrator of the novel, moreover, is that they are rogues in a rogue-fool configuration and that both, in this respect, cash in on the comedy of repetition. It is repeated roguery, and the reader, like Myrrhine's husband, is repeatedly shown to be the fool.

Tristram Shandy further links this comedy of repeated deferral to unambiguously sexual themes, the narrative refusal to come to the point echoing or reflecting a sexual beating about the bush on the part of the fictive figures. The novel's sexuality is indeed displaced both by the narrative motion, which constantly defers the moment of revelation, and by a metaphoric movement that hides the bawdiness beneath a mask of verbal decorum. This double displacement comes to light in the account Trim gives Toby of the circumstances in which he first fell in love:

> My wound was then in a fair way of doing well—the inflammation had been gone off for some time, but it was succeeded with an itching both above and below my knee, so insufferable, that I had not shut my eyes the whole night for it.
> Let me see it, said she, kneeling down upon the ground parallel to my knee, and laying her hand upon the part below it—it only wants rubbing a little, said the Beguine; so covering it with the bed cloaths, she began with the forefinger of her right hand to rub under my knee, guiding her fore-finger backwards and forewards by the edge of the flannel which kept on the dressing.
>
> ·
>
> The young Beguine, continued the corporal, perceiving it was of great service to me—from rubbing, for some time, with two fingers—proceeded to rub at length, with three—till by little and little she brought down the fourth, and then rubbed with her whole hand: I will never say another word, an' please your honour, upon hands again—but it was softer than satin—
>
> ·
>
> The fair Beguine, said the corporal, continued rubbing with her whole hand under my knee—till I feared her zeal would weary her—"I would do a thousand times more," said she, "for the love of Christ"—In saying which, she passed her hand across the flannel, to the part above my knee, which I had equally complained of, and rubbed it also.
> I perceived, then, I was beginning to be in love—
> As she continued rub-rub-rubbing—I felt it spread from under her hand, an' please your honour, to every part of my frame—
> The more she rubbed, and the longer strokes she took—the more the fire kindled in my veins—till at length, by two or three strokes longer than the rest—my passion rose to the highest pitch—I seized her hand—
> —And then, thou clapped'st it to thy lips, Trim, said my uncle Toby—and madest a speech.
> Whether the corporal's amour terminated precisely in the way my uncle Toby described it, is not material; it is enough that it contained in it the essence of all the love romances which ever have been wrote since the beginning of the world.[62]

The narration of Toby's own sexuality is characterized by similarly repetitive deferral, as the reader—with a curiosity equal to that of Widow Wadman—impatiently waits for the "revelation" as to where Toby sustained his war-wound. The final exposure is likewise subject to a "metaphorical" displacement playing on the ambivalence of the word "where"—Toby sustained his war-wound at Namur. Fooled again!

Wycherley's bawdy Restoration comedy *The Country Wife* makes use of a comparable double displacement. Just as the moment of Aristophanic detumescence is displaced spatially and temporally (offstage and after the final curtain), and just as Sterne too juxtaposes metaphoric and temporal displacement, so Wycherley brings together spatial and metaphorical shifts in the famous "china" episode, in which a sexual pun allows the mask of social decorum to be superficially kept in place (deceiving Sir Jasper), while permitting the spectator to see through the verbal facade. The displacement is at the same time spatial in that it is offstage that Horner shows Lady Fidget his piece of china. The two of them return to their company after the event:

Lady Fidget.   And I have been toiling and moiling for the prettiest piece of china, my dear.
Horner.   Nay, she has been too hard for me, do what I could.
Mrs. Squeamish. Oh, lord, I'll have some china too. Good Mr. Horner, don't think to give other people china, and me none; come in with me too.
Horner.   Upon my honour, I have none left now.
Mrs. Squeamish. Nay, nay, I have known you deny your china before now, but you shan't put me off so. Come.
Horner.   This lady had the last there.
Lady Fidget.   Yes indeed, madam, to my certain knowledge, he has no more left.
Mrs. Squeamish. O, but it may be he may have some you could not find.
Lady Fidget.   What, d'ye think if he had had any left, I would not have had it too? for we women of quality never think we have china enough.

(Act 4, scene 3)

Beneath the feigned refinement of their verbal chinaware, it is clear that it is more a matter of tupperware.

Beaumont's *The Knight of the Burning Pestle* demonstrates even more patently how the open sexuality of the phallic rite has been sublimated into the bawdy pun, the sexual subtext "hidden" behind a mask of gallantry. Here, however, it is a more translucent mask. The Burning Pestle with which Rafe symbolizes his knighthood is thus metaphorically linked to a syphilitic pizzle, and a correspondingly salacious subtext consistently rears its flaming head throughout the play, from the early comments made by the Citizens that Rafe will "discharge himself" (acquit himself in his acted role as a knight, but also ejaculate) to Rafe's own chivalrous references to the "casket and purse" of the ladies he seeks to defend. As he tells Mistress Merrythought:

Rafe. Farewell, fair lady, and your tender squire.
       If, pricking through these deserts, I do hear
       Of any traitorous knight who through his guile
       Hath light upon your casket and your purse,
       I will despoil him of them and restore them.

Mistress Merrythought. I thank your worship.
Rafe. Dwarf, bear my shield; squire, elevate my lance;
    And now farewell, you Knight of holy Bell.

(Act 3)

This saucy subtext is echoed by the Citizens (*Wife.* "Give me a penny i'th' purse while I live, George." *Citizen.* "Ay, by lady, cony, hold thee there") and reaches a syphilitic peak in the sequence of ribald puns forging metaphoric connections between weaponry and sex, as Rafe surveys his company:

Rafe.	Let me see your piece, neighbour Greengoose; when was she shot in?
Greengoose.	An't like you, master captain, I made a shot even now, partly to scour her, and partly for audacity.
Rafe.	It should seem so certainly, for her breath is yet inflamed; besides, there is a main fault in the touch-hole, it runs and stinketh; and I tell you moreover, and believe it, ten such touch-holes would breed the pox in the army.

(Act 5)

Falstaff and Pistol similarly brandish their verbal weaponry in the second part of *Henry IV*. In this case, however, the smut is linked less to the realm of self-mockingly syphilitic imagery than to the sort of sexual aggression that Freud attributed to the *Zote*. Aristophanes's characters too can produce puns of an equally aggressive and male order. Greek culture of the time drew a particularly sharp line between serious and humorous discourse as regards the propriety of language, and, given such strict demands for decorum, blatant bawdiness evidently became all the more necessary as a vicarious release for the ordinary man. *The Acharnians* features a sustained quibble on the double meaning of the Greek word χοῖρος (young pig/twat) as a Megarian tries to sell his daughters, disguised as pigs, to Dikaiopolis. The wordplay is extended to exploit the fact that the young pig has not at the moment got a tail, that it will acquire a big, thick, red one later, that it will become more hairy, that it would be nice to sacrifice it to Aphrodite, that its flesh is delicious when skewered on a spit,.... Such verbal weaponry has the subtlety of a howitzer and may well be interpreted as a male act of sexual violation, an aggressive denudation of a female body reduced to the level of an economic, sexual, or comestible commodity. The example in question is indeed male humor in a society so unashamedly male-dominated that, given the play context, it need hardly even disguise its penetratingly phallic intentions. In other respects, however, Aristophanes was reasonably balanced in the sexuality of his comedy: the male genitals are as regularly "exposed" by the comic Muse as the female.

Aristophanes further displaces his phallic fun not merely into the sphere of verbal intercourse but also into the realm of "prop" comedy. The big artificial floppy stage willy, a perpetual source of mirth, is characterized by the same sort of versatility and fluid functionality as words are. Equally useful as a joystick or a handrope, the stage phallus constitutes a sort of *practical pun* in its flexibility, the metaphorical displacement being of an applied rather than a verbal kind.

Although Aristophanes may tend at times towards the scarcely veiled crudity of the χοῖρος type, he does not tie himself down to any particular formula. *Lysistrata*, for example, starts with the sort of "is it big?" joke that could have turned in an appearance alongside the naughty-but-nice second-team stalwarts. The sexual pun may thus range from the brashly male arsenal of phallic firearms, through Boccaccio's cheekily irreligious innuendo, to coy euphemism, nudges, winks, and narrative gaps, the sexuality in each case being masked in a different manner and to a different extent. Whereas Aristophanic bawdiness was permissible simply because of the play context, other puns require a more thorough lexical muffling in order to escape the eagerly snipping censor's scissors of the social superego. In Anthony Burgess's *Inside Enderby* (1963), to take but one literary example, Enderby is described (on three occasions) as snarling "for cough," concealing the "nasty" four-letter word beneath a mask of conversational normality.[63] Children's TV is apparently an ideal opportunity for smuggling in a healthy dose of subversive bawdiness unbeknown to (most of) its viewers, as *Captain Pugwash* displayed with its cast of pirates including Master Bates and Seaman Staines.[64]

Joyce, as we have seen, disguises his naughtiness behind a recondite use of foreign languages or what is seemingly a torrent of incomprehensible gibberish. In the following passage from *Finnegans Wake*, Shem (in the form of the devilish Glugg, alias Joyce) resolves to take to writing, laying bare to the entire (untired) world (of Leinster, Munster, Connacht, and Ulster) the secrets of his gaffer and gammer:

He would bare to untired world of Leimuncononnulstria (and what a strip poker globbtrottel they pairs would looks!) how wholefallows, his guffer, the sabbatarian (might faction split his beard!), he too had a great big oh in the megafundum of his tomashunders and how her Lettyshape, his gummer, that congealed sponsar, she had never cessed at waking malters among the jemassons since the cluft that meataxe delt her made her microchasm as gap as down low. So they fished in the kettle and fought free and if she bit his tailibout all hat tiffin for thea. He would jused sit it all write down just as he would jused set it up all writhefully rate in blotch and void, yielding to no man in hymns ignorance, seeing how heartsilly sorey he was, owning to the condrition of his bikestool. And, reading off his fleshskin and writing with his quillbone....[65]

Writing here exposes itself as a hidden (somewhat urinary) sexuality, both writing and sex after all being signs of the fall (be it Adam's, Lucifer's, Wall Street's, Finnegan's, or Humpty Dumpty's). Half-concealed beneath or within its lexical deluge is a fluid network of references to strip poker, pairing, holes, beardsplitters (which beard?), great big ohs, big bottoms (megafundum), cesspits, making water (or malt, or both at the same time), clefts, deltas, cleaving implements, microchasms.... Glugg's or Joyce's writing is itself, moreover, an act of contrition, a confession undertaken in and on a *Beichtstuhl*, yet in turn seemingly associated with sexual or excremental discomfort, his stool (bikestool) producing sores as well as causing him to be sorry—and involving a possibly rather painful use of the fleshskin (foreskin or *Fläschchen*, bottle of ink) and the quillbone.

Joyce reestablishes a traditional alliance of sexuality and lexical inventiveness, an alliance that had culminated earlier in the comedy of Rabelais with its abundance of coinages for the act of copulation: words such as *rataconniculer*, *bouttepoussenjambier*, and *sacsacbezevezine-masser*.[66] Indeed, this element of dynamic, productive innovation characterizes not only Rabelais and Joyce but also the *popular* imagination, typified by its spawning of wacky names, say, for the female genitalia: "flapdoodle," "prickpocket," "fart-daniel," "intercrural trench," "grove of eglantine," "hypogastric cranny," and "yard measure" are just a few of scores of possibilities given by one source.[67]

Yet such verbal creativity, epitomized in the figure of Rabelais's Panurge, is not exhausted in mere word-invention: it is also manifest as a displacement of the sexual into the domain of the fantasy. Panurge is above all a linguistic virtuoso, a perpetual performer whose imaginative and narrative resourcefulness comes to light in the bawdy tales with which he entertains both Pantagruel and the reader. Witness the extremely indelicate Aesopian fable of the lion who, having been wounded by a hatchet blow, has his wound wiped clean by a benevolent carpenter. Strolling innocently through the forest afterwards, the lion comes across an old woman who at the sight of him tumbles over backwards for fright, her dress and petticoats all a-rumple, exposing her "what-d'ye-call-it" to general view. The tale continues:

> When he saw this, the lion ran up out of pity to see if she had done herself any harm and, at the sight of her whatsitsname, said:
> "Oh, poor woman, who gave you that wound?"
> As he was speaking, he noticed a fox, whom he called over with the words:
> "Brother fox, over here, over here, you are needed!"
> And when the fox came over, he said to him:
> "Brother fox, look, my friend, someone has given this good woman a wicked

wound between her legs, there's a conspicuous cleft in the flesh. Look how big the gash is: from the bum to the navel it measures four, if not a good five and a half hands. It must have been a hatchet-blow, and I fear it may be an old wound. To keep the flies off it, you must wipe it well, I beseech you, inside and out. You have a fine, long tail: wipe it, my friend, wipe it, I implore you, and in the meantime I shall go and find some moss to stuff in it; for in this way we are meant to aid and support one another. Wipe it hard, my friend, like this, wipe it well, for this wound needs a frequent wiping, or else the woman will not feel well. Now wipe it well, my wee brother, wipe away. God has given you a whopping tail, as weighty and as wide as you could wish; wipe hard, and do not weary. A willing wiper who wipes without wavering and keeps on wiping with his whopper will never be worried by flies. Wipe away, my ballocky fellow, wipe away...."[68]

As with the insistent rubbing motion that informs Trim's (account of his) first love, the repetitive narrative movement of Panurge's tale here imitates the repetitive sexual movement of the fox's tail. Again we are brought back to our own Aesopian hobbyhorse, and once again it is Barthes who has something to say on the phenomenon of narrative repetition and its erotic potential: "Repetition itself engenders *jouissance*.... In short, the word may be erotic under two opposed conditions, both of them excessive: if it is repeated to excess, or by contrast if it is unexpected, succulent on account of its novelty."[69] It is as if language, a sort of surrogate or sublimated sexuality, even comes to *enact* that for which it is a replacement, in turn becoming "erotic" either through its rhythmic repetitiveness or its unanticipated creativity.

In the case of Rabelais, moreover, the link between sexual or textual repetition and sexual or textual innovation becomes an explicit thematic problem, for repetition itself is characterized by a radical ambivalence. Rabelaisian repetition is on the one hand productive, self-generating, and a symbol of fecundity, change and motion, while on the other it can easily degenerate into empty, sterile, and unproductive reiteration of the same. This ambiguity is concretized in the two lists of bollock epithets in the *Tiers Livre*, the cornucopian vitality of the first list countered by the imagery connoting sterility and debility in the second.

The comedy of grotesque or surreal sex is not restricted to Rabelais. In *The Death of Fergus* of Irish legend, Fergus (man) and Bébó (leprechaun) have sexual intercourse even though she is only three fists tall and his ithyphallus measures seven fists. If the pun and the euphemism are forms of sexual understatement, this irreal exaggeration is a step in the other direction, that of overstatement. Such extravagance is an essential trait of Panurge's sexuality, typified by the flight of architectural fancy in which he designs a city wall consisting of female *callibistrys*, ideal after all for absorbing male weapons, but also a slight on the promiscuity of Parisian women (who are easier to lay than bricks). Tongue-in-someone-else's-cheek overstatement also informs Panurge's own sexual performance, or rather his nonperformance, for Panurge's achievements are all verbal. His wooing of the Parisian lady is a sexual catastrophe, but pure entertainment, staged for the pleasure of Pantagruel and the absent spectator. And are we really to believe that Panurge has blissomed 417 Parisian ladies in the nine days previously? In this respect, the Panurge of book 2—equipped with his unwearying wanger—can be seen as the archetypal boaster, his sexual windiness typified by the oversize codpiece he wears, the symbolic antithesis to the full, fertile, verdantly fructifying one sported by Gargantua in book 1.[70] Panurge's "true" sexuality is masked by his hyperbolic verbal codpiece; or rather—for Panurge is a natural actor—his true sexuality *is* his mask. Panurge's bravado shows him to be a cousin of the sexual braggart (*sexueller Maulheld*) of German carnival comedy and not unrelated to the swaggering soldier, the *miles gloriosus* descended from Plautus's Pyrgopolynices and perpetuated in the Spanish *capitano* (Spavento) of the commedia.

In the case of Panurge above all, it seems that acting and performing is the *form* of his sexuality, histrionic and openly fantastic as this is. As such, Panurge may indeed be taken as a symbol of "fallen" sexuality in general in that he shows it to be a necessarily social act, a performance. Panurge's sexuality is the sexuality of an every man jack, it being his self-awareness that distinguishes him in allowing him to milk the explicitly theatrical potential of the act. Volpone is another sexual actor, incessantly either playing a role or voyeuristically/sadistically watching Mosca do so. His attempt to woo Celia is his chief rhetorical flourish and remains at this level until he grows tired of her refusals. At this point he resorts to bathetic threats of rape: "I should have done the act, and then have parleyed. Yield, or I'll force thee" (3.7). As one who glories more in the cunning purchase of his wealth than in the glad possession, however, Volpone is still able to savor the performance and the deception *for its own sake*—even after it has all gone wrong and he has been unmasked as a rogue and had to rely on Mosca to save his skin. Volpone gratefully applauds the acting skills of the trickster Mosca:

> *Volpone.* Good wits are greatest in extremities.
> *Mosca.*   It were a folly, beyond thought, to trust
>   Any grand act unto a cowardly spirit:
>   You are not taken with it, enough, methinks?
> *Volpone.* O, more, than if I had enjoyed the wench:
>   The pleasure of all woman-kind's not like it.

> (Act 5, scene 2)

For Volpone, histrionic pleasure in a sense comes to replace sexual pleasure (even if there is a pinch of irony in Volpone's words, or an at-

tempt to put on a brave face—itself another pose). Indeed, acting impotence, Volpone in the end seems to be taken over by his role, his
growing weakness symbolized not just by his amatory failure with Celia,
nor by the signs of physical infirmity he shows at the beginning of the
final act (infirmity that up until then he had been feigning), but also by
the fact that he is outmaneuvered by his servant Mosca. The differences
between Volpone and Panurge are that, whereas Panurge is performing
for us (or for Pantagruel), Volpone is ultimately always motivated by self-
interest and that, whereas Panurge is a funster, Volpone is portrayed as a
reprehensible rogue. In a moment of weakness, Volpone does have an
attack of "genuineness" at the beginning of the fifth act. Ironically, however, this "genuineness" takes the form of an involuntary continuation of
his role as an invalid and is every bit as rhetorical. Like Panurge, Volpone
proves unable to stop acting.

An interesting (if digressive) light is thrown upon the relationship
between imitation, play, and mating by the example of dolphins. Psychologists see the mimetic impulse as playing a decisive part in the cow
dolphin's choice of mating partners during courtship displays performed
by sexually excited bull dolphins. In systematic studies of free-ranging
dolphins, it has further been noted how "both partners engage in closely
co-ordinated formation swimming, in which both simultaneously adopt
identical postures prior to mating attempts." Such observations have led
psychologists to propose "that imitation of the behavioural posture of the
partner may provide the stimulus for selective mating responses or, at
least, may serve to reinforce social bonds and to strengthen group cohe-
siveness."[71] The analogy with these subaquatic sexual comedies returns
us to the notion of an original sexuality inherent in the theatre and thematically latent in the fictional acting that takes place onstage as play-
within-play. Such mimetic "foreplay" comes to light even more clearly in
the battles of wit traditional in much romantic and Restoration comedy.
In this respect, wit, with its posturing and sparring, may be seen as a displacement of sexuality, or sexual mimicry, into the domain of *verbal* skill.

The sort of male-female repartee in evidence in such comedies as *Much
Ado* and *The Way of the World* not only represents a turning of the social
tables, therefore, but also operates as a sign of conjugal compatibility.
Conversational competence seems both to symbolize and anticipate sexual competence, the implication being that Beatrice and Benedick or
Millamant and Mirabell will make good couples and have lots of children.
The following dialogue between Mirabell and Millamant on the twin
subjects of love and cruelty demonstrates the complementarity of their
bantering wit, as they playfully attack one another in measured and controlled speech, developing one another's imagery, forging witty similitudes, neither of them yielding an inch.

Millamant.	... one's cruelty is one's power, and when one part with one's cruelty, one parts with one's power; and when one has parted with that, I fancy one's old and ugly.
Mirabell.	Ay, ay, suffer your cruelty to ruin the object of your power, to destroy your lover—and then how vain, how lost a thing you'll be? Nay, 'tis true: you are no longer handsome when you've lost your lover; your beauty dies upon the instant: for beauty is the lover's gift; 'tis he bestows your charms—your glass is all a cheat....
Millamant.	... One no more owes one's beauty to a lover, than one's wit to an echo: they can but reflect what we look and say; vain empty things if we are silent or unseen, and want a being.
Mirabell.	Yet, to those two vain empty things, you owe two of the greatest pleasures of your life.
Millamant.	How so?
Mirabell.	To your lover you owe the pleasure of hearing yourselves praised; and to an echo the pleasure of hearing yourselves talk.

(Act 2, scene 5)

This conversational "rite" as it were seals the marriage of the two true wits. A similar process has been described in *Love's Labour's Lost*, where the battle of wits consists in part in appropriating the words spoken by one's verbal opponent and finding a meaning in them that was not intended: "To reapply or develop a given metaphor has the same effect as to reapply or develop the pattern of sound in a given set of words.... The point (the characters) make is that to use one another's words in banter is like making love; each makes meaning out of what the other provides physically. They notice *in medias res* that there is the same sort of sequence of taking advantage and acquiescing: the process of taking liberties with each other's words goes with a kind of verbal hiding and showing."[72] A further bond between wit and sex is unearthed by the play's own wit, the punning sportiveness that uses pricks and marks (the Elizabethan equivalents of shafts and scores) to build a metaphorical bridge linking the two areas and connecting both to the sphere of archery and combat. That wit may indeed so easily turn into invective and abuse is again indicative of the overlap between sex and hostility.

One of the most remarkable (if parodic) examples of such verbal compatibility is presented by Büchner's thoroughly unusual comedy *Leonce und Lena*, in which Lena bowls Leonce over by making the right responses at the right time, flattering his (pseudo-?) morbidity and his sense of romantic ennui with a welter of macabre imagery:

Lena.	The moon is like a sleeping child, whose golden locks have fallen about its lovely face. Oh, its sleep is death. See how the angel of death reposes on its dark pillow and the stars burn around it like candles....
Leonce.	Stand up in your white dress. Escort the corpse through the night and sing its requiem.

Lena.   Who speaks there?
Leonce. A dream.
Lena.   Dreams are blessed.
Leonce. Then be blessed with a dream and let me be your blessed dream.
Lena.   The most blessed dream is death.
Leonce. Then let me be your angel of death. Let my lips touch your eyes like
           his pinions. *He kisses her.* Beautiful corpse, you lie so lovely on the
           black pall of night that nature comes to hate life and falls in love with
           death.

                                                                    (Act 2, scene 4)

Overwhelmed by this conversational experience and "losing" himself in
his partner, Leonce seeks to consummate the manifest sensuality of their
oral exchange by *dying* (a blatantly orgasmic image), and more specifically by *drowning* (as crassly parodic as Bri's "waves breaking on
rocky shore" cliché). The ultimate bathetic anticlimax comes when
Leonce is rescued and the romantic suicide attempt proves abortive.
Within minutes, Leonce has rolled over and dropped off to sleep.

Coincidentally or not, connections between wit and sex seem to exist
not merely in terms of wit's function (as an aphrodisiac), but also in
structural terms, as a number of theorists have implied by their own
choice of metaphor in definitions or descriptions of wit. Jean Paul is renowned for his definition of *Witz* as "the disguised priest who couples
[*kopuliert*] every pair,"[73] a metaphor cited by Freud who likewise sees in
the *Witz* an economical means of bridging gaps between disparate ideas,
a way of unearthing identity within difference. Freud then goes on to
quote Vischer's supplement to Jean Paul's metaphor: "He is happiest
marrying those pairs whose relatives disapprove of the union."[74] Like a
mini-happy-ending, the marriage, frowned upon by the in-laws, thus represents the overcoming of an obstacle. For Dr. Johnson, wit was "the
unexpected copulation of ideas," perhaps unwittingly implying that it is
the ideas, not the priest, who are now doing the copulating, indeed even
that wit is a case of sex *before* marriage (i.e., unexpected), while the
French poet Paul Valéry was to equate the pun with sex *outside* marriage,
claiming that "great gods have been born of a pun, which is a sort of
adultery."[75] In the past, moreover, "wit" has been used not only in its
intellectual sense but also to refer to the vagina and the penis. Whereas
the familiar word meaning intelligence may be traced back to the Old
English *witan* "to know," to the Latin *videre* "to see," to the Greek
(*v*)*idea* "I see," and ultimately to the Sanskrit *veda* "I know," the other
"wit" seems to have been derived from the Latin *vitalia membra* and
might now be referred to as the vitals. Correspondingly, the French word
vit formerly had the meaning of "a mans yard; a beasts pizle," and *vite*

was "a womans etc."[76] This point puts a new perspective on the claim that a display of wits might serve as foreplay to sexual activity to come. It is possible that Shakespeare is playing on this ambiguity in various passages in *Love's Labour's Lost*, pervaded as the play is by implied associations between wit and sex. Seeking inspiration for a cunning witticism, for example, Mote invokes his father's wit and his mother's tongue (might his mother have been a fellatrice?). Elsewhere, Costard and the Princess spar bawdily:

> *Costard.* God dig-you-den all! Pray you, which is the head lady?
> *Princess.* Thou shalt know her, fellow, by the rest that have no heads.
> *Costard.* Which is the greatest lady, the highest?
> *Princess.* The thickest and the tallest.
> *Costard.* The thickest and the tallest! It is so—truth is truth.
> An your waist, mistress, were as slender as my wit,
> One o' these maids' girdles for your waist should be fit.
> Are not you the chief woman? You are the thickest here.
> *Princess.* What's your will, sir? What's your will?
>
> (Act 4, scene 1)

Will, after all, could also have a libidinous meaning.

In the case of wit, the element of sexuality occurs in such a displaced form that it may escape anyone's notice except theoretical hobbyhorse riders. Perhaps it is time to turn to more openly "shocking" forms of comedy, to areas of comic sexuality that have been or still are regarded as taboo, abnormal, or morally wrong, as exemplified by the forthright sexual unorthodoxy of ritual clowns and scapegoats. The position in Western civilization is complicated by the fact that the early Christian Church, under the influence of the very personal outlooks of leading church thinkers such as Tertullian, Jerome, and Augustine, came to see sex itself as morally wrong or fundamentally disgusting. For the church fathers, it was sinful to find enjoyment in it, and the only permissible form of intercourse was the purposefully procreative one-up-one-down, male-on-top marital bash, carried out in literal and figurative obscurity. Other positions were considered "unnatural" because they were seen to be modeled on animal intercourse, constitutive of an inversion in the male-female hierarchy or they were suspected of being contraceptive in intention and effect.[77] Given such medieval ignorance and silence, it is not surprising that sex itself came to be regarded as grotesque—the ridiculous bouncing of the buttocks described by Lady Chatterley—a marked contrast with the beneficial and naturally positive qualities attributed to it by Taoism ("If in one night a man can have intercourse with more than ten women it is best"[78]) and Hinduism. Regarding sex as natural, these creeds were remarkable for their enlightenment and advanced learning, typified by the poetically euphemistic Chinese sex manuals and the more matter-of-fact, less metaphorical Hindu *Kamasutra*. In oppressive and intolerant cultures, by contrast, any reference to sex will have a greater potential to shock, surprise, or embarrass its audience (possibly into laughter) than where openness and insight carry the day. The need for release from repressive silence or abstinence is a function of the cultural climate. The sexually scatological comedy of Alfred Jarry is clearly an attempt to *épater les bourgeois* of buttoned-up, late-nineteenth-century Europe, while, in a different comic field, Joe Orton's brazenness fulfills an analogously shocking function in the Britain of the sixties.

For the early church fathers, the major sexual sin was contraception (whether involving anal or oral intercourse, "poisons creating sterility," or coitus interruptus), and the sexual dark ages saw the suppression of all the contraceptive knowledge developed since Aristotle (who had recommended a blend of olive oil and cedar oil, lead ointment, or frankincense) and a return to magic and superstition.[79] Given these circumstances, such devices as condoms, which were beginning to be used as a contraceptive in the seventeenth and eighteenth centuries, not surprisingly acquired a certain "shocking" potential (now being combatted by the media as a response to AIDS), although as a comic device they were some way beneath the standard of most decent, self-respecting bourgeois comedy. Fortunately, Grabbe's comedy *Scherz* is self-respectingly *in*decent and, as such, provides an example of condom comedy when the schoolmaster tries to use them to entice the Devil into a trap. This association of condoms and the Devil mockingly illustrates the moral status of the sheath, but the effect is abruptly deflated at the same time, for the bait does not function properly, the Devil being distracted by the smell of the boozy schoolmaster:

Devil.	I can smell two things here! On the left something indecent, something child-preventative. On the right something pissed, something child-educative.
Schoolmaster.	A pox on it, he wouldn't be referring to *me* by any chance?
Devil.	(*going towards the condoms*) The indecent thing is powerfully drawing me towards it, (*turning back in the direction of the schoolmaster*) but the pissed thing is tempting me every bit as much ... (*stops*)—if only I knew which of the two was the more immoral! (*sniffs around more vigorously*).
Schoolmaster.	(*very scared*) Hang it! My conscience!
Devil.	I've got it: the pissed, child-educative thing to my right is the more wicked, while the indecent, child-preventative thing to my left is by comparison a very model of innocence!

(Act 3, scene 5)

Luckily for the schoolmaster, he is able to ward off the Devil with a piece of pew stolen on a drunken nocturnal visit to the church, and the Devil in the end does go for the johnnies.

Another of the sexual practices prohibited by the Church was masturbation: indeed Christian society was the first Western society to do so, later theologians interpreting the biblical tale of Onan, who was slain by the Lord for spilling his seed (because he refused to inseminate his brother's wife), as a story about "self-abuse" rather than coitus interruptus.[80] The theme is notable for its absence from most traditional comedy—although it does come to hand in the Shakespearean bawdy quip: witness the earlier quotation from *Love's Labour's Lost*, where bowling, rubbing, and "having one's hand in" all mask a masturbatory meaning. Yet it is only this century that comedy has produced figures such as Ignatius J. Reilly and John Self, who have turned whacking off into an art form and a full-time pleasure and proclaimed the universal, deeply democratic quality of the handjob ("In the end," as Self phrases it, "you've got to hand it to handjobs").[81] Both these figures are huge, amoral slubberdegullions, to whose antisocial innards the narrative form (free indirect style and first person narrative respectively) grants the reader privileged access and with whom we may, therefore, ultimately associate. Their fictional status and their ethical ambivalence, however, do leave open the possibility of distance rather than (or as well as) identification as an equally viable response, for as a case of coming unscrewed the madness of masturbation shares the equivocacy (as well as the egalitarianism) of other modes of folly. It is significant, though, that they are both creations of the last thirty years, as if the comic possibilities of the theme had previously been stifled because it was simply too disgusting, too close to the boner. Many people would doubtless still feel this to be the case. Even Brecht's openly bisexual Baal seems to have regarded masturbation either as an unmentionable or as beneath his level, seeking in his expressionistic elementalism a cosmic union with nature, but nevertheless stopping short to ask why one cannot sleep with the plants. Philip Roth's figure Portnoy (an American creation of the sixties) would have answered: but you can! Indeed, the narrator's compulsive tunnel vision imaginatively transposes any convenient orifice to its rightful position at the juncture of a pair of female legs:

> "Oh shove it in me, Big Boy," cried the cored apple that I banged silly on that picnic. "Big Boy, Big Boy, oh give me all you've got," begged the empty milk bottle that I kept hidden in our storage bin in the basement, to drive wild after school with my vaselined upright. "Come, Big Boy, come," screamed the maddened piece of liver that, in my own insanity, I bought one afternoon at a butcher shop and, believe it or not, violated behind a billboard on the way to a bar mitzvah lesson.[82]

The candor with which Portnoy relates his experiments in the field explodes both the old-fashioned ethical mask that proclaims that such things should not be done and the mask of discursive decorum that would have it that such things should not be talked about. The effect generated by the comic release is further heightened by techniques of repetition and exaggeration, Portnoy being not merely a masturbator but a monomanic masturbator.

Zoophilia may in a sense be viewed as an extension of Lenny Bruce's principle that if desperate enough we'll schtup anything. Although bestiality may be making the best of a bad job, however, it is a practice traditionally condemned by Western civilization as the depths of depravity and unnaturalness. An illuminating variation on this approach to the phenomenon comes to light in John Barth's *The Sot-Weed Factor*, where Henry Burlingame's intimacy with a sow called Susie is not presented as a misplaced or perverse act of brute sexual lust, but as a manifestation of an all-encompassing cosmophilia that again leaves Baal standing. After the clearing up of a classic minicomedy of misunderstanding, in which Ebenezer initially believes the lover in question to be a (human) whore, Ebenezer's prudery incites Timothy Mitchell (alias Burlingame) to the following reflections on the theme of "naturalness" in sexual proclivities:

> Methinks Dame Nature's not so nice as thee, sir. I grant ye that a rabbit-hound in heat seeks out a bitch to mate with, but doth he care a fig be she turnspit or mastiff? Nay, more, by Heav'n, he'll have at any partner, be't his bitch, his brother, or his master's boot! His urge is natural, and hath all nature for its target—with a hound-bitch at the bulls-eye, so to speak. I have seen yonder spaniels humping sheep....[83]

Not only is the episode a burlesque of conventional amour and Susie a porcine parody of the ravished damozel, the comic potential of this "shocking" act of abnormality is further exploited by having the point of rupture in the mask of sexual decorum coincide with a moment of enlightenment as Ebenezer and reader alike finally grasp the situation and Susie comes padding out from the dark corner that had hidden her from narrative sight. The "moral" jolt is thus superimposed upon a satisfying comic moment of *dis*illusionment or *un*deception (which retrospectively unveils a number of pleasing situational ironies into the bargain), permitting the reader to enjoy the surprise in defiance of any residual moral qualms.

The effect of Tim's cogent argumentation, moreover, is thematically to "positivize" what otherwise might have been unequivocally damned as an unnatural practice. Sordid zoophilia is thereby converted into the romantic cosmophilia of a "Suitor of Totality, Embracer of Contradictories,

Husband to all Creation, ... Cosmic Lover."[84] The universal passion he defends so eloquently is an idealization and intensification of what the hung-up, twentieth-century Portnoy was to regard as a complaint:

> I love the world, sir, and so make love to it! I have sown my seed in men and women, in a dozen sorts of beasts, in the barky boles of trees and the honeyed wombs of flowers; I have dallied on the black breast of the earth, and clipped her fast; I have wooed the waves of the sea, impregnated the four winds, and flung my passion skywards to the stars![85]

The deep-seated ambiguity informing the novel's presentation of zoophilia/cosmophilia is underscored by its embodiment in the completely protean figure of Henry Burlingame, whose identity in general is as mutable and versatile as his sexuality in particular. Burlingame is the ultimate natural actor, and even pig-loving Tim Mitchell is but a part he periodically plays, the "genuineness" of his carnal claims remaining as much of a mystery as Panurge's histrionic sexual performances. We never really *know* that he has gone the whole hog. In the course of the novel, he appears in at least eight guises other than "himself," and, as Henry, he preaches a Heraclitean flux both in general and in personal terms:

> 'Tis but a grossness of perception, is't not, that lets us speak of *Thames* and *Tigris*, or even *France* and *England*, but especially *me* and *thee*, as though what went by those names or others in time past hath some connection with the present object? I'faith, for that matter how is't we speak of *objects* if not that our coarse vision fails to note their change? The world's indeed a flux, as Heraclitus declared: the very universe is naught but change and motion.[86]

If this self-aware mercuriality ("your true and constant Burlingame lives only in your fancy," he tells Ebenezer elsewhere),[87] endows him with both the "wisdom" of the sceptical philosopher and the "folly" of the amoral natural actor, it also ultimately means that Henry ends up being everyone, yet no one, an ambivalence of plenitude and absence that may pose an existential threat to other, less literary fools. It is the same ambivalence that characterizes his sexuality, hovering as this does between ebullient pansexuality and mysterious impotence (and even his loved one Anna is still a virgin). His sexuality, indeed his identity as a whole, remains a riddle, not just a physiological absence within the fiction, but a hermeneutical absence holding the reader in unresolved suspense, teasingly deferring a revelation of its true nature. The "truth" about the comic fool is that behind his mask there is everything and nothing at all.

In the form of heterosexual satyriasis, obsessive sexuality offers itself for comic use not so much as a deviation, abnormality, or evil (it being, after all, a sign of manly spunk) as because of its tendency to become

predictable and repetitive. Feydeau's Rugby typifies such repetitive ran-
diness, laughable for the mechanical reliability with which he enquires
whether anybody has called for him and the repeated frustration that
follows (in conjunction with his caricatural English features, such as his
inability to speak French). Aristophanes likewise incarnates this combination of sexual obsession and social incompetence in a foreign figure,
the same sort of passing of the buck that has since led to such expressions
as *le vice allemand* (homosexuality), *le vice anglais* (flagellation), French
letters, and French kisses. Aristophanes's riggish Scythian in *Women at
the Thesmophoria* would thus have satisfyingly fulfilled contemporary
expectations regarding Scythian conduct. This predictability is complemented by his accent (as with Rugby) and by the fact (as with Rugby)
that he is also presented as a fool, his obsession making it relatively easy
for Mnesilochus to outwit him by luring him away with a scantily clad
dancing girl.

Female insatiability has also been subject to appropriation by the
comic Muse, but more in the guise of permissiveness and in connection
with the celebratory theme of cuckoldry than as the target of normative
mockery. Aristophanes, for example, presents the women of Athens as
randy and bibulous, but their sexual zeal is always characterized by a fun-
loving naturalness, while Boccaccio's women have the full authorial seal
of approval when they go metric in response to the wizened old yards of
husbands two or three times their age. Feydeau's Amélie (in *Occupe-toi
d'Amélie*) is nonchalantly amoral in her pursuit of carnal pleasure
(though she is not mocked for being a nymphomaniac), but it is only one
step from such figures to the ambivalence of Wedekind's Lulu, who embodies the anarchic creative/destructive energies so often associated in
the male mind with Woman. Having been hidden behind an ethical veil
for a couple of millenia, Woman assumes the status of an Unknowable
and shares the radical ambiguity of Folly, Madness, Utopia, and Chaos.

This ambiguity is embodied in the parodic sex films of Russ Meyer,
whose big-breasted vixens tyrannize would-be machos sporting square
faces and extremely low IQs. These women generate a mixture of admiration and fear, functioning both as objects of desire and as threats to
male sexuality, presages of male impotence. Meyer's parody of sex and
violence works by exaggeration and crass overstatement, symbolized in
the hyperbolically curvacious contours (tending towards infinity) of his
heroines and in his use of camp symbolism and badly simulated sex. Yet
Meyer's films are a prime illustration of the way parody may become indistinguishable from and dependent upon that which is being parodied.
The films themselves *are* violent and pornographic, and Meyer seems to
celebrate rather than scorn what he parodies. The question of how pornography can be comic is obviously dependent upon a definition of the

limits of pornography. If by pornography is meant textual, theatrical, or cinematic material in which sexual stimulation is the prime aim, then it is unlikely to be comic (at least in intention). Industrialized soft-core pornography in particular presupposes a *normalization* or *homogenization* of the body, which is presented in a sort of prepacked stereotypicality as boringly predictable as frozen food packaging. Just as eroticism was seen to share with comic sauciness its hints and half-revelations (i.e., understatement), however, so other types of pornography may well overlap with "comic" overstatement. Sade's *Justine* falls into this category, as the heroine (the virtuous antithesis to her sister Juliette as well as to Meyer's vamps) is dragged from one male member to the next during the course of her penile servitude, eventually coming face to face with an elephantine pizzle described in the following ithyphallic terms: "His love-truncheon, which I had only too many occasions to see and feel, combined a foot in length with more than eight inches circumference. This instrument—stiff, sinewy, perpetually foaming, and on which huge veins could be seen which made it even more horrific—remained up in the air throughout the five or six hours the session lasted, without drooping for a minute." Yet worse is to come; depicting another encounter only thirty pages later, she finds it necessary to assure her listener: "Oh, Madame! Never had anything the equal of it sullied my vision up till then, and whatever the preceding descriptions may have been, this surpassed everything I have been able to depict, as the imperious eagle eclipses the dove."[88]

In general pornography is fundamentally conservative, but also much more reassuring and flattering to the male ego than either Meyer or Sade. This is typified by the *Playboy* sex cartoons where women are above all caricatured by being given large breasts and big buttocks.[89] Such caricature is inherently reactionary since it exploits and reaffirms popular prejudice and cheap stereotype, debasing women to a mechanically predictable *object* of male amusement and also creating an image of "sexy" woman subservient to particular male fantasies. The *Playboy* sex-kitten is young, shaped like a dumb-bell(e) and sexually available. Such portrayal is manifestly essentialist, reducing the essence of Woman to its caricatural distortion by masculine desire. Angela Carter writes that pornographers "are the enemies of women only because our contemporary ideology of pornography does not encompass the possibility of change, as if we were the slaves of history and not its makers." Pointing out, moreover, that pornography is like satire in its "inbuilt reactionary mechanism," Carter describes how "pornography reinforces the archetypes of (the woman's) negativity ... simply because most pornography remains in the service of the status quo. And that is because its elementary metaphysic gets in the way of real life and prevents us seeing real life."[90] Rather like comedy, that is, pornography generates a *play* context displaced from the real. Yet pornographic play is a reassuring realm of male supremacy (not unlike the men's institutions where the Freudian *Zote* verbally rapes its female victim), and its play context—or ontological ambiguity—hides or dilutes what in the real world would be considered its immorality or deviance (as aggressive voyeurism). It's all just a bit of harmless fun—or so it seems. What is also striking about the *Playboy* brand of sexuality is the chaste concealment of the male genitals: the magazine is robustly heterosexual in outlook (though of course this can by no means be claimed of all pornography).

A similar sort of aggressively male fusion of comedy and pornography was the hallmark of the American "burlesque" show, a brand of popular theatre owing much to the rough, rowdy, and riotous English music-hall tradition, which developed in the course of the nineteenth century. Like the comic strip, moreover, the burlesque (at which an actual theatrical burlesque was but rarely performed) seems to have exerted a major influence upon the loud, excessive sexual comedy of Russ Meyer. It was a predominantly male, predominantly drunken "sex-and-comedy cocktail"[91] presenting acrobats, magicians, stripteasing, abrasive stand-up comedians, and leggy chorus girls. It too was fundamentally conservative in its sexual outlook, almost every joke getting its laughs at the expense of incipient or overt homosexuality, while the more original performers were lured away by legitimate theatre, cinema, radio, or television.[92] Jokes about homosexuality are indeed the most common example of the capacity of sexual laughter to act normatively, confirming and conserving existent mores, mocking what is considered to be deviant and different. This is laughter at its more brutish, bullyingly normalizing us into sexual conformity. Homosexuality has of course not always been seen as unnatural or a "sin against nature." In Judeo-Christian civilization the attitude developed out of the ambiguous biblical story of Sodom in conjunction with revulsion at Greek habits, a series of theological and socio-political factors converging to turn the homosexual into a danger to the state and the Church.[93] The thirteenth-century theologian Aquinas strengthened the aversion to homosexuality by "proving" that it was unnatural, a seal on the fate of homosexuals for centuries to come. The French went on burning homosexuals long after they had stopped burning witches, and the death penalty was enforceable for sodomy in England up until 1861.[94] Modern society still seems to be pervaded by the belief that it is a perversion of natural drives. In terms of Freud's second topographical model, the homosexual joke demonstrates the extent to which the sexually aggressive energies channeled into the *Witz* may spring from the superego as much as from the id.

Of course, the id may be secretly (or openly) celebrating as well (or instead), the pleasure-seeking subsystem laughing *with* that which is laughed *at* by the superego. The explicitly "revolutionary" or marginal gay theatre known as the "Ridiculous," which developed off-off-Broadway from the sixties onwards, flamboyantly cocks a snook at the repressive and vindictive cultural superego, flaunting a volatile carnal ebullience that revels in burlesque transvestism and sexual mercuriality ("I'm trisexual. I'll try anything"[95]). While the unproblematic and norm affirmative celebration of sexuality implied by the happy ending, for example, has traditionally been stoutly monogamous and heterosexual (how often has Jack ended up having, say, Jill's brother, or—to take Puck's metaphor literally—how often has man ended up with his mare?), modern theatre is thus by no means compelled to conform in this respect. Ronald Tavel's *Gorilla Queen* (1967), featuring the transsexual Queen Kong, is propelled towards what is obviously a parody of the conventional matrimonial happy ending—a shotgun wedding absolutely flexible in its sexual permutations: "I pronounce you man and wife, or man and man, or ape and man, or queen and woman, or queen and man, or queen and queen, or ape and ape up and up." Such marginal theatre has indeed tended to move in the direction of Ubuesque antitheatre (dispensing in toto with plot, coherence, and identity) rather than integrate any more orthodox modification of the traditional comic "Jack gets Jill" formula. The result has been a pansexual pandemonium of camp irreverence, where *all* inhibitions seem to go by the board.

The perennial ambivalence of the phenomenon is perhaps best indicated within the tradition of comic theatre by the example of transvestism, which not only tends to be metonymically associated with homosexuality but likewise implies the sexual mutability normally suppressed by our adoption of a single, unequivocal sexual identity. As early as Aristophanes's *Women at the Thesmophoria*, for example, both Agathon and Cleisthenes are held up to (by Aristophanic standards relatively gentle) ridicule for their mincing effeminacy, yet down through the ages sexual cross-dressing has also played a consistent part in comic trickery and deception. In the same Aristophanic play, Mnesilochus dresses up as a woman in order to save Euripides's skin, an early comic case of what was to be an ever-recurrent topos of males dressed up as females and females as males. Here, admittedly, part of the comedy consists in the recognition that Mnesilochus is *acting*, the fact that we see through his mask to his "true" sexual identity. Yet this is not the whole story. Throughout the centuries, switches in sex-roles have been a widespread form of cultural play (in carnival and saturnalian festivities for example).[96] Sexual reversal seems to constitute an essential aspect of comic release, as the cultural mask of unilinear sexual identity is rejected for a while to give vent to our potentially polymorphous sexuality. The swapping of gender in a certain sense shows the arbitrariness of the mask, the conventionality structuring social comportment in general and sexual comportment in particular. At least part of the comedy of sexual disguise in the theatre may be derived from a celebratory circumvention of the rigors of convention.

Gone with the Wind

One of the oldest of all taboos relates to menstruation. Ever since prehistoric times man has attributed magical properties to menstrual blood as a response to his bamboozlement about its origins and significance. The mystical importance of *all* blood, coupled with the fear generated by the inexplicability of this particular phenomenon, seems to have made man naturally wary of this sign of female difference and otherness. The enforced isolation of menstruating women has been a recurrent response down the years, as the original taboo was gradually transformed into a pretext for keeping women in their place and surrounding them with an aura of mysterious unknowability. The female period thus became linked with imagery of contamination and came to symbolize the sinfulness and degeneracy of the woman's body, the menstruating female enjoying approximately the same social status as a witch. The women of Babylon in ancient times were ritually unclean for the statutory six days of their monthly period, defiling everything they touched, while the Hebrews opined that, if a man touched the bed, chair, or clothes of a woman during her period, he was contaminated for the rest of the day.[97] In his *Natural History*, Pliny summarizes the antique view that contact with menstruation blood causes fruit to go off, new wine to turn sour, grass to dry up, trees to lose their fruit, iron to rust, air to grow dark, and dogs to become rabid, a whole series of "apocalyptic" consequences perpetuated as an established element of medieval thought.[98] Gratian, whose *Decretals* on church discipline stem from the twelfth century, treated these not inconsiderable side effects as the reason for the exclusion of women from priesthood. The period appears thus to have been singled out as a target for a rampant misogyny manifest in the appraisal of Tertullian, a third-century theologian, that woman is a "temple built on a sewer." Blatantly passing the theological buck, in *On the Cult of Femininity* he inveighs against Eve as a representative of Woman in general, pronounced guilty by divine authority for leading Man astray where even the Devil himself had not been able to prevail. As such, she is no less than "the Devil's gateway."[99] The New Testament puts it: "A woman should learn in quietness and full submission. I do not permit a woman to teach or to have authority over a man; she must be silent. For Adam was formed first, then Eve. And Adam was not the one deceived; it was the woman who was deceived and became a sinner" (1 Tim., 2:12–14). Augustine's damning verdict on Original Sin likewise makes both the womb and its entrance responsible for the evil committed on earth. It is evident that the woman's body is something that must needs be hidden, her voice silenced, that she be confined to a concealed nonexistence similar in fact to that of the fool in its potential ambivalence. Woman herself must be covered by the social mask.

Even if enlightened Western society has magnanimously stopped pointing an accusatory finger at women for having their periods, and the monthly bleeding no longer in itself constitutes a breach of ethical norms, there persists a reluctance to talk about it in many quarters. It is a nasty, ugly, messy affair, and should be flushed down the discursive lavatory with all those other conversational no-nos issuing from down below. It is this silence surrounding menstruation that accounts for the fact that serious, British, late nineteenth-century medicine was still unsure whether the touch of a menstruating woman could turn a ham rancid or not. Menstruation humor explodes this mask of unenlightened decorum which has hidden the theme for so many millenia. A relatively new sphere in the history of comedy, it may often work by embarrassing its audience into laughter, yet at the same time it is a theme of particular relevance to feminists, who see in it a means of celebrating rather than denigrating the female body.

If the humor were created with the idea that menses is dirty, smelly, ugly and shameful (the traditional attitude that society has inculcated), it would have been female humor. Since, however, the underlying attitude is that menses is normally and naturally female; since, moreover, the attitude is that menses is not to be hidden (as shameful) but to be joked about (as normal) or even celebrated (as naturally female), the humor is deeply feminist. Not by explicit statement but by implicit posture, the expression of such humor attacks the unhealthy and oppressing idea cultivated for thousands of years that women's bodies are foul.[100]

Once again, a tension between festive celebration and derisive revulsion may be seen to be at work.

Corresponding to the affirmative perspective of modern women, we find a celebratory female (proto-feminist?) gesture in ancient Greek mythology.[101] Mourning the loss of her daughter Persephone to the Underworld, the Greek goddess of fertility, Demeter (a sort of Mother Earth or "Geo-mater"), is—according to the orphic tradition—brought to laughter by the sight of her maid/wet nurse, Baubo (or Iambe), exposing her vulva. Here the female body may at one level be interpreted as providing a source of surprised mirth through its emergence from concealment. Yet the gesture means more than this, for it can also be understood to console Demeter for the loss of her child by reminding her of her fertility, her capacity to produce further offspring, by celebrating the creativity and fecundity of the female body. That the exposure of the vulva assumes the import of a symbolic gesture of solidarity among women is implied not only by the orphic description of the act as one that is repeated in the future (i.e., a ritual performance) but also by the *Homeric Hymns to Demeter*, which attribute the gesture not to Baubo but (in slightly less obscene form) to Iambe, whose name clearly indicates her connection with the satirical *iambic* verses reputed to have been performed at female rites such as the *Thesmophoria*. Displaying the vulva to a man by contrast has frequently acquired the symbolic function of an insult, or even a bewitchment. A number of comic moments, therefore, seem to converge: the formal element of surprise coupled with the pleasurable transgression entailed by the sight of what is normally condemned to epistemological obscurity, *plus*—in the case of the vulva as opposed to the phallus—a special female "topsy-turvy" solidarity celebrating what is customarily despised or derided by male discourse.

A brilliant modern day variant on period comedy turns up in one of the manically ranted comic monologues of Ben Elton, who stands the sexual order on its head by imagining what a difference it would make if it were the *men*—with beery boastings down the pub about how much they bleed ("I was so heavy last month I needed a blood transfusion")—who had the periods instead of the women. Tampons would be available on the N.H.S., for a start. Given the possibility of this celebratory context and the association of the curse not with filth but with fecundity, it is perhaps no coincidence that the German romantic poet Novalis described wit itself as the *menstruum universale*,[102] a monthly cleansing of our vision as it were, an intellectual period embodying the promise of *ingenium*, creativity and mental fertility.

If female menstruation now has comic potential through being considered *ugly* as opposed to *wrong* (and our vitals themselves tend not to be our most stunningly beautiful anatomical features), then the same goes for the realm of scatology, which disrupts an aesthetic rather than an ethical set of norms. The colon (to adopt a typographical idiom) can be every bit as comic as the period. That this area is itself intrinsically coupled with the sphere of sexuality is betokened by the multifunctionality of the genitalia, an attribute of course shared with that paragon of verbal versatility, the pun. The vision of the world pervading Brecht's *Baal*, for example, is colored by an awareness of this link between procreation and excrement. Ekart finds himself unable to take God seriously for having coupled the reproductive organ and the urethra in the biological jigsaw puzzle, and the romantic idealization that normally masks or beautifies creation and procreation is unceremoniously shattered by Brecht's two iconoclasts, who see the world as God's poo.

In *Finnegans Wake*, Joyce too blurs the boundary between the sexual and the urinary activities through a permanent punning equivocation that makes it impossible to be certain whether van Hoother "laying cold hands on himself" is in fact micturating or masturbating or even—amid the oneiric fluidity of the (w)hole proccss—doing both. The fact that his genitals serve him doubly indeed echoes a radical duality structuring the entire work under the thematic aegis of Giordano Bruno's coincidence of opposites. Once more, reproduction/creation and excretion/destruction are all part of the same vicus of recirculation. Joyce's novel is further striking for bringing the same measure of lexical creativity into the sphere of the urinary as it does with the sexual. This network of puns is based primarily upon such *pee* and *wee* surrogates as "peas" and "peace" (wee peep, peewee, wious pish, peteet peas, pious Eneas, poing her pee, posspots, spilleth peas, bistrispissing, trispass through minxmingled hair, Trickspissers vill be pairsecluded, wetting his widdle) and also on variants of *making water* (they made whole waters, mouths making water, making wind and water, on the makewater, the mingling of our meeting waters), plus a polyglottal range of foreign sources incorporating the Irish word *mun*, the Persian *shash*, the Japanese *shoben*, and the Latin root of micturition *mingere* (your dirty minx, Minxy Cunningham, comminxed, Minxy was a Manxmaid, a minx from the Isle of Woman).[103] If *Finnegans Wake* were to have a moral (which it doesn't), it would perhaps be that you should look before you leak.

Freud makes it clear that excremental humor shares its origins with sexual laughter, infantile sexuality being akin to a polymorphous cesspit where the two areas remain undifferentiated. "The sexuality which forms the content of the bawdy joke comprises more than just what is peculiar to each sex: it also includes those features common to both sexes to which feelings of shame extend, in other words the excremental in its broadest sense. All this however is incorporated by childhood sexuality, for which there exists a cloaca, so to speak, in which what is sexual and what is excremental can only be distinguished with difficulty, if at all."[104] Clearly, therefore, any distinction between an "ethical" and an "aesthetic" mask is tenuous to say the least, and it is perhaps more helpful to regard the latter as an aspect of the former as opposed to a separate category. As the mask metaphor would have it, our toilet training is but one branch of the process of socialization that drums into the anarchic little monster starting out in life that there is a time and a place for excrement, just as there is a time and a place for sex and a time and a place for aggression. As with sexuality, the natural sensual enjoyment gained from defecation is restrained, limited, and ordered by a social superego, but a vicarious escape from this order can be experienced in the comic mode. Hence the mirth caused when our culturally inculcated toilet role—with its tendency to rub, chafe, and be a pain on the whole—is ripped or dropped at an unexpected moment.

Of course, toilet humor has tended to be pooh-poohed by po-faced coprophobics down the centuries. In *The Assemblywomen*, Aristophanes has Blepyrus try—and fail—to move his bowels onstage and even ask the audience if anyone with experience in bottoms would mind helping him relieve his intestinal blockage. But this is immediately followed up by a mock-deprecatory rejection of such comedy by Blepyrus, a gesture that (half-)disowns such execrable humor—although not until after it has won a few laughs. Even though Aristophanes at times pretends to look down or turn up his nose at this level of fecal fun, this has not convinced his critics. In a comparison of Aristophanes and Menander Plutarch refers to the "verbal diarrhoea" of the former, claiming that the hoi polloi are attracted by this, while the educated find it loathsome. The implication is evident: only the uncivilized fail to be offended at the sight of the feces behind the social mask. Ben Jonson (living, by the way, at a time when "excrement" was something grown on the upper lip) likewise laid into Aristophanes for "reducing all witt to the originall Dungcart,"[105] although, ironically enough, it has in turn been posited by Edmund Wilson that the pedantically classical erudition and the vindictive and aggressive orderliness of Jonson's own comedy are themselves symptomatic of a fixation with the sadistic anal stage of psychosexual development.[106] Wilson even speculatively brings Jonson's own malodorous strain (released in *The Poetaster*, *The Alchemist*, and *The Famous Voyage*) into context with the claims of psychologists that "explosive bowel evacuations" can function as surrogates for discharges of normally pent-up fury or rage. But here we are perhaps getting bogged down in the slipstream of our pansexual hobbyhorse....

One of the most reliable ways of raising a titter is by means of the well-(or ill-)timed fart. The "talking anus" is a widespread motif in medieval folk humor,[107] one of its most notorious practitioners being Dante's chief-demon, Malacoda, who acknowledges his subordinate demons by blowing his own intestinal trumpet at the close of the twenty-first canto of *Inferno*: "Ed elli avea del cul fatto trombetta." Flatulence is associated with devils and demons in the popular imagination, but also—ultimately—with fools, a linkage illustrated by the common etymological root of the two words in the Latin *flare*, to blow. Fools are empty-headed fellows, blathering bellows blowing out hot air; they are windiness incarnate. The predominant comic characteristic of Grimmelshausen's naive fool Simplicissimus, for example, is his petomanic propensity. The noxious odors for which he is responsible function as a particularly potent form of party pooping and earn him a beating for his labors. But, if flatulence is the signal of a fool, it is the fool in his capacity as an *unmasked*, i.e., unspoiled, human being. In the context of Grimmelshausen's novel, Simplicissimus's smelly but innocent contribution to the occasion contrasts with the sinful, debauched folly of the older guests, and the whiffy guff strikes the reader as a cogent and an honest social retort.

Not only is flatulence a more or less explosive release from the socially decorous role we are normally constrained to play, therefore, it also has an undeniable communicative value, one that has come naturally to generations of schoolchildren who have used the fart to comment upon the educational establishment. Clive James explains the technique: "The whole secret of raising a laugh with a fart in class is to make it sound as if it is punctuating, or commenting upon, what the teacher is saying."[108] Anthony Burgess describes one such comment unintentionally made by his protagonist Enderby at a pompously inflated literary prize-giving event:

> Enderby, preoccupied with the need to suppress his body's noises, heard only fragments of an exquisitely bad poem and he nodded approvingly to show that he considered Sir George to have made a very good choice of an illustrative example of very bad poetry. As the last line scrannel-piped wretchedly out, Enderby felt a particularly loud noise coming, so he covered it with a laugh.
>
> Ha ha (perrrpf) ha.
>
> Sir George was rather surprised than displeased. He gaped down at Enderby for five seconds and then scanned his typescript tremblingly, as if fearful that something scatological had stolen ambiguously in. Reassured, he frowned on Enderby, his patches of skin shaking, and then took breath for the peroration. As he opened his mouth, Enderby, with infelicitous timing, gave vent.
>
> Brrrbrrrpkrrrk.
>
> Shem Macnamara said, "And as good and succinct a piece of criticism as ever I heard."[109]

Enderby's clamorous colon facetiously punctuates the proceedings, debunking poetic haughtiness by dragging the attention back down below the belt with insistent repetition. Bowel movements are above all bathetic.

Enderby's anal ululations also give Burgess the opportunity to indulge in a pleasurable bout of verbal inventiveness, hinting at a common etiological origin to the comedy generated by flatulence and by gibberish or unstoppable loquacity. The nonsensical babblings of the dadaist Kurt Schwitters were likewise but the product of a passage of wind through one of the human orifices, yet they too created a comic effect by *parodying* normal speech. The belch, furthermore, may operate in a similar way to the fart, a sign of indecorum, grossness, or parodic disrespect on the one hand, but also (possibly) of naturalness or of unsophisticated honesty. It may equally be enjoyed for the pure *sound* of its grotesque or ugly musicality. This is the case in Aristophanes's *The Frogs*, where Dionysus tries to out-burp the chorus of frogs (and succeeds).

Part of the comedy in Enderby's instance is the monomania and exaggeration accompanying his wind, the "cloacal obsession" that colors the entire outlook of this "past master on visceral dysfunctions."[110] The hyper-bolus not only informs his conception of his own innards ("the kitchen-gods fighting") but pervades the imagery of the whole novel, a narratorial obsession coming to merge with or repeat that of the protagonist in a sympathetic free indirect style: "Stealthily the sky had, above their searching heads, been clouding over. There was a greenish look in the atmosphere as though the atmosphere proposed, sooner or later, to be sick."[111] Across the Atlantic (and around the same time) Ignatius J. Reilly is lavishing equally compulsive attention upon his pyloric valve, which, proving to be every bit as troublesome, temperamental, and antisocial as Enderby's, is personified into one of the major figures of the novel: "Since the attempted arrest and the accident, he had been bloating for almost no reason at all, his pyloric valve snapping shut indiscriminately and filling his stomach with trapped gas, gas which had character and being and resented its confinement. He wondered whether his pyloric valve might be trying, Cassandralike, to tell him something." Later we learn of the selfsame valve that it was "executing several maneuvers that exceeded in originality and violence anything it had done before."[112]

In various less prudish eras and areas, the excremental has more or less unashamedly taken its place on stage. Just as Blepyrus's constipation is turned into a public matter, French medieval farce plays games of swapping and confusion with bottles of wine and urine, while Pulcinella of the commedia shatters the theatrical illusion by merrily micturating on stage. In more modern times, Beckett's Vladimir goes offstage to do his business, yet this nevertheless draws attention to stage convention, as well as social convention, in a like manner: verisimilar characters have infinitely capacious bladders, or at any rate they never seem to need to interrupt the "action" by taking a leak. The comedy of the Freudian cesspit is taken to its extreme by Jarry's extremely infantile Ubu. Indeed the scatological element, particularly in *Ubu Cocu*, is so direct and unsubtle that it tends to be viewed as meiely disgusting, and not really all that funny. *Ubu Roi* opens with Ubu's infamous cry of *Merdre!* (shite!), and in this play Ubu, armed with toilet brush ("balai innommable") and sporting the phallic gorbelly that again fuses the sexual and the excremental, proves himself to be a voracious shite-eater. But this is nothing compared to the fourth act of *Ubu Cocu*, which reaches a cloacal climax without parallel when

Ubu takes his seat on the lavatory only for it completely to disintegrate under his weight. The fact that half the cast, including Mère Ubu, her lover Memnon, and Père Ubu's Conscience, all happen to be in the earth closet at the time in no way perturbs the coprophagous hero. When Memnon ventures to poke his head up, Ubu simply shoves him back down and continues with business as usual. Incoherent and crass it may be, but as regards pure antitheatre, the Dadaists who were to come a few years later could go no further in blowing a raspberry at conventional theatrical norms.

Just as Jarry parodies decorous bourgeois theatre in general by dragging it through the *merdre*, in *Peace* Aristophanes mocks a specific drama, Euripides's *Bellerophon*, by transposing its imagery into the base sphere of defecation, transforming Euripides's Pegasus into a dung beetle. Like the skillfully timed fart that takes the wind out of overblown scholarly discourse, such comedy exploits the fact that excrement—together with the wind movements it generates and the accompanying cacophony—is considered to be nasty, ugly, and smelly. As such, scatological humor takes on a special significance as a means of degradation, and pranks, tricks, and deceptions frequently tend to toe the bottom line. Furthermore, corresponding to the age-old metonymic link between laughter and urine (Wycherley's Sparkish reports that a group of listeners be-pissed themselves for laughing at a jest of his), an even stronger and more timeworn bond exists between fear and feces. In Aristophanes's times, the laxative attributes of fear were a common motif, "dying oneself brown" (for example) serving as a widespread metonym for being afraid, and even in the twentieth century the motif has reared its (ugly) bottom in the cowardly figure of Ubu (in *Ubu Roi*).

As much as anywhere, the excremental runs (or trots) consistently through the bowels of Rabelais's *Gargantua* and *Pantagruel*, and the lily-livered Panurge of book 4 once again testifies to the metonymic coupling of fear and its bodily manifestations, a debasement of cowardice and of fear itself. In the final chapter of the book, he is so frightened by a cannon salute fired from Pantagruel's fleet that, terrorized by mystic fantasies as he cowers in the ship's storeroom, he drops his load on the spot. Rabelais takes this opportunity to grant the reader a learned disquisition on the subject, starting with a medical analysis:

> The retentive capacity of the nerve which controls the muscle known as the sphincter—the arse-hole in other words—had been relaxed by the intense fear accompanying his fantastic visions, coupled with the thunder of the cannonades, which is more frightening in the interior of the ship than on deck. For one of the symptoms and effects of fear is that it generally opens the gateway of the seraglio temporarily retaining the faecal matter.[113]

Rabelais reinforces this account with "historical" anecdotes to prove his point. Yet Panurge has the last word, cheerfully recovering his spirits to deny his fear, demonstrate once more his logorrheic powers with a litany of synonyms for shit, and enjoin us to have a drink:

> "Are you saying that I'm frightened?" replied Panurge. "Not in the least. By God, I'm more courageous than if I'd just swallowed all the flies put in pies in Paris from St John's Day to All Saints' Day. Ha, ha, ha! But ho! What the devil is this? Do you call it crap, turds, crottels, shit, friants, droppings, faecal matter, excrement, ordure, dung, stools, fumets, stronts, waggying or werderobe? It's Hibernian saffron, that's what I think. Ho, ho, ho! Hibernian saffron, that's it! Let's have a drink!"[114]

Scatological laughter is here not only a debasement of fear, but also an overcoming of it.

In spite of the potential ambivalence of the motif, fecal humor has primarily been employed over the years as a means of degradation and humiliation, even if a relatively harmless one. The timeless gesture of displaying the buttocks is still to be found as a sign of contempt among sports fans, as is the idea of (you) "not being fit to wipe my arse." The element of abasement is made clear by the sort of scatological mockery in *Simplicissimus*, admittedly set against the background cruelty of the Thirty Years' War, where a vanquished impostor is forced to kiss the arses of three sheep as a token of his shame. Being made to eat this particularly unsavory kind of humble pie again unearths the sinister proximity of humor and humiliation.

It is in a similar spirit when Boccaccio has Fiammetta relate the story of Andreuccio who, swindled by a trickstress pretending to be his sister, is unceremoniously flushed out of her house via the cesspit (full of ordure— as Boccaccio/Fiammetta zestfully points out), and it is noticeable that Fiammetta's listeners in the narrative frame of the *Decameron* all find Andreuccio's ordeals essentially amusing and not in the least loathsome, nauseating, or sick. On the eighth day, the gracious Filomena enthusiastically tells of the trick Bruno and Buffalmacco play on Calandrino, whereby they skillfully oblige him to eat a dog doodah to prove his honesty, and again, as Boccaccio explicitly recounts, this story has the charming, intelligent, sophisticated, gently-bred ladies and young men of the day shaking with mirth. Chaucer's *Miller's Tale* is a tale of jolly rogerings in which the carpenter's young wife Alisoun deceives her aged husband and goes to bed with the student Nicholas, but also takes the chance to play a dirty trick upon another tiresome suitor by the name of Absolon, described as "somdeel squaymous of fartyng." Alisoun exploits the darkness of night (we readers sharing the amused enlightenment of the onlooking Nicholas) to entice Absolon to her window in the hope of a kiss:

This Absolon gan wype his mouth ful drie.
Derk was the nyght as pich, or as the cole,
And at the wyndow out she putte hir hole,
And Absolon, hym fil no bet ne wers,
But with his mouth he kiste hir naked ers
Ful savourly, er he were war of this.
Abak he stirte, and thoughte it was amys,
For wel he wiste a womman hath no berd.
He felte a thyng al rough and long yherd,
And seyde, "Fy! allas! what have I do?"
"Tehee!" quod she, and clapte the wyndow to,
And Absolon gooth forth a sory pas.

(*Canterbury Tales*, 1.3730–41)

When Absolon returns with a hot iron, bent on vengeance, Nicholas compounds the insult by dealing out a thunderous fart that almost blinds Absolon with its blast, but he is rewarded for his efforts with the sort of farcical comic strip blow on the backside that rocks his very fundaments. The excremental plays a more nauseating part in the pranks of Rabelais's Panurge, who delights in making fetid concoctions for the very purpose of pleasurably churning people's stomachs or besplattering his victims with yuck-pies.[115]

Much of the comic effect of the prank consists in the privileged immunity of the laughing spectator and the flattering impression he has of knowing better than the victim or fool. *The Miller's Tale* exemplifies this, the literal and metaphorical darkness in which Absolon gropes about compounding his ignominy and our superiority. The confusion of wine and urine in the French farce *Un Amoureux* works on similar principles, as do Boccaccio's *beffe* and the fake feces of the surrealists and Sex Pistols. In the Fake Dog Crap Sketch, Lenny Bruce explains (and is bamboozled by) the workings of this unsophisticated comic prop, once more (like Aristophanes) turning such humor to account by denigrating it:

It's really bizarre. It's fool-your-friend, hurt-your-friend, put a fly in his ice-cube.
"We have a cute little article here, it's, it's fake dog crap."
"*What?*"
"Yeah—fake dog shit—very humorous. Ya see, we take this fake dog crap and we put it on the stairs, see"—
"Now who would buy that?"
"Oh, there's a market for it."
"Well, it doesn't seem very humorous to—"

"Oh yeah—cause you can take it two ways, see? It's *double entendre*. It could be real dog shit or fake dog crap. And then we have this fake vomit—"

. . . .

"Look. I mean, just picture this. See, here's what happens. The guy comes home, see? The wife puts the fake dog shit on the stairs. The real vomit or the fake vomit or the real dog shit and the fake dog shit, see. And he comes home and goes
'*Yippee! Dog shit!*'
And he grabs it and goes
'Ahhh, it's *fake*! Oh, here's some vomit!'
That's fake too, and then he cries his eyes out—and that's the fun. That's after he drinks the fly in the sugar cube."
"Well, I dunno. That's certainly a weird kind of humor."[116]

Lenny Bruce's example implies that vomit possesses a comic potential analogous to that of the turd. Barfing is smelly and ugly for one thing, a social nonstarter, and is often linked, moreover, with the comic theme of inebriation. It is as if our antisocial bodily innards are explosively heaving their way past the cosmetic social mask that normally keeps such nastiness concealed. Two cases of graphically "sick" comedy come to mind. During the night of drunken revelry to which Simplicissimus contributes with his mind-blowing meteorism, Simplicissimus's Governor "shoots a fox" in a moment of respite, the unfortunate young simpleton finding himself caught in the crossfire and almost nauseated into returning fire. The strength of the narratorial stomach, however, is evidenced by the comic gusto with which he enumerates the former contents of the Governor's belly as the eponymous hero carries away the bowl of swill. The whole episode is recounted with an irony as subtle as the Thirty Years' War:

> [My master] commanded me to carry away the fox, which, as it was in a silver basin, did not strike me as anything despicable, but as a bowl full of enough ragout to feed four men, which it was not at all fitting to throw away. In addition I knew full well that my master had stored nothing nasty in his stomach, but delightful and delicate pastries, as well as all sorts of pies, fowl, wild game and domestic livestock, all of which could still be nicely distinguished and recognized.[117]

Martin Amis produces a comic hyper-bolus to describe a similar episode in *Money*, where John Self, after a typically gargantuan drink binge, throws up during a business meeting:

> Halfway through my synopsis the cork of nausea abruptly popped in my throat. I only just made it to the adjacent can, which was large and acoustical: my imitation of an exploding hippopotamus came through the closed door in full quadrophonic (as Fielding later explained). I got one or two funny glances on

my return, but I just butched it out and I don't think it did me any harm. If I were them, I'd enjoy the spectacle.[118]

By narrating the incident with the aid of an exaggerated comic simile, Amis not only generates a comedy of identity or recognition (for other slobbish Selfs who have mimicked exploding pachyderms in their time) and confirms the bulldozingly predictable comedy of Self's self-destructive character, he simultaneously—through the surreality of the image—transposes the episode from the everyday world of functional rationality into the realm of grotesque and violent fantasy. While iterating the repetitious identity of the hero (an identity we *share* to the extent that we empathize or identify with him), the description may also jolt or surprise us with the freakish extravagance of its imagery.

An area of bodily ugliness that generates a comparable degree of squeamishness is the olfactory, churning out as it does those phlegmatic bogeymen collectively known as snot. Again, Martin Amis provides us with a comically overstated description of the phenomenon, this time in *The Rachel Papers*, where Charles takes especial delight in a series of prodigiously messy coughing fits:

One particularly illustrious fit ended when a huge, wriggling blob of gilbert leapt from my mouth and smacked solidly against the bathroom wall—better than *five feet* away. I focused my eyes; it was enormous; it looked like—what are they called? bolasses?—the weighted lassoos employed by South American cowpokes. Soon, I thought, soon, just by coughing in the direction of their legs, I'd be able to trip up old ladies in the street.

It also enriched the texture of my phlegm: I whoofed up goo pretzels, fried slugs, pixie's nylons.[119]

The comic vigor of the account results both from Amis's hyperbolic imagination and from the blatant breach of the taboo that disallows public appearances or social performances by snot, which for the bulk of the cultural comedy is condemned to keep a low profile and not draw attention to itself. Lenny Bruce likewise cocks a snook at our nasal inhibitions:

Alright. I'm going to do something you never thought I'd do on stage. I'm going to do a bit now that I was arrested for. I'm going to tell you the dirtiest word you've ever heard on stage. It's just *disgusting*!

I'm not going to look at you when I say it, cause this way we won't know who said it. I may blame that cat over there. It's a four-letter word, starts with an 's' and ends with a 't' . . .

The word is—Oh, I'm going to *say* it and just get it *done* with. I'm tired of walking the streets.

(*Whispers*) "Snot!"

I can't look at you. But that's the word: snot. I know a lot of my friends are thinking now,

"He's so clever, and then, for a cheap laugh, he says 'snot.' He don't need that, that disgusting character."[120]

Bruce's response to the social institutions that get up his nose is to pick it, probing the boundary between the funny and the disgusting and at the same time drawing attention to his own awareness of the question whether he is being comic or sick. The boundary itself becomes Bruce's theme, but, by ironically working it into his semitheoretical routine ("I mean, there's certain things that's funny, and there's certain things that are downright disgusting"[121]), he straddles it and claims it for the realm of comedy, enabling his hung-up audience to laugh both about snot and about its hang-ups about snot. Bruce's rhetorical hawk rips off the social mask of decorum, propriety, and niceness, but, as an unmasking, it also grants us access to truth. This truth is a purely bodily one, and Bruce himself parodies the truthfulness of his comic revelation by reducing it to the level of sheer triviality. Nevertheless, the truth it is:

> But do you know anything about snot? Except that every time you heard it you go *Phah!* Or *Ich!* Or *Keeriste!?* ...
> Suppose I tell you something about snot, something that was so unique about snot that you'd go:
> "Is that the *truth* about snot?"
> "Look, I'm gonna lie to ya? That's *right.* That's about snot."
> . . . .
> Well, I've done some research about snot. How about this about snot: *you can't get snot off a suede jacket!*[122]

In the sphere of bodily ugliness, it is perhaps Enderby's stepmother who takes the digestive biscuit. She is an embodiment of fleshly grotesquery, her gargantuan body completely bursting the aesthetic straitjacket that normally hides our seething, gurgling, churning innards behind a mask of cosmetic fixity. Enderby describes her with a passionate revulsion:

> She picked her teeth with old tram-tickets, cleaned out her ears with hairclips in whose U-bend ear-wax was trapped to darken and harden, scratched her private parts through her clothes with a matchbox-rasping noise audible two rooms away, made gross sandwiches of all her meals or cut her meat with scissors, spat chewed bacon-rind or pork-crackling back on her plate, excavated beef-fibres from her cavernous molars and held them up for all the world to see, hooked out larger chunks with a soiled sausage-finger, belched like a ship in the fog, was sick on stout on Saturday nights, tromboned vigorously in the lavatory....[123]

It is telling that Enderby, himself hardly a model of intestinal tranquillity, should deem these habits so loathsome: not only does he lack the distance to be able to view this unmasked fleshliness with dispassion, his loathing is compounded by a number of personal sexual tensions. Her ebullient carnality comes to symbolize for him the ugliness of the sexual act itself, a development for which he holds her responsible with her habit of "emerging in a ladylike belch or a matchstick picking of teeth from behind the most cool and delectable facade."[124] Her flamboyant grotesqueness has shattered the illusion of beauty required for social and sexual intercourse, revealing the mucilaginous glob underneath.

Pubic hair is a further such sphere of normally hidden bodily "ugliness." The comedy to which its discursive appearance can consequently give rise is typified by the sketch in which the stand-up comedian Billy Connolly asks the question why pubes stop growing when they do (how do they *know* when to stop?) and imagines the repercussions if this were not the case: wouldn't it be fab and groovy if ...? Such a monologue is of course virtually unquotable: its impact is above all visual as Connolly— the archetypal shaggy joketeller—demonstrates his (hirsute) point with exaggerated gesture and infectiously wide-eyed credulity. Taking a theme that is usually half-hidden from sight by the lingerie of sexual propriety, Connolly modulates and works through the range of its comic possibilities like hairs on a G-string. Ben Elton meanwhile makes the point that pubes refuse to be kept in concealment by propriety's skimpy pose-pouch anyway, for they get EVERYWHERE: "There is no corner of creation they haven't colonized. Open a book, wallop! there's a pubic hair...." And the bar of soap is of course their home from home ("I think they put them in at the factory"). It is the attraction of pubic humor that doubtless explains the near universal popularity in British society of signs for pubic transport, pubic footpaths, and pubic toilets (to let).

Earthily carnal comedy clearly has its roots in the grotesque, the taboo areas of the body corresponding to the parts and the exudations that mediate between the self and the nonself: pubes, excrement, urine, semen, monthly blood, vomit, mucus. The grotesque has indeed been designated a *"Gestaltung des Es,"* a form expressive of the id,[125] a structuring of what comes to light when the cultural superego normally ordering and shaping and defining our perception is pushed to one side for a while. Accordingly, it may denote the sort of artistic unshapes and misformations that often characterized the Renaissance vision of demons, devils, and fallen souls. In Michelangelo's sketches for a treatment of The Last Judgement, for example, the damned are portrayed as fantastically deformed, the act of transgression itself entailing a concomitant loss of formal coherence and unity.[126] The grotesque either transcends or affronts our classificatory system, depending on our point of view, for the diabolical figures are neither man nor beast. They resist the reassurances of orderly categorization, rather like those unsettlingly gungy mediations between body and world. The devil himself is a rent in the cosmic/cosmetic order, a purulent pimple that cannot be hidden by the divine makeup. From this perspective, grotesque ugliness becomes linked in an associative chain with bad or evil, while the aesthetic category of "bad taste" implies (in its badness) a parallel set of value judgements—ugly *and* morally wrong.

To the extent that, in everyday terms at least, ugliness is considered to be less *harmful* than evil, however, it measures up to one of the first criteria ascertained as central to comedy, and it is perhaps for this reason that a number of theorists have directed their attentions towards it. Bohtz, for example, suggests that the object of laughter is the ugly in its deviation from the Idea;[127] comedy arises from the imperfection of the material world, mere appearance failing to live up to the ideals of the Idea (reality). Here Bohtz is applying a Platonic-Christian model that is the exact inverse in structure and evaluation of the Schopenhauerian one derived from Kant and Eastern mysticism and stressing that the world of human ideas is but an appearance masking the fluidity of things as they really are. The German theorist Jünger too takes as a presupposition for his study of the comic that there is "nothing comic in which ugliness isn't implicated,"[128] even while admitting that not all that is ugly is comic. But Jünger's theory is one of those not very nice, Bergsonian ones: laughter represents the triumph of beauty over ugliness, the crushing victory of norm conformity over deviance. It contains the aggressive social message: be beautiful, or we'll rearrange your face! Fortunately—again—this is only half of the story. Comic laughter can relativize and celebrate "ugliness," just as it can celebrate farts, snot, belches, periods, and bits of dirt in the corner of one's fingernails.

Nevertheless, uglification, or the act of making ugly, does play an important role in derision and mockery, in much the same way as does scatological debasement. Cicero points out in *De Oratore* (55 B.C.) that people are frequently turned into the butt of mockery by being compared with an object more ugly than they, for laughter is engendered when ugliness is compared with even greater ugliness[129] or, as Quintilian would have it, when a similitude is pinpointed that links the object of scorn to something baser or more lowly than itself.[130] Caricature likewise consists in a process of rendering grotesque or repulsive and is a public pillorying to which well-known figures and notabilities are particularly prone. Once more, the comic recognition of identity is concomitant with an element of distortive difference. That it is often the bodily protuberances and cavities of these figures that are exaggerated and deformed (noses, mouths, ears, or—in traditional ritual caricature—penis, vagina and anus) brings us back to the realm of specifically bodily grotesqueness.

Physical decrepitude can itself be turned into a comic object, as demonstrated by the first part of Beckett's description of the Lynch family in *Watt*:

There was Tom Lynch, widower, aged eighty-five years, confined to his bed with constant undiagnosed pains in the caecum, and his three surviving boys Joe, aged sixty-five, a rheumatical cripple, and Jim, aged sixty-four years, a hunchbacked inebriate, and Bill, widower, aged sixty-three years, greatly hampered in his movements by the loss of both legs as the result of a slip, followed by a fall, and his only surviving daughter May Sharpe, widow, aged sixty-two years, in full possession of all her faculties with the exception of that of vision. Then there was Joe's wife née Doyly-Byrne, aged sixty-five years, a sufferer from Parkinson's palsy but otherwise very fit and well, and Jim's wife Kate née Sharpe aged sixty-four years, covered all over with running sores of an unidentified nature but otherwise fit and well.[131]

The list goes on and on and on. Beckett uses techniques of repetition and accumulation to engender a snowball effect of human deformity, while also lending the whole portrayal a sort of jaunty objectivity that removes it from the sphere of mockery. While it cannot be claimed that the Lynches would make a strikingly beautiful sight by common standards, the forthright bluntness of the comic litany is a refreshing rejection of the beautifying and falsifying mask of aesthetic conformity distorting "conventional" literature. The Lynch family may not be much to look at, but it has an earthy, if rather decomposing, truthfulness about it (a sense of humus), an integrity shared by the narration.

Jokes about physical defects can quickly become tasteless, sick, and offensive in a much more malevolent way than jokes about farts and snot, and this applies not only to quips at the expense of the handicapped, but also to jokes about pain in general, death, and catastrophe. Such laughter obviously offers an emotional release in bringing to the conversational or discursive surface themes that are usually deemed taboo and kept underground. It is an opportunity to shock, moreover, and—as the metaphor would have it—a moment of vicarious freedom for our natural malice. At the same time, however, such jokes can undeniably serve as a means of *coming to terms* with areas of anxiety, negotiating taboo topics, and exploring emotional responses to those existential matters which define and delimit our very identity. The black comedy of *A Day in the Death of Joe Egg*, for example, revolving as it does around a "human parsnip," is not a tasteless and irreverent attempt to *épater les bourgeois*, but a demonstration of the way humor may be necessary (as an emotional anesthetic) to help people cope with pain and death. Here the sequences of minicomedies within the comedy, played by Bri and Sheila, work as distance-generating factors both for them (in their relationship to their handicapped daughter) and for us (in our relationship to them), and they are coupled with a goodly measure of illusion-rupturing metatheatre that facilitates further dissociation on the part of the spectator from the more harrowing or brutal aspects of the goings-on. At the end of the first act, for example, the human parsnip herself skips onstage to tell the audience that an interval is to follow, and both her parents separately pour their heart out to the spectators, such a device creating a tension of immediacy (through its directness) and distance (through its breach of the dramatic illusion). While Bri thus strives to explain his emotional situation in "a way that will prevent a sudden stampede to the exit-doors" (1), Sheila likewise ends up qualifying her outpourings with a reference to us: "Even when I *am* a bit down, I shouldn't normally talk about it to a lot of complete strangers" (1). Notably, another self-referential moment in the play even takes exception to its own jokes, querying the palliative attributes of such distance-creating comedy:

> *Sheila.*   We know one—a man of seventy-six, just become a Boy Scout. They said they wouldn't have him any longer in the Cubs.
> *Freddie.* These jokes. May I say my piece about these jokes? They've obviously helped you see it through. A useful anaesthetic. But. Isn't there a point where the jokes start using *you*?
> *Sheila.*   I thought you were going to speak to Bri about—
> *Freddie.* Please. This first. Isn't that the whole fallacy of the sick joke? It kills the pain but leaves the situation just as it was?
>
>   (Act 2)

9
The Cognitive Mask

Theoretical Nothings

The description of the grotesque as a form expressing the id points up a new link between the comic and a realm of radical otherness, of metaphysical madness. Comic "ugliness" comes to light as a chink in the mask not only of ethical and aesthetic order, but also of conceptual and perceptual structure. The grotesque play with forms and structures yields us a glimpse of the unknowable. This subchapter is an attempt to place these rather abstract sounding ideas in a broadly philosophical context centered on Kant.

Freudian metaphors have already provided a model for describing the comedy of norm deviance, which constitutes a dropping of (or rupture in) the social mask to reveal a "true" self, the id or unconscious. A variant on the model takes into account that this "true" self is always ultimately a purely negative or vacuous notion: as soon as antisociality sees itself or is seen as a positive phenomenon, it has necessarily trapped itself in a framework of social meaningfulness and interaction. All we can know is the mask; what is behind the mask is inconceivable, or there is nothing there. For this model, the act of deviance can only ever stand in a symbolic relationship to the "hidden" truth.

Freud was aware of the Kantian origins of his theory, which had been transmitted via a hefty dose of Schopenhauerism, and it is the Kantian metaphor that will perhaps prove most helpful in illustrating how comedy may emerge from a rent in the cognitive mask of conception and perception. Freud himself alludes to the relationship between the unconscious and the Kantian thing-in-itself: "Just as Kant warned us not to overlook the subjective nature of our perception or take our perception to be identical with the unknowable object of perception, so psychoanalysis exhorts us not to substitute the perception of consciousness for the unconscious psychical process which is its object. As with the physical, the psychical need not in reality be as it appears to us."[1] In this same essay, Freud describes the unconscious in terms that stress its unknowability, an unknowability shared with the *Ding an sich*: "How are we to come to a knowledge of the unconscious? We of course know it only as consciousness, after it has undergone a transformation or translation into consciousness.... The unconscious processes only become knowable for us under the conditions of dreams or neuroses.... In themselves they are unknowable."[2] In the *Kritik der reinen Vernunft*, Kant makes the claim that space, time, and the categories of the understanding are merely forms necessarily imposed by our cognitive faculties upon our perception and conception of the world. The world *appears* to us as structured by such principles as causality (an effect being of necessity preceded by a cause) and permanence of substance (a quantum of substance being permanent).[3] These epistemological principles, however, have absolutely no bearing on the way the world is in itself, independent of our cognition: behind the *appearance* of time, space, causality, and permanence of substance, the *reality* of the thing as it is in itself remains completely unknowable.

Kant's model is a subtle one. As he emphasizes in the *Prolegomena*, he has not reduced the entire spatio-temporal world of substance and causality to the status of mere illusion (*Schein*), but to that of appearance (*Erscheinung*). Herein lies his difference from most idealists. Kant's handy use of a nice distinction in the German language enables him to attribute to the world of appearance an ambivalent ontological status analogous to that of theatrical performance: it would be misleading to say either that it is simply real or simply illusory, so perhaps in a sense it is both. While theatrical performance is thus real in that its actors are objectively existent beings and to this extent the onlooker is not wrapped up in a subjective world of hallucinatory delusion, it is unreal insofar as what is witnessed is "just pretend." Likewise, Kant's "appearance" is to be distinguished from mere "illusion" (or subjective delusion),[4] yet nor is it to be confused with the "thing-in-itself," reality as it is in independence of our cognizance of it. In what follows, an appropriation of Kant's metaphor will draw attention to the comic potential of rupturing this mask of cognitive appearances, playing with the rules of causality and substance, the forms of time and space. If the world really is a stage, then such comedy offers metatheatrical treats of a somewhat different order from those encountered so far.

Kant is not the only philosopher to have "relegated" causality to the status of mere appearance. Hume saw in causality a connection imposed by the mind between things that have recurrently been experienced in conjunction, and, like Kant, Hume was making a primarily epistemological point. All we can know in experience, he claims, is this constant conjunction of perceived properties, not any "real" or "necessary" causal relation. The human mind has a natural disposition to form habits,

however, and—aided by patterns and repetitions—we naturally anticipate that those conjunctions of phenomena experienced in the past will
recur in like manner in the future. "In all single instances of the operation
of bodies or minds, there is nothing that produces any impression, nor
consequently can suggest any idea, of power or necessary connexion. But
when many uniform instances appear, and the same object is always followed by the same event; we then begin to entertain the notion of cause
and connexion. We then *feel* a new sentiment or impression, to wit, a
customary connexion in the thought or imagination between one object
and its usual attendant."[5] Causation is but a habit of expectation, a
"fiction of the imagination," by which Hume does *not* mean a lie but a
mental construct attributable to the habit-forming makeup of our cognitive apparatus. Although adding a cautionary word of warning, Hume too
employs a theatrical metaphor to elucidate his argument:

> The mind is a kind of theatre, where several perceptions successively make
> their appearance; pass, repass, glide away, and mingle in an infinite variety of
> postures and situations. There is properly no *simplicity* in it at one time, nor
> *identity* in different, whatever natural propension we may have to imagine that
> simplicity and identity. The comparison of the theatre must not mislead us.
> They are the successive perceptions only, that constitute the mind; nor have we
> the most distant notion of the place where these scenes are represented, or of
> the materials of which it is composed.[6]

The human mind is a theatre in which the identities of the characters
have to be added by the spectator, it would seem, a chaotic spectacle
indeed at which the onlooker must invent his own plot.

It was Hume's disconcerting notion that causation is a contingent habit
or fiction that gave Kant the prod in the philosophical ribs to jerk him out
of his dogmatic dozing and launch him into his critical career. He responded by turning Hume's "natural disposition of the mind" into a
necessary precondition for knowledge, an a priori rule of the understanding. Following Kant (and Schopenhauer), Nietzsche likewise regards causation as a fiction and, in the openly Schopenhauerian early
work *Die Geburt der Tragödie*, he praises his German predecessors for
their revelation that time, space, and causality "in actual fact only served
to elevate mere appearance, the work of Maya, to the unique and highest
reality, putting it in the place of the inner and true essence of things and
thereby rendering impossible any genuine knowledge of the latter."[7]
Causality is a mask or veil obstructing our vision of the way things really
are. Nietzsche later comes to reject such *Hinterweltereien* or worlds-
behind-worlds as the Kantian thing-in-itself or Schopenhauer's Will, yet
the fictional status of causality remains significant to his philosophical
perspective(s). He at times even turns what Kant had interpreted as a

synthesizing faculty into an actively creative role, stressing the psycho-logical importance of the subject's delusive belief that the world he has created is in fact the true reality-in-itself. The subject here resembles a playwright watching his own play but forgetting that he is responsible for having written it.

The later Nietzsche especially puts more and more emphasis on the notion characteristic of Heraclitus's thought and of Eastern mysticism that all is in flux, the specifically human concepts of a "cause," a "thing," or a "substance" being but fictive straitjackets striving to impose a dis-tortively rigid form upon the fluidity of the world. Indeed, Nietzsche's attack on causality was launched in conjunction with one on substance or matter and on mechanistic determinism in general in terms that seem to anticipate certain of the claims of the quantum theory of this century. Causation was to be condemned as a misleading concept precisely insofar as it implied a *something* doing the causing and a *something* upon which the causing was being done. Once the ingredients from the mechanistic worldview have been eliminated from the scene, however, "we are left not with things, but dynamic quanta, which exist in a relationship of ten-sion with all other dynamic quanta, whose essence consists in their rela-tionship with all other quanta."[8]

Rejecting the idea of final, indivisible "atoms" to which all matter can ultimately be reduced, Nietzsche takes up the thread of the Eastern mysticism which had influenced Schopenhauer so profoundly. According to the Hindu and Buddhist religions, the belief that reality comprises discretely existent "things" or "objects" is an illusion created by the magic of *Maya* on the mind. Space, causality, and time (insofar as it is divided into separate "moments") are equally illusory. By contrast with the Hellenic tradition of philosophical thought (excluding such ex-ceptional figures as Heraclitus and Giordano Bruno), Eastern thought—including Taoism as well as Hinduism and Buddhism—sees reality as characterized by perpetual flow or change, as a play of forces lying be-yond the inflexible bounds or bondage of human conceptuality. If the occidental tradition privileges substance and stasis, the oriental lays greater emphasis on relation, on the holistic fluidity of a dynamic web of interaction.

The quantum physics of the twentieth century—with its radical under-mining of the notion of fundamental units of substance—has incidentally wrenched open anew the age-old dichotomy between appearance (which behaves in accordance with the classical laws of physics) and reality (which does not). According to Heisenberg's uncertainty principle, it is impossible to know where an atomic or subatomic particle is located *and* to know its velocity at one and the same time; indeed, the very concept of an atom with a definite location and velocity is meaningless. Quantum theory claims that at a subatomic level matter instead shows "tendencies to exist," which can only be understood in terms of so-called probability amplitudes (superpositions of coexistent "alternative possibilities" added together with complex number weightings, i.e., weightings that include imaginary numbers such as the square root of minus one). Although useful conceptions at the everyday level at which classical physics is applicable (the level that *appears* to us), causality and substance are not adequate with respect to the microscopic reality, which consists in the particle's potential to be located at any number of places. We are thus brought back to the old mask/face dichotomy of actuality and potential, our logical rationality only functioning in terms of actuality (a unit of substance either is located at a specific place or it is not—*basta!*) and veiling from us the potentiality inherent in reality (a subatomic "particle" may be here, *and* it may be there, *and* it may be somewhere else, ...).

This duality based on actuality and potentiality can easily be blown up to a macroscopic level as well, serving as a purely logical model to complement the epistemological or metaphysical metaphors of appearance and reality. Here it takes the form of one of the traditional "laws of thought," known as the law of identity, which dictates that everything is what it is—or that if something is true, it is true. A cat, for example, is incontestably a cat, a rose a rose, a shadow a shadow; if it rains, it rains, and so on. This tautological self-identity is a precondition for any cognitive activity. The correlative of this law is what is known as the law of contradiction, according to which nothing can simultaneously have and not have the same property, and a proposition and its negation cannot both be true: if it is raining, then it is not the case that it is not raining. In this sense, every actual fact amounts to a limitation or definition imposed upon the infinitude of possibility: if my carpet is a dirty brown with nasty splodges on it, then it is not blue, green, nor a prettily patterned motley kept in the best of nick—nor indeed any other color (ad infinitum). This "appearance" of logical identity underpinning all rational thought is so comprehensive that if something is the case, then it simply cannot not be so; the notion of possibility becomes vacuous as soon as it is divorced from actuality or ceases to be seen as contingent upon it. Nonetheless, we have already come across the power of the pun and the metaphor, exploding the bounds of logic, to open up a nonsense world in which things are not what they are.

While Eastern thought—like the quantum physical model—has tended to accentuate that its conception of reality (while transcending temporality) is also essentially dynamic, the Western tradition, in the wake of Pythagoras and Plato, has generally based its philosophy upon an ontological distinction between appearance and reality wherein the latter is considered to be nontemporal and time itself secondary or unreal by comparison, for example, with the timeless truths of mathematics. In the opinion of Bertrand Russell, indeed, "mathematics is ... the chief source of the belief in eternal and exact truth, as well as in a super-sensible intelligible world. Geometry deals with exact circles, but no sensible object is *exactly* circular; however carefully we may use our compasses, there will be some imperfections and irregularities. This suggests the view that all exact reasoning applies to ideal as opposed to sensible objects; it is natural to go further, and to argue that thought is nobler than sense, and the objects of thought more real than those of sense-perception."[9]

Corresponding to such a duality, a number of German romantics formulated theories of comedy in which material appearance stands in (comic) opposition to the timeless reality of the Idea. In his lectures on aesthetics of 1829, Solger explained comedy as the result of a contradiction between appearance and Idea arising when the latter acquires "existence" through its necessary material embodiment. It is a sign of the fallibility of the existent world as opposed to the immutable perfection of ideality: laughter is a response to imperfection. For Vischer, the comic is a prank played by appearance upon the Idea, a cheeky attempt to trip it up.[10] Here the comedy amounts to a bathetic deflation of the Idea's pretensions, yielding the pleasure of witnessing the sublime take a tumble at the hands of some lowly piece of materiality from the existent world.

The real or true tends thus to be viewed either as a realm of absolute timelessness, as with Plato and the Christian tradition, or a sphere of absolute flux, as in Eastern mysticism (and its European adherents), typified by the mercurial Hindu figure of Siva, the Lord of the Dance and a symbol of dynamic fluidity. As theoretical or theological constructs, however, pure flux and pure stasis alike are limiting or liminal concepts, *Grenzbegriffe* that form a boundary to the domain of rational thought and merge into one another (as boundaries do). The reason for this is their unknowability, the negativity that removes them from the orbit of actual positive experience: it is just as impossible to shed or transcend all static human conceptuality (for we are prisoners of our cognitive limitations) as it is to know the Platonic Idea through sensible experience. Even dissenting mystics would concur that what they know is in a sense inexpressible.

Philosophical models especially have accentuated the negative quality of the nontemporal, noncausal, nonspatial, insubstantial thing-in-itself or noumenon.[11] Kant, for example, denies even the possibility of any knowledge of it, attributing to the receptive constitution of the knowing subject the entire spatio-temporal framework of the natural world, and thereby ignoring the problems of talking of a non-spatio-temporal thing-in-itself "affecting" the cognitive faculties of a subject ("affecting" being a word with an explicitly spatio-temporal application). Kant in fact draws what he sees as an essential distinction between two uses of the term "thing-in-itself": a negative one, referring to it as a thing insofar as it is not an object of our empirically-based cognition, and a positive one, denoting a positively conceived object of nonempirical cognition or of what he terms intellectual intuition, a faculty we as humans do not possess.[12] On closer inspection, however, the positive noumenon emerges as essentially negative too: such a concept, necessarily outside the bounds of human experience, is utterly empty, and Kant himself takes it as an example in his definition of various sorts of Nothing.[13]

The two aspects of the Kantian noumenon are fundamentally related. In its negative application, it denotes the world insofar as it is *un*known and can*not* be known; in its positive use, its unknowability smuggles in the implication that it is something which could be known given a higher form of human intuition (e.g., God). Like any nothing, this positively conceived thing-in-itself is wholly polymorphous, yet its conception necessarily requires the imposition of a defined (definite or definitive) form: it can only be "visualized," that is, as some phenomenon taken from experience, as is the case with an anthropomorphic God or a somewhat less than anthropomorphic Devil. Even the term "thing-in-itself" is a misnomer, sneaking into our conception of the unknowable the notion of "thinghood," which has its roots firmly in the realm of time, space, and causality. The thing-in-itself is no thing, nor an event, and even to say it is nothing leads us astray.

Given the pure negativity of the real implied by the Kantian model, how on earth can comedy come anywhere near revealing it to us? One possible answer—implied by both Schopenhauer and Freud[14]—would be that there are degrees of negativity or unknowability. Schopenhauer, for example, takes the Kantian thing-in-itself, dubs it the Will, and asserts that we know it by analogy with our own (antisocial and instinctually monstrous) will. The contention that unknowability is quantifiable is of course doomed to be riddled with contradictions. Then again, so is any claim about what cannot be known; indeed, the very act of making such a claim is self-defeatingly contradictory. If all this seems rather nonsensical, this is because we have reached one of the points where comedy and theory about comedy start to converge. Like any attempt to conceptualize the inconceivable, comedy can only yield access to it in the necessarily *displaced* form of nonsense. The mask metaphor would then hold that comic play with the structures of our perception, such as causality, comes to represent, symbolize, or imitate the chaotic or dynamic unfathomability of the world.

This suggestion is supported by the fact that both Kant and Schopenhauer utilize what could be called a two-tiered model, involving masks upon masks. Schopenhauer's own theory of the ridiculous is built upon the idea of a disparity between the world as it reveals itself to perception and our conceptual ordering of it, the concept functioning like a mask whose inflexibility opens up an incongruity between concept and percept, the abstract and the immediate. Here it is still the empirical (i.e., the psychological) that concerns Schopenhauer. It is at a different level, however, when Schopenhauer depicts comedy as an affirmation of the Will to Life, for in this case what is being asserted or celebrated is the *ontological* thing-in-itself, the unknowable, irrational, primarily sexual force beyond the individuating mask of representation, beyond the grasp of empirical perception and conception.[15]

Kant's model is two-tiered in a similar way to Schopenhauer's. On one level, Kant distinguishes between intuition (*Anschauung*) and understanding (*Verstand*) in a way roughly analogous to Schopenhauer's empirical dichotomy between what is perceived (*Wahrnehmung*) and the concept (*Begriff*). On a different level is his "ontological" distinction between appearance and reality, according to which the cognitive mask, comprising both perception and conception, hides an unknowable reality.[16] Whereas the "empirical" or "psychological" mask is wobbly (it is wobbled by nonsense), the "ontological" one cannot be breached. Experience always remains trapped in its own spatio-temporality.

Kant's own theory of laughter works at a psychological level, when it is not being downright physiological: laughter is generated by an element of nonsensicality, something distinctly displeasing to Kant's personified Understanding. It is the sudden transformation of an expectation into nothing which gets the Understanding's goat, whereupon the body takes over and starts vibrating violently.... Notably, however, Kant's own phrasing may be interpreted as betraying an awareness of the interaction of the two levels of masks. Kant's definition, after all, does not refer to the sudden transformation of an expectation into its *opposite*, but into *nothing*. This point should not be overemphasized, for Kant himself did not capitalize "*nichts*": he used the word as an indefinite pronoun, not as some vague substantive abstraction. Nevertheless, Kant's terminology was seized upon by the post-Kantian aesthetics of Bouterwek, who saw the risible nonsensicality as the product of a "logisches Null."[17] Just as Ritter was to see the comic as proclaiming the existence of that which is defined negatively, Bouterwek's point is that the disconcerting appearance of something that is not something can only be accommodated by laughter. Whereas sensible discourse refers to the "real world," nonsense refers to nothing or to "nothing"—or at least to nothing sensible.

The upshot of all this is that the cognitive mask can conveniently be regarded as two-tiered, comprising both a conceptual level and a perceptual level, just as the ethical mask was seen to present itself either as a mask of decorum hiding the "natural" or as a mask of normality hiding the "unnatural," and just as the social actor proved to constitute both the mask that he *wears* (at times) and the mask, or sequence of masks, that he *is* (always). In all three cases, the latter mask is at a certain level impregnable and can best be understood as hiding nothing/"nothing."

If comic play and comic lawlessness are regarded as imitating or symbolizing the unfathomability of the world, then it is evident that they can quickly take on a theological significance. William F. Lynch, S.J., interprets the comic in such a manner, seeing it as going "below all the categories within which the most of life is spent" and enabling us to penetrate through "the surfaces and the forms of things (to) their true being which is also an incredible non-being." Comedy seems to move towards some formless ontological essence *beyond* man, according to Father Lynch, a realm that can most fittingly be described negatively and is compatible with the chaotic perspective of the comic fool, but the sworn enemy of what he calls the "univocal mind."[18]

Outside the theatre, the traditional conception of "magic" has been intrinsically associated with the arcane workings of a hidden divinity, and events that appear to occur without cause tend to be viewed as supernatural. Indeed, the nineteenth-century British pantomime, characterized as it was by a whole complex of gadgets, props, and traps that could "do the impossible," frequently employed these devices not only for transformations and timely exits during the harlequinade, but also to conjure the surprise presence of a supernatural agent. The mystical belief that drawing back the veil of *Maya* and experiencing a break in the chain of causation exposes an entity only accessible to intuition would of course take a critical battering at the hands of the supremely sober Kant, for whom the whole business would be the work of a noumenal nothing getting too big for its boots. Nevertheless, as shown by the comic fool who is *nobody* because he is *everybody*, being nothing is just another way of being everything.

Of course, this negativity can equally become linked with diabolic or satanic imagery, as is the case for example with the romantic grotesque, which presented a terrifying devil and generated threateningly infernal laughter.[19] This ambivalence (which corresponds to the unresolvable tension between static and dynamic conceptions of the absolute) is a necessary constituent of our relationship to radical otherness. Ruskin, aware of the interplay of the ludicrous and the fearful in the grotesque, comments upon this tension between horror and sublimity, maintaining that "if the objects of horror in which the terrible grotesque finds its materials were contemplated in their true light, and with the entire energy of the soul, they would cease to be grotesque, and become altogether sublime."[20] An excess of the ludicrous or playful, however, results in a type of grotesque classified not as "terrible" but as "sportive," which in its more noble forms may be an "elaborate and luscious form of nonsense," but is liable to degenerate into an "artistical pottage, composed of nymphs, cupids, and satyrs, with shreddings of heads and paws of meek wild beasts, and nondescript vegetables."[21] The visions pervading the ignoble grotesque are warped by the decay and dissolution that goes hand in hand with sin. Baffling our cognitive faculties in their attempts to classify or categorize, such grotesqueries represent things that can best be described as "non-things," perched unsteadily on the boundary between form and soupy formlessness. In the visual arts of the Reformation, monstrosities of this order indeed came to designate not only fallen souls in general but the Devil himself. This is exemplified by Erhard Schön's portrait of "Der Teufel mit der Sackpfeife" (1535), in which a diabolically reptilian nonshape—sporting a lasciviously leering one-eyed physiognomy in the region where his genitals might otherwise have been expected—is depicted as using the head of a (Lutheran) cleric as something akin to a bagpipe. As Harpham's study of the grotesque puts it: "The quality of grotesqueness arises not so much from the specific contents of the image as from the fact that it refuses to be taken in whole because it embodies a confusion of type. If we did not have the word *devil*, a category which ... serves as a storage-place for demonic non-things, we would have no word for it at all."[22]

Describing the Nondescript

The comic glimpse of nonevents, as of nonthings, is likely, therefore, to strike us as distinctly frightening. A rupture in the chain of causality in everyday surroundings (suppose my slab of homemade fudge spontaneously combusts) will disconcert rather than amuse us. If our attempt to invent a fiction of causality to explain it away remains unsuccessful, if we are unable to rationalize the irrationality out of existence (I never was very good at cooking anyway), then we shall be forced either to question our sanity (I must be mad, I shouldn't have eaten those mushrooms) or to attribute the event to a supernatural "cause"—that is, a noncause. This is an unnerving option, to say the least. Schopenhauer describes the *Grausen* (horror or dread) that may take hold of a person when he or she begins to realize the depths of frightening unfathomability from which one is only separated by the reassuring mask of individuation with its ordered compartmentalizations and differentiations. This feeling comes upon its victims "when some [*irgendein*] chance happening calls the principle of individuation into question by seeming to constitute an exception to the principle of sufficient reason in one or other [*irgendein*] of its forms: for example, when some [*irgendein*] change seems to take place without cause, or a dead person come back to life, or in some other way [*sonst irgendwie*] the past or future seems to be present or the faraway near."[23] Schopenhauer betrays that he is dealing with an area beyond the reach of philosophy and of experience in general by sprinkling his account with a glut of indefinite adjectives and adverbs (*irgendein, irgendwie*). Indeed, he cannot really know what he is talking about.

Transposed into the safety of the theatre, displaced into a play context, however, the fear or horror generated by the irrational can be overcome in the guise of laughter. Nietzsche interprets Aristophanic comedy, a brand of comedy in which flights of fancy recurrently disrupt any sense of causal order, as functioning in this manner: "The comic as the artistic discharge from the nausea of the absurd."[24] Laughter here serves as the response to or as a release from a nasty bout of the existential butterflies. The irrationality that evokes *Grausen* in Schopenhauer is not so far removed from what Freud terms the uncanny (*das Unheimliche*). Suggesting a variety of causes for this sense of the uncanny, including excessive repetition, a breakthrough of residual animism (normally suppressed social irrationalism) or a return of infantile sexual complexes, Freud points out that much of what is uncanny in life is not so in literature and concludes his essay by specifying how the uncanny is processed into comedy by means of ironic distance in the works of Nestroy and Wilde. It is an exposure of what is normally hidden that may give such an impression of uncanniness, as Freud's citation of Schelling illustrates: "We call uncanny everything which was supposed to stay in secrecy, in concealment, in latency, and has emerged."[25] Structurally analogous, the uncanny and the comic diverge in that in life one is at the mercy of repetition and the irrational, whereas the comic artist, like the theatrical spectator, is able to use *distance* to process and control those forces normally hidden or repressed.

The irrational may thus be primarily refreshing in its effect, especially if it turns up in the milder, less threatening form of the merely unhabitual. Incongruous juxtapositions and unusual or unexpected happenings may engender a healthy renewal of perspective, a reawakening of the imagination, without necessarily entailing the traumatic horror associated with more oppressively inexplicable irrationality. How Madius, and following his lead Descartes, found a basis for laughter in *admiratio* or wonder springing from *novitas* or novelty has already been considered. This century, the Russian formalist Schlovsky has maintained that art itself ruptures the mask of habitual perception, brushing aside the smoke screen of automaticity that stultifies daily life. By the technique of *ostranenie*, which presents things dissociated from their habitual context, art defamiliarizes them, and thereby makes the stone stony again.[26] Schlovsky indeed characterizes this as a capturing of the Becoming of a thing, while

Brecht—whose *Verfremdungseffekt* may be regarded as a stepchild of *ostranenie*—understood it as a means of throwing into question the causality of events.[27] When art has in its turn become automatic, moreover, parody moves in and defamiliarizes *it* by toying with and exposing narrative habits normally taken for granted. Beckett, a master of the inexplicable, portrays the phenomenon of defamiliarization in a way that couples the idea of habit and the mask metaphor: "When (the object) appears independent of any general notion and detached from the sanity of a cause, isolated and inexplicable ..., then and only then may it be a source of enchantment. Unfortunately Habit has laid its veto on this form of perception, its action being precisely to hide the essence—the Idea—of the object in the haze of conception/pre-conception."[28] Causal habit masks or conceals the way things "really" are.

As implied by Madius's "*admiratio*" and Beckett's "enchantment," irrationality—particularly in its more patently nonsensical manifestations—is more than a therapeutic renewal, it is also a release. In *Über Wahrheit und Lüge*, Nietzsche depicts art and fantasy as an intellectual saturnalia, a joyful period of freedom for the intellect from its slavish subordination to truthfulness and rationality, an opportunity for it to mix its metaphors, muck about with concepts, try its hand at forbidden patterns of thought. *Menschliches, Allzumenschliches* contains a paragraph that is even clearer on the matter. The joy of nonsense, writes Nietzsche, "frees us momentarily from the constraints of necessity, expediency, and conformity with experience, in which we usually see our inexorable masters. We play and laugh whenever our expectations (which normally keep us anxious and tense) are exploded without any harm being done. It is the joy of the slave at the saturnalia."[29] Nonsense and the irrational create a sort of epistemologically topsy-turvy world: normally slaves to deterministic causality and logical necessity, we are granted a carnivalesque period of mastery in which our fantasy carries the day over the relentless predictability of the world. Schopenhauer too sees the incongruity ensuing from a disparity between concept and percept as a jubilantly inversive triumph of intuition or concrete immediacy over the tyranny of reason, intuition indeed being the primary of the cognitive faculties but as a rule subdued by the dictates of rational order. "This victory won by intuitive knowledge over thought gives us pleasure.... The sight of this strict, unremittingly taxing pedant Reason for once being found wanting is therefore bound to be a source of delight to us. The countenance of laughter is consequently very closely related to that of joy."[30] Mind you, the reign of the intellect in Schopenhauer is illusory at the best of times: elsewhere he stresses repeatedly that the intellect is in fact but an unfortunate servant of the domineering (but blind) will. In this sense, incongruity is truthful in the way it throws light on the inadequacies and unmasks the pretensions of reason.

Of course, one need not go to the theatre for a dose of such irrationality: it can all be staged within the head. The break in the binding chain of causality, which gives rise to *Grausen* in Schopenhauer, has a markedly different effect on the seemingly sovereign rationality of Kant, who lays greater weight on the negative character of the thing-in-itself and for whom any particular wayward perception does not intimate the existence of a whole new realm behind the epistemological curtain, but is demoted to the rank of subjective illusion, a mere "Spiel der Vorstellungen" or play of images.[31] Kant incidentally uses the same term to designate those mental chimera which move him to laughter.[32] If it is not a subjective fancy, he might of course be dreaming.[33]

The world of the dream is a world of unreason and absurdity that—when not threatening—can indeed frequently take a turn for the comic. Moreover, the Freudian model points up a whole gamut of analogies with the *Witz*: the dream constitutes a parallel processing of the unknowable energies of the unconscious for a start, and the dream-work (*Traumarbeit*) that does this processing is distinctly similar to the joke-work (*Witzarbeit*) that performs a comparable service in presenting our unconscious drives in a socially acceptable guise. The technique of condensation (*Verdichtung*) is common to both, for example, with the consequence not only that dreams are on occasions very witty in their exploitation of uncharted verbal resources of polysemy and homophony,[34] but also that they generate a graphic equivalent of the pun—the grotesque. In this instance, visual forms are fused and merged by means of a condensation of those features they have in common, the resultant grotesquery being a single form that—like the pun—has two or more significations at once. Freud refers to this as overdetermination:[35] each element of the dream content signifies a *plurality* of diverse material from among the latent psychic ingredients. The dreamworld is furthermore a realm where the laws of causality, logical necessity, and the excluded middle (*A* is *B* or *A* is not *B*) are blatantly infringed.

A space such as this, where irrationality and the preposterous call the tune, may also be artificially engendered, by drink or by drugs. Grotesque visions and works of comic fantasy have for this reason often been interpreted as the creations of a hallucinating fancy, just as Hoffmann's poetic grotesquery struck Baudelaire as visions of inebriety and Ruskin judged the "brutal mockery" and "insolent jest" of the Grotesque Renaissance to be "the perpetuation in stone of the ribaldries of drunkenness."[36] One of Edgar Allan Poe's most hallucinatory short stories, "The Angel of the Odd," is narrated by a figure who, for all his asseverations to the contrary, soon reveals himself to be as stoned as a gargoyle. Conversing with a bottle-shaped hallucinatory visitant ("a personage nondescript, although not altogether indescribable"[37]), he initially expresses his scepticism regarding unlikely events or singularities such as one reads in the papers, but quickly finds himself caught up in and the narrator of a whirl of improbabilities yet more ludicrous than any journalistic invention. Even his attempt to put an end to the trauma by drowning himself is sidetracked by the eccentricity of a drunken crow, who makes off with the "most indispensable portion" of his clothing:

> Postponing, therefore, for the present, my suicidal design, I just slipped my nether extremities into the sleeves of my coat, and betook myself to a pursuit of the felon with all the nimbleness which the case required and its circumstances would admit. But my evil destiny attended me still. As I ran at full speed, with my nose up in the atmosphere, and intent only upon the purloiner of my property, I suddenly perceived that my feet rested no longer upon *terra firma*; the fact is, I had thrown myself over a precipice, and should inevitably be dashed to pieces but for my good fortune in grasping the end of a long guide-rope, which depended from a passing balloon.[38]

These blatant improbabilities are of course taken by the reader to be the figment of an extremely well-oiled imagination, yet implicit thematic parallels suggest that the reader and the daydreaming drunkard may in fact be two of a kind. It is while *reading* a batch of soporific literary banality that leaves him feeling a little stupid that the narrator first looks to the bottle, and it is in a newspaper that he comes across the initial unlikelihood against which he bridles. To the extent that the reader dismisses as fictions the alcohol-induced improbabilities that are to follow, therefore, he adopts the sceptical position originally held by the inebriate who denies or is ignorant of his inebriation. Yet while the sceptical reader corresponds to the sort of drunkard who—like the narrator at the outset—refuses to believe in his fictive visitations, the gullible reader who suspends disbelief in the catalogue of unlikelihood, by contrast, shares the perspective of the drunken narrator once he is carried away by his fantasies. Either way, it appears, the folly of drunkenness (and of reading) has been subtly relativized and perhaps implicitly universalized. The issue is complicated by a parallel blur between dream and waking:

> My dreams were terrifically disturbed by visions of the Angel of the Odd. Methought he stood at the foot of the couch, drew aside the curtains, and, in the hollow, detestable tones of a rum puncheon, menaced me with the bitterest vengeance for the contempt with which I had treated him. He concluded a long harangue by taking off his funnel-cap, inserting the tube into my gullet, and thus deluging me with an ocean of Kirschwasser, which he poured in a continuous flood from one of the longnecked bottles that stood him instead of an

arm. My agony was at length insufferable, and I awoke just in time to perceive that a rat had run off with the lighted candle from the stand.[39]

Drunken dreams, dreams about drunkenness, and dreams about drunken dreams (etc.) merge into a boozy artistical pottage. Dreaming or awake, drunken or sober, reading or drinking, knowledge about the truth-value of one's perceptions seems out of the question: the witness of an unlikelihood can never ultimately be sure whether he is confronted with a dream, a drunken delusion, a narrative fiction, or simply the unfathomability of the world.

Comedy is perhaps made to sound more exciting than it actually is by the Nietzschean claim that drama in general has its (logical? chronological?) roots in the *Rausch* or intoxication of Dionysian celebration, the ritual frenzy in which the mask of Apollonian individuation, discontinuity, and moderation is ripped off and the boundaries of selfhood and existence transcended in an orgiastic swell of dissolution. Yet radical alterity of vision does seem to be common to both (certain sorts of) intoxication and (certain sorts of) surreal or grotesque comedy. Oscar Wilde describes the effects of absinthe in terms that link the frightening and the funny:

> After the first glass, you see things as you wish they were. After the second, you see things as they are not. Finally you see things as they really are, and that is the most horrible thing in the world ... I mean disassociated. Take a top-hat! You think you see it as it really is. But you don't, because you associate it with other things and ideas. If you had never heard of one before, and suddenly saw it alone, you'd be frightened, or laugh. That is the effect absinthe has, and that is why it drives men mad.[40]

The hallucinator sees things removed from the context that lends them a reassuringly habitual meaning (as is the case with *ostranenie*), and this—via the route of negation—is associated in Wilde's mind with a perception of things "as they really are." Absinthe-mindedness is an intuitive vision of the thing-in-itself.

This perspective validates the speculation as to whether Alice's trip into Wonderland is psychedelic in origin (Carroll himself possibly having had experience with laudanum). Alice does indeed consume some particularly mysterious potions and cakes, and who is to deny that the mushroom on top of which the Caterpillar sits smoking his hookah is in fact a magic one. The juxtaposition of incongruities that may be effected by hallucinogenics has its roots in the same bisociative potential—an ability to combine "two hitherto unrelated cognitive matrices"[41]—that Koestler judged to be essential to both punning and scientific discovery. Baudelaire illustrates the degree to which hashish can turn even the dullest of dullards into rampant punsters: "It sometimes happens that people not cut out for wordplay at all improvise endless strings of puns, highly improbable juxtapositions of ideas, enough to drive the greatest masters of this bizarre art round the bend."[42]

In *Fear and Loathing in Las Vegas*, Hunter S. Thompson's foray into the depths of hallucinatory humor—narrated in manic hyperbole—exposes once again the proximity of grotesquely distorted vision and sheer terror, here compounded by a hefty portion of paranoia ("No flowers in this town. Only carnivorous plants").[43] Given the vacillation between comedy, wonder, and naked fear generated by the acid experience, it is not surprising that, particularly in the sixties, it has often come to be associated with revelatory access to religious truth or some spiritual thing-in-itself. Thompson's revelations, however, are secular in orientation. Like Poe, he uses the experiences brought on by his cargo of "heinous chemicals" to show the sanity of the "normal" world turned on its head and to question the boundary between reason and madness. His binge of delusive folly unveils the folly of Las Vegas, as he comes to the conclusion that it is "not a good town for psychedelic drugs. Reality itself is too twisted."[44] N. F. Simpson performs a similar feat of reversal in *A Resounding Tinkle*, in which—adopting the hallucinatory perspective—he proves reality to be an illusion caused by mescalin deficiency and sanity an illusion caused by lack of alcohol. The result is an exuberant relativism: when mescalin is the rule and not the exception, mescalin deficiency is indeed a form of madness. From the perspective of the tripper, the "normal" point of view is as comic and absurd as the psychedelic vision is to the nontripper, and reality is as ludicrous as illusion is to the sane and the sober-minded.

The irrational, therefore, throws up the question whether we are drunk, dreaming, or mad. Comedy relieves us of the worry by transposing us into the realm of play and using tricks to create the impression of the impossible. This constitutes a shift from unsettling self-delusion to a context of intentional delusion that (half-)admits its delusive nature. Theatrical props, tricks, and acrobatics can thus be employed to defy the laws of physics, allowing the fool or clown to appear and disappear through floor and walls and feign the same freedom from the limitations of deterministic causality as from the bondage of social norms. In the Covent Garden pantomime of the first half of the nineteenth century, it was the figure of Harlequin who embodied this capacity to do the impossible. An exceptionally agile dancer and tumbler, he would leap through trapdoors in "solid" scenery and spring to astonishing heights under the propulsion of machinery beneath the floor. Moreover, he was empowered to perform stage magic by means of his celebrated bat, charming his pursuers or setting them helplessly dancing, and above all using his baton to transform his surroundings. These effects, seemingly spontaneous, of course had their causes backstage, being the special responsibility of the stage machinist with his hidden devices such as the "falling flap" and the "rise and sink" technique.

In the case of the falling flap, the scenery to be metamorphosed is covered with canvas flaps that, on being released, either expose what is concealed or reveal the painting on their own obverse side. A later development of this prop allowed changes from an original object to a new one and back to the old one, employing a mechanism not unlike the adjustable louvres of a venetian blind. Interestingly, in *Harlequin and Don Quixote*, this permitted the audience to witness the same apparitions as the foolish Don himself, to share his madness. As the *Morning Post* reported of the event:

> In order that the audience may enter into the wild imaginings of the Knight-errant, and understand the motives of his actions, it has been most ingeniously contrived that his fancies should be realized for a moment, and that the objects should immediately after resume their natural shape. Thus, in the adventure of the windmill, no sooner has *Don Quixote* cast his eye upon it, than it turns into an immense giant, and the flour sacks become as many distressed damsels who implore his pity. But whilst he turns to take his lance and shield, the giant resolves itself again into a windmill and the ladies into sacks.[45]

The heroic madman, of course, fails to notice any difference, and is dealt a painful thrashing at the hands-cum-sails of the mill. Using scenery designed in two parts, the "rise and sink" technique involved whisking the upper part into the oblivion of the flies and at equally considerable speeds dropping the lower portions through slots (known as slotes) into the cellarage. One such "rise and sink" transformation, for example, changed Pantaloon's postchaise posthaste into a lumbering wheelbarrow, whipping the top part into the flies and sinking the bottom into the cellar to reveal the wheelbarrow behind.[46] In addition to these magical devices, the excitement of the harlequinade or chase (Pantaloon or Clown in pursuit of Harlequin and Columbine) was augmented by a whole array of traps, such as the "star trap," which projected the actor through the stage floor as if from nowhere (or "Nowhere"?), and the "vampire trap," which snapped to after he had flung himself through it, as if he had passed through a solid object.[47]

In the world of cinema, Harpo Marx proves himself in the same tradition, when he produces from within his tatty coat a series of cups of coffee, a feather, an axe, a stuffed moosehead, a range of flags, and a four-course meal.[48] The camera indeed has an even greater potential than the

stage for lying, a fact exploited by the French film pioneer, Georges Mé-
liès, who used techniques of superimposition and reversal to play with the
flow of time and create a surreal world in which heads can be inflated and
then deflated, and where causality can be made to work backwards.
Forms and figures are distorted and transformed with cheekily subversive disrespect for order and stasis, as exemplified by *Le Brahmane et
le Papillon* (1901), in which a randy brahman, having transformed a
giant caterpillar into a butterfly-fairy, is himself then metamorphosed
into a creepy-crawly before he has had a chance to realize his ulterior
motives.[49]

Irrationality and the impossible may furthermore be displaced into the
realm of the written or spoken word, here constituting a verbal rather
than a visual incongruity.[50] The nonsense world of Alice with its rocking-
horse-flies, snap-dragon-flies, and bread-and-butter-flies epitomizes such
verbal surrealism, Tenniel's illustrations guiding us in the visualization of
this fantasy, although he does run into difficulties with the depiction of
the Cheshire-Cat's grin (without the cat). On such occasions, verbal
magic shows a conceptual sleight of hand that leaves our faculty for visual
reproduction straggling, for such nonsense in the end really does refer to
nothing but nothing. This applies, moreover, not only to the sort of grotesque formations found in Wonderland and through the looking-glass,
but also to the unalloyed gibberish characteristic of Edward Lear, who
wrote a letter to a friend that ended "Okul scratchabibblebongibo, viddle
squibble tog-a-tog, ferrymoyassity amsky flamsky ramsky damsky crockle-
fether squiggs" and was signed "Flinkywisty pomm—Slushypipp."[51]
Even where the syntactical structure of the sentence is slightly more in
evidence, as in such propositions as "the gostak distims the doshes,"[52]
the words that apparently function as nouns still make no actualized or
specific reference to the "real" world—and consequently *could* mean
anything. Another category of nonsense, typified by semantic contradiction of the kind found in Chomsky's celebrated example "Colourless
green ideas sleep furiously," also draws attention to its own properties as
language, both semantic and phonological, yet without finally pretending
to "refer" to anything other than itself, for the contradictions and illog-
icalities that leap out at us at the same time thwart any attempts at definite or definitive visualization. The abstract noun *Nothing*—which also
refers to nothing—can itself constitute a special kind of nonsense peculiar
to waxings philosophical.

The world of nonsense in Wonderland and through the looking-glass is
a highly ordered nonsense, resulting as it so often does from the following
of an illogical premiss to its logical conclusion. In his muddle-mindedness,
the White King for example responds to a bout of faintness by eating a
bagful of hay:

Alice was glad to see that it revived him a good deal. "There's nothing like eating hay when you're faint," he remarked to her, as he munched away.

"I should think throwing cold water over you would be better," Alice suggested: "—or some sal-volatile."

"I didn't say there was nothing *better*," the King replied. "I said there was nothing *like* it." Which Alice did not venture to deny.[53]

The logic seems perfectly reasonable at first sight:

1. There's nothing like hay for faintness.
2. The King wishes to put an end to a spell of faintness.
3. The King eats hay.

The premiss, however, proves to have been misunderstood, both by Alice and (in all probability) by the reader. Understood "correctly" (in the literal sense meant by the King), the logic breaks down, and the King can be said to be behaving absurdly or irrationally. Shakespeare's *Love's Labour's Lost* offers similarly logical illogicality in a snippet of dialogue between Berowne and Costard:

> *Berowne.* Stay, slave. I must employ thee.
> As thou wilt win my favour, good my knave,
> Do one thing for me that I shall entreat.
> *Costard.* When would you have it done, sir?
> *Berowne.* This afternoon.
> *Costard.* Well, I will do it, sir. Fare you well.
> *Berowne.* Thou knowest not what it is.
> *Costard.* I shall know, sir, when I have done it.
> *Berowne.* Why, villain, thou must know first.
> *Costard.* I will come to your worship tomorrow morning.
> *Berowne.* It must be done this afternoon.
>
> (Act 3, scene 1)

A superficial mask of logic, which glides sneakily from the fact that Costard will know what the chore is after he has done it to the assumption that he need therefore not be told beforehand, conceals an antilogic that will allow Costard to get away without having to put himself out for Berowne. If he has not been told what he has to do, after all, he cannot be expected to do it. Costard's antilogic thus also incorporates the inexorable logic of cheeky disobedience and good old-fashioned laziness. His faulty reasoning is thoroughly rational.

It was to do justice to this inevitable interplay of reason and unreason, logic and illogicality, sanity and madness, that von Hartmann amended Kant's comment about the laughter caused by nonsense (*Widersinn*) to point out that a remnant of sense always shines forth from the comic nonsense. Santayana makes a parallel remark with respect to the form-lessness of the grotesque, which can never be absolute: "If this confusion is absolute, the object is simply null; it does not exist aesthetically, except by virtue of its materials. But if the confusion is not absolute, and we have an inkling of the unity and character in the midst of the strangeness of the form, then we have the grotesque. It is the half-formed, the per-plexed, and the suggestively monstrous."[54] The comic breach in the scaffolding of logic or in the chain of causality can only function as a *symbol* for the purely chaotic, a synecdochic part for the unfathomable hole, that utterly theoretical or theological Nothing. The most irrational and disorderly aesthetic events assume a rational, social meaning because of their context, and even the garbled warblings of the Dadaists inad-vertently acquire a significance as art through their self-stylization as anti-art, just as Lear's gibberish both parodies normal communication and gains a meaning and a beauty of its own in its phonological immediacy.

While normal, functional discourse—proud possessor of a single un-equivocal meaning—gives the illusion of direct access to an unambiguous Truth (being presumed to be true unless it paradoxically proclaims itself otherwise), neither nonsense nor gibberish pretend to be transparent. Instead they comically direct attention towards *themselves* as phenomena, as conceptual or material "masks" that exist insofar as they appear in their own right, but are only contingently or arbitrarily attached to any specific semantic content seen as sited "behind" the mask. One may have to search for the sense within nonsense, or it may hit one in the eye, but it is impossible to take it for granted in the way that everyday language al-lows and encourages. Referring to the comic writers of Modernism (Joyce, Faulkner, Stevens, and Beckett), moreover, it has been written that the "comedians of language want to make us aware of the wrongness of language, its comically stumbling attempts to contain the flow of real-ity, and at the same time make us aware of the ability of language, through the acknowledgement of its wrongness, to achieve an expression of reality that could not otherwise be achieved."[55] Although such authors may tend to see language as masking or distorting a fluid and dynamic reality (as conceived—under the influence of Schopenhauer—by Berg-son), it may equally be claimed that self-referential language, like other forms of nonsense, in referring to nothing except itself exposes that be-neath the mask of language lies—Nothing. This applies not only to gib-berish and semantic self-contradiction, but also to the compulsive self-referentiality of the *nouveau roman*, which can be summed up in the nonsensically or paradoxically self-referential proposition "This sentence is a lie/fiction." Utterly vacuous in referential terms, this statement pre-sents itself instead as a conceptual grotesquery that forbids access to any truth except the half-truth of its own opacity.

This verbal opacity comes to light in the surreal litany of similes Rabelais has Xenomanes use in his depiction of Quaresmeprenant or Lent.[56] This huge list moves from the internal organs (his brain, for example, being like a male fleshworm's left bollock, his mammillary attachments like a big shoe, his pineal gland like a bagpipe, his palate like a mitten, his pylorus like a pitchfork, his spermatic vessels like puff-pastries, his colon like a goblet), via his mental attributes (his memory being like a game-bag, his common sense like a bumble-bee, his intelligence like slugs emerging from strawberries,...), to his external organs (his member being like a slipper, his testicle-muscles like a tennis-racket, his beard like a lantern, his tongue like a harp, his optic nerves like a tinder-box, ...), and on to his amazing bodily processes (if he spat, it was basketfuls of artichokes; if he blew his nose, it was salted eels; if he belched, it was oysters in their shells; if he farted, it was brown leather boots; if he slobbered, it was communal ovens,...). The pleasure of this enumeration derives from a verbal ebullience and an incantatory repetitiveness that has its origins in carnivalesque procession. Its gratuitous nonsensicality and utter inconceivability turn Quaresmeprenant into a purely lexical construct. In mimetic terms, he has absolutely no shape at all, instead comprising mere emptiness or absence, windy nothingness. By exposing its own fictive nature, such language by implication unmasks the illusionism of normal discursive fiction (which consists in pretending not to be a fiction). Refusing to permit that *enargeia* which gives the reader the delusion of being a spectator at a visually definite or definable scene,[57] it spotlights *itself* as a verbal phenomenon.

If such comic nonsense operates by drawing attention to itself as language, causality can have an analogous effect when it becomes obtrusive and excessively predictable, a patterned accumulation developing a surreality of its own. This is causality focusing upon its own excesses, just as the verbal repetition of the Rabelaisian litany seems to revel in its sheer superfluity. While on the one hand yielding the reassuring satisfaction of predictability, the mask of identity and repetition distorts itself into a grotesque self-parody. Buster Keaton's comedy frequently exemplifies such surreal exaggeration. In *Seven Chances* (1925), the film comes to a frenetic climax in which Buster (seeking a wife) is pursued first by one bride, then two, then a handful, before being run all over town by a vast mob of rampaging women in white. This snowball effect is then displaced into the nearby countryside where what starts off as a solitary stone pushed downhill in Buster's direction turns into a monumental barrage of boulders bearing down on him. In the marvellous short film *Cops* (1922), Buster is put to flight by a rampant pack of gormless policemen; in *Go West* (1925) it is a herd of cattle who overrun the town, while in *Steamboat Bill Jr.* (1928), Buster's acrobatic genius manifests itself in a hyperbolic cyclone scene that takes on the quality of nightmarish distortion (except it is too funny).

Even before Keaton's *Cops*, cinematic history had exploited the comedy of the mad chase in the celebrated figures of Mack Sennett's Keystone Kops, who whizzed around with a manic energy, hurtling headlong into one another, yet bouncing apart unhurt. The pantomime of the early nineteenth century had likewise taken special pleasure in introducing the newly formed ranks of the blue-coated Metropolitan Police force into the mayhem of the harlequinade, generating the satisfyingly retributive comedy of mauling and deriding the prototypical boys in blue. Like their cinematic successors, these upholders of the law chase about the place like deranged puppets and are shown to be purely mechanical, uncomprehending in their anonymity, and stunningly brainless, a perpetuation of an anti-authoritarian comic tradition that plays on the dullness of squires and magistrates and is indeed traceable back to Shakespeare and beyond. With the pace speeded up to forty-two frames per second in the filmic madness of the Keystone Kops, however, a frenzied paranormality could be created in which these human chains of cops in pursuit would fly through the film like a pack of very fast truncheon-wielding dominoes, before colliding and piling up in a blurred heap of uniforms and bodies.

A distinction has been drawn between contingent and necessary causality, which might go some way towards explaining this phenomenon. Whereas strict determinism posits a necessary chain of causal determination, this view may be modified to permit the possibility of mutually independent chains of causation, each in itself strictly determined but not necessarily interdetermined. An "accident" results at the confluence of two or more such independent causal chains, and this is the point at which the Keystone Kops meet their downfall. Whether such "contingent determinism" is philosophically coherent or not, it is certainly more helpful in describing the way things *seem*, the pileup of peelers being an intersection or conjunction of two autonomously moving chains, be these regarded as human chains or chains of causation. Causality here *draws attention* to itself as causality, for each chain displays an obtrusive inevitability that often simultaneously moves in the direction of the surreal. Yet the comic effect also springs from a different source: the overview of the spectator observing from a position of elevated distance. If the contingency of the collision is but the appearance or the way things seem to the finite participant caught up in the immediacy of his own chain of causation, the superior knowledge of the aesthetic onlooker enables him to perceive the underlying necessity determining events in "reality." The onlooker can see that two marauding chains of constabulary causation are doomed to crash (say, round the corner of a house), just as the laughing gods enjoy privileged access to a vision of the fatalistically determined order of events. It is the gloating superiority of the ironic perspective.

Ionesco's antitheatrical comedy is not only a parody and an explosion of linguistic and dogmatic bondage, it also mockingly shatters the laws of physics. Dominated by an overriding sense of the habit the human mind has of using cliché, ideological dogma, and logical order to mask the tragic absurdity of a meaningless world, his comedy exposes the senseless ontological disarray that normally remains comfortingly concealed. Just as the surreal cinematic madness of Buster Keaton and of the Keystone Kops had taken the causal chain ad absurdum, Ionesco parodies causality by excessive accumulation and repetition, using linguistic patterns in *La Cantatrice chauve*, proliferating chairs in *Les Chaises*, and a contagious epidemic of people turning into rhinoceroses in *Rhinocéros*. In conjunction with this, absurd breaches in causality parody the laws of physics by blatantly infringing them. In *La Cantatrice chauve*, the clock typifies this tendency with its absolute randomness and unpredictability (soon becoming predictably unpredictable), striking seven, followed by three, followed by two-one, followed by twenty-nine, ... The parody of causality even merges into a parody of the laws of inductive reasoning. Having twice answered the doorbell to find nobody there, Madame Smith is reluctant to go a third time and only yields unwillingly to the argumentation of Monsieur Smith:

> *M. Smith.* Whenever *I* visit anyone, I ring the doorbell to go in. I think that everybody does likewise and that every time the doorbell rings it's because there's someone there.
>
> *Mme. Smith.* That's true in theory. But in reality things happen differently, as you saw just now.
>
> . . . .
>
> Well, I'll go and have a look. You can't say I'm pig-headed, but you'll see there's nobody there. (*She goes and opens the door, then closes it again*). You see, nobody there.
>
> . . . .
>
> *The doorbell rings again.*
>
> *M. Smith.* Listen, the doorbell. There must be somebody there.
>
> *Mme. Smith.* (*in a fit of anger*) Don't make me go and open the door again. You've seen it doesn't do any good. Experience teaches us that whenever we hear the doorbell ring, it's because there's nobody there.
>
> (Scene 7)

When the fourth ring of the doorbell is followed by the entrance of a fireman searching for a fire or domestic calamity to give him something to do, Madame Smith maintains that only the first three cases are valid for inductive reasoning, while the fireman himself ventures the more cautious conclusion that when there is a ring at the door, sometimes there is somebody there—and sometimes nobody.

Beckett too creates effects whereby the completely inexplicable may shock, surprise, or startle the onlooker into laughter, as is the case with the spontaneous combustion of Winnie's parasol in *Happy Days*. Influenced by the claim attributed to Democritus that nothing is more real than nothing, Beckett portrays his characters vainly striving to fill in the existential nothingness with habit, cliché, and language, but the combustion of the parasol confounds such measures, nothingness as it were blowing its own ontological trumpet. The "deeper" truth of such comedy is that the world is disordered, chaotic, and meaningless, and it is only a fiction of the human mind if it seems otherwise.

Starting with Jarry at the turn of the century, himself inspired by the absurdity of Grabbe writing in Germany eighty years earlier, a major strand of twentieth-century comedy has exploited the inexplicable, the irrational, and the absurd. Quite apart from Beckett and Ionesco, the Italian futurist Marinetti, himself the creator of an Ubuesque play *Le Roi Bombance* (1905), produced an articulate plea for a spectacularly "shocking" form of theatre in his manifesto *Il Teatro di Varietà* (1913). Beside audience participation, anti-academic primitivism, an "ironical decomposition" of hackneyed conceptual prototypes, freedom from all tradition, and a coupling of erotic stimulation with the devastating deflation of idealized love, this theatrical blueprint advocates the destruction of "all our conceptions of perspective, proportion, time and space."[58] In the manifesto *La cinematografia futurista* (1916), he proposes a variety of comically absurd tricks and fantasies, visualizing (for example) an oversize nose imposing silence upon a thousand congressional fingers by the ringing of an ear, while two policemen's moustaches arrest a tooth. Such fantasy clearly dissociates its objects from the habitual context that makes them familiar and unworthy of further attention. Whether considered amusing, fantastic, disturbing, refreshing, or merely silly (and a waste of time and space), the theatre and the cinema as Marinetti imagines them are remarkable in their transgression of both moral and spatio-temporal bounds. Indeed, it is not so far from his grotesque impossibilities to the surreal cartoons of Terry Gilliam, which frame and punctuate *Monty Python's Flying Circus* with cheerfully dismembered limbs and animated objects that concertina through space and time and blow a protracted raspberry at the laws of physics. Because of its flexibility, the cartoon seems to be an ideal medium for such madness: very silly, but very, very funny. Shortly after Marinetti's programmatic proposals, Apollinaire was likewise being very silly in *Les Mamelles de Tirésias*, designated a "surrealist drama," in which Thérèse spontaneously grows a beard and discards her breasts as she turns into a man. In this world without temporal logic not only does Thérèse's husband succeed in having 40,049 babies in one day, but these babies—even as they lie there squealing—have already led active and fulfilling lives (one, for example, having written a best-seller).

In the surreal world where objects can fly about without any respect for causal law and order, the theory propounded by Schelling is perhaps of relevance. Starting from the assumption that comedy consists in "the upturning of every possible relationship based upon opposition," he posits that the highest comedy involves the reversal of the relationship of necessity and freedom. Whereas normally it is the object that is determined by necessity and the (human) subject who is essentially free, in comedy the subject appears bound by the laws of necessity (perhaps owing to the predictability caused by self-deception or monomanic inflexibility), while the inanimate object seems free to whirl about in a world of lawless liberty.[59] Auden describes one of his categories of comic contradiction in strikingly similar terms: "The operation of physical laws upon inorganic objects associated with a human being in such a way that it is they who appear to be acting from personal volition and their owner who appears to be the passive thing."[60] As with Schelling, it is an inversion in the relationship between human subject and nonhuman object that is being depicted: the subject has as it were become an object and the object a subject. Auden gives the example of a man and an umbrella that, as if off its own bat, blows inside out. This may be perceived, of course, as a reversal not just in the subject-object relationship, but also in the concomitant master-servant hierarchy. Whereas it is usually the case that the subject is master and the inanimate object at his or her beck and call, in comedy the object proves recalcitrant, and perhaps even carries the day. Emerson's short essay on "The Comic" presents a comparable situation: "It affects us oddly ... to see things turned upside-down, or to see a man in a high wind run after his hat, which is always droll. The relation of the parties is inverted—hat being for the moment master, the bystanders cheering the hat." In these situations, according to Emerson, "the majesty of man is violated. He, whom all things should serve, serves some one of his own tools."[61] A world in which objects are given free rein is a variation on the topsy-turvy world. Causal anarchy calls into question the sovereignty of the cognitive subject.

Of course, the irrational and acausal need not be restricted to the inanimate. Unmotivated, nonfunctional conduct in human beings may strike us as a sort of psychological breach in causation, even if it can always be presumed to have some underlying physiological cause—or a hidden psychological one. The "silly walks" of the *Monty Python* team (John Cleese, Graham Chapman, Eric Idle, Terry Jones, Michael Palin) typify the phenomenon of utterly imbecilic nonfunctionality. At the sight of John Cleese's legs going shooting off at virtually impossible angles (and they do seem to be all over the place), it is not only our expectations regarding what natural circumstances cause people to do that go for a burton, but the mask of behavioral normality that permits us, as a rule, to anticipate rationality or utility in what people do. In addition, the pin-striped suits and bowler hats worn by the ranks of the silly walkers re-inforce the *appearance* of sanity and social conventionality in order to make the break with the norm all the more comically obtrusive. *At Last the 1948 Show*, in which the pre-Pythonesque sixties silliness of Cleese and Chapman joined with Tim Brooke-Taylor (future Goody) and Marty Feldman, produced a comparable scene of pin-striped, bowler-hatted barminess in the sketch "Let's Speak English." Four city gents are sitting formally around a table:

> *No. 1.* I am a chartered accountant.
> *No. 2.* I am a chartered accountant.
> *No. 3.* I am a chartered accountant.
> *No. 4.* I am a gorilla.
> *No. 1.* The teapot is on the trolley.
> *No. 2.* The teapot is on the trolley.
> *No. 3.* The teapot is on the trolley.
> > *No. 4 gets to his feet, picks up trolley and places it on the table, smashing teacups ad lib.*
> *No. 4.* The trolley is on the table—and it goes through the window.[62]

Number four proceeds to bung the trolley through the window, pour tea over the other three, and then thoroughly demolish the place, before taking his seat again. Number one wonders about becoming a gorilla as well.

It is perhaps possible to distinguish those phenomena which seem to arise without having been caused from other aspects of the surreal such as the grotesque, the incongruous, or the fantastic, the former playing specifically with the concept of temporal order, the latter playing with other kinds of conceptual order. A parallel may illustrate the proximity as well as the difference implicit in the distinction. Just as time is frequently conceived as unilinear in form, for it has only one dimension (or *is* only one dimension) and a seemingly irreversible direction, so language too—especially speech, its traditionally privileged manifestation—can be vi-sualized as a temporal or unilinear succession of units of meaning or of sound. While play with causation constitutes a break in the unilinearity whereby only one event can occur at one place at any one time or one cause can only have one effect, metaphors, puns, and iconographic gro-tesques that signify two things at once likewise amount to breaches in the (illusion of) discursive unilinearity which would have it that only one thing can be signified at a time.

In the case of metaphors, it is indeed only the element of identity or similarity, the area of common semantic ground *shared* by tenor and vehicle (or "figurative" and "literal" meaning), that makes positive cognition or re-cognition possible (whereas for puns it is often just a phonological yoke that pulls the disparate components together). The metaphorical proposition "the man was a lion" has a cognitive value only as long as the two metaphorically related components are regarded as sharing some semantic attribute such as bravery. If I were to venture the more abstruse claim that my goldfish was a dustbin lid, for example, or a can of baked beans, the unearthing of a common property would clearly be much less likely (though not impossible—they might smell similar or have a comparable color). Taken literally, the propositions are absurd, for the components linked together are *different*, and it is in this respect— taken literally—that the propositions may start to be viewed as surreal or fantastic (in their resistence to *enargeia*). Alice's bread-and-butter-fly is a grotesque pun formation, whose composition depends upon the tenuity of the *butter* morpheme shared by bread-and-butter and butterfly, while the difference between the two terms, their incongruity and incompatibility, places the invention emphatically in the realm of nonsense. The bread-and-butter-fly is a verbal equivalent to the iconographic grotesque, a mixed formation that is *both* bread-and-butter *and* butterfly, and therefore neither, and therefore nothing. When Buster Keaton, doing a spot of underwater repair work in *The Navigator*, takes advantage of a passing swordfish to have a swordfish-fight, the surreality is of the same order. The swordfish is both a sword and a fish. Taking a pun literally, Buster enacts its visual equivalent.

The "transformation" scenes springing from Harlequin's bat in nineteenth-century pantomime have likewise been described as unearthing "visual similes,"[63] disclosing a concealed or latent likeness between the initial object and the product of the metamorphosis and thereby making possible a recognition of similarity or similitude within difference. The transformation of a group of judges or magistrates into a gaggle of cackling old women, for example, is not mere chaotic disorderliness, but intimates a satiric barb directed both at the magistrates in question and at magistrates in general (or, alternatively, at old women in general). Even more than Harlequin, however, it was the role of Clown, so irreplaceably occupied by Grimaldi, that came to embody the inventive fertility of the visual simile, for Clown was a perpetual practitioner of practical puns and ad hoc improvizations. Mayer explains the principle:

> Unlike Harlequin's trickwork, which required backcloths or built-up pieces abruptly transformed at the slap of his bat, Clown's visual similes were elaborate 'tricks of construction.' A trick of construction was based on the same assumption which permitted Harlequin's tricks, that one object shared a hidden

kinship with another, and that it was the job of the pantomime comic to reveal this relationship. The trick of construction, however, began in a different manner, frequently with the theft of what first appeared to be a hodgepodge of items. Gradually, as the stolen and borrowed articles pile up, Clown would begin to arrange or assemble them into some kind of order: a grotesque human form, a carriage, a travesty of a military uniform, a sailing vessel, an outlandish animal. Frequently, as Clown stood back to admire his creation, Harlequin would surreptitiously animate it, terrifying the astounded Clown.[64]

One example sees Clown as a recruiting sergeant in vain search of victims. Helping himself to pots, barrels, and jars, the archetypal practical punster arranges them to resemble soldiers in file, whom he then puts through their drill—before being frightened out of his wits when they spring to life and march off. Another of the best-loved tricks of construction entailed Clown dressing the corpse of Pantaloon in the bodily parts of a motley jumble of animals, creating a beast known as a "Nondescript" (although not altogether indescribable). This animal—consisting of all animals—ends up a nonanimal, a type of absurd nonthing not so far removed from the devils of the Reformation and the Renaissance ragout of "nondescript" vegetables and miscellaneous bodily members. It is popular enough to live on in such pantomime variations as the "cameleopard"—another portmanteau animal comprising a camel and a leopard, but, by a nice etymological quirk, perhaps coming closest to a chameleon in its mercurial nondescriptness.

The greater the degree of difference between two unsuspecting concepts, the greater the effect of incongruous or fantastic surreality obtained by brutally yoking them together verbally or visually. It is for this reason that André Breton elevates boldness of metaphor to the forefront of the surrealist enterprise, writing in *Les Vases communicants* (1932): "Comparing two objects as remote from one another as is possible or by any other method bringing them together in a sudden and striking way, this remains the highest task to which poetry can aspire.... The stronger the element of immediate dissimilarity seems to be, the more it should be overcome and denied."[65] The temerity of the surreal metaphor verges on madness or hallucinating drunkenness. While the factor of *identity* yields the reassuring pleasure of cognition, of recognition (viz., "getting the joke"), it is the incompatible *difference* that takes the compound in the direction of unknowability and nonexistence. Quaresmeprenant, we are told, has a spleen like a quail-decoy, saliva like a shuttle, a bladder like a catapult (and the neck of which is like a bell's clapper), an abdomen like an Albanian's hat; his sperm is like a hundred small nails, his deliberations like a sack of barley, his volition three nuts on a plate, his feet guitars, his navel a fiddle, and if he yawned, it was pots of chickpeas,...[66] The two components of the myriad of similes used to describe him as a rule have nothing in common, so it is impossible to say anything positive about Quaresmeprenant's spleen, bladder, abdomen, sperm, etc. Just as we cannot really give a definitive form to our visualizations of a snapdragon-fly or a swordfish-fight, Quaresmeprenant is ultimately a grotesque nothing, a verbal monstrosity. Much of the comic pleasure consists in trying to picture these absurdities, or—in the visually more explicit cinematic medium—in watching Buster Keaton's concretization of the impossible. An analogous effect is achieved in nonsensical jokes of the "elephant" variety: how do you get four elephants in a mini? Easy, two in the front, two in the back.

It was Aristophanes who created some of the most celebrated fantasies within the comic tradition—visions of the world in which dung beetles can ascend to the gods and the birds can assume their rightful position of sovereignty over man and god alike. This sense of fantasy and freedom led the German romantic Friedrich Schlegel—in his enthusiasm for the Old Comedy—to the insight that causal consistency is much too cumbersome for Aristophanic ebullience with its transcendence of all the barriers, bonds and boundaries of normal life: "Complete causal coherence, inner dramatic necessity and unity are far too ponderous for a light and diverting rush of inebriation."[67] It was doubtless this same Aristophanic *Rausch*, even if less light and frothy and more deeply Dionysian, that prompted Nietzsche to forgive Hellenic culture its (Socratic) sins on account of having produced an Aristophanes.[68] As Dürrenmatt puts it, Aristophanic *Einfall* (fancy) transforms the world into a comedy, while begetting a magical poetry of the theatre and "a higher transparency of things"[69] only paralleled (in his opinion) by the likes of Nestroy in recent centuries. *Lumpazivagabundus*, with its magical frame, exemplifies this realm of comic enchantment dreamt up by Nestroy.

In the case of Aristophanes, however, the dreamlike quality is enhanced by glaring inconsistencies and contradictions within the plays themselves, which run their course with jaunty indifference to the laws of physics and psychology. Proponents of verisimilar coherence in drama would here level charges of "unconvincingness" or "failures of structure," rather than attribute these unlikelihoods to the ingenious ways of a surreal fantasy. In *Lysistrata*, for example, the wives of Athens go on sex-strike to dissuade their husbands from their military preoccupations. Yet what difference would this make if all the men were away at war anyway? Aristophanes shows the men reduced to walking erections in a matter of days, yet conveniently leaves out of account all the boys, men, and *het-airai* who could have lent a hand in this time of crisis. Not that these points ultimately matter. Such inconsistencies can be explained by the fact that—by contrast with Plautine comedy—comedy of the Aristophanic stamp is primarily *episodic*, seeking to exploit the comic potential of a given situation or miniplot, rather than build up the framework of an ordered comic plot in its organic entirety, a plot based on intrigue and deception and reliant upon a higher level of psychological verisimilitude. But if an episodic structure, coupled with authorial sloppiness, may end up spawning one kind of unrealistic effect, the Plautine comedy of intrigue that has developed since Old Comedy may well produce another, for an excess of contrived machinations and manipulations of plot can also function as a *parody* of causality. The extravagant coincidences and chance encounters characteristic of the comedy of intrigue can thus be understood, like the Keystone Kops, as a confluence of disparate causal chains (i.e., separate linear plot developments), but as a rule without the apparent inevitability of the Kops' collisions. Inordinate intrigue and arbitrarily orchestrated coincidence—which lends itself so easily to parody—tends merely to seem too far-fetched to be true. One German critic has described this tendency as visibly taking the principle of causality ad absurdum.[70] Although much comedy does indeed imply that there is an order in the way of the world, an overdose of order may quickly turn into a parody of order.

Excessive flukes—bumping into one's father and one's twin independently after twenty years of separation following a shipwreck that left all its survivors in the mistaken belief that everybody else had been drowned—are frequently part of the happy ending and therefore linked less with a sudden and obtrusively startling breach in causality than with a general aura of unreality, the "holiday humor" which has over the years been a prerequisite for a certain type of festival comedy. This comic unreality constitutes a transposition of reality into a play context where the laws of nature can be surreptitiously circumvented—provided this is done in the name of a happy ending. The "guarantee" of a happy ending means we are free to laugh at short-term mishaps because our aesthetic overview assures us that all the inextricably knotted strands of discrete causation are directed towards a single point of convergence that will also be a denouement (for only when all the strands have been brought together can they be unraveled).

A somewhat different order of comic unreality is engendered by the comic giants' tales featuring such figures as Finn (in Irish legend) and Rabelais's Gargantua and Pantagruel. When we read tall stories like those of Gargantua, who accidently eats six pilgrims in a salad, or of the narrator of *Pantagruel*, who spends six months exploring his protagonist's mouth, in this time discovering twenty-five inhabited kingdoms there (a theme taken up by *At Last the 1948 Show*, where a dentist clambers into his patient's mouth to blast out a molar but encounters the objections of a band of Welsh miners situated in the throat[71]), it is likely that, while enjoying the flight of fancy as an escape from the bondage of normal spatial proportion, we simultaneously reject it as a mere fiction or illusion. In part at least, such laughter is a sign that we know better, that we are not taken in by the deception and can see through the fictive lies. What emerges is a tension between a suspension of disbelief which allows us comic release from the bonds of reason on the wings of Rabelais's soaring imagination, and the sceptical satisfaction of refusing credence, keeping our rationally down-to-earth feet on the ground. Just as moral transgression often requires an aesthetic frame in order to become comic, so logical and rational transgression is most likely to be comic if it can also—if need be—be recognized as an escape. Distance and identification again hover in equilibrium.

An appreciation of grotesque shapes and figures thus tends to be accompanied by an awareness of their impossibility and the enjoyment of nonsense attended by an implicit acceptance of its nonsensical status. When nonsense is believed (as is more often the case with children), it functions less as comedy than as a scene of wonderment and rapture, a Wonderland like the one Alice wanders and wonders through. The comedy of the faulty logic permeating Alice's adventures requires an acknowledgement both of its internal consistency (its rightness) and of its flawed premiss (its wrongness). The episode of the Cheshire Cat's grin, for example, which continues to be visible after the rest of the cat has disappeared, is based on the faulty assumption that any word functioning as a noun must have a concrete thing of which it is the signifier. So is the Red Queen's claim that if a dog loses its temper, then wanders off, the temper remains. Once this common philosophical fallacy (the fallacy of reification) is accepted, the episodes have a perfectly acceptable internal logic of their own. The same applies to the Mad Hatter's assertion that Alice must be on bad terms with Time because she beats it when she learns music. The comic effect of such nonsense is based not merely on a retreat into irrationality, but also—in the midst of the madness—a rediscovery of rationality in the internal logic.

In his writings on the ridiculous, Schopenhauer describes this category of comic nonsense or absurdity in terms of the concept/percept distinction already encountered, the conceptually tenable proving to be impossible to perceive or intuit. Talking about a grin that outlasts its face, for example, does not obviously infringe any grammatical structure, but it simply cannot be pictured. We cannot know how it would look. Schopenhauer himself offers a rather wordy explanation of the adventures of Münchhausen as

> impossible (actions), presented to the audience as having really taken place. In these cases, of course, the facts are clothed in such a fashion that when thought in the abstract, and thus comparatively a priori, they appear possible and plausible; but afterwards, when it comes to the intuition (*Anschauung*) of the in-

dividual case, that is a posteriori, the impossibility of the matter and the absurdity of its postulation come to the fore and provoke laughter on account of
the conspicuous incongruity between what is intuited and what is thought.[72]

Schopenhauer cites Münchhausen's claim to have used a frozen stream of
his own urine, solidified in midflow, as a rope to reappropriate the dagger
he had dropped when chased up a tree by an aggressive bear, and the
Rabelaisian tale of musical notes frozen into a horn and then defrosting,
as well as the traditional anecdote of two lions who eat one another up
until only their tails remain. He could just as easily have mentioned the
episode where Münchhausen pulls himself and his horse out of a quagmire—by his own hair. All of these are palpable impossibilities that we
do not believe, transparent lies that do not fool us ... or do they?

Just as Rabelais's narrator repeatedly assures his readers of his utter
truthfulness (wishing epilepsy, leg-ulcers, and dysentry upon those who
doubt him), and Poe's drunken narrator constantly denies or plays down
his inebriation (viz., "the very few glasses of Lafitte which I had sipped"),
Münchhausen too goes to remarkable lengths to convince us of the veracity of his tales, attacking the mendacity of a rival raconteur and relating
with overzealous approval the fate of two crooks strung up by their legs
for spinning yarns. The narratorial claim that one is not lying (or not
drunk or not mad) subtly complicates the tension between scornful disbelief and a willing suspension of disbelief. On one level, it functions as a
straightforward asseveration of truth (encouraging the reader to sit back,
as it were, forget any doubts, and enjoy the story). On another level,
however, the protestations themselves alert our attention to the *possibility* of falsehood, by implication comically turning the reader's gullibility
into a theme of the fiction. The proposition "I am not lying" is tantamount to an assertion "But I might be ...," a playful pretence of seriousness that is at the same time an admission of playfulness, rather like
the stand-up comedian's "No, seriously...." At this stage, we are
launched back towards the liar's paradox with all its logical and epistemological convolutions.

The ethical ambivalence of narratorial lying, which is both condemned
and seen through as falsehood and celebrated as a manifestation of man's
creative faculty, is echoed in the ambivalent truth-status of fiction itself.
Fiction indeed may be regarded as something akin to a mutually acknowledged half-lie, typified by the liar's paradox which confesses its own
falsehood and by the anti-illusionistic comic drama which spotlights the
techniques of its own illusionism. The comedy of impossibility may in
turn itself contribute to the devices and tricks of anti-illusionism and
metatheatre. When a stage event occurs without an apparent cause,

therefore, this generally functions less as a breach in the spectator's own "ontological" illusion than—because of the dramatic context—as a breach in the theatrical illusion. Theatrical impossibilities consequently tend to present themselves not as real impossibilities, but as stage stratagems or illusions that the spectator is lucky enough to recognize as such, or "see through." The unsettling aspect of the irrational in real life, where we lack the overview that permits us to explain it away as a trick of the props, is in the theatre diluted into comedy. The theatre of Bertolt Brecht, for example, makes explicit use of the capacity of fantasy to rupture the dramatic illusion.[73] In *Der Gute Mensch von Sezuan*, the ludicrous descent of the gods on their garish pink stage-prop clouds serves as a biting parody of the *deus ex machina* (both the prop and the underlying theological notion), at one and the same time disrupting the theatrical illusion and exposing that the "unfathomable" gods themselves are but the chimerical figments of a theatrical imagination. At the end of the play, battered and humiliated, they gratefully return to their native Nothingness.

Nonsensical and absurd theatre is in this way inextricably bound up with antitheatre, with theatre that admits its playfulness rather than pretend its illusion is reality. The following is part of a plot dreamt up for a drama by Mollfels in Grabbe's *Scherz*:

> The masses weep, the bells toll, the Princess laments as if she were already in the very clutches of the Devil, and everything crashes in utter desperation from the stage. Hereupon Ossian enters and eats a sandwich. When he has finished, the scene is transformed into the reception-chamber of the imperial palace.... In one corner of the chamber are two hoses which are thoroughly incensed with one another and on the point of poisoning themselves for sheer gall; nearby hangs a plush doublet leafing through an encyclopaedia and drinking a cup of tea. Meanwhile, however, a hypochondriacal brush bent on vengeance is prowling around and making bloodthirsty gestures.
>
> (Act 2, scene 4)

A dramatic offering to the Goddess of Boredom, this play (although only narrated, not enacted) anticipates the loopy excesses of the surrealists by a hundred years and functions as a parody both of the orderly run-of-the-mill course of the world in general and of theatrical convention and more specifically the play within which it stands as a sort of "play"-within-a-play.

Tieck's *Kater*, a play pervaded by metatheatrical wit, exemplifies the links in a different way: in the play-within-the-play in which Puss appears, the human attributes of the tomcat annihilate any chance of a reasonable illusionism, as indeed is pointed out by a confused and disconcerted spectator. Another onlooker is left wondering whether he is dreaming, drunk, or mad. Like Grabbe's Devil, Puss possesses an incongruous double identity as both puss and person (a kind of grotesque or walking pun). He eats, talks, wears boots, and is quick-witted, and Gottlieb on one occasion inadvertently refers to him as a man; yet he is furry, has a taste for nightingale and, when the play disintegrates into dramatic disorder, he springs up an adjacent pillar with feline agility. This human/cat duality conveniently corresponds to an actor/character or real/fictive duality, however, Puss at one level coming over as simply a puss, while at another level striking us as *really* being a man acting a puss. The tension between belief and disbelief regarding the dramatic illusion thus parallels the tension in the audience's attitude to the causal and conceptual order. That all this takes place at one remove and both play and audience are internalized within the "real" play, does not alter the basic configuration: instead it draws even more bamboozled attention to the problematic interaction of spectator, illusion, and reality.

Bottoms Up

Tieck's playful fusion of theatrical levels—as when Hanswurst asks the public what they think of the play and the public respond that there *is* no public in the play—is a logical impossibility, a sophisticated conceptual grotesquery and one that Tieck explores in still more detail in *Die Verkehrte Welt*, where the characters swap theatrical levels with blithe disregard for verisimilitude. The play is an unparalleled rejection of dramatic illusion, causality, consistency, and coherence, prefiguring Jarry's *Ubu* cycle in its sheer dramatic chaos. The particularly Ubuesque naval battle between Pantaloon and Harlequin typifies the manner in which anti-illusionism comes to coincide with breaches in causation, when the soldiers "swimming" about in the "water" suddenly stand upright and walk to shore: walking on water is a piece of piss when the water exposes itself as a stage prop. Actors join the spectators, spectators become actors, and when Skaramuz gets into difficulties in the fiasco of a finale, the audience intervenes in the pell-mell to ensure an ending to their taste. The actor-audience reversal epitomizes Tieck's topsy-turviness, creating an overriding impression that the characters, in both the play and the play-within-the-play, have escaped the control of the playwright and are roaming about in a realm of fictional anarchy. Yet the traditional motif of the world-upside-down is also briefly touched upon, manifest in the rebellion of the sheep who want to shear the shepherds and the declaration of Skaramuz (playing Apollo) that under his rule children need no longer respect their parents.

These two topsy-turvy configurations are but two of many such motifs that have their origins in a range of "World Upside Down" broadsheets popular in the late Middle Ages. The connection between comedy and reversal is one we have repeatedly stumbled across in this chapter and elsewhere, be it a reversal in the relationship between master and servant, subject and object, or actor and audience or a transposition considered in terms of conceptual primacy, social power, or spatial, temporal, or volitional position. If topsy-turviness can be viewed as a subcategory of the grotesque or nonsensical in its displacement of the chaotic or the soupily inconceivable into form or structure, it is a displacement that involves the generation of a new, inverted order and consequently gives the onlooker or reader the comic satisfaction of recognizing a new set of patterns. Yet just as the "political" inversion of master and slave or servant implicitly reveals the arbitrary distribution of social roles condemning one person to subservience and one to dominance, so the "perceptual" or "conceptual" inversion of expected patterns may be interpreted as betraying the arbitrariness of our cognitive mask.

A comprehensive example of the organizational logic of the topsy-turvy world is provided by the Venetian broadsheet of *Il Mondo alla Riversa* from the 1560s, which in a sequence of illustrations depicts: a cart going before its horse, an ass washing its master's head, a sheep shearing a shepherd, ladies following a servant, a horse driving a man, women making war, ships traveling on land, a husband spinning while the wife is armed, son beating father (with the aid of mother), a patient examining his doctor, a gypsy having his fortune told by his client, a gentleman serving animals at table, a peasant ordering his master to hoe, an inverted globe, a peasant contradicting a sage, old men playing with childish toys, a child instructing his elders, land animals being hunted in the sea, seed being sown in the waters, airborn fish attacking birds in the sea, fish living on land and in the sea, mouse chasing cat, crow attacking falcon, hare eagle, chicken fox, goat lion, an ox with a lyre serenading an ass, an ass riding a miller, a donkey driving a laden master, an ox driving men at a plough, an ox slaughtering a butcher, and a peasant riding horseback while the king walks.[74] As David Kunzle has shown, the most common categories of inversion are those involving the relationship of human to human (master to servant, husband to wife, child to father), human to animal (miller to ass, butcher to ox), animal to animal (cat to mouse, eagle to hare), or of animal to element (as when fish take to land, birds to water). In addition to these may be found rarer inversions between animal and object (horse before cart), object and object (a tower placed inside a bell), and human and object (anvil hitting a smith), together with a general category of miscellaneous absurdities and incongruities that do not strictly speaking involve hierarchical inversions but that fill up the broadsheets with nonsensical fantasy (animals depicted in incongruous human activity).[75] Again, social and political reversals emerge as analogous to a perceptual surreality that plays with (and reorganizes) the order of the world.

One type of reversal to which the iconographic comedy of the broadsheets does not have access is *temporal* reversal, an inversion in the unilinearity of causal order that reorganizes its elements into a new, back-to-front form, rather like a diachronic jigsaw puzzle taken apart and put back together the wrong way around. The comedy is normally dependent upon a recognition of its aberrant relationship to the original or conventional order. Tieck's *Verkehrte Welt*, for example, starts with its epilogue ("Now, gentlemen, how did you like our play?") and concludes with its prologue ("You are about to see a play here"), the topsy-turvy world once more combining with metatheatrical (self-) parody. Alice too comes across varying degrees of temporal reversal. In Wonderland, where the laws of causality or of sufficient reason are perhaps best summed up by the March Hare's "Why not?" in response to Alice's "Why?," the temporal order is by and large forward moving, apart from the Red Queen's hysterical proteron "Sentence first—verdict afterwards."[76] The temporal preposterousness is more consistent through the looking-glass, although here too it is patchy. One particular patch of backwardness occurs before the White Queen has pricked her finger:

> ... the Queen began screaming, so loud that [Alice] had to leave the sentence unfinished. "Oh, oh, oh!" shouted the Queen, shaking her hand about as if she wanted to shake it off. "My finger's bleeding! Oh, oh, oh, oh!"
>
> Her screams were so exactly like the whistle of a steam-engine, that Alice had to hold both her hands over her ears.
>
> "What *is* the matter?" she said, as soon as there was a chance of making herself heard. "Have you pricked your finger?"
>
> "I haven't pricked it *yet*," the Queen said, "but I soon shall—oh, oh, oh!"
>
> "When do you expect to do it?" Alice asked, feeling very much inclined to laugh.
>
> "When I fasten my shawl again," the poor Queen groaned out: "the brooch will come undone directly. Oh, oh!" As she said the words the brooch flew open, and the Queen clutched wildly at it, and tried to clasp it again.
>
> "Take care!" cried Alice. "You're holding it all crooked!" And she caught at the brooch; but it was too late: the pin had slipped, and the Queen had pricked her finger.
>
> "That accounts for the bleeding, you see," she said to Alice with a smile. "Now you understand the way things happen here."
>
> "But why don't you scream *now*?" Alice asked, holding her hands ready to put over her ears again.
>
> "Why, I've done all the screaming already," said the Queen. "What would be the good of having it all over again?"[77]

Notably, however, although the White Queen screams *before* she has pricked herself, the act of pricking proceeds in the normal temporal direction, so the effect is not truly one of watching a film run backwards. Moreover, despite describing herself as "living backwards," her memory works in both directions, not just forward.

The temporal reversal is (at times) linked with a type of volitional reversal, as a result of which willing something produces the contrary effect, as when Alice on one occasion sets off towards the Red Queen and promptly loses sight of her. In the company of the Red Queen, Alice has to run herself breathless just to reach a destination they arrived at ten minutes ago, the Queen explaining that "it takes all the running *you* can do, to keep in the same place."[78] It has been pointed out that the looking-glass presents a world that is strictly predetermined, Alice's role having been planned in advance.[79] Such predestination makes the White Queen's knowledge of the future logically possible, and the fact that Alice has to run at full pace just to stay in the same place can be viewed as a signal of volitional impotence in the face of the predestined course of events. This conjunction of determinism and volitional helplessness is equally prevalent in Martin Amis's *Time's Arrow*, where the entire sequence of narrated events runs backwards from end to beginning:

> Oh, the disgusted look on women's faces as they step backwards through a doorway, out of the rain. Never watching where they are going, the people move through something prearranged, armed with lies. They're always looking forward to going places they've just come back from, or regretting doing things they haven't yet done. They say hello when they mean goodbye.[80]

Of course, the narrative "thought" obligingly moves in our direction: it has to, for all thought—the reader's as much as the narrator's—is dependent upon and a symptom of the forward flight of time's arrow. Yet even this need not be taken as an inconsistency, for the narrative is written not oral, and—as the narrator points out—writing, like art, seems to transcend time's arrow in a way not accessible to speech. Its static nature lends it an essential timelessness.

In the novel's first half especially, Amis's topsy-turvy narrative brilliance is above all comical, the reader enjoying the recognitive pleasure of unearthing sense in the nonsense, unraveling and identifying daily motions set in reverse gear:

> Is it just me, or is this a weird way to carry on? All life, for instance, all sustenance, all meaning (and a good deal of money) issues from a single household appliance: the toilet handle. At the end of the day, before my coffee, in I go. And there it is already: that humiliating *warm* smell. I lower my pants and make

with the magic handle. Suddenly it's all there, complete with toilet paper, which you use and then deftly wind back on to the roll. Later, you pull up your pants and wait for the pain to go away.... Then the two cups of decaff before you hit the sack.[81]

The temporal reversal further produces a topsy-turvy world of inverted values in which giving becomes taking, falling becomes rising, breaking mending, and destroying creating. We witness "[a] child's breathless wailing calmed by the firm slap of the father's hand, a dead ant revived by the careless press of a passing sole, a wounded finger healed and sealed by the knife's blade."[82] Pimps are the good guys, while doctors massacre people, and as for cabs:

They're always there when you need one, even in the rain or when the theatres are closing. They pay you up front, no questions asked. They always know where you're going. They're great. No wonder we stand there, for hours on end, waving goodbye, or saluting—saluting this fine service. The streets are full of people with their arms raised, drenched and weary, thanking the yellow cabs. Just the one hitch: they're always taking me places where I don't want to go.[83]

Taking us back to the protagonist's wartime activities, however, the second half of the novel consists in an eerily gruesome modulation on the topsy-turvy theme, one that stifles the comic force of narrative reversal. Here it is the "unreversed" reality that is upside-down, for the holocaust with which the reader is confronted is in itself the most frighteningly apocalyptic *mundus inversus* imaginable.

Auden elucidates the comedy of temporal reversal in a way that sheds additional light on its connection with volitional reversal: "When a film is run backwards, reversing the historical succession of events, the flow of volition is likewise reversed and proceeds from the object to the subject. What was originally the action of a man taking off his coat becomes the action of a coat putting itself on a man."[84] Such volitional reversal is an inversion in the relationship (or hierarchy) of (willing) subject and (willed) object—that epistemological equivalent of the master-slave configuration—and is clearly, from the common sense point of view, utter nonsense. The reversal of subject and object in their *grammatical* capacities produces an even more whimsical effect in the Hans Sachs ditty, adapted by Grimmelshausen in *Teutscher Michel*, that tells of a village that sat in a peasant, this peasant being in the habit of using a breadroll to eat his milk and spoon and harnessing four carts to his horse. As for his place of abode, his kitchen was situated in the hearth and his corner had four houses.[85] This verbal topsy-turvying of subject and object hides conceptual impossibility beneath its plausible grammatical inversions, taking the motif of the world-upside-down even further into the realm of inconceivability.

The borderline between the social or political aspect of topsy-turvydom and its fantastic or nonsense element is necessarily rather indistinct and has undergone shifts in accordance with context-specific historical factors that affect the extent to which its readers wish to imagine the possibility of social change or to escape into a fantasized sphere of impossibility. As the world-upside-down broadsheets developed over the years, for example, they became more dominated by the element of surreality which in the Middle Ages had played a marginal role, maximum incongruity coming to replace actual reversals during the course of the eighteenth and nineteenth centuries.[86] Pigs read newspapers, horses play chess, elephants thresh corn, and castles hover in midair, as the motif moves back in the direction of the αδυνατα or *impossibilia*, the sequence of impossibilities imagined by Virgil and the ancients.[87]

At the beginning of this century, however, Jarry's *Ubu Enchaîné* represents a remarkable combination of social and perceptual inversions in a deluge of topsy-turvy nonsense. In this play, Ubu decides to become a slave in order to wield his tyranny, at one swoop transforming his domain into a comic dominion where the slaves do the commanding. Having been on the receiving end of a standard Ubuesque beating, Ubu judges this to be a *rise* in his social status, and, while in prison, he is hailed as king by an English tourist, three free men, and his fellow convicts. This is a world in which the army corporal has to say the opposite of what he means in order to have his wishes carried out, where soldiers are required to be systematically disobedient, and where the laws of physics are so inconsequential that nail scissors can be used (for example) to cut open Mère Ubu's ball and chain. A topsy-turvy revolt is the play's climactic lowpoint, perpetrated by the masters and free men, all of whom demand the right to become slaves. It results in a mad search for balls and chains to wear, the air reverberating with cries of "Long live servitude!" Ubu is threatened with freedom, but fortunately manages to escape as a convict.

Just as nonsense may either be celebrated as a flight from the tyranny of reason or mocked as a deviation from the order of sense and truth, so the motif of the world-upside-down contains an intrinsic ambiguity that has a number of facets. Laurel and Hardy's film *Saps at Sea* shows sporadic glimpses of topsy-turviness that are comic for their structured nonsensicality. These function, by and large, as episodic gags existing with relative autonomy from the rest of the proceedings, flashes of madness that startle the onlooker into laughter. Witness the wash-basin from which water comes out of the right tap if you turn on the left one and the left tap if you turn on the right one, or the flat where the fridge plays music if you open the door, but the radio is frozen over. Yet the fantasy of a world-upside-down, when the focus of a more consistent thematic attention, may also come to be equated with a utopian vision of the way things might be or might have been, a land of pure possibility. Virgil's pastoral poetry, for example, presented the imagined attributes of a bucolic Arcadia where lamb and lion live in harmony and the soil needs no harrowing. Impossible juxtapositions symbolize a now unknowable or unrealizable social condition, a cultural thing-in-itself defined by its difference from the way the world actually is. As with Aristophanes, who created topsy-turvy societies with women on top or birds in the ascendant, the impossible inversions merge with festive fantasies, cornucopian dreamlands of peace and perpetual revelry. Influenced by the broadsheets, Johann Ulrich von König's play *Die Verkehrte Welt*, which predates Tieck's version by over a hundred years, incorporates the theme to proffer what amounts to a criticism of contemporary moral and literary conventions, presenting the "topsy-turvy" world as in fact the world the right way up. It is a world, for example, in which the protagonists Harlekin and Skaramuz bump into a female doctor who—madness of madnesses!—treats her patients according to the dictates of nature and experience rather than rely upon the fusty charlatanry of books. The apparently topsy-turvy utopian vision thus satirizes the genuinely topsy-turvy reality by showing an alternative to throw into relief the folly of things as they are.

Christian Weise's *Lustspiel von der Verkehrten Welt* (1683) is also evidently influenced by the broadsheets, presenting sheep wanting to shear their shepherd, a miller carrying his ass, a child rocking his grandfather in the cradle, pupils teaching their master, and a patient drugging his doctor. Yet Weise's satire of the way of the contemporary world is launched from a perspective diametrically opposed to König's in that the inverted world he depicts is in fact presented as a satiric *per*version of the way things should be, a deviation from the social norms that ought to carry the day. The biblical association of turning the world on its head with wickedness and sin (viz., Psalms 146:9, Isaiah 24) is perpetuated in the message of such topsy-turvy conservatism, which—founded upon a complacent acceptance of the ruling order—functions along the lines: beat your wife and kids, or they'll beat you,... In the satirical songs of the *Carmina burana*, the topsy-turvy motif is also used as a means of satirizing the real world, portraying it as a crass deviation from the desirable (normal, traditional) order, the way things *used* to be. Here, however, it is moral implications rather than principles of control that are brought to the fore. Upended by the corrupting force of money, this *mundus inversus* is a world where the rich are poor, the truth false (no. 3), folly is eloquent, sweetness is bitter, the worthless is expensive, the lame can jump, and the

deaf can hear (no. 11). Inversion even characterizes the relationship between appearance and reality. Not only is what *is* the opposite of what
ought to be, the way things *seem* is also the opposite of the way things *are*.
In a sinful world where all are masked, and society's turpitude is concealed behind a veil of virtue, the satiric poems of the *Carmina burana*
assume the function of unmasking such hypocritical vice:

> While honey drips down from their lips, in their heart gall lies;
> Not everything is honey that appears in honey's guise.
> . . . .
> While virtue's always on the tongue, in the act is sin;
> Behind a snow-white cloak they hide a pitch-back soul within.
>
> (no. 42)

In this satirical function the world-upside-down is a grotesque caricature
of reality rather than a yearning dream of unreality. It is not far from
satirically distortive visions of a negatively judged reality to dystopian
fantasy. One such poem written by Theophile de Viau in the sixteenth
century was to influence the surrealists:

> This stream runs back up to its source . . .
> The sun has become a black dot,
> The moon, I see, is going to fall,
> This tree has moved from the spot[88]

The broadsheets themselves at times display a dystopian or grotesquely
unsettling aspect, typified by the image of the pig slicing open the
butcher, and topsy-turvy figures are even incorporated into apocalyptic
fantasies on the principle that the end of the world would witness everything turned on its head: if you can't keep control of your wife and kids
(it might be inferred) then we are all doomed!

All in all, a number of possibilities come to light. If the *mundus inversus* is taken as representing the real world, then it tends to be distorted
by caricature and by implication defined as perverse. Alternatively it may
be presented as fantasy and understood as a utopian ideal that, although
appearing to our corrupt vision in the guise of an inverted world, is in fact
an inversion of a perverted reality and thus an inversion of an inversion.
Or again, it may take on the aura of a negative or dystopian fantasy, an
inversion and perversion of a reality itself regarded as relatively stable
and desirable. Whether positive, negative, or hovering between in an
area of ethical neutrality or indeterminacy like the nonsensical flights of
fancy that are primarily escapist, such visionary creations demonstrate
that the existing order need not be permanent. With regard to the
broadsheets, which tend to be grotesque rather than utopian, David

Kunzle describes the ambivalence in the following terms: "The essential ambivalence of the (world-upside-down) permits, according to circumstances, those satisfied with the existing or traditional social order to see the theme as a mockery of the idea of changing that order round, and, at the same time, those dissatisfied with that order to see the theme as mocking it in its present, perverted state. But the discontented have another alternative—to see the (world-upside-down) as a promise of revenge."[89]

Just as the Cretan liar's paradoxical proposition that all Cretans are liars implicitly undermines its own veracity, the "deeper" truth of such topsy-turvy comedy is perhaps, therefore, the paradoxical one that there is no "deeper" truth, that the "deeper" truth is a windy absence. If comedy recurrently shows that the slave is a master and that freedom is a sort of slavery—that good is bad and vice can be a type of virtue—then freedom and bondage, good and evil, become a matter of perspective: the question of whether the world is upside-down or not depends on which way up *we* are. The possibility of seeing a world that is not distorted by our own perspective, by the prismatic mask that shapes and structures our cognition, is a utopian dream, and utopia—as its etymology betrays—is a no-place, a theoretical or theological nowhere that can best be pictured as peopled with Nobodies like Panurge, Falstaff, and Harlequin, and Nondescripts like Quaresmeprenant, the cameleopard, and the bread-and-butterfly.

Notes

These endnotes contain all secondary and theoretical sources, together with all primary ones except references to drama and poetry. In the case of drama and poetry, I have wherever possible given act and scene numbers or line numbers within the text itself. Where the play is not so divided, notes are used. In the case of novels, where I felt it would be helpful, I have supplemented the notes with volume and chapter numbers. Translations are mine, except where otherwise indicated.

Introduction

1. Theodor Lipps, quoted in Otto Rommel,"Die wissenschaftlichen Bemühungen um die Analyse des Komischen," in *Wesen und Formen des Komischen im Drama*, ed. R. Grimm and K. L. Berghahn (Darmstadt: Wiss. Buchges., 1975), 20.
2. Oliver Goldsmith, "An Essay on the Theatre; or a Comparison between Laughing and Sentimental Comedy" (1773), in *The Collected Works of Oliver Goldsmith*, 5 vols., ed. A. Friedman (Oxford: Clarendon Press, 1966), 3:212. Voltaire uses similar phrasing in his article "Art Dramatique" in the *Dictionnaire philosophique*.
3. Laurent Joubert, *Traité du Ris* (1579; Geneva: Slatkine Reprints, 1973), 42.
4. Helmuth Plessner, "Lachen und Weinen," in his *Philosophische Anthropologie* (Frankfurt-am-Main: S. Fischer Verlag, 1970), 126.
5. Quoted in Walter Redfern, *Puns* (Oxford: Basil Blackwell, 1984), 169.
6. Jean Paul Richter, *Vorschule der Ästhetik*, ed. J. Müller (1804; Leipzig: Felix Meiner, 1923), 99.
7. See especially essays by Jerome S. Bruner, "Nature and Uses of Immaturity" (1972), and J. Watson, "Smiling, Cooing and 'The Game'" (1972), in *Play—Its Role in Development and Evolution*, ed. J. S. Bruner, A. Jolly, and K. Sylva (Harmondsworth: Penguin, 1976), 28–64 and 268–76.
8. J. A. R. A. M. van Hooff, "A Comparative Approach to the Phylogeny of Laughter and Smiling" (1972), in *Play*, 130–39, I. Eibl-Eibesfeldt, *Grundriß der Vergleichenden Verhaltensforschung*, 6th ed. (Munich: Piper, 1980), 206–13.
9. Hans Robert Jauss, "Zum Problem der Grenzziehung zwischen dem Lächerlichen und dem Komischen," in *Das Komische*, ed. W. Preisendanz and R. Warning (Munich: Fink, 1976), 361–72.
10. See Bruner, "Nature and Uses of Immaturity"; see also K. Groos, "The Play of Man: Teasing and Love-Play" (1901), and R. Fagen,"Modelling How and Why Play Works" (1975), in *Play*, 28–64, 68–83, and 96–118.
11. Gregory Bateson, "A Theory of Play and Fantasy" (1955), in *Play*, 121.
12. Northrop Frye, *An Anatomy of Criticism* (Princeton: Princeton University Press, 1957), 68.

13. Viktor Sklovskij, *Theorie der Prosa*, trans. Gisela Drohla (Frankfurt-am-Main: Fischer Taschenbuch Verlag, 1984), 130.

14. Frye, *Anatomy of Criticism*, 46.

15. Dante, *Literary Criticism of Dante Alighieri*, trans. R. S. Haller (Lincoln: University of Nebraska Press, 1973), 100–101.

16. Jonathan Culler, *Structuralist Poetics* (London: Routledge and Kegan Paul, 1975), 136.

17. Plato, *Politicus; Philebus*, trans. H. N. Fowler (Loeb Classical Library, 1925), 337.

18. Aristotle, *The Poetics*, trans. W. Hamilton Fyfe (Loeb Classical Library, 1932), 19–21.

19. Charles Lamb, "On the Artificial Comedy of the Last Century," in his *The Works of Charles Lamb*, 12 vols., ed. W. MacDonald (London: Dent, 1905), 1:285.

20. Henri Bergson, *Le Rire* (Paris: Presses Universitaires de France, 1940), 3–4 and 103–4.

21. Quoted in Maurice Charney, *Comedy High and Low* (New York: Oxford University Press, 1978), 176.

22 Friedrich Nietzsche, *Menschliches, Allzumenschliches* in his *Werke*, ed. G. Colli and M. Montinari (Berlin: de Gruyter, 1967), 4:3:102. Plessner's gloss is cited in Otto Best, *Der Witz als Erkenntniskraft und Formprinzip* (Darmstadt: Wiss. Buchges., 1989), 105.

23. See "Introduction" to *Humour in Society: Resistance and Control*, ed. C. Powell and G. E. C. Paton (London: Macmillan, 1988), xiii–xxii.

24. Anton Zijderveld, *Humor und Gesellschaft* (Graz: Styria, 1976), 144.

25. Friedrich Schiller, *Über naive und sentimentalische Dichtung*, in his *Werke*, 45 vols., ed. Lieselotte Blumenthal and Benno von Wiese (Weimar: Bölhau, 1962–), 20:446.

26. Richard Schechner, *Between Theater and Anthropology* (Philadelphia: University of Pennsylvania Press, 1985), 302ff.

27. Ibid., 305.

28. Ibid., 296.

29. Plato, *Politicus; Philebus*, 341.

30. Ernst Robert Curtius, *Europäische Literatur und lateinisches Mittelalter* (Bern: Francke, 1948), 148–50.

31. Manfred Schmeling, *Das Spiel im Spiel* (Rheinfelden: Schäuble, 1977), 27.

32. John Barth, *The Sot-Weed Factor* (London: Panther Books, 1965), 640 (bk. 3, chap. 11).

33. The distinction between social and cognitive levels is not intended to carry any epistemological cargo, but is simply for ease of analysis.

34. Kant's important distinction between *Erscheinung* (appearance) and *Schein* (illusion) need not concern us at this stage, the significant point being that both exist in an opposition to the real. Chapter 9 of this essay, "The Cognitive Mask," will deal with the matter more thoroughly.

35. Arthur Schopenhauer, *Die Welt als Wille und Vorstellung*, in his *Sämtliche Werke*, 5 vols., ed. W. F. von Löhneysen (Frankfurt-am-Main: Suhrkamp, 1986), 2:415 and 462–66.

36. Arthur Schopenhauer, *Über die Vierfache Wurzel des Satzes vom Zureichenden Grunde*, in his *Sämtliche Werke*, 3:171.

37. G. W. F. Hegel, *Ästhetik*, 2 vols., ed. F. Bassenge (Berlin: Aufbau, 1965), 2:552.

Chapter 1. Mask and Repetition

1. C. K. Taylor and G. S. Saayman, "Play and Imitation in Dolphins" (1973), in *Play*, 241.

2. Jean Piaget, "Mastery Play" (1951), in *Play*, 166–71.

3. F. W. J. v. Schelling, *Philosophie der Kunst*, in his *Werke*, 3 vols. (Leipzig: Fritz Eckardt, 1907), 3:359–66.

4. Sigmund Freud, "Der Witz und seine Beziehung zum Unbewußten" (1905), from *Psychologische Schriften*, in his *Studienausgabe*, 10 vols., ed. A. Mitscherlich, A. Richards, and J. Strachey (Frankfurt-am-Main: S. Fischer, 1970), 4:116.

5. Frye, *Anatomy of Criticism*, 276.

6. At a political level, the words also point to the vicious circularity of despotism. From this perspective the melancholic ennui pervading the play is being parodied (as a privilege of the idle).

7. See Sigmund Freud, "Das Unheimliche" (1919), from *Psychologische Schriften*, in his *Studienausgabe*, 4:260. Freud also linked his notion of the *Unheimliche*, or the uncanny, with a repetition of what is suppressed and described the compulsion to repeat as one of the commonest symptoms of neurotic behavior.

8. W. G. Moore, *Molière: A New Criticism* (Oxford: Oxford University Press, 1949), 34–35.

9. Bergson, *Le Rire*, 22: "Les attitudes, gestes et mouvements du corps humain sont risibles dans l'exacte mesure où ce corps nous fait penser à un simple mécanique." The German theorist Schütze had earlier made the similar point that "auf der Bühne stets komisch wirke, was den Menschen zu einer Sache zu machen scheine und die Ahnung von einem Mechanismus gebe...." See Rommel, "Die wissenschaftlichen Bemühungen um die Analyse des Komischen," 10.

10. Bergson, *Le Rire*, 15.

11. Thomas Hobbes, *Leviathan*, ed. C. B. Macpherson (Harmondsworth: Penguin, 1968), 124–25.

12. Hegel, *Ästhetik*, 2.552.

13. Laurence Sterne, *The Life and Opinions of Tristram Shandy, Gentleman*, ed. Graham Petrie and with an introduction by Christopher Ricks (Harmondsworth: Penguin, 1967), 43 (vol. 1, chap. 7).

Chapter 2. Mask and Acting

1. Henry Fielding, *Completed Works*, 16 vols., ed. W. E. Henley (London: Heinemann, 1903), 1:21–22.

2. Terence Cave, *Recognitions: A Study in Poetics* (Oxford: Clarendon Press, 1988), has rigorously explored the critical odyssey undergone by the term *anagnorisis*. In my sketchy reference to the comic uses of the term, I have, of course, here ignored the many important differences between various definitions, concerning for example what exactly it is that is recognized (nominal identity, genealogical identity, intentions or motivations), who it is that is recognized (self or others), and who is doing the recognizing (characters or audience). Relevant in this context is the recognizing done by the spectator.

3. For the quotations from Donatus-Evanthius, Dionysius of Thrace, Robortello, Dryden, and Frye, see Cave, *Recognitions*, 50–51, 52, 79, 138, and 192.
4. Quoted in Giacomo Oreglia, *The Commedia dell'Arte*, trans. Lovett F. Edwards (London: Methuen, 1968), 74.
5. Nietzsche, *Menschliches, Allzumenschliches*, in his *Werke*, 4:3:186.
6. Moore, *Molière*, 39, 83, and 121. Moore's model thus assumes abnormality to be the mask and normality to be the face or underlying reality. Although an excellent model for explaining Molière, it of course overlooks the possibility that normality might just itself be a mask.
7. Jean-Paul Sartre, *L'Etre et le néant* (Paris: Gallimard, 1943), 84.
8. See Edward Erwin, "Psychoanalysis and Self-Deception," in *Perspectives on Self-Deception*, ed. Brian P. McLaughlin and Amélie Oksenberg Rorty (Berkeley: University of California Press, 1988), 228–45.
9. Ibid., 237.
10. Sartre, *L'Etre et le néant*, 95.
11. Ibid., 102.

Chapter 3. Language as a Mask

1. Martin Heidegger, *Sein und Zeit* (Tübingen: Niemeyer, 1986), 168.
2. Ibid., 252 and 255.
3. Ibid., 169.
4. Miguel de Cervantes Saavedra, *The Adventures of Don Quixote*, trans. J. M. Cohen (Harmondsworth: Penguin, 1950), 742 (pt. 2, chap. 43).
5. Friedrich Nietzsche, *Über Wahrheit und Lüge im Aussermoralischen Sinne*, in his *Werke*, 3:2:374.
6. Harold Pinter, "Writing for the Theatre," in his *Plays: One* (London: Eyre Methuen, 1976), 14–15.
7. Cyra McFadden, *The Serial* (London: Picador, 1980), 73 (chap. 19).
8. Ludwig Wittgenstein, *Philosophische Untersuchungen* (no. 38), in his *Werkausgabe*, 8 vols. (Frankfurt-am-Main: Suhrkamp, 1984), 1:260.
9. Roman Jakobson,"Closing Statement: Linguistics and Poetics" (1958), in *Style in Language*, ed. T. Sebeok (London: John Wiley and Sons, 1960), 350–77; "The poetic function projects the principle of equivalence from the axis of selection into the axis of combination. Equivalence is promoted to the constitutive device of the sequence" (358).
10. François Rabelais, *Oeuvres complètes*, ed. Guy Demerson et al. (Paris: Seuil, 1973), 92 (bk. 1, chap. 19).
11. Ibid., 466–67 and 472–74 (bk. 3, chaps. 26 and 28).
12 See Terence Cave, *The Cornucopian Text: Problems of Writing in the French Renaissance* (Oxford: Clarendon Press, 1979), 212–22.
13. Anthony Burgess, *Inside Mr. Enderby*, in his *Enderby* (Harmondsworth: Penguin, 1982), 13–16.
14. James Joyce, *Ulysses* (Harmondsworth: Penguin, 1969), 254–56.
15. James Joyce, *Finnegans Wake* (London: Faber and Faber, 1960), 183.
16. On *enargeia*, see Cave, *The Cornucopian Text*, 27–28 and 150.
17. Samuel Beckett, *Watt* (London: Picador, 1988), 27.
18. Vivian Mercier, *The Irish Comic Tradition* (London: Oxford University Press, 1962), 80.

19. Ibid., 97.

20. George E. C. Paton, "The Comedian as Portrayer of Social Morality," in Powell and Paton, eds., *Humour in Society: Resistance and Control*, 218.

21. Freud, "Der Witz und seine Beziehung zum Unbewußten," in his *Studienausgabe*, 4:25.

22. Redfern, *Puns*, 95.

23. Jakobson, "Closing Statement: Linguistics and Poetics," 370.

24. Redfern cites the distinction made by Hughes and Hammond between puns, which are "irrational, capricious, arbitrary," and play on words, which is "rational, erudite;" Redfern, *Puns*, 17.

25. Lewis Carroll, *Alice's Adventures in Wonderland and Through the Looking-Glass*, ed. Roger Lancelyn Green (Oxford: Oxford University Press, 1982), 91–92 and 100.

26. Quoted in Tony Staveacre, *Slapstick: The Illustrated Story of Knockabout Comedy* (London: Angus and Robertson, 1987), 115.

27. John Locke, *An Essay Concerning Human Understanding*, ed. P. H. Nidditch (Oxford: Clarendon Press, 1975), 156.

28. Hobbes, *Leviathan*, 135.

29. La Rochefoucauld, *Maximes et Réflexions diverses* (Paris: Gallimard, 1976), 59.

30. See Best, *Der Witz als Erkenntniskraft und Formprinzip*, 25–26, 39, 41, 64, 75, 83, and 88.

31. Ibid., 81.

32. Schopenhauer, *Die Welt als Wille und Vorstellung*, in his *Werke*, 1:107–8.

33. Ibid., 1:105.

34. G. B. Milner, "Homo Ridens: Towards a Semiotic Theory of Humor and Laughter," *Semiotica* 1, no. 5, (1972): 18.

35. Rabelais, *Oeuvres complètes*, 303 (bk. 2, chap. 21).

36. Ibid., 282 (bk. 2, chap. 16).

37. I am using the word *trope* as the general designation for the rhetorical technique whereby one term stands in for another. *Figures* are clusters of such terms. *Metaphors*, where the two terms have a semantic feature in common (a point of similarity), and *metonymy*, where the two terms are linked by a common context (a point of contiguity), are the two main subcategories of trope. *Synecdoche*, the rhetorical use of a part to designate the whole or the whole to designate a part, may be seen as a further subcategory either of metaphor or of metonymy. The important point is that, traditionally at least, metaphors and metonyms are characterized by the fact that their elements have something in common, be it an attribute or a context. *Simile* is a comparison that is explicitly stated. Max Black's interaction theory of metaphor is right to stress the way the interaction of the frame (syntagmatic context) and the focus (the tropical term itself) may itself generate the area of common ground. The German romantic poet Novalis had likewise drawn attention to the creative potential of wit.

38. Arno Schmidt, *Aus dem Leben eines Fauns* (Frankfurt-am-Main: Fischer Taschenbuch Verlag, 1973), 57.

39. Ibid.

40. Ibid., 112.

41. Richard Brautigan, *The Hawkline Monster* (London: Arena, 1987), 134.

42. Bergson, *Le Rire*, 88.

43. See Barry Fantoni, ed., *Private Eye: Colemanballs: 5* (London: Corgi Books, 1990).

44. See chapter 9.

45. Wayne Booth, *The Rhetoric of Fiction* (Chicago: University of Chicago Press, 1961), 304.

46. Empson's terms, quoted in D. C. Muecke, *Irony and the Ironic* (London: Methuen, 1982), 8.

47. Quintilian, *Institutio Oratoria*, trans. H. E. Butler (Loeb Classical Library, 1960), 485.

48. Sterne, *Tristram Shandy*, 528 (vol. 8, chap. 15).

49. Ibid., 525 (vol. 8. chap. 11).

50. Joachim Ritter, "Über das Lachen" (1940), in his *Subjektivität* (Frankfurt-am-Main: Suhrkamp, 1979), 62–92; 74.

51. Staveacre, *Slapstick*, 145.

52. Joyce, *Finnegans Wake*, 296 and 298.

53. Ibid., 533.

54. René Girard, *La Violence et le sacré* (Paris: Grasset, 1972), 217 and 250.

55. Redfern, *Puns*, 3 and 18.

56. Ibid., 120.

57. Jacques Lacan, "L'instance de la lettre dans l'inconscient ou la raison depuis Freud" (1957), in his *Ecrits 1* (Paris: Editions du Seuil, 1966), 260.

58. G. W. F. Hegel, *Wissenschaft der Logik*, in his *Werke*, 20 vols., ed. E. Moldenhauer and K. M. Michel (Frankfurt-am-Main: Suhrkamp, 1986), 6:202–7.

59. Joyce, *Finnegans Wake*, 437 and 364. See also his *Ulysses*, 568.

60. Joyce, *Finnegans Wake*, 3, 614.

61. Giovanni Boccaccio, *Decameron*, ed. Cesare Segre (Milan: Mursia, 1966), 391 (6:4).

62. Best, *Der Witz als Erkenntniskraft und Formprinzip*, 25.

63. Oscar Wilde, *The Picture of Dorian Gray*, ed. Peter Ackroyd (Harmondsworth: Penguin, 1985), 69, 45, 28, 231, and 129.

64. Immanuel Kant, *Kritik der Urteilskraft*, in his *Werke*, 12 vols., ed. W. Weischedel (Frankfurt-am-Main: Suhrkamp, 1957), 10:437.

65. Quoted in Richard Ellmann, *Oscar Wilde* (London: Hamish Hamilton, 1987), 482.

66. Ibid., 329.

67. Wilde, *The Picture of Dorian Gray*, 66.

68. Joe Orton, *The Orton Diaries*, ed. John Lahr (London: Methuen, 1986), 209.

69. See Brecht, *Der kaukasische Kreidekreis* (from *Stücke 8*, in his *Werke*, 24 vols., ed. W. Hecht et al., Frankfurt-am-Main: Suhrkamp, 1992), scene 2; Martin Amis, *Money* (Harmondsworth: Penguin, 1985), 215; Molière, *Le Malade imaginaire* (in his *Oeuvres complètes*, Paris: Seuil, 1962), 3.3.

70. Redfern, *Puns*, 150.

71. Carroll, *Alice*, 80.

72. Rabelais, *Oeuvres complètes*, 72–73 (bk. 1, chap. 11).

Chapter 4. Cracking the Mask

1. See M. T. Herrick, *Comic Theory in the Sixteenth Century* (Urbana: University of Illinois Press, 1950), 44; René Descartes, *Les Passions de l'âme* (art. 178), in his *Oeuvres et lettres*, ed. A. Bridoux (Paris: Gallimard, 1953), 780.

2. Cave, *Recognitions*, 58, 79n., 113, and 119.

3. Cicero, *De Oratore* (Loeb Classical Library, 1948), 389: "Cum aliud exspectamus, aliud dicitur. Hic nobismet ipsis noster error risum movet" (my own translation).

4. Quintilian, *Institutio Oratoria*, 485.

5. See David Farley-Hills, *The Comic in Renaissance Comedy* (London: Macmillan, 1981), 6.

6. Moore, *Molière*, 39.

7. Martin Amis, *London Fields* (Harmondsworth: Penguin, 1990), 57.

8. Martin Amis, *The Rachel Papers* (Harmondsworth: Penguin, 1984), 45.

9. Schopenhauer, *Die Welt als Wille und Vorstellung*, in his *Werke*, 2:465–66.

10. Ibid., 2:656.

11. Ibid., 2:731.

12. Amis, *Money*, 15.

13. Ibid., 204.

14. Curtius, *Europäische Literatur und lateinisches Mittelalter*, 433.

15. This translation is given in K. J. Dover, *Aristophanic Comedy* (Berkeley: University of California Press, 1972), 74.

16. Rabelais, *Oeuvres complètes*, 322 (bk. 2, chap. 27).

17. Descartes, *Les Passions de l'âme* (art. 70), 728.

18. Jauss writes that "der komische Held ist nicht an sich selbst, sondern vor einem Horizont bestimmter Erwartungen, mithin im Hinblick darauf komisch, daß er diese Erwartungen oder Normen negiert." In Hans Robert Jauss, "Über den Grund des Vergnügens am komischen Helden," in *Das Komische*, ed., Preisendanz and Warning, 105.

19. Aristophanes, *Women at the Thesmophoria*; I am here quoting David Barrett's Penguin translation, entitled *The Poet and the Women* (Harmondsworth: Penguin, 1964), 138–39.

Chapter 5. Rupturing the Illusion

1. See Hans Jakob Christoffel von Grimmelshausen, *Der abenteuerliche Simplicissimus* (Berlin: Verlag neues Leben, 1985), 36 (bk. 1, chap. 10); Petronius, *The Satyricon*, and Seneca, *The Apocolocyntosis*, trans. J. P. Sullivan (Harmondsworth: Penguin, 1977), 46.

2. Mikhail Bakhtin, *Rabelais and His World*, trans. Hélène Iswolsky (Bloomington: Indiana University Press, 1984), 7.

3. Eckehard Catholy, *Das deutsche Lustspiel: Vom Mittelalter bis zum Ende der Barockzeit* (Darmstadt: Wissenschaftliches Buchgesellschaft, 1968), 67–75.

4. C. L. Barber, *Shakespeare's Festive Comedy* (Princeton: Princeton University Press, 1959), 36.

5. Luigi Pirandello, *Sei Personaggi in cerca d'autore; Enrico IV* (Milan: Arnoldo Montadori, 1984), 104–7.

6. Ibid., 107–8.

7. Amis, *Money*, 71.

8. Ibid., 246–47.

9. Sterne, *Tristram Shandy*, 364 and 526 (vol. 5, chap. 13 and vol. 8, chap. 11).

10. Quoted in David Esrig, *Commedia dell'arte: eine Bildgeschichte der Kunst des Spektakels* (Nördlingen: Greno, 1985), 165.

11. Ibid., 174.
12. Schechner, *Between Theater and Anthropology*, 308–9.
13. Amis, *Money*, 46, 286, and 293.
14. See, for example, F. M. Cornford, *The Origin of Attic Comedy* (1914) ed. T. H. Gaster (New York: Doubleday, 1961), 276.
15. "Schauen" and "gucken" both mean "to look" in German; the French pronunciation of *Piper* is homophonous with "peeper."
16. Enid Welsford, *The Fool: His Social and Literary History* (1935) (New York: Doubleday, 1961), xii, 250 and 233.
17. J.-C. Aubailly, *Le monologue, le dialogue et la sottie* (Paris: Champion, 1976), 353.
18. Quoted in Culler, *Structuralist Poetics*, 139.
19. Sterne, *Tristram Shandy*, 202 (vol. 3, chap. 20).
20. Ibid., 123, 240, and 285 (vol. 2, chap. 8, vol. 3, chap. 38, and vol. 4, chap. 13).
21. Ibid., 82 (vol. 1, chap. 19).
22. Amis, *Money*, 215.

Chapter 6. Discarding the Social Mask

1. Michael D. Bristol, *Carnival and Theater* (London: Methuen, 1985), 4.
2. See Introduction to *Comedy: Developments in Criticism*, ed. D. J. Palmer (London: Macmillan, 1984), 9.
3. Catholy, *Das deutsche Lustspiel*, 11.
4. Joubert, *Traité du Ris*, 21.
5. Welsford, *The Fool*, 127.
6. See Michel Foucault, *Histoire de la Folie* (Paris: Plon, 1961). I quote throughout from the abridged, English version, *Madness and Civilization: A History of Insanity in the Age of Reason*, trans. Richard Howard (London: Tavistock, 1971), 74. Foucault's chronological distinctions are rather shaky, so I have taken the easy way out and ignored them, concentrating instead on structures of folly stripped to such a level of abstraction that they can be taken as "timeless."
7. R. D. Laing, *The Divided Self* (Harmondsworth: Penguin, 1965), 39. See also 42ff.
8. Foucault, *Madness and Civilization*, 94–95.
9. See also Carol Clark, *The Vulgar Rabelais* (Glasgow: Pressgang, 1983), 79–90.
10. Angela Carter, *The Sadeian Woman* (London: Virago, 1979), 9.
11. Wilde, *The Picture of Dorian Gray*, 26–27.
12. Amis, *The Rachel Papers*, 72 and 77.
13. McFadden, *The Serial*, 19 (chap. 4).
14. Foucault, *Madness and Civilization*, 107.
15. Ibid., 115–16.
16. Nikolai Gogol, *Dairy of a Madman and Other Stories*, trans. Ronald Wilks (Harmondsworth: Penguin, 1972), 35 and 37–38.
17. Foucault, *Madness and Civilization*, 188–89.
18. Laing, *The Divided Self*, 102–5.
19. Ibid., 163.
20. R. D. Laing, *Self and Others* (Harmondsworth: Penguin, 1971), 52.

21. Aubailly, *Le Monologue, le dialogue et la sottie*, 521–23.
22. Angela Carter, *Nights at the Circus* (London: Picador, 1985), 116.
23. Bristol, *Carnival and Theater*, 38.
24. Martin Esslin, *The Theatre of the Absurd*, rev. ed. (Harmondsworth: Penguin, 1980), 368.
25. Culler, *Structuralist Poetics*, 137: "Comedy exists by virtue of the fact that to read something as a comedy involves different expectations from reading something as a tragedy or as an epic."
26. Ibid.
27. Bakhtin, *Rabelais and his World*, 81–82.
28. Schelling, *Werke*, 3:361.
29. Cervantes, *Don Quixote*, 527 (pt. 2, chap. 10).
30. Friedrich Dürrenmatt, "Theaterprobleme," from *Theater: Essays, Gedichte und Reden*, in his *Werkausgabe*, 30 vols. (Zürich: Diogenes, 1985), 24:61.
31. Quoted in Moore, *Molière*, 21.
32. Kant, *Kritik der Urteilskraft*, in his *Werke*, 10:437.
33. Quoted in Rommel, "Die wissenschaftlichen Bemühungen um die Analyse des Komischen," 6.
34. This is one of the central points made by Bakhtin in his study of Rabelais.
35. E. Mason and R. Ellmann, eds. *The Critical Writings of James Joyce* (London: Faber and Faber, 1959), 144.
36. Rainer Warning, "Elemente einer Pragmasemiotik der Komödie," in *Das Komische*, ed. Preisendanz and Warning, 290.
37. Welsford, *The Fool*, 253.
38. Oreglia, *The Commedia dell'Arte*, 36–43.
39. Erasmus, *Praise of Folly*, trans. Betty Radice (Harmondsworth: Penguin, 1971), 76.
40. Aubailly, *Le monologue, le dialogue et la sottie*, 418.
41. Welsford, 226.
42. Sandra Billington, "'Suffer Fools Gladly': The Fool in Medieval England and the Play *Mankind*," in *The Fool and the Trickster*, ed. Paul V. A. Williams (Cambridge: Brewer, 1979), 36–54.
43. On the *agroikos*, see Frye, *Anatomy of Criticism*, 172–75.
44. See Catholy, *Das deutsche Lustspiel*, 39.
45. Cervantes, *Don Quixote*, 516 (pt. 2, chap. 8).
46. Ibid., 916 (pt. 2, chap. 70).
47. Hegel, *Ästhetik*, 2:554, 552, 553, and 570.
48. Warning, "Elemente einer Pragmasemiotik der Komödie," 325.
49. Ritter, "Über das Lachen," 76.
50. Ibid., 78–79.
51. Bernard Spivack, "Falstaff and the Psychomachia," *Shakespeare Quarterly* 8 (1957):449–50.
52. Barber, *Shakespeare's Festive Comedy*, 58ff.
53. G. R. Hibbard, *Thomas Nashe: A Critical Introduction* (London: Routledge and Kegan Paul, 1962), 96.
54. W. H. Auden, "The Prince's Dog," in his *The Dyer's Hand and Other Essays* (New York: Random, 1962), 195.
55. See Introduction to the Arden edition of *King Henry IV Part 2*, ed. A. R. Humphreys (London: Methuen, 1967), lv.
56. See James George Frazer, *The Golden Bough: A Study in Magic and Religion*, abridged edition (London: Macmillan, 1922), 573.

57. Charney, *Comedy High and Low*, 172.
58. Quoted in Robert M. Torrance, *The Comic Hero* (Cambridge: Harvard University Press, 1978), 305.
59. Ibid., 306.
60. Quoted in Karl Miller, *Doubles: Studies in Literary History* (Oxford: Oxford University Press, 1985), 35.
61. *Letters of John Keats*, ed. Robert Gittings (Oxford: Oxford University Press, 1970), 157.
62. Quoted in Miller, *Doubles*, 219.
63. Keats's term: see *Letters*, 43.
64. Rabelais, *Oeuvres complètes*, 534 (bk. 3, chap. 46).
65. Ibid., 300–5 (bk. 2, chap. 21).
66. Richard Alewyn, *Probleme und Gestalten: Essays* (Frankfurt-am-Main: Suhrkamp, 1982), 28–29.
67. Felicity Firth, "Comedy in Italy," in *Comic Drama: The European Heritage*, ed. W. D. Howarth (London: Methuen, 1978), 75.
68. Oreglia, *The Commedia dell'Arte*, 71.
69. Charles Baudelaire, "De l'essence du rire," in his *Oeuvres complètes*, 11 vols., ed. J. Crépet (Paris: Conard, 1923), 1:389–90.
70. David Mayer III, *Harlequin in His Element: The English Pantomime, 1806–1836* (Cambridge: Harvard University Press, 1969), 45–47.
71. Ibid., 262.
72. Paul Radin, *The Trickster: A Study in American Indian Mythology* (New York: Schocken, 1972), xxiv.
73. C. G. Jung, "On the Psychology of the Trickster Figure," trans. R. F. C. Hull, in Radin, *The Trickster*, 200.
74. Radin, *The Trickster*, 168–69.
75. Bertolt Brecht, "Baal," from *Stücke 1*, in his *Werke*, 24 vols., ed. W. Hecht, et al. (Frankfurt-am-Main: Suhrkamp, 1989), 29, 91, and 126.
76. Hegel, *Ästhetik*, 2:570.
77. Hobbes, *Leviathan*, 141–42.
78. Freud, "Der Witz und seine Beziehung zum Unbewußten," in his *Studienausgabe*, 4:120.
79. Ibid.
80. Kant, *Kritik der Urteilskraft*, in *Werke*, 10:440.
81. Ibid.
82. Schiller, *Werke*, 20:417. Notably, Schiller finds the intentional, conscious rejection of the social mask (*Naive der Gesinnung* as opposed to the *Naive der Überraschung*) to be moving rather than funny.
83. Jaroslav Hasek, *The Good Soldier Svejk*, trans. Cecil Parrott (Harmondsworth: Penguin, 1974), 31–32 (bk. 1, chap. 4).
84. Grimmelshausen, *Simplicissimus*, 109 (bk. 1, chap. 32).
85. Ibid., 132 (bk. 2, chap. 5).
86. Ibid., 148–49 (bk. 2, chap. 10).
87. See Welsford, *The Fool*, 79ff.
88. Lamb, *Works*, 1:282, 285.
89. Paton, "The Comedian as Portrayer of Social Morality," 207.
90. Quoted in Wolfgang Dreßen, "Possen und Zoten: Ausflüge unter die Gürtellinie," in *Lachen, Gelächter, Lächeln*, ed. D. Kamper and Chr. Wulf (Frankfurt-am-Main: Syndikat, 1986), 150.

91. George Meredith, "An Essay on the Idea of Comedy and the Uses of the Comic Spirit" (1897), in his *Works*, 27 vols. (London: Constable, 1910), 23:46.

92. Elder Olson, *The Theory of Comedy* (Bloomington: Indiana University Press, 1968), 18.

93. See Ritter, "Über das Lachen," 78.

94. Jean Paul Richter, *Vorschule der Ästhetik*, 125.

95. Dover, *Aristophanic Comedy*, 125–26.

96. See Ann Jefferson, *The Nouveau Roman and the Poetics of Fiction* (Cambridge: Cambridge University Press, 1980), 144.

97. John Kennedy Toole, *A Confederacy of Dunces* (Harmondsworth: Penguin, 1981), 1–2 (chap. 1).

98. Ibid., 282–83 (chap. 12).

99. Ibid., 36 (chap. 2).

100. Ibid., 27–28 (chap. 2).

101. Ibid., 110 and 185 (chaps. 5 and 9).

102. Ibid., 157–58 (chap. 7).

103. Ibid., 263 (chap. 12).

Chapter 7. The Political Mask

1. Bakhtin, *Rabelais and his World*, 10.

2. Ibid., 81.

3. Joubert, *Traité du Ris*, 18–19.

4. Bristol, *Carnival and Theater*, 71.

5. Schopenhauer, *Aphorismen zur Lebensweisheit*, in his *Sämtliche Werke*, 4: 379.

6. Bristol, *Carnival and Theater*, 113. The argument of the following paragraph is indebted to Bristol.

7. Ibid., 126.

8. Dante, *Literary Criticism*, 100–1.

9. Quoted in the "Documentation Thématique" to Alain-René Lesage, *Turcaret*, ed. Bernard Blanc (Paris: Larousse, 1973), 150.

10. Alewyn, *Probleme und Gestalten*, 37.

11. Cervantes, *Don Quixote*, 800 (pt. 2, chap. 51).

12. In Wilde's *A Woman of No Importance* (from his *Works*, 15 vols. [New York: AMS, 1972]), Lord Illingworth says: "The history of women is the history of the worst form of tyranny the world has ever known. The tyranny of the weak over the strong. It is the only tyranny that lasts" (Act 3).

13. Mrs. Allonby makes the point in *A Woman of No Importance*, act 1.

14. See Reay Tannahill, *Sex in History*, rev. ed. (London: Sphere Books, 1989), 254–59.

15. Peter Brand, "Disguise in Renaissance Comedy, with Illustrations," in *Comparative Criticism: An Annual Journal*, ed. E. S. Shaffer (Cambridge: Cambridge University Press, 1988), 86.

16. Ian Donaldson, *The World Upside-Down* (Oxford: Oxford University Press, 1970), 12.

17. Meredith, *Works*, 23:15.

18. Ibid., 31.

19. Ibid.
20. G. W. F. Hegel, *Phänomenologie des Geistes*, in his *Werke*, 20 vols., ed. E. Moldenhauer and K. M. Michel (Frankfurt-am-Main: Suhrkamp, 1986), 3:541–44.
21. Dover, *Aristophanic Comedy*, 32.
22. Bristol, *Carnival and Theater*, 35.
23. Zijderveld, *Humor und Gesellschaft*, 180.
24. Bergson, *Le Rire*, 72.
25. Barbara A. Babcock, Introduction to *The Reversible World: Symbolic Inversion in Art and Society*, ed. B. A. Babcock (Ithaca: Cornell University Press, 1978), 22.
26. Natalie Zemon Davis, "Women on Top: Symbolic Sexual Inversion and Political Disorder in Early Modern Europe," in *The Reversible World*, 171.
27. The drinking songs of the *Carmina burana* are a different kettle of fish, but do not explicitly employ the topos of inversion.

Chapter 8. The Ethical Mask

1. George Bernard Shaw, *Man and Superman: A Comedy and a Philosophy* (Harmondsworth: Penguin, 1946), 146.
2. Hobbes, *Leviathan*, 185–86.
3. Plato, *Politicus; Philebus*, 339.
4. Descartes, *Les Passions de l'âme* (art. 126), 753. See also 780.
5. Meredith, *Works*, 23:46.
6. Welsford, *The Fool*, 80ff.
7. Mercier, *The Irish Comic Tradition,* 7 and 105.
8. Nietzsche, *Zur Genealogie der Moral* (2:16), in his *Werke*, 6:2:338–39.
9. Cornford, *The Origin of Attic Comedy*, 113.
10. Redfern, *Puns*, 92.
11. Rabelais, *Oeuvres complètes*, 119 (bk. 1, chap. 25).
12. Barth, *The Sot-Weed Factor*, 460–66 (pt. 2, chap. 31).
13. Rabelais, 126–27 (bk. 1, chap. 27).
14. Antonin Artaud, *Le Théâtre et son double*, in his *Oeuvres complètes*, 11 vols. (Paris: Gallimard, 1961–74), 4:39 and 109.
15. Eugène Ionesco, *Notes et contre-notes* (Paris: Gallimard, 1962), 13.
16. Quoted in Mayer, *Harlequin in his Element*, 44.
17. Quoted in András Horn, *Das Komische im Spiegel der Literatur* (Würzburg: Königshausen und Neumann, 1988), 161.
18. Eric Bentley, *The Life of The Drama* (London: Methuen, 1966), 297.
19. Staveacre, *Slapstick*, 48.
20. Bakhtin, *Rabelais and his World*, 148.
21. See Charney, *Comedy High and Low*, 58–59.
22. Joubert, *Traité du Ris*, 16 and 20.
23. Freud, "Der Witz und seine Beziehung zum Unbewußten," in his *Studienausgabe*, 4:98.
24. Ibid., 96.
25. Ibid., 159 and 193.
26. Freud, "Das Ich und das Es" (1923), from *Psychologie des Unbewußten*, in his *Studienausgabe*, 3:320.

27. Freud, "Der Witz und seine Beziehung zum Unbewußten," in his *Studien-ausgabe*, 4:93.

28. Dürrenmatt, "Theaterprobleme," in his *Werkausgabe*, 24:61.

29. Roland Barthes, *Le Plaisir du texte* (Paris: Editions du Seuil, 1973), 19.

30. Freud, "Drei Abhandlungen zur Sexualtheorie" (1904–5), in *Sexualleben*, in his *Studienausgabe*, 5:100.

31. Bertolt Brecht, *Schriften zum Theater*, 7 vols., ed. W. Hecht (Frankfurt-am-Main: Suhrkamp, 1963), 5:111.

32. Sterne, *Tristram Shandy*, 572 (vol. 9, chap. 1).

33. Jean Genet, "Comment jouer *Les Bonnes*," introduction to *Les Bonnes* (Paris: Gallimard, 1947), 8.

34. Schechner, *Between Theater and Anthropology*, 298ff.

35. Ibid., 301.

36. Barthes, *Le Plaisir du texte*, 45.

37. Ibid.

38. Friedrich Schlegel, "Vom ästhetischen Werte der griechischen Komödie" (1794), in his *Kritische Ausgabe*, 38 vols., ed. E. Behler (Munich: Schöningh, 1979), 1:30.

39. Northrop Frye, "The Argument of Comedy" (1949), in *Comedy: Developments in Criticism*, ed. D. J. Palmer, 74.

40. Schopenhauer, *Die Welt als Wille und Vorstellung*, in his *Sämtliche Werke*, 1:173.

41. Ibid., 2:730.

42. Ibid., 2:656.

43. Ibid., 2:562.

44. Ibid.

45. Freud, "Der Witz und seine Beziehung zum Unbewußten," in his *Studien-ausgabe*, 4:105.

46. Wilde, *The Picture of Dorian Gray*, 26.

47. Wilhelm Reich, *Die Sexuelle Revolution* (Frankfurt-am-Main: Fischer, 1971), 43.

48. Ibid., 95.

49. Ibid., 23.

50. Michel Foucault, *La Volonté de Savoir, Vol. 1: Histoire de la Sexualité* (Paris: Gallimard, 1976), 133. I have quoted from the English translation, *The History of Sexuality*, trans. Robert Hurley (Harmondsworth: Penguin, 1981), 101.

51. Ibid., 136 (103 in translation).

52. Freud, "Drei Abhandlungen zur Sexualtheorie," in his *Studienausgabe*, 5:134.

53. Tannahill, *Sex in History*, 402.

54. Lenny Bruce, *The Essential Lenny Bruce*, ed. John Cohen (London: Papermac, 1987), 176.

55. Quoted in Staveacre, *Slapstick*, 142.

56. Bruce, *The Essential Lenny Bruce*, 170.

57. Quoted in Staveacre, *Slapstick*, 147.

58. Freud, "Der Witz und seine Beziehung zum Unbewußten," in his *Studien-ausgabe*, 4:100 and 103.

59. Ibid., 95.

60. Plessner, "Lachen und Weinen," in his *Philosophische Anthropologie*, 119.

61. Sterne, *Tristram Shandy*, 101 (vol. 1, chap. 25).

62. Ibid., 548–49 (vol. 8, chap. 22).

63. Burgess, *Inside Mr. Enderby*, 84 and 119 (x2).

64. It certainly passed me by, but I am assured of the truth of the matter by a number of completely unreliable sources.

65. Joyce, *Finnegans Wake*, 229.

66. Rabelais, *Oeuvres complètes*, 48, 303, and 596 (bk. 1, chap. 3, bk. 2, chap. 21, bk. 4, chap. 5).

67. Kit Schwartz, *The Female Member* (London: Robson, 1989), 8ff.

68. Rabelais, *Oeuvres complètes*, 278 (bk. 2, chap. 15).

69. Barthes, *Le Plaisir du texte*, 67–68.

70. Terence Cave sees the ambivalence of the codpiece or *braguette*, like the narrative repetition, as figuring the ambivalence of a fallen text: "The textual surface is a rhetorical *braguette* enacting, through the cornucopian analogy, a plenitude; but at the same time it also undercuts this plenitude by introducing its own thematic inversion." More specifically, "while the text as cornucopia delights in its own productivity, its generative movement depends on its fictionality, on its lack of origin or grounding" (Cave, *The Cornucopian Text*, 187).

71. Taylor and Saayman, "Play and Imitation in Dolphins," 240.

72. Barber, *Shakespeare's Festive Comedy*, 101.

73. Jean Paul Richter, *Vorschule der Ästhetik*, 173.

74. Freud, "Der Witz und seine Beziehung zum Unbewußten," in his *Studienausgabe*, 4:15.

75. Redfern, *Puns*, 53 and 59.

76. H. A. Ellis, *Shakespeare's Lusty Punning in "Love's Labour's Lost"* (The Hague: Mouton, 1973), 104.

77. Tannahill, *Sex in History*, 142.

78. Ibid., 156.

79. Ibid., 143–44.

80. Ibid., 65–66.

81. Amis, *Money*, 388.

82. Philip Roth, *Portnoy's Complaint* (Harmondsworth: Penguin, 1986), 21.

83. Barth, *The Sot-Weed Factor*, 341 (pt. 2, chap. 21).

84. Ibid., 516 (pt. 3, chap. 2).

85. Ibid., 343 (pt. 2, chap. 21).

86. Ibid., 137 (pt. 2, chap. 3).

87. Ibid., 345 (pt. 2, chap. 22).

88. D. A. F. de Sade, *Justine, ou Les Malheurs de la vertu*, ed. Béatrice Didier (Paris: Livre de Poche, 1973), 367–68 and 396–97.

89. See Gail Dines-Levy and Gregory W. H. Smith, "Representations of Women and Men in *Playboy* Sex Cartoons," in *Humour in Society*, 234–59.

90. Carter, *The Sadeian Women*, 3, 16, and 17.

91. Staveacre, *Slapstick*, 23.

92. Elmer M. Blistein, *Comedy in Action* (Durham, N.C.: Duke University Press, 1964), 85–86.

93. Tannahill, *Sex in History*, 148.

94. Ibid., 373–75.

95. Quoted in Ruby Cohn, *New American Dramatists 1960–1980* (London: Macmillan, 1982), 126.

96. See Davis, "Women on Top: Symbolic Sexual Inversion and Political Disorder in Early Modern Europe," 152.

97. Tannahill, *Sex in History*, 56.

98. Geburg Treusch-Dieter, "Das Gelächter der Frauen," in *Lachen, Gelächter, Lächeln*, 138.

99. Tertullien, *La Toilette des femmes* (*De cultu feminarum*), trans. Marie Turcan (Paris: Editions du cerf, 1971), 42–47.

100. *Pulling Our Own Strings*, ed. Gloria Kaufman and Mary Kay Blakely (Bloomington: Indiana University Press, 1980), 14.

101. See Georges Devereux, *Baubo, la vulve mythique* (Paris: Godefoy, 1983).

102. Novalis, *Schriften*, 5 vols., ed. P. Kluckhohn and R. Samuel (Stuttgart: W. Kohlhammer, 1960), 2:434.

103. Bernard Benstock, *Joyce-Again's Wake: An Analysis of "Finnegans Wake"* (Seattle: University of Washington Press, 1965), 276–81.

104. Freud, "Der Witz und seine Beziehung zum Unbewußten," in his *Studienausgabe*, 4:93.

105. Ben Jonson, "Timber, or Discoveries," in his *Works*, 11 vols., ed. C. H. Herford, P. Simpson, and E. Simpson (Oxford: Clarendon Press, 1925–52), 8:644.

106. See Edmund Wilson, "Morose Ben Jonson," in *Ben Jonson: A Collection of Critical Essays*, ed. J. A. Barish (Englewood Cliffs, N. J.: Prentice-Hall, 1963), 60–74.

107. Curtius, *Europäische Literatur und lateinisches Mittelalter*, 434.

108. Quoted in Miller, *Doubles*, 424.

109. Burgess, *Inside Mr. Enderby*, 49–50.

110. Ibid., 57 and 114.

111. Ibid., 17 and 141.

112. Toole, *A Confederacy of Dunces*, 26–27 and 317 (chaps. 2 and 13).

113. Rabelais, *Oeuvres complètes*, 763 (bk. 4, chap. 67).

114. Ibid., 765–66 (bk. 4, chap. 67).

115. Ibid., 281 (bk. 2, chap. 16).

116. Bruce, *The Essential Lenny Bruce*, 35–36.

117. Grimmelshausen, *Simplicissimus*, 110–11 (bk. 1, chap. 33).

118. Amis, *Money*, 65.

119. Amis, *The Rachel Papers*, 190.

120. Bruce, *The Essential Lenny Bruce*, 33.

121. Ibid., 200.

122. Ibid., 33–34.

123. Burgess, *Inside Mr. Enderby*, 26.

124. Ibid., 27.

125. Wolfgang Kayser, *Das Groteske: Seine Gestaltung in Malerei und Dichtung* (Oldenburg: Gerhard Stalling Verlag, 1957), 199.

126. Geoffrey Harpham, *On the Grotesque: Strategies of Contradiction in Art and Literature* (Princeton: Princeton University Press, 1982), 6–7.

127. Rommel, "Die wissenschaftlichen Bemühungen um die Analyse des Komischen," 15.

128. Friedrich Georg Jünger, *Über das Komische* (Frankfurt-am-Main: Klostermann, 1948), 11.

129. Cicero, *De Oratore*, 398.

130. Quintilian, *Institutio Oratoria*, 468.

131. Beckett, *Watt*, 98.

Chapter 9. The Cognitive Mask

1. Freud, "Das Unbewußte" (1915), from *Psychologie des Unbewußten*, in his *Studienausgabe*, 3:130.

2. Ibid., 125 and 146.

3. In the "Analogies," Kant tries (and, many would argue, fails) to prove these as *scientific* principles. Of more lasting importance have been Kant's *epistemological* insights that the concept of an objective event presupposes something permanent in perception and the notion of a necessary (causal) order in the relevant perceptions and in what is perceived.

4. In his introduction to the "Transcendental Dialectic" in the *Kritik der reinen Vernunft*, Kant distinguishes "empirischer Schein," or empirical delusion, in which the judgement is led astray by the influence of the imagination, from "transcendentaler Schein," or transcendental delusion, in which categories of human understanding are mistakenly assumed to pertain, not to cognition, but to things as they are in themselves (4:308–11).

5. David Hume, *An Enquiry Concerning Human Understanding*, in his *The Philosophical Works*, 4 vols., ed. T. H. Green and T. H. Grose (1886; reprint, Darmstadt: Scientia Verlag Aalen, 1964), 2:64–65.

6. David Hume, *A Treatise of Human Nature*, in his *The Philosophical Works*, 1:534.

7. Nietzsche, *Die Geburt der Tragödie*, in his *Werke*, 3:1:114.

8. Nietzsche, *Nachgelassene Fragmente*, in his *Werke*, 8:3:51.

9. Bertrand Russell, *A History of Western Philosophy* (London: George Allen and Unwin, 1946), 55.

10. See Rommel, "Die wissenschaftlichen Bemühungen um die Analyse des Komischen," 12–20.

11. Of course, this need not be so. Just as quantum physicists describe their subatomic reality in statistical terms, empirically minded philosophers such as Locke and Russell, while denying that we are sensibly aware of things as they really are, do not go to the drastic lengths of cutting us off from any empirical knowledge of them. This is (in theory at least) accessible to science, in the form of the language of sense data, and it is still a knowledge of spatio-temporal objects.

12. Immanuel Kant, *Kritik der reinen Vernunft*, in his *Werke*, 3:277.

13. Ibid., 3:306–7.

14. Freud, "Das Unbewußte," in his *Studienausgabe*, 3:130.

15. Bergson, influenced by Schopenhauer, fuses these two levels in his essay on laughter. Indeed, both his theory of comedy and his metaphysics are in many ways analogous to Schopenhauer's. Bergson speaks of reality—and of the human self—as a restless, shifting flux, a creative mobility that cannot be done justice by the static spatiality of concepts and that can only be known by what he refers to as intuition, as opposed to analysis. Like Schopenhauer, he sees the target of laughter as a rigidity that distorts the fluidity of real life, a mask that—by oversimplification—warps and contorts the dynamic reality. Whereas for Schopenhauer it is a conceptual rigidity that has this effect (in his theory of the ridiculous), for Bergson it is a mechanical rigidity, the predictable tendency to repetition that is characteristic of behavioral fixation.

16. Strictly speaking, things are not quite as straightforward in Kant as I have pretended for the sake of simplicity: Kant's troublesome inner/outer (self/world) duality in particular often leaves it unclear whether he is referring to an empirical self (the inner sense) or a transcendental self. More so than Schopenhauer, moreover, Kant would see himself as making points about epistemology rather than psychology, even though his phrasing is often markedly psychological.

17. Quoted in Michael Wetzel, "Die Räsonanz des Ego oder: Warum und worüber im Königsberg des 18. Jahrhunderts gelacht wurde," in *Lachen, Gelächter, Lächeln*, 176.

18. Quoted in Fred M. Robinson, *Comedy of Language: Studies in Modern Comic Literature* (Amherst: University of Massachusetts Press, 1980), 12.

19. Bakhtin, *Rabelais and his World*, 41.

20. John Ruskin, *The Stones of Venice*, in his *Works*, 39 vols., ed. E. T. Cook and Alexander Wedderburn (London: George Allen, 1904), 11:178.

21. Ibid., 11:162.

22. Harpham, *On the Grotesque*, 6.

23. Schopenhauer, *Die Welt als Wille und Vorstellung*, in his *Werke*, 1:482.

24. Nietzsche, *Die Geburt der Tragödie*, in his *Werke*, 3:1:53.

25. Freud, "Das Unheimliche," in his *Studienausgabe*, 4:248 and 264.

26. Sklovskij, *Theorie der Prosa*, 13.

27. Brecht, *Schriften zum Theater*, 5:292.

28. Quoted in Robinson, *Comedy of Language*, 134.

29. Nietzsche, *Menschliches, Allzumenschliches*, in his *Werke*, 4:2:176.

30. Schopenhauer, *Die Welt als Wille und Vorstellung*, in his *Werke*, 2:131. Schopenhauer is here extending even further Kant's problematic separation of the cognitive faculties into intuition and understanding.

31. Kant, *Kritik der reinen Vernunft*, in his *Werke*, 3:230.

32. Kant, *Kritik der Urteilskraft*, in his *Werke*, 10:437.

33. Kant, *Kritik der reinen Vernunft*, in his *Werke*, 3:236.

34. See chapter 3.

35. Freud, "Über den Traum" (1901), in his *Gesammelte Werke*, 18 vols. (London: Imago, 1942), 2/3:666.

36. Baudelaire, "De l'essence du rire," 1:394; Ruskin, *The Stones of Venice*, 11:135.

37. Edgar Allan Poe, *Comedies and Satires*, ed. David Galloway (Harmondsworth: Penguin, 1987), 177.

38. Ibid., 183.

39. Ibid., 181.

40. Quoted in Ellmann, *Oscar Wilde*, 441.

41. Arthur Koestler, "Association and Bisociation" (1967), in *Play*, 644. See also Koestler's *The Act of Creation* (London: Arkana, 1989), 45 and 59.

42. Quoted in Redfern, *Puns*, 112.

43. Hunter S. Thompson, *Fear and Loathing in Las Vegas; A Savage Journey to the Heart of the American Dream* (London: Paladin, 1972), 57.

44. Ibid., 49.

45. Quoted in Mayer, *Harlequin in his Element*, 113.

46. Ibid., 114.

47. Staveacre, *Slapstick*, 89.

48. Ibid., 91.

49. Thomas Brandlmeier, "Das Groteske im Kino," in *Lachen, Gelächter, Lächeln*, 234.

50. Such distinctions can be misleading, but it is clear that there is *some* difference in effect between witnessing an absurdity in the first person and simply being told or reading about it. Tenniel's illustrations to Lewis Carroll's *Alice* books illuminate both the proximity of the verbal and the visual and the limitations of the visual in depicting certain verbal absurdities.

51. Anthony Burgess, "Nonsense," in *Explorations in the Field of Nonsense*, ed. Wim Tigges (Amsterdam: Rodopi, 1987), 19.

52. Cited in C. K. Ogden and I. A. Richards, *The Meaning of Meaning*, 10th ed. (London: Routledge and Kegan Paul, 1969), 46.

53. Lewis Carroll, *Alice*, 201.

54. Quoted in Harpham, *On the Grotesque*, 15.
55. Robinson, *Comedy of Language*, 175.
56. Rabelais, *Oeuvres complètes*, 665–70 (bk. 4, chaps. 30–32).
57. Cave, *The Cornucopian Text*, 27, 150, and 208–9.
58. F. T. Marinetti, *Teoria e Invenzione Futurista* (Milan: Montadori, 1968), 80–91 and 138–44.
59. Schelling, *Philosophie der Kunst*, 3:359–61.
60. W. H. Auden, "Notes on the Comic," in *The Dyer's Hand*, 373.
61. Ralph Waldo Emerson, "The Comic," in his *Works*, ed. G. Sampson, (London: George Bell and Son, 1906), 3:270.
62. Staveacre, *Slapstick*, 134.
63. Mayer, *Harlequin in his Element*, 39.
64. Ibid., 48.
65. André Breton, *Les Vases communicants* (1932) (Paris: Gallimard, 1955), 148.
66. Rabelais, *Oeuvres complètes*, 665–70 (bk. 4, chaps. 30–32).
67. Schlegel, "Vom ästhetischen Werte der griechischen Komödie," in his *Kritische Ausgabe*, 1:31–32.
68. Nietzsche, *Jenseits von Gut und Böse*, in his *Werke*, 6:2:43.
69. Dürrenmatt, "Die alte Wiener Volkskomödie," from *Theater: Essays, Gedichte und Reden*, in his *Werkausgabe*, 24:28.
70. Warning, "Elemente einer Pragmasemiotik der Komödie," 293.
71. Staveacre, *Slapstick*, 38.
72. Schopenhauer, *Die Welt als Wille und Vorstellung*, in his *Werke*, 2:128.
73. Brecht, *Schriften zum Theater*, 3:154.
74. David Kunzle, "The World Upside Down," in *The Reversible World*, 45.
75. Ibid., 42.
76. Carroll, *Alice*, 67 and 108.
77. Ibid., 176–77.
78. Ibid., 141 and 145.
79. See Peter Heath, *The Philosopher's Alice* (London: Academy, 1974), 147.
80. Martin Amis, *Time's Arrow* (Harmondsworth: Penguin, 1992), 51.
81. Ibid., 18–19.
82. Ibid., 34.
83. Ibid., 74.
84. Auden, "Notes on the Comic," 373.
85. See Werner Welzig, "Ordo und verkehrte Welt bei Grimmelshausen," in *Der Simplicissimusdichter und sein Werk*, ed. G. Weydt (Darmstadt: Wissenschaftliches Buchgesellschaft, 1969), 373.
86. Kunzle, "The World Upside Down," 58.
87. Curtius, *Europäische Literatur und lateinisches Mittelalter*, 105.
88. Quoted in ibid., 107.
89. Kunzle, "The World Upside Down," 88.

Bibliography

Comic Works

Amis, Martin. *London Fields*. Harmondsworth: Penguin, 1990.

———. *Money*. Harmondsworth: Penguin, 1985.

———. *The Rachel Papers*. 1973; Harmondsworth: Penguin, 1984.

———. *Time's Arrow*. Harmondsworth: Penguin, 1992.

Amoureux, Un. In *Farces du Moyen Age*. Edited by André Tissier. Paris: Flammarion, 1984.

Apollinaire, Guillaume. *L'Enchanteur pourrissant*. Edited by Michel Décaudin. Paris: Gallimard, 1972.

Ariosto, Ludovico. *La Lena*. Edited by G. Davico Bonino. Turin: Einaudi, 1981.

Aristophanes. *The Knights. Peace. The Birds. The Assemblywomen. Wealth*. Translated by Alan H. Sommerstein and David Barrett. Harmondsworth: Penguin, 1978.

———. *Lysistrata. The Acharnians. The Clouds*. Translated by Alan H. Sommerstein. Harmondsworth: Penguin, 1973.

———. *Plays*. With an English translation by B. B. Rogers. 3 vols. Cambridge: Harvard University Press (Loeb Classical Library), 1960–63.

———. *The Wasps. The Poet and the Women. The Frogs*. Translated by David Barrett. Harmondsworth: Penguin, 1964.

Artaud, Antonin. *Oeuvres complètes*. 11 vols. Paris: Gallimard, 1961–74.

Barnes, Peter. *The Ruling Class*. 1969; London: Heinemann, 1980.

Barth, John. *The Sot-Weed Factor*. 1961; London: Panther Books, 1965.

Beaumarchais. *Théâtre*. Paris: Flammarion, 1965.

Beaumont, Francis. *The Knight of the Burning Pestle*. Edited by Michael Hattaway. London: Ernest Benn, 1969.

Beckett, Samuel. *Endgame*. London: Faber and Faber, 1958.

———. *Happy Days* (bilingual edition). Edited by James Knowlson. London: Faber and Faber, 1978.

———. *Waiting for Godot*. London: Faber and Faber, 1956.

———. *Watt*. 1953; London: Picador, 1988.

Blake, William. *The Complete Poems*. 2nd ed. Edited by W. H. Stevenson. London: Longman, 1989.

Boccaccio, Giovanni. *Decameron*. Edited by Cesare Segre. Milan: Mursia, 1966.

Brant, Sebastian. *Das Narrenschiff*. Rev. ed. Edited by Manfred Lemmer. Tübingen: Niemeyer, 1968.

Brautigan, Richard. *The Hawkline Monster*. 1974; London: Arena, 1987.

Brecht, Bertolt. *Stücke 1–10*. In *Werke*. 24 vols. Edited by W. Hecht et al. Frankfurt-am-Main: Suhrkamp, 1989– .

Bruce, Lenny. *The Essential Lenny Bruce*. Edited by John Cohen. London: Papermac, 1987.

Büchner, Georg. *Werke und Briefe*. Munich: Deutscher Taschenbuch Verlag, 1980.

Buckingham, George Villiers, 2nd duke of. *The Rehearsal*. In *Three Restoration Comedies*, edited by G. G. Falle. New York: St Martin's Press, 1964.

Bürger, Gottfried August. *Wunderbare Reisen zu Wasser und zu Lande, Feldzüge und lustige Abenteuer des Freiherrn von Münchhausen*. Frankfurt-am-Main: Insel, 1976.

Burgess, Anthony. *Inside Mr. Enderby*. In *Enderby*. Harmondsworth: Penguin, 1982.

Carmina burana. With a German translation by Carl Fischer and Hugo Kuhn. Munich: Deutscher Taschenbuch Verlag, 1979.

Carroll, Lewis. *Alice's Adventures in Wonderland and Through the Looking-Glass*. Rev. ed. Edited by Roger Lancelyn Green. Oxford: Oxford University Press, 1982.

Carter, Angela. *Nights at the Circus*. London: Picador, 1985.

Cervantes Saavedra, Miguel de. *The Adventures of Don Quixote*. Translated by J. M. Cohen. Harmondsworth: Penguin, 1950.

Chaucer, Geoffrey. *Canterbury Tales*. Rev. ed. Edited by A. C. Cawley. London: Dent, 1975.

Chauldronnier, Un. In *Farces du Moyen Age*. Edited by André Tissier. Paris: Flammarion, 1984.

Congreve, William. *Comedies*. Edited by Anthony G. Henderson. Cambridge: Cambridge University Press, 1982.

Coover, Robert. *Spanking the Maid*. 1982; London: Paladin, 1988.

Corneille, Pierre. *L'Illusion comique*. Edited by Marc Fumaroli. Paris: Larousse, 1970.

Dante Alighieri. *La Divina Commedia. Inferno*. Edited by Guiseppe Villaroel et al. Milan: Arnoldo Montadori, 1985.

Dürrenmatt, Friedrich. *Romulus der Große*. Vol. 2 of *Werkausgabe*. 30 vols. Zürich: Diogenes, 1985.

Eichendorff, Joseph von. *Die Freier*. Stuttgart: Reclam, 1982.

Everyman. Edited by A. C. Cawley. Manchester: Manchester University Press, 1961.

Fantoni, Barry, ed. *Private Eye: Colemanballs: 5*. London: Corgi Books, 1990.

Farce nouvelle nommée la Folie des Gorriers. In *Recueil général des Sotties*. 3 vols. Edited by E. Picot. Paris: Didot, 1902–12.

Feydeau, Georges. *Théâtre complet*. 9 vols. Paris: du Bélier, 1948–56.

Fielding, Henry. *Completed Works*. 16 vols. Edited by W. E. Henley. London: Heinemann, 1903.

Fo, Dario. *Morte accidentale di un anarchico*. Turin: Einaudi, 1974.

Genet, Jean. *Le Balcon*. 1956; Paris: Gallimard, 1979.

Gogol, Nikolai Vasilcvich. *Diary of a Madman and Other Stories.* Translated by Ronald Wilks. Harmondsworth: Penguin, 1972.

———. *The Government Inspector.* Translated by D. J. Campbell. London: Sylvan Press, 1947; London: Heinemann, 1980.

Goldsmith, Oliver. *Collected Works.* 5 vols. Edited by A. Friedman. Oxford: Clarendon Press, 1966.

Grabbe, Christian Dietrich. *Scherz, Satire, Ironie und tiefere Bedeutung.* Edited by Alfred Bergmann. Stuttgart: Reclam, 1970.

Griffiths, Trevor. *Comedians.* Rev. ed. London: Faber and Faber, 1979.

Grimmelshausen, Hans Jakob Christoffel von. *Der abenteuerliche Simplicissimus.* Berlin: Verlag neues Leben, 1985.

Gryphius, Andreas. *Absurda Comica oder Herr Peter Squenz.* Edited by Herbert Cysarz. Stuttgart: Reclam, 1954.

Handke, Peter. *Publikumsbeschimpfung und andere Sprechstücke.* Frankfurt-am-Main: Suhrkamp, 1966.

Hasek, Jaroslav. *The Good Soldier Svejk and his fortunes in the World War.* Translated by Cecil Parrott. Harmondsworth: Penguin, 1974.

Holberg, Ludvig. *Jeppe vom Berge, oder Der verwandelte Bauer.* Translated by Hermann Engster. Stuttgart: Reclam, 1980.

Hubsch vasnachtspil, Ein. Play no. 31 in vol. 1 of *Fastnachtspiele aus dem fünfzehnten Jahrhundert.* 4 vols. Edited by Adelbert von Keller. Stuttgart: Bibliothek des Litterarischen Vereins, 1853.

Ionesco, Eugène. *Rhinocéros.* Paris: Gallimard, 1959.

———. *Three Plays. La Cantatrice chauve. La Lecon. Les Chaises.* Edited by H. F. Brookes and C. E. Fraenkel. London: Heinemann Educational Books, 1965.

Jarry, Alfred. *Tout Ubu.* Edited by Maurice Saillet. Paris: Livre de Poche, 1985.

Jonson, Ben. *Works.* 11 vols. Edited by C. H. Herford, P. Simpson, and E. Simpson. Oxford: Clarendon Press, 1925–52.

Joyce, James. *Finnegans Wake.* 1939; London: Faber and Faber, 1960.

———. *Ulysses.* 1922; Harmondsworth: Penguin, 1969.

Kleist, Heinrich von. *Der zerbrochne Krug. Ein Lustspiel.* Edited by Alexander von Bormann. Munich: Goldmann, 1983.

König, Johann Ulrich von. *Die verkehrte Welt. Ein Lustspiel.* Hamburg, 1746.

Lesage, Alain-René. *Turcaret.* Edited by Bernard Blanc. Paris: Larousse, 1973.

Machiavelli, Niccolò. *Mandragola.* Edited by G. Davico Bonino. Turin: Einaudi, 1980.

Mankind. In *The Macro Plays: The Castle of Perseverance. Wisdom. Mankind.* Edited by Mark Eccles. London: Oxford University Press, 1969.

Marivaux. *Le Jeu de l'amour et du hasard.* Edited by Pierre Michel. Paris: Bordas, 1980.

Marlowe, Christopher. *The Complete Plays.* Edited by J. B. Steane. Harmondsworth: Penguin, 1969.

McFadden, Cyra. *The Serial.* 1977; London: Picador, 1980.

Middleton, Thomas. *A Mad World, My Masters.* Edited by Standish Henning. Lincoln: University of Nebraska Press, 1965.

Molière. *Oeuvres complètes*. Paris: Seuil, 1962.

Mumming at Hertford. In *English Moral Interludes*. Edited by Glynne Wickham. London: Dent, 1976.

Nashe, Thomas. *Works*. 5 vols. Edited from the original texts by Ronald B. McKerow. Reprint. Edited by F. P. Wilson. Oxford: Basil Blackwell, 1958.

Nestroy, Johann. *Der böse Geist Lumpazivagabundus oder das liederliche Kleeblatt. Der Talisman. Freiheit in Krähwinkel*. Edited by Thomas Rothschild. Munich: Goldmann, 1983.

Nichols, Peter. *A Day in the Death of Joe Egg*. London: Faber and Faber, 1967.

Oreglia, Giacomo. *The Commedia dell'Arte*. Translated by Lovett F. Edwards. London: Methuen, 1968.

Orton, Joe. *The Complete Plays*. London: Eyre Methuen, 1976.

Petronius. *The Satyricon*. And Seneca. *The Apocolocyntosis*. Translated by J. P. Sullivan. Harmondsworth: Penguin, 1977.

Pinget, Robert. *L'Hypothèse. Abel et Bela*. Paris: Minuit, 1987.

Pinter, Harold. *Plays: One*. London: Eyre Methuen, 1976.

Pirandello, Luigi. *Sei personaggi in cerca d'autore. Enrico IV*. Milan: Arnoldo Montadori, 1984.

Plautus. *The Pot of Gold and other plays*. Translated by E. F. Watling. Harmondsworth: Penguin, 1965.

———. *Works*. 5 vols. With an English translation by Paul Nixon. Cambridge: Harvard University Press (Loeb Classical Library), 1930–38.

Poe, Edgar Allan. *Comedies and Satires*. Edited by David Galloway. Harmondsworth: Penguin, 1987.

———. *Great Tales and Poems*. New York: Pocket Books, 1951.

Rabelais, François. *Oeuvres complètes*. Edited by Guy Demerson et al. Paris: Seuil, 1973.

Robbe-Grillet, Alain. *La Maison de rendez-vous*. Paris: Minuit, 1965.

Roth, Philip. *Portnoy's Complaint*. 1967; Harmondsworth: Penguin, 1986.

Rudelsberger, Hans, trans. *Altchinesische Liebeskomödien*. 1923; Zürich: Manesse, 1988.

Sade, D. A. F. de. *Justine, ou les malheurs de la vertu*. Edited by Béatrice Didier. Paris: Livre de Poche, 1973.

Schmidt, Arno. *Aus dem Leben eines Fauns*. 1953; Frankfurt-am-Main: Fischer Taschenbuch Verlag, 1973.

Scudéry, Georges de. *La Comédie des comédiens*. Edited by Joan Crow. Exeter: University of Exeter Press, 1975.

Shakespeare, William. *As You Like It*. 2nd ed. Edited by Agnes Latham. London: Methuen, 1975.

———. *Comedy of Errors*. Edited by R. A. Foakes. London: Methuen, 1962.

———. *Hamlet*. Edited by Harold Jenkins. London: Methuen, 1982.

———. *The First Part of King Henry IV*. Edited by A. R. Humphreys. London: Methuen, 1960.

———. *The Second Part of King Henry IV*. Edited by A. R. Humphreys. London: Methuen, 1966.

————. *Love's Labour's Lost*. Edited by John Kerrigan. Harmondsworth: Penguin, 1982.

————. *The Merchant of Venice*. 7th ed. Edited by John Russell Brown. London: Methuen, 1961.

————. *A Midsummer Night's Dream*. 3rd ed. Edited by Harold F. Brooks. London: Methuen, 1979.

————. *Much Ado About Nothing*. Edited by A. R. Humphreys. London: Methuen, 1982.

————. *Twelfth Night*. 2nd ed. Edited by J. M. Lothian and T. W. Craik. London: Methuen, 1975.

Shaw, George Bernard. *Man and Superman: a Comedy and a Philosophy*. 1903; Harmondsworth: Penguin, 1946.

Sheridan, Richard Brinsley. *Dramatic Works*. London: Oxford University Press, 1946.

Simpson, N. F. *A Resounding Tinkle*. 1958; London: Faber and Faber, 1968.

————. *One Way Pendulum: A Farce in a New Dimension*. 1960; London: Faber and Faber, 1988.

Sottie pour le Cry de la Basoche. In *Recueil général des Sotties*. 3 vols. Edited by E. Picot. Paris: Didot, 1902–12.

Ein spil von eim thumherrn und einer kupplerin. Play no. 37 in vol. 1 of *Fastnachtspiele aus dem fünfzehnten Jahrhundert*. 4 vols. Edited by Adelbert von Keller. Stuttgart: Bibliothek des Litterarischen Vereins, 1853.

Sterne, Laurence. *The Life and Opinions of Tristram Shandy, Gentleman*. Edited by Graham Petrie. Harmondsworth: Penguin, 1967.

Sternheim, Carl. *Die Hose: Ein bürgerliches Lustspiel*. Darmstadt: Luchterhand, 1976.

Stoppard, Tom. *The Real Inspector Hound*. 2nd ed. London: Faber and Faber, 1970.

————. *Rosencrantz and Guildenstern are Dead*. London: Faber and Faber, 1967.

Swift, Jonathan. *Poems*. Rev. ed. 3 vols. Edited by Harold Williams. Oxford: Clarendon Press, 1958.

Swinburne, Algernon Charles. *Poems*. 6 vols. London: Chatto and Windus, 1904.

Thompson, Hunter S. *Fear and Loathing in Las Vegas: A Savage Journey to the Heart of the American Dream*. London: Paladin, 1972.

Tieck, Ludwig. *Werke*. 4 vols. Edited by Marianne Thalmann. Darmstadt: Wissenschaftliche Buchgesellschaft, 1963–66.

Toole, John Kennedy. *A Confederacy of Dunces*. Harmondsworth: Penguin, 1981.

Virgil. *The Eclogues. The Georgics*. Translated by C. Day Lewis. Oxford: Oxford University Press, 1983.

Voltaire. *Candide, ou L'optimisme*. Edited by André Morize. Paris: Didier, 1957.

Wakefield Pageants in the Towneley Cycle, The Edited by A. C. Cawley. Manchester: Manchester University Press, 1958.

Wedekind, Frank. *Erdgeist. Die Büchse der Pandora*. Munich: Goldmann, 1980.

Wilde, Oscar. *The Picture of Dorian Gray*. Edited by Peter Ackroyd. Harmondsworth: Penguin, 1985.

————. *Three Plays*. London: Eyre Methuen, 1981.

————. *Works*. 15 vols. New York: Lamb, 1909. Reprint. New York: AMS, 1972.

Wycherley, William. *The Country Wife*. Edited by John Dixon Hunt. London: Ernest Benn, 1973.

Zuckmayer, Carl. *Der Hauptmann von Köpenick*. Frankfurt-am-Main: Fischer Taschenbuch, 1961.

Theoretical Works

Alewyn, Richard. *Probleme und Gestalten: Essays*. Frankfurt-am-Main: Suhrkamp, 1982.

Aristotle. *Poetics*. With an English translation by W. Hamilton Fyfe. London: Heinemann (Loeb Classical Library), 1932.

Artaud, Antonin. *Oeuvres complètes*. 11 vols. Paris: Gallimard, 1961–74.

Aubailly, Jean-Claude. *Le Monologue, le dialogue et la sottie*. Paris: Champion, 1976.

Auden, W. H. *The Dyer's Hand and Other Essays*. New York: Random, 1962.

Babcock, Barbara A., ed. *The Reversible World: Symbolic Inversion in Art and Society*. Ithaca: Cornell University Press, 1978.

Bakhtin, Mikhail. *Rabelais and his World*. Translated by Hélène Iswolsky. Bloomington: Indiana University Press, 1984.

Barber, C. L. *Shakespeare's Festive Comedy: A Study of Dramatic Form and its Relation to Custom*. Princeton: Princeton University Press, 1959.

Barthes, Roland. *Le Plaisir du texte*. Paris: Seuil, 1973.

Baudelaire, Charles. "De l'essence du rire." In *Oeuvres complètes*. 11 vols. Edited by J. Crépet. Paris: Conard, 1923.

Benstock, Bernard. *Joyce-Again's Wake: An Analysis of "Finnegans Wake."* Seattle: University of Washington Press, 1965.

Bentley, Eric. *The Life of the Drama*. London: Methuen, 1966.

Bergson, Henri. *Le Rire*. Paris: Presses Universitaires de France, 1940.

Best, Otto. *Der Witz als Erkenntniskraft und Formprinzip*. Darmstadt: Wissenschaftliche Buchgesellschaft, 1989.

Billington, Sandra. "'Suffer Fools Gladly': The Fool in Medieval England and the Play *Mankind*." In *The Fool and the Trickster*, edited by Paul V. A. Williams. Cambridge: Brewer, 1979.

Blistein, Elmer M. *Comedy in Action*. Durham, N.C.: Duke University Press, 1964.

Booth, Wayne. *The Rhetoric of Fiction*. Chicago: University of Chicago Press, 1961.

Brand, Peter. "Disguise in Renaissance Comedy, with Illustrations." In *Comparative Criticism: An Annual Journal*, edited by E. S. Shaffer. Cambridge: Cambridge University Press, 1988.

Brecht, Bertolt. *Schriften zum Theater*. 7 vols. Edited by W. Hecht. Frankfurt-am-Main: Suhrkamp, 1963.

Breton, André. *Les Vases communicants*. 1932; Paris: Gallimard, 1955.

Bristol, Michael D. *Carnival and Theater: Plebeian culture and the structure of authority in Renaissance England*. London: Methuen, 1985.

Bruner, Jerome S., Alison Jolly, and Kathy Sylva, eds. *Play—Its Role in Development and Evolution*. Harmondsworth: Penguin, 1976.

Burgess, Anthony. "Nonsense." In *Explorations in the Field of Nonsense*, edited by Wim Tigges. Amsterdam: Rodopi, 1987.

Carter, Angela. *The Sadeian Woman*. London: Virago, 1979.

Catholy, Eckehard. *Das deutsche Lustspiel: Vom Mittelalter bis zum Ende der Barockzeit*. Darmstadt: Wissenschaftliche Buchgesellschaft, 1968.

Cave, Terence. *The Cornucopian Text: Problems of Writing in the French Renaissance*. Oxford: Clarendon Press, 1979.

———. *Recognitions: A Study in Poetics*. Oxford: Clarendon Press, 1988.

Charney, Maurice. *Comedy High and Low*. New York: Oxford University Press, 1978.

Cicero. *De Oratore*. London: Heinemann (Loeb Classical Library), 1948.

Clark, Carol. *The Vulgar Rabelais*. Glasgow: Pressgang, 1983.

Cohn, Ruby. *New American Dramatists 1960–80*. London: Macmillan, 1982.

Cornford, F. M. *The Origin of Attic Comedy*. Edited by T. H. Gaster. 1914; New York: Doubleday, 1961.

Culler, Jonathan. *Structuralist Poetics*. London: Routledge and Kegan Paul, 1975.

Curtius, Ernst Robert. *Europäische Literatur und lateinisches Mittelalter*. Bern: Francke, 1948.

Dante Alighieri. *Literary Criticism of Dante Alighieri*. Translated by R. S. Haller. Lincoln: University of Nebraska Press, 1973.

Descartes, René. *Oeuvres et Lettres*. Edited by A. Bridoux. Paris: Gallimard, 1953.

Devereux, Georges. *Baubo, la vulve mythique*. Paris: Godefoy, 1983.

Donaldson, Ian. *The World Upside-Down*. Oxford: Oxford University Press, 1970.

Dover, K. J. *Aristophanic Comedy*. Berkeley: University of California Press, 1972.

Dürrenmatt, Friedrich. "Theaterprobleme." In *Theater: Essays, Gedichte und Reden*. Vol. 24 of *Werkausgabe*. 30 vols. Zürich: Diogenes, 1985.

Eibl-Eibesfeldt, I. *Grundriß der vergleichenden Verhaltensforschung*. 6th ed. Munich: Piper, 1980.

Ellis, H. A. *Shakespeare's Lusty Punning in "Love's Labour's Lost."* The Hague: Mouton, 1973.

Ellmann, Richard. *Oscar Wilde*. London: Hamish Hamilton, 1987.

Emerson, Ralph Waldo. "The Comic." In vol. 3 of *Works*, edited by G. Sampson. London: George Bell and Son, 1906.

Erasmus. *Praise of Folly*. Translated by Betty Radice. Harmondsworth: Penguin, 1971.

Erwin, Edward. "Psychoanalysis and Self-Deception." In *Perspectives on Self-Deception*, edited by Brian P. McLaughlin and Amélie Oksenberg Rorty. Berkeley: University of California Press, 1988.

Esrig, David. *Commedia dell'arte: eine Bildgeschichte der Kunst des Spektakels*. Nördlingen: Greno, 1985.

Esslin, Martin. *The Theatre of the Absurd.* Rev. ed. Harmondsworth: Penguin, 1980.

Farley-Hills, David. *The Comic in Renaissance Comedy.* London: Macmillan, 1981.

Fielding, Henry. *Completed Works.* 16 vols. Edited by W. E. Henley. London: Heinemann, 1903.

Foucault, Michel. *The History of Sexuality. Volume One: An Introduction.* Translated by Robert Hurley. Harmondsworth: Penguin, 1981.

―――. *Madness and Civilization: A History of Insanity in the Age of Reason.* Translated by Richard Howard. London: Tavistock, 1971.

Frazer, James George. *The Golden Bough: A Study in Magic and Religion.* Abridged edition. London: Macmillan, 1922.

Freud, Sigmund. *Studienausgabe.* 10 vols. Edited by A. Mitscherlich, A. Richards, and J. Strachey. Frankfurt-am-Main: S. Fischer, 1969–72.

―――. "Über den Traum." In vol. 3 of *Gesammelte Werke.* 18 vols. Edited by Anna Freud et al. London: Imago, 1942.

Frye, Northrop. *An Anatomy of Criticism.* Princeton: Princeton University Press, 1957.

Genet, Jean. "Comment jouer *Les Bonnes.*" Introduction to *Les Bonnes.* Paris: Gallimard, 1947.

Girard, René. *La Violence et le sacré.* Paris: Grasset, 1972.

Goldsmith, Oliver. *Collected Works.* 5 vols. Edited by A. Friedman. Oxford: Clarendon Press, 1966.

Grimm, R., and K. L. Berghahn, eds. *Wesen und Formen des Komischen im Drama.* Darmstadt: Wissenschaftliche Buchgesellschaft, 1975.

Harpham, Geoffrey. *On the Grotesque: Strategies of Contradiction in Art and Literature.* Princeton: Princeton University Press, 1982.

Heath, Peter. *The Philosopher's Alice.* London: Academy, 1974.

Hegel, G. W. F. *Ästhetik.* 2nd ed. 2 vols. Edited by Friedrich Bassenge. Berlin: Aufbau, 1965.

―――. *Werke.* 20 vols. Edited by E. Moldenhauer and K. M. Michel. Frankfurt-am-Main: Suhrkamp, 1986.

Heidegger, Martin. *Sein und Zeit.* 1922; Tübingen: Niemeyer, 1986.

Herrick, M. T. *Comic Theory in the Sixteenth Century.* Urbana: University of Illinois Press, 1950.

Hibbard, G. R. *Thomas Nashe: A Critical Introduction.* London: Routledge and Kegan Paul, 1962.

Hobbes, Thomas. *Leviathan.* Edited by C. B. Macpherson. Harmondsworth: Penguin, 1968.

Horn, András. *Das Komische im Spiegel der Literatur.* Würzburg: Königshausen und Neumann, 1988.

Howarth, W. D., ed. *Comic Drama: The European Heritage.* London: Methuen, 1978.

Hume, David. *The Philosophical Works.* 4 vols. Edited by T. H. Green and T. H. Grose. 1886. Reprint. Darmstadt: Scientia Verlag Aalen, 1964.

Ionesco, Eugène. *Notes et contre-notes.* Paris: Gallimard, 1962.

Jakobson, Roman. "Closing Statement: Linguistics and Poetics." 1958. In *Style in Language*. Edited by T. Sebeok. London: John Wiley and Sons, 1960.

Jefferson, Ann. *The Nouveau Roman and the Poetics of Fiction*. Cambridge: Cambridge University Press, 1980.

Jonson, Ben. *Works*. 11 vols. Edited by C. H. Herford, P. Simpson, and E. Simpson. Oxford: Clarendon Press, 1925–52.

Joubert, Laurent. *Traité du Ris*. 1579; Geneva: Slatkine Reprints, 1973.

Joyce, James. *Critical Writings of James Joyce*. Edited by E. Mason and R. Ellmann. London: Faber and Faber, 1959.

Jünger, Friedrich Georg. *Über das Komische*. Frankfurt-am-Main: Klostermann, 1948.

Kamper, D., and Wulf, Chr., eds. *Lachen, Gelächter, Lächeln*. Frankfurt-am-Main: Syndikat, 1986.

Kant, Immanuel. *Werke*. 12 vols. Edited by W. Weischedel. Frankfurt-am-Main: Suhrkamp, 1957.

Kaufman, Gloria, and Mary Kay Blakely, eds. *Pulling Our Own Strings*. Bloomington: Indiana University Press, 1980.

Kayser, Wolfgang. *Das Groteske: Seine Gestaltung in Malerei und Dichtung*. Oldenburg: Gerhard Stalling Verlag, 1957.

Keats, John. *Letters of John Keats*. Edited by Robert Gittings. Oxford: Oxford University Press, 1970.

Koestler, Arthur. *The Act of Creation*. 1964; London: Arkana, 1989.

Lacan, Jacques. *Ecrits 1*. Paris: Seuil, 1966.

Laing, R. D. *The Divided Self: An Existential Study in Sanity and Madness*. 1959; Harmondsworth: Penguin, 1965.

———. *Self and Others*. 2nd ed. Harmondsworth: Penguin, 1971.

Lamb, Charles. "On the Artificial Comedy of the Last Century." In *Works*. 12 vols. Edited by W. MacDonald. London: Dent, 1905.

Rochefoucauld, La. *Maximes et Réflexions diverses*. 2nd ed. Edited by Jean Lafond. Paris: Gallimard, 1976.

Locke, John. *An Essay Concerning Human Understanding*. Edited by P. H. Nidditch. Oxford: Clarendon Press, 1975.

Marinetti, F. T. *Teoria e Invenzione Futurista*. Edited by Luciano De Maria. Milan: Arnoldo Montadori, 1968.

Mayer III, David. *Harlequin in his Element: The English Pantomime, 1806–36*. Cambridge: Harvard University Press, 1969.

Mercier, Vivian. *The Irish Comic Tradition*. London: Oxford University Press, 1962.

Meredith, George. "An Essay on the Idea of Comedy and the Uses of the Comic Spirit." 1897. In vol. 23 of *Works*. 27 vols. London: Constable, 1910.

Miller, Karl. *Doubles: Studies in Literary History*. Oxford: Oxford University Press, 1985.

Milner, G. B. "Homo Ridens: Towards a Semiotic Theory of Humor and Laughter." In *Semiotica* 1, no. 5 (1972).

Moore, W. G. *Molière: A New Criticism*. Oxford: Oxford University Press, 1949.

Muecke, D. C. *Irony and the Ironic*. 2nd ed. London: Methuen, 1982.

Nietzsche, Friedrich. *Werke. Kritische Gesamtausgabe.* 20 vols. Edited by G. Colli and M. Montinari. Berlin: de Gruyter, 1967– .

Novalis. *Schriften.* 5 vols. Edited by P. Kluckhohn and R. Samuel. Stuttgart: W. Kohlhammer, 1960.

Ogden, C. K., and I. A. Richards. *The Meaning of Meaning.* 10th ed. London: Routledge and Kegan Paul, 1969.

Olson, Elder. *The Theory of Comedy.* Bloomington: Indiana University Press, 1968.

Orton, Joe. *The Orton Diaries.* Edited by John Lahr. London: Methuen, 1986.

Palmer, D. J., ed. *Comedy: Developments in Criticism.* London: Macmillan, 1984.

Pinter, Harold. "Writing for the Theatre." In *Plays: One.* London: Eyre Methuen, 1976.

Plato. *Politicus; Philebus.* With an English translation by H. N. Fowler. London: Heinemann (Loeb Classical Library), 1925.

Plessner, Helmuth. "Lachen und Weinen." In *Philosophische Anthropologie.* Frankfurt-am-Main: S. Fischer, 1970.

Powell, Chris, and George E. C. Paton, eds. *Humour in Society: Resistance and Control.* London: Macmillan, 1988.

Preisendanz, Wolfgang, and Rainer Warning, eds. *Das Komische.* Munich: Fink, 1976.

Quintilian. *Institutio Oratoria.* With an English translation by H. E. Butler. Cambridge: Harvard University Press (Loeb Classical Library), 1960.

Radin, Paul. *The Trickster: A Study in American Indian Mythology.* New York: Schocken, 1972.

Redfern, Walter. *Puns.* Oxford: Basil Blackwell, 1984.

Reich, Wilhelm. *Die Sexuelle Revolution.* Frankfurt-am-Main: Fischer Taschenbuch Verlag, 1971.

Richter, Jean Paul. *Vorschule der Ästhetik.* Edited by J. Müller. 1804; Leipzig: Felix Meiner, 1923.

Ritter, Joachim. "Über das Lachen." 1940. In *Subjektivität.* Frankfurt-am-Main: Suhrkamp, 1979.

Robinson, Fred M. *Comedy of Language: Studies in Modern Comic Literature.* Amherst: University of Massachusetts Press, 1980.

Ruskin, John. *Works.* 39 vols. Edited by E. T. Cook and Alexander Wedderburn. London: George Allen, 1904.

Russell, Bertrand. *A History of Western Philosophy.* London: George Allen and Unwin, 1946.

Sartre, Jean-Paul. *L'Etre et le néant.* Paris: Gallimard, 1943.

Schechner, Richard. *Between Theater and Anthropology.* Philadelphia: University of Pennsylvania Press, 1985.

Schelling, F. W. J. v. *Werke.* 3 vols. Leipzig: Fritz Eckardt, 1907.

Schiller, Friedrich. *Über naive und sentimentalische Dichtung.* In vol. 20 of *Werke.* 45 vols. Edited by Lieselotte Blumenthal and Benno von Wiese. Weimar: Böhlau, 1962– .

Schlegel, Friedrich. "Vom ästhetischen Werte der griechischen Komödie." 1794. In vol. 1 of *Kritische Ausgabe.* 38 vols. Edited by E. Behler. Munich: Schöningh, 1979.

Schmeling, Manfred. *Das Spiel im Spiel.* Rheinfelden: Schäuble, 1977.

Schopenhauer, Arthur. *Sämtliche Werke.* 5 vols. Edited by W. F. von Löhneysen. Frankfurt-am-Main: Suhrkamp, 1986.

Schwartz, Kit. *The Female Member.* London: Robson, 1989.

Sklovskij, Viktor. *Theorie der Prosa.* Translated by Gisela Drohla. Frankfurt-am-Main: Fischer Taschenbuch Verlag, 1984.

Spivack, Bernard. "Falstaff and the Psychomachia." In *Shakespeare Quarterly* 8 (1957).

Staveacre, Tony. *Slapstick: The Illustrated Story of Knockabout Comedy.* London: Angus and Robertson, 1987.

Tannahill, Reay. *Sex in History.* Rev. ed. London: Sphere Books, 1989.

Tertullien. *La Toilette des femmes (De cultu feminarum).* Translated by Marie Turcan. Paris: Editions du cerf, 1971.

Torrance, Robert M. *The Comic Hero.* Cambridge: Harvard University Press, 1978.

Welsford, Enid. *The Fool: His Social and Literary History.* 1935; New York: Doubleday, 1961.

Welzig, Werner. "Ordo und verkehrte Welt bei Grimmelshausen." In *Der Simplicissimusdichter und sein Werk,* edited by G. Weydt. Darmstadt: Wissenschaftliche Buchgesellschaft, 1969.

Wilson, Edmund. "Morose Ben Jonson." In *Ben Jonson: A Collection of Critical Essays,* edited by J. A. Barish. Englewood Cliffs, N.J.: Prentice-Hall, 1963.

Wittgenstein, Ludwig. *Werkausgabe.* 8 vols. Frankfurt-am-Main: Suhrkamp, 1984.

Zijderveld, Anton. *Humor und Gesellschaft. Eine Soziologie des Humors und Lachens.* Translated from the Dutch by Diethard Zils. Graz: Styria, 1976.

Index